This item cannot be checked out

REFERENCE

Word 2013

ABSOLUTE BEGINNER'S GUIDE

Sherry Kinkoph Gunter

800 East 96th Street,
Indianapolis, Indiana 46240

Word 2013 Absolute Beginner's Guide

ISBN-13: 978-0-7897-5090-7
ISBN-10: 0-7897-5090-2

Library of Congress Control Number: 2013940326

Printed in the United States of America

First Printing: July 2013

Trademarks

Warning and Disclaimer

Bulk Sales

Que Publishing offers excellent discounts on this book when ordered in quantity for bulk purchases or special sales. For more information, please contact

U.S. Corporate and Government Sales
1-800-382-3419
corpsales@pearsontechgroup.com

For sales outside the United States, please contact

International Sales
international@pearsoned.com

Editor-in-Chief
Greg Wiegand

Acquisitions Editor
Michelle Newcomb

Development Editor
Robin Drake

Managing Editor
Sandra Schroeder

Project Editor
Mandie Frank

Copy Editor
Paula Lowell

Indexer
Lisa Stumpf

Proofreader
Dan Knott

Technical Editor
Vince Averello

Editorial Assistant
Cindy Teeters

Cover Designer
Matt Coleman

Compositor
Mary Sudul

Contents at a Glance

Introduction 1

Part I   Word Basics

1   Getting to Know Microsoft Word 5

2   Basic Word Operations 19

3   Setting Up Accounts and Services 35

Part II   Building Simple Documents

4   Document Basics 55

5   Template Basics 71

6   Adding Text 81

Part III   Making Documents Look Impressive

7   Formatting Text 95

8   Formatting Paragraphs 107

9   Formatting Pages 127

10   Advanced Formatting 143

Part IV   Adding Visual Interest with Tables, Charts, and Graphics

11   Adding Tables to Word Documents 161

12   Editing Tables 171

13   Adding Charts, Graphs, and Diagrams 193

14   Adding Simple Graphic Elements 217

15   Inserting Pictures and Videos 237

16   Fine-Tuning Your Graphics 259

Part V   Using Specialized Word Tools

17   Tools for Longer Documents 291

18   Using Proofreading Tools 315

19   Printing Documents 333

Index 361

Online Elements

20   Collaborating, Reviewing, and Sharing Documents

21   Using Word on the Internet

Table of Contents

Introduction 1

Who This Book Is For 2

How This Book Is Organized 2

Conventions Used in This Book 3

I Word Basics

1 Getting to Know Microsoft Word 5

Introducing Word 6

What's New in Word 2013? 8

Starting Word 9

Exploring the Program Window 11

Finding Help with Word Issues and Topics 14

Exiting and Closing in Word 16

2 Basic Word Operations 19

Working with the Ribbon 20
    Using Ribbon Elements 21
    Hiding and Displaying the Ribbon 24

Working with the Quick Access Toolbar 25

Using Context Menus and Toolbars 26

Dealing with Dialog Boxes 27

Working with Word View Modes and Zoom Tools 29
    Changing View Modes 29
    Zooming Your View 32

3 Setting Up Accounts and Services 35

Introducing Web and Cloud Connectivity 36

Using a Microsoft Account 39
    Signing In 39
    Adding and Switching Accounts 41

Customizing Your Account 42
    Customizing Your Account Picture 43
    Changing the Background and Theme 46

Adding Services 47

Adding Apps 50

II Building Simple Documents

4 Document Basics **55**

Starting a New Document 56

Saving Documents 58
    A Word About File Types 60
    Other File-Saving Options to Consider 62

Opening and Closing Documents 62

Viewing Multiple Documents 65

Moving, Copying, and Pasting Data Between Files 66

Assigning Document Protection 67

5 Template Basics **71**

Understanding Templates 72

Applying a Template 72

Finding More Templates 76

Saving Templates 78

6 Adding Text **81**

Typing and Editing Text 82

Selecting Text 84

Moving and Copying Text 85
    Cutting and Pasting Text 86
    Copying and Pasting Text 86
    Using the Mini Toolbar 87
    Working with the Clipboard Pane 87

Adding Text with Quick Parts 88
    Inserting a Quick Part 89
    Creating Your Own Quick Parts 91

Inserting Symbols 92

III Making Documents Look Impressive

7 Formatting Text **95**

Applying Boldface, Italics, and Underline 96

Changing the Font 98

Changing the Point Size 100

Using the Font Dialog Box 102

Adding Color to Text 103

Copying Formatting from One Place to Another 104

8 Formatting Paragraphs **107**

Controlling Alignment 108

Indenting Text 110
    Simple Indents 111
    Custom Indents 111
    Special Indents 112
    Setting Indents with the Ruler 112

Setting Tabs 115

Using Bulleted and Numbered Lists 118

Controlling Spacing 120
    Line Spacing 121
    Paragraph Spacing 123
    Character Spacing 125

9 Formatting Pages **127**

Setting Margins 128

Creating Columns 130

Changing Vertical Alignment 132

Adding Headers and Footers to a Document...............134
   Adding Headers and Footers 135
   Adding Page Numbers.......................................138

Inserting Pages, Breaks, and Sections 139
   Inserting Pages 139
   Inserting Breaks 140

10 Advanced Formatting **143**

Applying a Theme 144

Applying Styles..146
   Choosing Style Sets 149
   Assigning Styles...150
   Creating New Styles...151

Adding Special Effects...152
   Inserting Drop Caps...152
   Applying Text Effects 153
   Adding a Watermark...154

Adding Borders and Shading..156
   Adding Text Borders...157
   Adding Page Borders 158
   Adding Shading...159

IV Adding Visual Interest with Tables, Charts, and Graphics

11 Adding Tables to Word Documents.........................**161**

Inserting a Basic Table...162

Inserting and Creating Quick Tables.............................165

Drawing a Custom Table...167

Inserting Excel Spreadsheets as Tables.........................169

12 Editing Tables...**171**

Selecting Table Parts 172

Changing Column Widths and Row Heights.....................173
   Resizing by Dragging.......................................173
   Using the Tab Tools...174
   Using the Table Properties Dialog Box 175

Adding and Deleting Columns and Rows 176

Adding and Deleting Cells 180

Merging and Splitting Table Cells 181

Changing Cell Alignment and Margins 184

Repositioning and Resizing Tables 186

Dressing Up a Table with Table Styles and Borders 188

13 Adding Charts, Graphs, and Diagrams **193**

Working with SmartArt 194
    Inserting SmartArt 196
    Customizing SmartArt Graphics 197
    Changing Layouts, Colors, and Styles 202
    Formatting SmartArt 203

Inserting Charts 205
    Understanding the Chart Types 206
    Understanding Chart Parts 207
    Inserting a Chart 209
    Entering Chart Data 210
    Editing Charts 212

14 Adding Simple Graphic Elements **217**

Drawing Shapes 218
    Repositioning and Resizing Shapes 222
    Formatting Shapes 223

Inserting WordArt Objects 226

Inserting Text Box Objects 231

15 Inserting Pictures and Videos **237**

Understanding Picture File Types 238

Inserting Images from the Internet 240
    Using Pictures from Office.com 242
    Searching for Pictures Using Bing 244
    Searching for Pictures on SkyDrive 246

Inserting Your Own Pictures 248

Capturing Screenshots 250

Embedding Videos 254

16 Fine-Tuning Your Graphics **259**

Resizing, Positioning, and Wrapping Text Around Graphics 260

Rotating and Flipping Objects 267

Layering and Grouping Objects 270
Layering Objects 271
Grouping Objects 275

Adding Picture Styles and Borders 276

Adding Flourishes with Effects 279
Assigning Effects 279
Applying Artistic Effects to Pictures 281

Cropping Pictures 282

Adjusting Pictures 285
Correcting Picture Problems 285
Tweaking Colors 286
Removing Backgrounds 287

V Using Specialized Word Tools

17 Tools for Longer Documents **291**

Structuring Documents with Outline View 292

Inserting Footnotes and Endnotes 297

Adding Captions 299

Inserting Cross-References 301

Creating an Index 302

Creating a Table of Contents 306

Inserting Bookmarks 307

Navigating Long Documents with the Navigation Pane 310

18 Using Proofreading Tools **315**

Highlighting Text with a Highlighter Pen 316

Inserting Comments 317

Finding and Replacing Text 319

Checking Spelling and Grammar 322

Using AutoCorrect 324

Using the Word Thesaurus 327

Researching and Translating Words 328

Checking a Document for Hidden Data 330

19   Printing Documents **333**

Previewing and Printing a Document 334
     Previewing Pages 335
     Managing Print Settings 336

Controlling Page Setup 342

Printing Envelopes and Labels 343
     Printing Envelopes 343
     Printing Labels 346

Using Word's Mail Merge Tool 349

Index **361**

Online Elements

20   Collaborating on and Reviewing Documents

Tracking and Reviewing Documents
     Turning on Tracking
     Working with Comments
     Reviewing Changes

Comparing Documents

Editing Portable Document Format (PDF) Files

Sharing Documents with Others

21   Using Word on the Internet

Emailing Documents

Turning Word Documents into Web Pages

Adding Hyperlinks

Working with SkyDrive
     Managing SkyDrive from Your Browser
     Using Word to Access SkyDrive

Using Web Apps

Bonus online chapters may be found on the Que product page http://www.quepublishing.com/ title/9780789750907 within the "Downloads" tab.

About the Author

Sherry Kinkoph Gunter has written and edited oodles of books over the past 20 years covering a wide variety of computer topics, including Microsoft Office programs, digital photography, and web applications. Recent titles include *Sam's Teach Yourself Facebook in 10 Minutes* and *Microsoft Office for Mac Bible*. Sherry began writing computer books back in 1992 for Macmillan, and her flexible writing style has allowed her to author for a varied assortment of imprints and formats. Her ongoing quest is to aid users of all levels in the mastering of ever-changing computer technologies, helping users make sense of it all and get the most out of their machines and online experiences. Sherry currently resides in a swamp in the wilds of east central Indiana with a lovable ogre and a menagerie of interesting creatures.

Dedication

To my Mr. Gunter for helping to keep the swamp somewhat quiet during work hours.

Acknowledgments

Special thanks go out to Michelle Newcomb for allowing me another wonderful opportunity to write about Word; to development editor Robin Drake, for her dedication and patience in shepherding this project; to copy editor Paula Lowell, for ensuring that all the i's were dotted and t's were crossed; to technical editor Vince Averello and project editor Mandie Frank, for offering valuable input along the way; and finally a big shout out to the production team for their talents in creating and assembling such a good-looking book.

We Want to Hear from You!

As the reader of this book, *you* are our most important critic and commentator. We value your opinion and want to know what we're doing right, what we could do better, what areas you'd like to see us publish in, and any other words of wisdom you're willing to pass our way.

We welcome your comments. You can email or write to let us know what you did or didn't like about this book—as well as what we can do to make our books better.

Please note that we cannot help you with technical problems related to the topic of this book.

When you write, please be sure to include this book's title and author as well as your name and email address. We will carefully review your comments and share them with the author and editors who worked on the book.

Email: feedback@quepublishing.com

Mail: Que Publishing
        ATTN: Reader Feedback
        800 East 96th Street
        Indianapolis, IN 46240 USA

Reader Services

Visit our website and register this book at quepublishing.com/register for convenient access to any updates, downloads, or errata that might be available for this book.

INTRODUCTION

Microsoft Word 2013 is the latest release of the world's number one word processing program. I know what you're thinking, "ugh, another product version I have to relearn." Having mixed feelings about any software program that offers new and improved features is not uncommon. On one hand, seeing what sort of changes Microsoft has made to the program is exciting, but on the other hand, learning it all over again might mean more time and effort on your part. Don't worry—whether you're a new user or a seasoned pro, you can get up and running fast with this latest version of Word with a little help from the book you're holding.

I'll explain everything. In fact, it will seem like I'm practically there beside you going over each feature. You'll be particularly happy to know we take regular snack breaks along the way. I am a big proponent of snack breaks, as long as you wipe up your sticky keyboard. As your own personal computer tutor, I'll show you how to utilize all the major features available in Word to help tackle different tasks you might experience at home, at work, or on the go. Whether you want to type up a company memo or build a grade "A" research paper, in this book you learn where to find what you need and make it work for you. We can all certainly pontificate 'til the cows come home about what a wonderful and powerful program Word is, but you just want to get your work done, so why not have a little fun along the way?

Who This Book Is For

Obviously, the first thing to figure out is whether this book is for you or not. You're in luck—I wrote it just for you. How can you be so sure? This book is for you if…

- You need to learn how to use Word's new tools and features fast without wading through a lot of exposition.

- You want easy-to-understand examples and instructions to help you see exactly what's going on with your own computer screen.

- You're curious to know how to start using all the cloud storage and cloud computing features now available to all Microsoft Word users and interested others.

- You're brand-spanking new to Word and not as confident as you would like to be using a word processing program.

- You're a long-time Word user and you need to find out what changed between the previous version of Word and this latest version.

- You want to learn all about Word without being bored to tears and/or potentially missing any snack breaks.

How This Book Is Organized

Microsoft Word 2013 Absolute Beginner's Guide is divided into six parts.

Part I, "Word Basics," introduces all the fundamental information you need to find your way around the new program window and its tools, plus set up your Microsoft account. That's right, you use an account now to access all that Microsoft has to offer online, all from within the Word program window.

Part II, "Building Simple Documents," shows you how to start creating documents, saving them to your cloud storage or on your computer, building documents out of templates, and using the various methods for adding text.

Part III, "Making Documents Look Impressive," introduces you to all the formatting tools you can apply to your documents to make them look polished and professional. Learn how to assign attributes to text, paragraphs, and entire pages, including changing fonts and sizes, controlling text positioning, and applying styles and themes.

Part IV, "Adding Visual Elements with Tables, Charts, and Graphics," shows you how to start inserting all kinds of illustrative elements into your documents, including building tables, diagrams, and adding pictures. You also learn how to draw your own artwork using shapes and snazzy text art.

Part V, "Using Specialized Word Tools," covers all the nifty features for working with longer types of documents, such as footnotes and bookmarks. This part of the book also demonstrates how to utilize proofing tools and how to print out your pages when everything's ready to commit to paper.

Wait—that's not all! There's a whole other part of the book waiting for you online! That's right, it's a bonus section just because readers like you deserve more (plus, there's so much stuff to tell you about Word, I couldn't fit it all into this book). Visit http://www.quepublishing.com/title/9780789750907 to learn how to share your Word documents with others, including how to collaborate with Word's tracking and revision tools, how to share your Word content over the Internet as well as bring Internet content into your documents. Yes, it's the book that keeps on giving!

Conventions Used in This Book

Microsoft Word 2013 Absolute Beginner's Guide uses a number of conventions to provide you with special information. These include the following elements:

TIP Tips offer suggestions for making things easier or provide alternative ways to perform a particular task.

NOTE Notes provide additional, more detailed information about a specific Word feature.

CAUTION Cautions warn you about potential problems that might occur and offer advice on how to avoid these problems.

So in summation, *Microsoft Word 2013 Absolute Beginner's Guide* is beautifully tailored to help you master this latest version of Word with minimal tediousness and maximum enjoyment. Go grab your favorite snack and let's not waste a moment more—you have word processing stuff to learn.

Bonus coverage available FREE on the World Wide Web!

- Share Word content online and integrate web content into your documents

- Access and edit your documents from anywhere through SkyDrive

Bonus chapters may be found on the Que product page http://www.quepublishing.com/title/9780789750907 within the "Downloads" tab.

IN THIS CHAPTER

- Learn a little about Word's history as a word processing program.
- Preview all the major changes made to Word 2013.
- Find out how to launch Word in Windows 7 and Windows 8.
- Acquaint yourself with the basic elements of the Word program window.
- Learn how to find help if you ever run into trouble using Word.

1

GETTING TO KNOW MICROSOFT WORD

If you have never worked with Microsoft Word before, you are in for a treat; and if you have worked with the program before, you'll be happy to know that this new version is better than ever. Microsoft Word is an amazingly powerful program and there's seemingly no end to the types of documents you can create with it. Oh, sure, you can type up a simple letter in a jiffy, but did you know you can use it for this:

- All kinds of reports, from year-end budget reports to company prospects and beyond
- Research papers, term papers, essays, and the like
- Résumés, business cards, and all manner of promotional materials
- Brochures, flyers, and newsletters
- Organized lists, menus, to-do sheets, and so on
- Personalized calendars for home, office, and school

- Greeting cards, postcards, and notecards

- Photo albums for every occasion

- Faxes, labels, and coordinated mailing materials

- Web pages—yes, even web pages!

That's just the tip of the proverbial iceberg! As you can see from this small list of typical projects, you can use Word to create a wide variety of documents for a multitude of purposes, even those that rely more on visuals than on text. Are you ready to see what you can do?

Introducing Word

Let's start with basic introductions, shall we? Meet Microsoft Word, the most popular word processing program in the known universe. Seriously. Some estimate a half a billion people use Word—500,000,001 counting you. Why is it so popular, you might wonder? Because it's intuitive, easy to use, loaded with features to make great-looking documents, and extremely reliable. As you are about to find out, Word is the powerhouse of the Microsoft Office suite of programs, and with it, you can rule the world—or at least present yourself through polished, professional-looking documents.

In case you are interested in its origins story, Microsoft Word traces its roots back to 1983 when it was launched as software called Multi-Tool Word for Xenix and MS-DOS. The name was soon shortened to Word, and thus began its climb to the top of the software charts. Today's Word—version 2013—has come a long way and through numerous version numbers, interface tweaks, and platforms, both Windows and Mac, to become the software it is now.

Word has reigned as the go-to program for businesses and organizations both large and small, allowing users to create all sorts of documents for professional use. As you can imagine, a versatile tool like Word is a great way to maintain efficiency in the workplace. You can easily share documents between people, and Word even offers reviewing tools to help you manage edits to the same document from several users.

However, Word is equally valuable to home users as well. For every office use, there is a home use for creating documents ranging from household budgets to school reports. If your work happens to span both office and home time, Word handily transitions your work between environments. You can easily email files, store them in the cloud (online storage services) to access them from any computer, and transport files on portable storage devices (such as USB flash drives and so forth).

Just about every form of Word through the years has shared the same fundamental layout, consisting of a big, empty area in the middle where you can type in text, and other less-intrusive areas along the edges of the program window to access commands to help you work with the text. As you can see in Figure 1.1, the same fundamental layout is true for Word 2013.

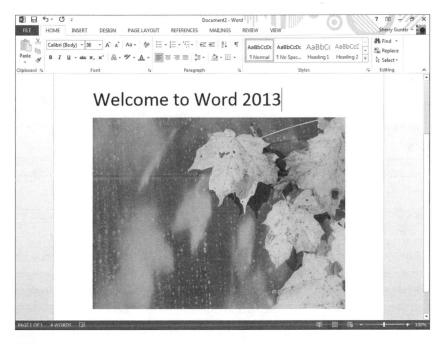

FIGURE 1.1

The new and improved Microsoft Word 2013.

NOTE If you're trying to figure out whether you want to purchase Word 2013 or not, here's what you need to know to help you make an informed decision. Microsoft Word 2013—and the entire Office 2013 suite of programs—can run on Windows 7 or Windows 8. It will not run on Windows XP or Vista. You can run Word on laptops, desktop computers, or tablets (with sufficient drive space and RAM). Word requires at least 1GB of RAM and 3GB of hard disk space. Word is available as a standalone program or as part of the Microsoft Office suite of productivity software. Word is also a part of the new Office 365, as cloud-based subscription software you can access on the Internet, for a monthly fee.

What's New in Word 2013?

Microsoft has made quite a few improvements to Word since its last rendition. For starters, it is retooled a bit to work with the new Windows 8 operating system. If your computer is one of the newer touchscreen models, you can utilize touchscreen techniques to interact with the program, such as selecting text using your finger to drag across the screen or tapping on the screen to activate a command. If your computer doesn't utilize touchscreen technologies, don't worry about it; you can use the traditional mouse, keyboard, or mousepad (on a laptop) methods to work in Word.

Here's a rundown of what else you can expect in the new Word 2013:

- A new, modern interface with a customizable watermark design in the upper-right corner.

- A new Start screen, also called a landing page, with quick access to recently used files, templates, and stored content.

- Speaking of templates, Word 2013 offers more than ever before. You can search for templates for every kind of document imaginable.

- New cloud connectivity—with an online connection and a Microsoft account, you can store documents online and access them from anywhere or any computer. Cloud connectivity includes Office 365 (a subscription-based software service) and SkyDrive (online file-hosting service).

- An improved Ribbon at the top of the program window that organizes commands.

- You can now add apps for Word and other Microsoft Office programs, such as dictionaries.

- The new Reading mode, which works great on a tablet, lets you browse a document like you're reading a book.

- Bookmarks let you pick up reading right where you left off in a document.

- You can now open PDF file formats and edit their content just like any other Word document.

- Improved markup tracking to help multiple users keep track of changes in a shared document.

- Improved graphics features to help you work with artwork and pictures you add to a document, including alignment guides to help you position graphics with your text.

- You can now insert online videos into your documents, such as content from YouTube.

There's more, but that's much of the big stuff. Let's get started by launching your own Word program.

Starting Word

You can start Word just like you start any other program on your computer. If you are using Windows 7, for example, you can apply any of these techniques:

- Click the **Start** button, type **Word**, and then click **Word 2013** at the top of the **Start** menu.

- Double-click the **Word** shortcut icon on the desktop (if there is one).

- Click the **Start** button, click **All Programs**, click **Microsoft Office 2013**, and then click **Word 2013**.

- Double-click any Word document file in Windows Explorer.

Figure 1.2 shows the Windows 7 Start menu with Word 2013 listed at top.

FIGURE 1.2

You can start Word using the Start menu in Windows 7.

If you are using Windows 8, try one of these methods:

- From the Windows 8 Start screen, type **Word**, and then from the Apps search screen, click **Word**.
- Click the tile for Word on the Start screen, and Word opens on the Desktop.
- In Desktop view, you can click Word's shortcut icon on the desktop, if available.

In Windows 8, Word launches over on the Desktop, which means you can minimize and maximize the program window, and the taskbar shows the open Word program icon.

 NOTE If you're new to Windows 8, try *Windows 8 Absolute Beginner's Guide*, available in fine bookstores online and off. It's sure to get you up and running fast with the latest Microsoft operating system.

After you open Word, the first thing you see is a landing page, also called a Start screen, shown in Figure 1.3. The Start screen is new to Word 2013. The screen lists any recent Word files you worked with, as well as templates to help you get started with making new documents. You can also access the **Open Other Documents** feature to look for other documents.

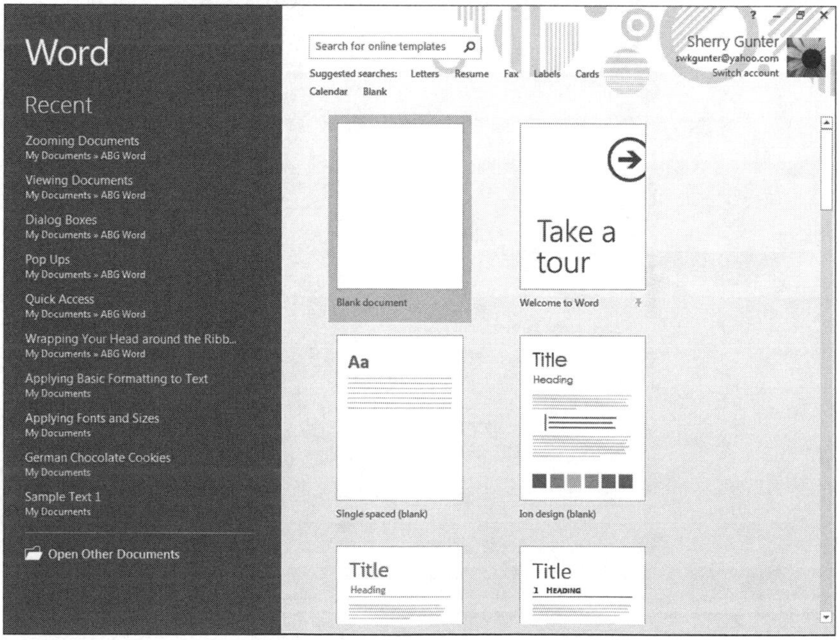

![Screenshot of Word's Start screen showing a list of recent documents on the left and template thumbnails on the right, including Blank document, Take a tour, Single spaced (blank), Ion design (blank), and more.]

FIGURE 1.3

Word's new Start screen is a jumping-off point for starting new documents or opening previously saved documents.

When presented with the Start screen, you can go a lot of different directions based on what you're trying to accomplish.

- If you want to open a document you've previously saved, you can look through the **Recent** list and click a document to open it.

- To open a file, click the **Open Other Documents** link to summon the Open screen where you can choose to open a document stored on your computer, SkyDrive, or other location.

- To create a new document based on a template, you can scroll through the selections and pick one that closely matches what you would like to make. If you can't find one you like, you can conduct an online search.

To help get things rolling, let's start by clicking the **Blank document** option on the Start screen. Doing so opens a new, blank document in the Word program window.

 NOTE I know you're not ready to close the program yet, but you'll learn the differences between closing the program window and simply closing a single document later in this chapter, just in case you were thinking about it already.

 TIP Tired of the Start screen? You can turn it off so that Word automatically starts a new, blank document every time you launch the program, thus skipping the extra window to jump through to start working in Word. To turn off the Start screen, click the **File** tab on the Ribbon, click the **General** options, and then deselect the **Show the Start screen when this application starts** check box. Click **OK** to apply the change. The next time you launch Word, you go right to a blank document. You can always turn the Start screen on again, if you want.

Exploring the Program Window

Microsoft Word shares a similar look and feel with all the Microsoft Office programs, including Excel, PowerPoint, and Outlook. The bonus in this news is that if you learn your way around one program, you can use the same techniques in another. Even if you don't plan on using any other Microsoft programs, the skills you learn in Word 2013 carry over into other non-Microsoft programs, too. Lots of other software manufacturers, for example, adopted the Microsoft Ribbon approach to organize and present commands and features.

If you're new to using Word, take a few moments and familiarize yourself with the program window's many nuances. Take a look at the blank document you opened, shown in Figure 1.4.

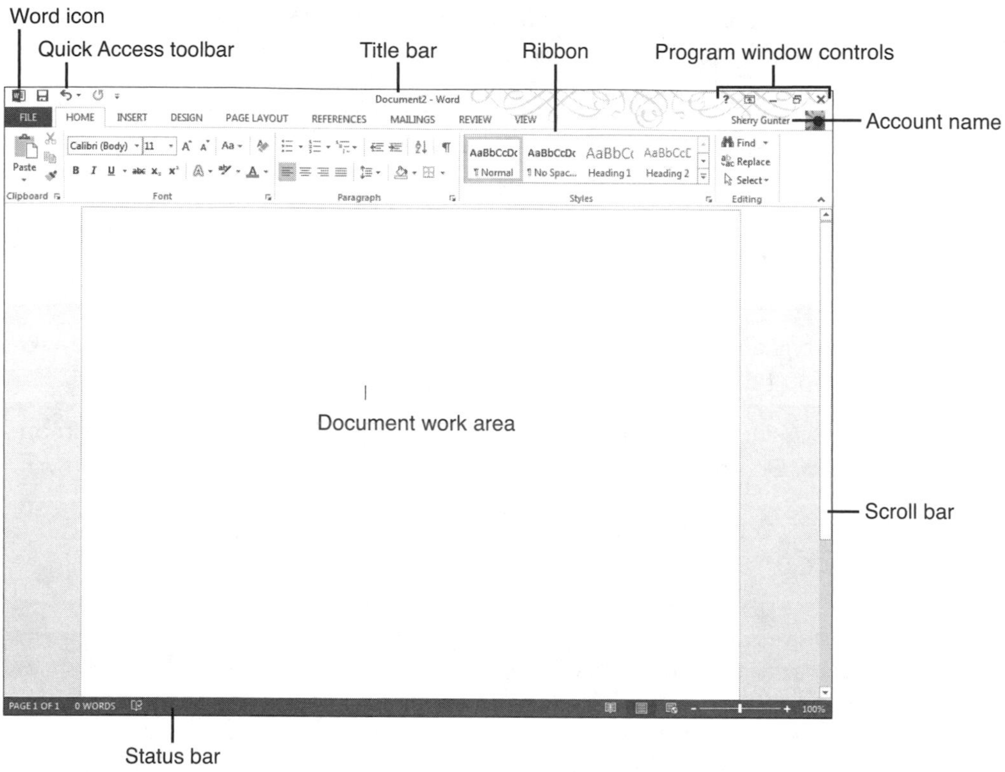

FIGURE 1.4

Here's an example of a blank document open in the Word program window.

Let's go over the various elements you see onscreen and what they're used for in Word:

- **Word icon** Click this icon to display a drop-down menu of program window controls, such as **Minimize** (reducing the window to an icon on the taskbar), **Maximize** (enlarging the window to optimize workspace), and **Close** (exiting the program).

- **Quick Access toolbar** Use this toolbar to quickly perform a common Word task, including saving a file, undoing or redoing an action. You can add other common tasks to the toolbar, too, such as the command for opening a file or printing.

- **Title bar** Look for the name of your document on the title bar. If you haven't named it yet, a default name appears, such as Document1 or Document2.

- **Ribbon**   The collapsible bar across the top of the document area houses most of the commands you need to work in Word. Related commands are grouped into tabs, and you click a tab to view its various commands.

- **Document work area**   The middle of the program window is where you do all your actual work, typing in text, formatting it to look nice, and so forth.

- **Scroll bar**   Use the scroll bar on the right side of the window to move around in your document. A horizontal scroll bar also appears if there's more to view in the window width.

- **Status bar**   The status bar displays information such as the number of pages in a document or the word count, and the right side of the status bar offers shortcuts to view modes and zooming tools.

- **Program window controls**   Use these controls to minimize, maximize, and close the program window. These same controls are also available through the Word icon. In addition to window controls, you'll find icons for accessing Help and collapsing/expanding the Ribbon.

- **Account name**   As part of the new cloud integration (online storage) Word lists your Microsoft account name and photo, which you can click to adjust account settings or switch user accounts.

Program windows are resizable and collapsible. You can resize the window by clicking the **Restore Down** icon (see Figure 1.5). This reduces the size of the window, as shown in Figure 1.6, and you can then drag it around by its title bar to move it. You can also click and drag a window corner to resize the Word window. To make it full-screen size again, click the **Maximize** button, which appears in place of the **Restore Down** button when the window is smaller in size. To minimize the window and hide it completely, click the **Minimize** button; click the Word document on the taskbar to view the Word window again.

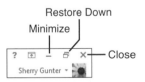

FIGURE 1.5

You can use the program window controls to control the actual window.

Maximize

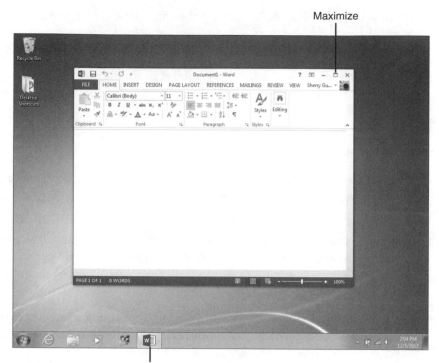

Click here to display the document window again

FIGURE 1.6

You can resize and move the Word window around the computer screen, as needed.

 TIP You can utilize window controls on all kinds of windows and dialog boxes you encounter while working with Word. For example, the **Close** button—displayed with an X—is handy for closing dialog boxes, tool palettes, panes, and more.

Finding Help with Word Issues and Topics

If you ever find yourself in a jam regarding a word-processing task, you can seek help through the Word Help feature. When activated, Help opens a special window you can use to look up topics, search online for additional resources, and generally learn more about the program or the feature you are working with at the time. With an online connection, Help taps into resources from the Microsoft Office website. Help offers tutorials, links to related topics, and a table of contents you can peruse.

To utilize Help, simply click the **Help** icon in the upper-right corner of the program window. As soon as you do, a Word Help window opens, as shown in Figure 1.7. You can scroll through the featured topics, if you like. You can click a link to learn more about a subject; Help displays additional information in another window, as shown in Figure 1.8.

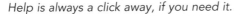

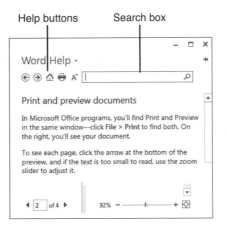

FIGURE 1.7

Help is always a click away, if you need it.

FIGURE 1.8

You can peruse the Help topics and use the navigation buttons at the top of the window to move around the Help.

After you open a Help window, here's what you can do:

- Use the navigation buttons (**Back** and **Forward**) at the top of the Help window to move back and forth between topics.

- Click the little icon that looks like a house, aptly named **Home**, to return to the main Help window you started in.

- If you're having trouble viewing the window's type size, you can click the **Text** button to toggle back and forth between regular and large type.

- Need to print out a help topic? Click the **Print** button.

- Use the **Search** box to search for keywords and topics.

- To close the Help window, click its **Close** button (the X in the upper-right corner of the window).

 NOTE Although the Help window offers lots of assistance in learning new commands and features, you might also open your browser window (such as Internet Explorer) and look around the Microsoft Office website (office.microsoft.com) for additional resources, forums, and other support help.

Exiting and Closing in Word

As it turns out, exiting and closing are two different things in some software programs, including Word. When you finish using Word, you can exit the program. When you finish a document, you can close it, but keep the program window open to work on more documents. One action completely closes a program, whereas the other keeps it open and simply closes the current file.

Closing the Word program window when you're done using it is actually a good idea. Keeping it running in the background does tend to use up some of your computer's processing power.

Regardless of whether you're exiting or closing, if you haven't saved your work yet, Word prompts you to do so, as shown in Figure 1.9. You can choose **Save** or **Don't Save**, or you can back out of the whole question by selecting **Cancel**.

Microsoft Word	✕
⚠ Want to save your changes to Document1?	
If you click "Don't Save", a recent copy of this file will be temporarily available.	
Learn more	
[Save] [Don't Save] [Cancel]	

FIGURE 1.9

If you haven't saved your work, Word prompts you to do so before exiting.

To close the current document, yet keep the program window open, follow these steps:

1. Click **File** on the Ribbon.

2. Click **Close** (see Figure 1.10).

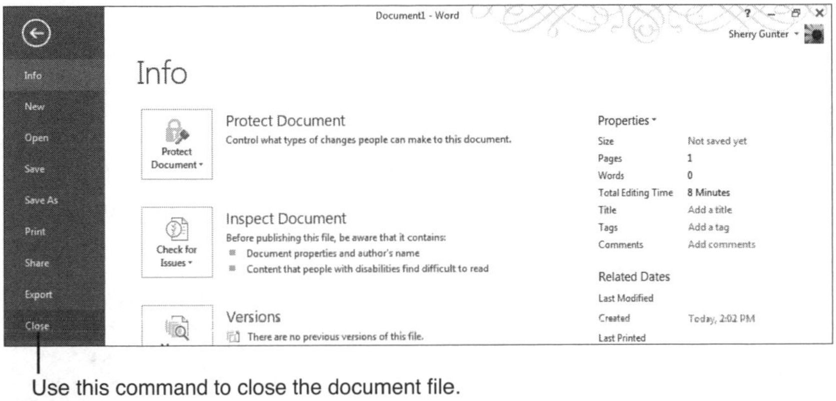

Use this command to close the document file.

FIGURE 1.10

The File tab opens this screen where you can find the Close command to close a document, but not the entire program.

To close the entire program window, use any of these methods:

- Click the **Close** icon in the upper-right corner of the program window.
- Click the **Word** icon in the upper-left corner and click **Close**.
- Right-click the Word document on the taskbar and click **Close window**.

As soon as you activate the **Close** command, Word closes entirely.

If you would rather just get the program window out of the way for a bit while you tackle other computer tasks, you can minimize the window. Minimizing the Word window reduces it to a button icon on the Desktop taskbar. To open it again, just click the icon.

THE ABSOLUTE MINIMUM

Now you know a little more about Word, and you're about to learn a whole lot more in the chapters to come. Meanwhile, here are a few items to take away from this chapter:

- Microsoft Word is the most famous word-processing program in the market today.

- Word 2013 includes a lot of exciting improvements, including a new reading mode and cloud connectivity.

- Word is super easy to launch, regardless of which operating system you're using, and the new Start screen lets you choose whether to start a new document based on a template or open an existing file.

- The program window layout is very intuitive; commands are located on the various tabs on the Ribbon, and the wide open area in the middle is where you type in text.

- You can use the Help feature to find help with Word topics and tasks, including tutorials and access to online support.

- Closing a document and closing a program are two different things.

2

IN THIS CHAPTER

- Learn how to work with the Ribbon of tools found at the top of the program window.

- Find out how to access the Quick Access toolbar squirreled away in the top-left corner.

- Acquaint yourself with context menus and toolbars.

- Learn how to deal with dialog boxes.

- Change your view with Word View modes and zoom tools.

BASIC WORD OPERATIONS

Before you jump in and start whipping up documents willy-nilly, taking some time to familiarize yourself with the basic methods Word offers to access tools, commands, and features is a good idea. Learning how to find your way to the commonly used commands and features now can help you speed up your work later. Microsoft Word presents commands, settings, and options through dialog boxes, context menus, toolbars, and the Ribbon. In many cases, you can access the same tools and features through several different avenues. For example, don't be surprised to find an Italics button on the Ribbon, in the Font dialog box, and on a mini toolbar that pops up from time to time. Although this might seem rather redundant at first, offering you several ways to accomplish the same task or action is simply a brilliant way to accommodate all kinds of users, including some who like making selections from a dialog box and others who like clicking things on a pop-up toolbar.

Another basic part of operating within Word is learning how to adjust your view of the document you are working on. You can switch view modes to change how a page is displayed onscreen, or use the zoom tools to change the level of magnification for viewing a document. Word's view modes and zoom tools are an essential part of helping you see what you're doing onscreen.

Working with the Ribbon

Introduced back in Word 2007, the Ribbon organizes commands and features into tabs listed across the top of the program window. Today's Ribbon is better than ever. If you haven't worked with the latest versions of Word in the past few years, you might be interested to know the Ribbon replaces the menus and toolbars of old. With the Ribbon format, related command buttons and features are organized into groups found within each tab. For example, if you display the **Home** tab, shown in Figure 2.1, you can find most of Word's formatting commands, such as font and size, alignment buttons, and styles. The **Insert** tab offers a plethora of items you can insert into a document, such as pictures, links, text boxes, and so forth. The various buttons, drop-down menus, and galleries found on the Ribbon tabs are grouped under labeled headings, such as **Font** or **Paragraph**, along the Ribbon's expanse.

Behold the mighty Ribbon

FIGURE 2.1

*The **Home** tab on the Ribbon displays various formatting tools and features.*

NOTE In regard to software lingo, lots of terms are interchangeable. For example, commands, features, settings, and options are all basically the same thing—selections you make in the program to perform a computer task. Sometimes this involves clicking an actual command button, such as **OK** or **Cancel**; other times this involves choosing from a variety of options to apply, such as clicking check boxes or radio buttons (the tiny circles with bullets) to turn items on or off. At the heart of it, all software programs are basically about taking your input, whether it's clicking buttons or typing in text, and turning it into something, such as a Word document.

Using Ribbon Elements

Using the Ribbon is a fairly straightforward procedure. All you have to do is click a tab name to view its contents. To activate a command or feature on the Ribbon, click on it. Let's say you type in a title at the top of your document and want to make it bold so it stands out from the rest of the page. To apply bold formatting to selected title text, you can click the **Bold** button (the button with a little bold B on it) found on the Ribbon's **Home** tab.

 NOTE   The Ribbon appears throughout the Microsoft Office suite of programs, such as Excel and PowerPoint, and it also appears in other programs as well. After you learn your way around the Ribbon in Word, you'll easily traverse the Ribbon format in other programs.

If you see a drop-down arrow—which is simply a downward pointing arrow icon—next to any Ribbon feature, you can click it to display a menu of additional choices or options. Figure 2.2 shows an example of a drop-down menu. After the menu drops, you can click a selection from the menu to apply it to your document.

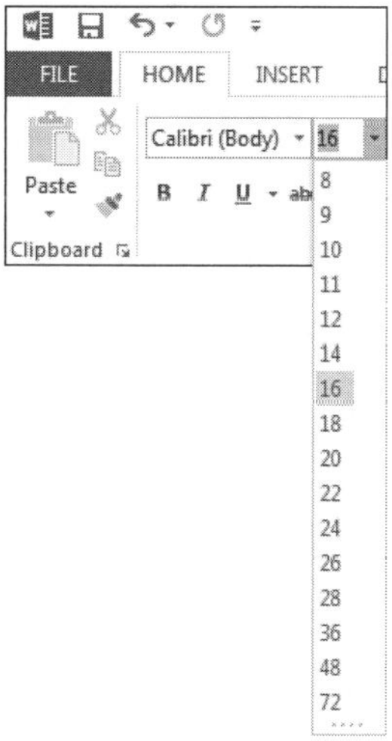

FIGURE 2.2

Drop-down menus offer a variety of selections you can make.

With some commands, such as font color, the command button shows the previously selected option, such as red. If you click the button instead of the drop-down arrow icon, you can apply the previously selected color to another area of your document without having to go through the process of selecting the color all over again. In other words, buttons like these retain the last selection until you designate another selection.

The Ribbon also features list boxes, called galleries, as shown in Figure 2.3. You can scroll through the gallery to view selections and click the one you want to apply.

FIGURE 2.3

Galleries list a variety of selections, such as styles you can apply.

You can also expand the gallery to view all the settings at one time, as shown in Figure 2.4.

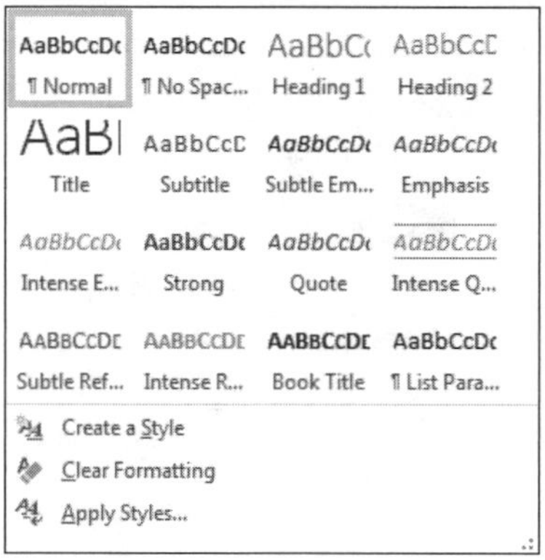

FIGURE 2.4

You can also open the gallery to view its contents.

Spinner arrows are also found on the Ribbon. For example, on the **Page Layout** tab, shown in Figure 2.5, you can click up and down arrow buttons to change the numeric settings for indents and spacing.

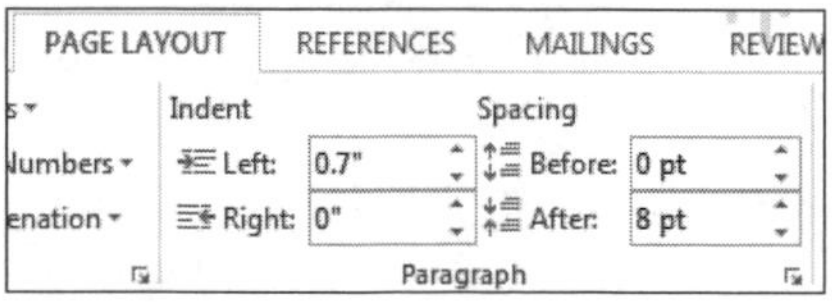

FIGURE 2.5

Use spinner arrows to adjust values.

Check boxes are also found on the Ribbon, specifically on the **View** tab. Simply check or uncheck a box to turn the feature on or off.

 NOTE The Ribbon got its name from its earliest concept of combining commands onto an area of the screen resembling a paper scroll-like strip. Although the Ribbon doesn't really work quite like a paper scroll today, it still offers easy, intuitive access to commands and features.

 TIP You might notice some groups of commands on a tab have a tiny icon in the bottom-right corner of the group. When clicked, this icon opens a dialog box where you can find additional and advanced commands. For example, if you click the **Paragraph** group's icon, the **Paragraph** dialog box opens with more spacing, indent, and line break settings. You can learn more about dialog boxes later in this chapter.

Here's a rundown of the main tabs found on the Ribbon:

- **File**—This tab opens a new screen of various file-related commands, such as Open, Save, and Print. Learn more about opening and saving files in Part II.

- **Home**—This tab organizes all the basic formatting commands for creating a document, including font, size, and alignment commands. Learn more about formatting in Part III.

- **Insert**—Use the commands on this tab to add elements to your document, such as clip art, text boxes, pictures, drawn shapes, video clips, and more. Learn more about adding graphic elements in Part IV.

- **Design**—Add flare to your document using Word's document formatting tools, including themes, watermarks, and page borders. Learn more about advanced formatting in Parts III and IV.

- **Page Layout**—Find all kinds of page layout controls on this tab, including margin settings, columns, page orientation, paragraph spacing, and other placement tools. Learn more about formatting pages in Part III.

- **References**—The tools on this tab help you to add footnotes, endnotes, citations and bibliography elements, table of contents, captions, index elements, and more. Learn more about building longer documents in Part V.

- **Mailings**—Use the tools on this tab to help generate mail merge documents and their various fields for customizing mass mailing materials. To learn more about mail merging, check out the additional online content for this book located at http://www.quepublishing.com/title/9780789750907.

- **Review**—Find Word's many proofing tools on this tab, including spell-checking options, grammar checking, and tools for collaborating on documents with reviewing and tracking marks. To learn more about sharing documents with other users, visit http://www.quepublishing.com/title/9780789750907 and find steps and techniques for using Word's reviewing features.

- **View**—You can find all the various ways to change your view of a document on this tab, including zoom tools, view modes, and window arrangement options for viewing more than one document at a time. Learn more about view modes later in this chapter.

- **Add-Ins**—If you install extra third-party add-in programs, such as specialized toolbars or features, you can find them listed in this tab. Learn more about add-ins and apps in Chapter 3, "Setting Up Accounts and Services."

In addition to these, task-specific tabs might also appear when you are working on an item such as a picture or drawn shape.

Hiding and Displaying the Ribbon

A lot of commands are available in Word, and placing them on various tabs on the Ribbon helps keep them organized. However, it also makes the Ribbon appear a bit intrusive at times because it holds so many things. You can easily hide the Ribbon and get it out of the way when you're working on documents. You can summon it back again with a click.

To hide the Ribbon, just double-click any tab name on the Ribbon. Word immediately hides the entire thing except for the tab names, shown in Figure 2.6. To display the Ribbon again, double-click a tab name.

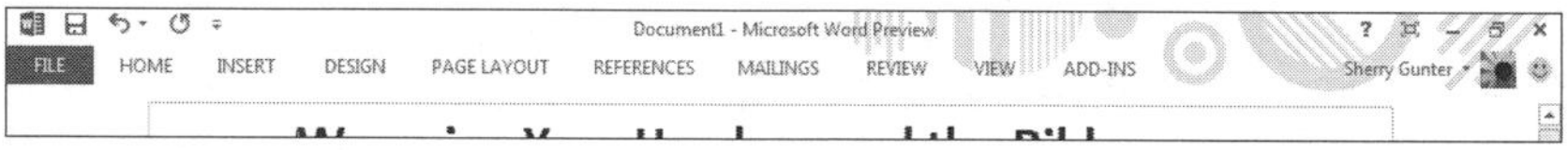

FIGURE 2.6

You can hide the Ribbon to free up screen space.

If you want the Ribbon to always appear locked in place, click the pushpin icon located at the far-right end, as shown in Figure 2.7. Click the same area to unlock the Ribbon again.

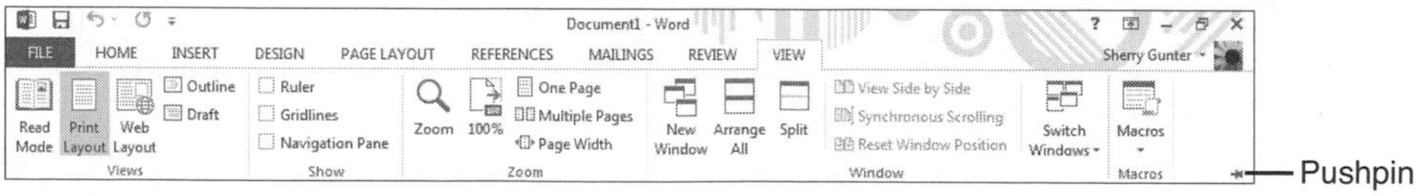

FIGURE 2.7

Look for the pushpin icon to pin the Ribbon in place.

TIP   Want to customize the Ribbon? You can add and subtract commands to suit the way you work. To find customizing options, right-click an empty area of the Ribbon or on a tab name and click **Customize the Ribbon**. This opens the **Word Options** dialog box to the **Customize Ribbon** tab where you can add and subtract commands, create new tabs, rename tabs, or reset to the default settings.

Working with the Quick Access Toolbar

Located in the top-left corner of the Word program window resides a small grouping of icon buttons called the Quick Access toolbar. These buttons give you quick access to common actions. By default, the Quick Access toolbar displays the **Save**, **Undo**, and **Redo** buttons, as shown in Figure 2.8. You can use these shortcut icons to quickly save a file, or undo or redo an action.

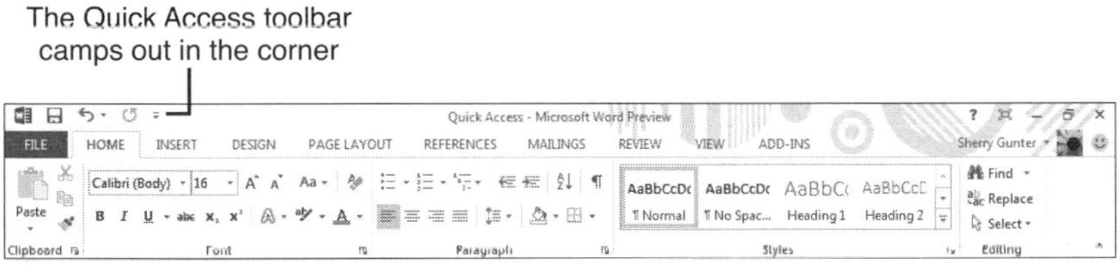

The Quick Access toolbar
camps out in the corner

FIGURE 2.8

Tucked away in the corner lurks the Quick Access toolbar.

You can also choose to display more or less shortcuts on the toolbar. Click the arrow icon at the end of the bar to display a drop-down menu (see Figure 2.9). Check marks next to the command names indicate the icons that appear on the toolbar. To add an icon, click the command name. To remove an icon, click it to uncheck it and delete it from the toolbar.

As you can imagine, placing shortcuts up at the top of your program window can be a timesaver if you find yourself performing the same tasks over and over again, such as printing files, and tire of looking through the Ribbon or other dialog boxes to find a command.

TIP   Want to customize the Quick Access toolbar? You can add an icon for a command you use the most. Click the arrow icon at the end of the Quick Access toolbar and choose **More Commands**. This opens the **Word Options** dialog box to the **Quick Access Toolbar** tab where you can add and subtract commands.

Click here to display the menu

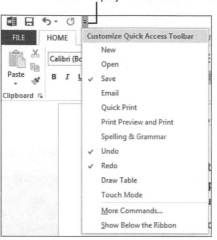

FIGURE 2.9

Use the drop-down menu at the end of the toolbar to specify which shortcut icons appear.

Using Context Menus and Toolbars

Microsoft Word offers several ways to apply commands related to the task at hand. Called context menus and toolbars, these features pop up and display shortcut commands pertaining to the item you are working with in a document.

For example, as soon as you select text in a document, a mini toolbar appears near the cursor. You can use this toolbar, shown in Figure 2.10, to quickly apply basic formatting commands. If you ignore the mini toolbar and keep working, it eventually disappears. To activate a command from the toolbar, simply click the button.

A pop-up toolbar offers shortcuts to popular formatting commands

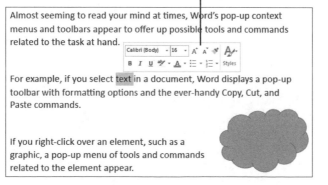

FIGURE 2.10

The mini toolbar offers shortcuts to common formatting commands, like Bold and Italics.

TIP You can turn off the automatic mini toolbar display if you do not find it helpful. To do so, click the **File** tab on the Ribbon, then click **Options**. The **Word Options** dialog box opens. Click the **General** category, then deselect the **Show Mini Toolbar on selection** check box and click **OK**. This turns the feature off. To turn it on again, revisit this dialog box and check the box again.

If you right-click while performing a task, such as entering text or editing a table, a context menu pops up listing commands related to what you're doing. For example, if you right-click a drawn shape (see Figure 2.11), the context menu includes commands for formatting the shape, adjusting its positioning, inserting a caption, and more. To make a selection from the context menu, click the command.

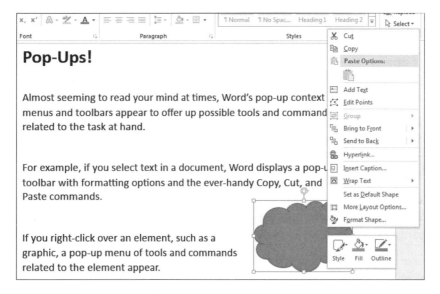

FIGURE 2.11

Context menus appear when you right-click in a document.

Dealing with Dialog Boxes

Dialog boxes are a basic part of just about every software program. Dialog boxes allow users to specify more input. Many of Word's dialog boxes offer more options for you to choose from before applying a feature, or present a variety of related settings all in one convenient spot. Figure 2.12 shows a typical dialog box. As you can see, it looks a lot like a form you might fill out.

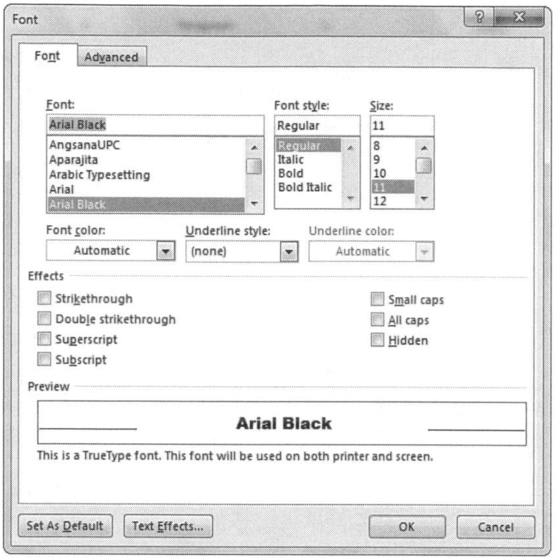

FIGURE 2.12

Dialog boxes require additional input from a user before implementing a feature or action.

Dialog boxes display many of the same tools found in the Ribbon, including buttons, list boxes, drop-down menus, spinner arrows, check boxes, and text boxes or *fields* in which you enter data. You can also find slider controls, tabs, and radio buttons among the many dialog boxes in Word.

The bottom of a dialog box typically has command buttons to execute the changes or to exit the box without changing anything. Click **OK** to execute the settings you specified, or click **Cancel** to forego the changes.

Some dialog boxes might include buttons that open additional dialog boxes. Tools and settings you find on Word's Ribbon might open dialog boxes as well. You are sure to encounter lots of dialog boxes as you work, but after you know what to expect from them and how to enter your input, you can handle them with ease.

 TIP You can move a dialog box around onscreen by clicking and dragging its title bar.

NOTE From time to time, Word also presents another type of box to you, called a prompt box. It looks like a dialog box in appearance, but generally it cautions you about a task or program need and offers some command buttons to choose from. For example, if you attempt to close a file you have not saved, Word prompts you to save your work. You can choose **Save**, **Don't Save**, or **Cancel** in the prompt box. Other prompt boxes just require an **OK** to confirm an action.

Working with Word View Modes and Zoom Tools

You can use Word's view modes to change the way you look at a document onscreen. You can also adjust the zoom level, or magnification, of your document to view more or less of your document on the screen. View modes and document zooming are handy features when you want to get a different view of your document pages, such as zooming in to make the text easier to read onscreen or switching to Read More mode to focus only on the text in a column format, much like reading a book. You can find all of Word's viewing tools conveniently located on the Ribbon's View tab.

Changing View Modes

A view mode refers to a screen display for viewing a document. By default, Word starts you out in Print Layout view. This mode is just one of five different view modes available in Word.

- **Read mode** Use this mode to hide all the tools and menus and focus on reading the document much like a book, with pages of text displayed as columns.

- **Print Layout** This mode displays your document in the middle of the screen surrounded by the Ribbon at the top, and scroll bars around the right and bottom edge. Basically, you can view all the elements in your document just as they appear in printed form.

- **Web Layout** If you are working with web pages in Word, this mode lets you see everything on the page just as it would appear in a browser.

- **Outline** If you are working with a large document, this view lets you see headings and subheadings in an outline format, with bullets and indents denoting levels in the document.

- **Draft** Use this view to see just the text in your document, minus all the graphic elements, and page layout elements such as headers and footers.

You can access Word's view modes several ways. If you simply want to choose between **Print Layout**, **Web Layout**, or **Read mode**, click the associated icon from the program window's status bar, as shown in Figure 2.13. This figure also shows the default Print Layout view.

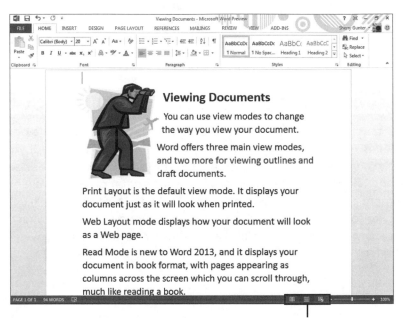

Click a view mode here

FIGURE 2.13

You can quickly choose a view mode from the status bar. This screen shows Print Layout mode.

 TIP   You can quickly find out the name of any Word button or icon by hovering the mouse pointer over it. This applies to the view icons on the status bar, too.

Figure 2.14 shows the same document using Web Layout view. Notice how the page content sprawls out without margin areas normally associated with documents.

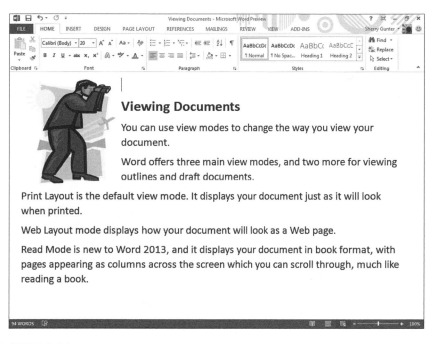

FIGURE 2.14

Here's the same document shown in Web Layout view mode.

Figure 2.15 shows the same document using Read mode. The Ribbon is no longer displayed, and the **Tools** and **View** tabs display menus when clicked. In this viewing mode, you can use the arrow icons on the left and right side of the page to move forward and backward a page, like turning pages in a book.

In addition to the view modes found on the status bar, you can also click the **View** tab on the Ribbon, as shown in Figure 2.16, and then click a view mode. In addition to the three main view modes, the View tab also features the **Outline** and **Draft** views.

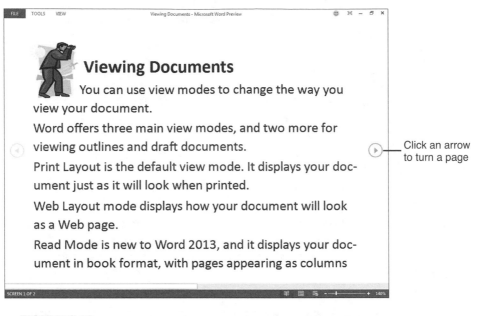

FIGURE 2.15

Here's the same document shown in Read mode.

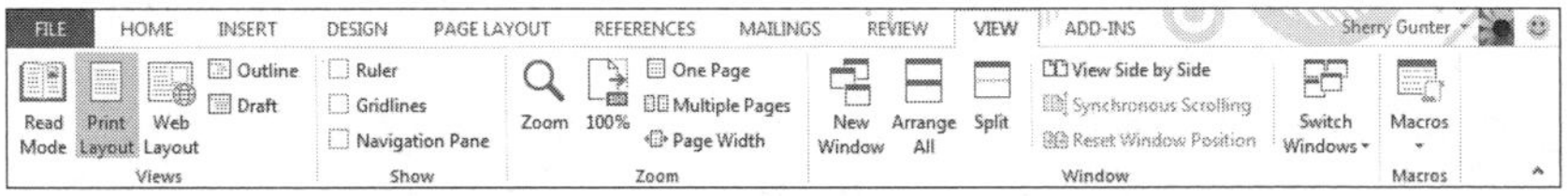

FIGURE 2.16

Use the View tab on the Ribbon as another route to switching views.

Zooming Your View

Magnifying tools have long been a staple of word-processing programs, allowing users to zoom in for a closer look at text and other document items, or zooming out for a bird's-eye view of a page. To make zooming easier than ever, you can drag the Zoom slider on the status bar (see Figure 2.17). Drag it left to zoom out or drag it right to zoom in. You can also click on the slider to adjust the zoom level. To return to 100%, click the middle of the Zoom bar.

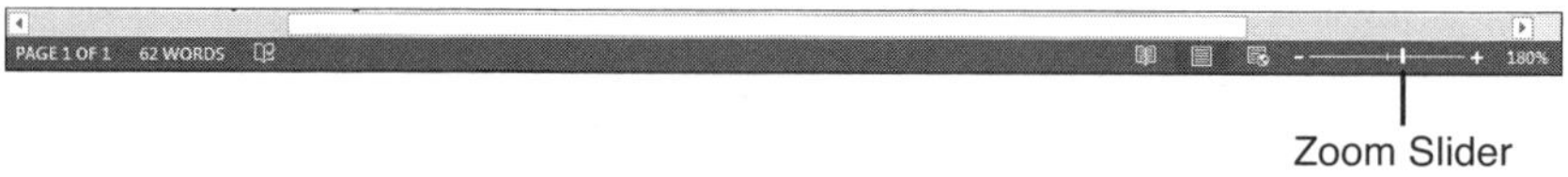

PAGE 1 OF 1   62 WORDS   180%

Zoom Slider

FIGURE 2.17

Drag the Zoom slider to zoom in or out.

You can also find **Zoom** controls on the **View** tab, as shown in Figure 2.18. Any time you want to return a page to 100% size, click the **100%** button. The View tab also lists options for viewing a single page, multiple pages, or full page width. To specify a specific zoom percentage, click the **Zoom** button to open the **Zoom** dialog box, shown in Figure 2.19.

FIGURE 2.18

The Ribbon's View tab offers more zoom options.

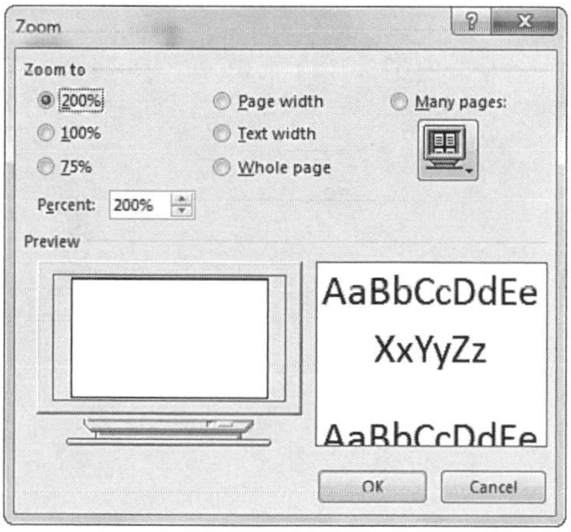

FIGURE 2.19

Use the Zoom dialog box to set a specific percentage for zooming a document, or choose from several presets, such as 200% or 75%.

From the Zoom dialog box, you can choose a percentage or type a number in the text box. Click **OK** to apply the new setting to the document.

THE ABSOLUTE MINIMUM

This chapter introduced you to several basic Word operations. Here are the key points to remember from this chapter:

- The Ribbon hosts all the tools and features you need to build, format, and work with documents. Click a tab to view its associated tools.

- Use the Quick Access toolbar in the upper-left corner to save a file, and undo and redo actions. You can also add and subtract buttons that appear on this toolbar to suit the way you work.

- You can right-click in a document to reveal task-related shortcuts via pop-up menus or toolbars.

- Use dialog boxes to enter additional settings and options.

- Word's view modes help you examine your document for different tasks, such as viewing how the document looks when printed or how a document looks as a web page.

- Word's Zoom tools change the magnification level for viewing a document. Use them to zoom in for a closer look or zoom out for a bird's-eye view.

IN THIS CHAPTER

- Learn the scoop about this whole "cloud" thing everybody's discussing.
- See how easy it is to sign into a Microsoft account.
- Explore ways to customize Word to suit your own style, such as picking out a really flattering account picture.
- Find out what services you can connect with Word to expand your document experiences.
- Discover the fun of shopping for more Word apps at the Office Store.

3

SETTING UP ACCOUNTS AND SERVICES

Microsoft Word 2013—and all the other applications in the Microsoft Office 2013 suite—offers better and faster ways than ever before to access your files and share them with others. Connecting with services, such as LinkedIn or Flickr, and sharing documents, pictures, and more, is also easier than ever. To use these new features, you need to set up a Microsoft account online. Chances are, if you've already installed Word, you've already taken steps to set up an initial account. In this chapter, you'll learn more about the connectivity options available and how to put them to use. I'll also explain this "cloud" stuff (which, strangely, has nothing to do with weather), help you find your way to additional services and apps, and show you how to customize your account.

Introducing Web and Cloud Connectivity

Everybody keeps talking about this "cloud" thing, but what exactly is it? Basically, it's really just the Internet. I know that's kind of a letdown and you were probably hoping it was a magical hard drive in the sky or something. Nope, it's just the Internet, but to be more specific, it's the ability to store and process computer data online rather than on your own computer. Cloud connectivity is really twofold—one part is *cloud storage*, taking your files, whether they are documents or pictures, and saving them to dedicated web servers. The other part is *cloud computing*, which is being able to run a computer program hosted on a web server. Both parts offer many advantages.

You're already using cloud storage if you have an email account someplace such as Google or Yahoo! (they store your email messages), or if you share photos on Flickr or Facebook (they store your photos). However, the real meat and potatoes of cloud storage are services dedicated to letting you store all of your data with them (sometimes for a fee, other times for free).

When you think about it, it's a brilliant idea. You don't have to worry anymore about where to store your files, how much storage space your hard drive has left, keeping up with what's on what flash drive or CD/DVD, or running out of storage space and needing to delete data to make room for more. Having someone else store your files safely is a pretty sweet deal. The final selling point is this—you can access your cloud storage from any computing device. Yes, *any* computing device! You don't have to use your home or office computer, you can use your smartphone, tablet, other computers, and so on. Plus, with cloud storage, you have a backup of all your files in case your hard drive crashes.

Cloud storage is a relatively new concept and many cloud-based services are popping up all the time. They work by offering you space on their servers to store all types of files. (*Web servers* are computers that host websites, storage, and applications.) Large companies, such as Microsoft or Amazon, have server "farms," or data centers, filled with thousands of servers. Most of the services charge a small monthly fee, and others are free, but limit the amount of storage. Examples of cloud storage services include Amazon's Cloud Drive, Dropbox, SugarSync, and Microsoft's very own SkyDrive.

 NOTE Why do they call it the *cloud*? The term comes from the way in which network engineers had to describe networks outside their own, such as the Internet, which they connected to but didn't necessarily control or know what was going on in the other networks. Real clouds are opaque, and network clouds are rather like this, too, because you can't really see how all the data moves across the Internet, but it does end up somewhere out the other side via all the connections. When the engineers would diagram the various devices and connections on their networks, they would draw the Internet portion of the network as a cloud.

Cloud computing—the other prong in cloud technology—uses the Web as a platform for applications. Rather than rely on installing programs on your computer to handle word processing or spreadsheet tasks, for example, you can use web-based applications to create and work with files. In other words, you're opening the program from the Web instead of on your own computer. When running applications on other computers on the cloud, less computing power is required from your own system. Microsoft Office is one such package available as a subscription service for both home and office users, called Office 365. You can access Office 365 from any computer, sort of like renting the software instead of buying it. The nice part of this sort of scenario is you no longer need to worry about upgrading versions of the software—updates and new features are available right away with cloud applications.

In light of the excitement over cloud storage and cloud computing, you need to be mindful of some things—*bandwidth* and *costs*. Sending email and viewing photos on the cloud doesn't require a great deal of bandwidth, but utilizing web-based applications, such as streaming movies or games, eats up your monthly bandwidth allocation fast. Make sure you are aware of the costs for going over the limit if you have a limit as part of your cloud services subscription or monthly fee.

WHAT IS BANDWIDTH?

Bandwidth refers to the amount of information that can be transmitted over a network connection. It's measured in speed, specifically bits per second, as in kilobytes (Kbps) at the low end or megabytes (Mbps) at the high end, with the *bits* being the pieces of data. Host providers, like your ISP (Internet service provider), rent out portions of their full-blown connection to you, and regulate how much you can use.

Out on the Internet, data travels quickly because everything is connected by cables and networks—think of it as a giant pipe in which information flows. As the end user, your connection is with your ISP and depending on your type of account, the connection might be very fast or somewhat slow. Because your provider has to pipe out the connection to numerous users besides you, your pipe size is much smaller and more restrictive in flow compared to the big pipe the ISP is connected to, so that's why a webpage might take longer to load in your browser window or a file to download onto your computer. Typically, if you want more bandwidth, you need a faster Internet connection, which usually costs more.

Microsoft products, such as Word 2013, tap into the power of cloud storage, too. For example, with a Microsoft account and an online connection, you can access Help files from Microsoft's online resources to learn more about a feature, or you can search through collections of clip art illustrations and stock photography to add visuals to your documents. You can also create a SkyDrive account (www.SkyDrive.com) and store your documents online. SkyDrive offers 7 GB of free storage; you can up that amount for additional fees.

Wait, there's more! Microsoft has cloud computing services to offer you, too! Office Web Apps offers browser-based versions of Microsoft programs, including Word (see Figure 3.1). Office Web Apps let you view and work with any of your Microsoft Office files. Office Web Apps are a free, online version of the Office suite and you can use them through the SkyDrive site, too. All it takes to use the apps is a Microsoft account (which used to be called a Windows Live Account). Mind you, the apps are not fully featured like a regular Word program window on your computer, or through a paid subscription with Office 365, but they're extremely useful nonetheless. The great thing about this feature is that your friends and colleagues who do not have Office installed can use SkyDrive and Office Web Apps to work on the files, too. This is a great way for you to share your documents with each other.

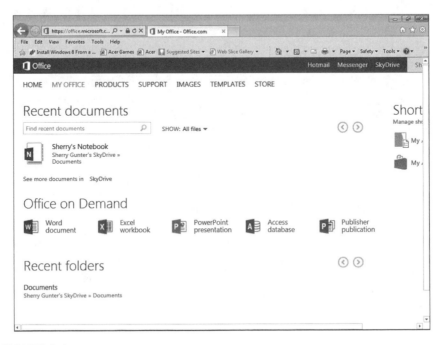

FIGURE 3.1

Using your web browser, log on to your My Office account to access SkyDrive, Office Web Apps, and more.

Using a Microsoft Account

When you create an account to start using Word, you enter user information about yourself, such as your name and email address. Let's talk about what you're getting into with such an account. A *Microsoft account* is a free, cloud-based account that lets you use SkyDrive (cloud storage), Hotmail (free email service), Skype (online video conferencing), and more. In fact, a Microsoft account gives you access to a wide range of services and tools, including productivity tools to help you manage files, and social tools that help you communicate and share with others. If you use a Microsoft service such as Hotmail or Messenger, you already have a Microsoft account, but if not, you can create a free one.

Your Microsoft account offers the following online services:

- **Email**   Outlook is the official email service, and you can use it with a Hotmail or Outlook email address, or use an email address you already have.

- **Messenger/Skype**   Use this service to send instant messages to your friends and contacts.

- **Calendar**   Keep track of important events and appointments, and share this data with others.

- **Office Web Apps**   Web-based versions of the popular Office suite, including Word, PowerPoint, Excel, and OneNote.

- **SkyDrive**   Not only is SkyDrive an online file storage space, but it's completely integrated with Office Web Apps.

- **Profile**   Create a public information page about yourself for viewing by other users who instant message you or contact you using email.

- **Windows Essentials Apps**   Includes Photo Gallery (photo viewer and editor app), Movie Maker (a simple video editing app), and Writer (blog editor).

You can learn more about these services on the Microsoft Office website (office. microsoft.com) and start your My Office account. Learn more about using Office Web Apps at http://www.quepublishing.com/title/9780789750907.

Signing In

Signing into your Microsoft account is pretty simple. If you sign out, for instance, you'll need to sign back in. As with a lot of online accounts, you need your email address and password to sign in. Follow these steps:

1.   Click the **Sign In** button (see Figure 3.2).

FIGURE 3.2

Look for the Sign In button to get started.

2. Type in your email address (see Figure 3.3).

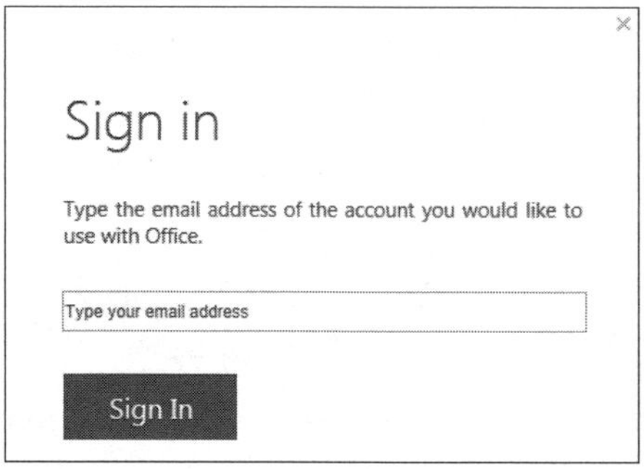

FIGURE 3.3

Click the box and type in your email address.

3. Type in your password (see Figure 3.4).

FIGURE 3.4

Next, type in your password.

4. Click **Sign In**.

Word logs onto your account and displays your user information, services you're using, and various account settings in a screen similar to the one in Figure 3.5.

Sign out link   Account name drop-down arrow

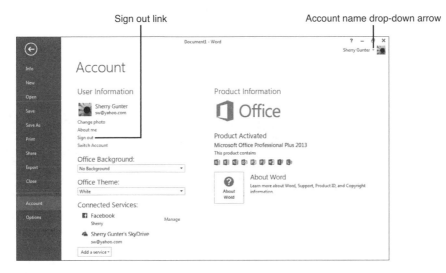

FIGURE 3.5

Account information and settings include your name, photo, and any customizing settings you have applied.

If you need to sign out again later, click the **File** tab and click **Account**, then click the **Sign out** link (see Figure 3.5). You can also click your account name drop-down arrow up in the right-corner of the program window and then click **Account settings** to open the same screen.

Adding and Switching Accounts

You can add multiple accounts and switch between them. This is helpful if you are sharing Word with other users in your household, for example. You can create an account for each one and they can customize their accounts the way they like.

To add an account, start by displaying the **Account** page again (see Figure 3.5). Click the **Switch Account** link to get things rolling. If you already know the other person's email and password, you set up an account for him, or he can take over your keyboard and do it himself. The same **Sign In** box appears that you encountered in Figure 3.3, and you have to enter the email address and the password. After the new account is created, it's automatically added to Word, too.

To switch between multiple accounts, click the **Switch Account** button on the **Account** page to display the **Accounts** box shown in Figure 3.6. Click the account you want to use in Word and you're ready to go. To add more accounts, you can click the **Add Account** button at the bottom of the **Accounts** box.

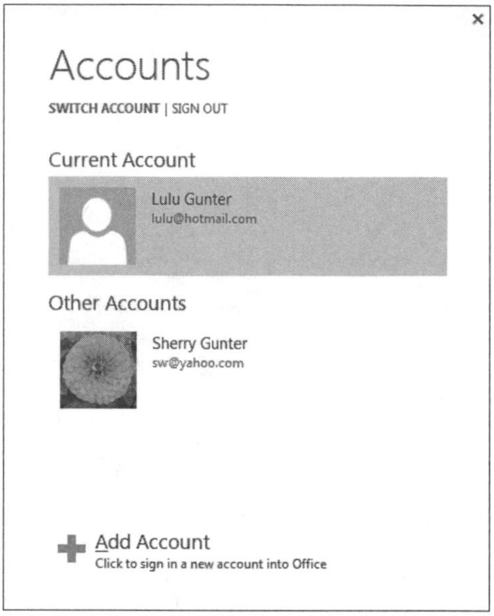

FIGURE 3.6

You can switch between accounts using the Accounts box.

You can also switch between accounts by clicking the account name drop-down arrow in the program window and choosing **Switch account**. This also opens the **Accounts** box.

Customizing Your Account

You can do a little customizing to make Word your own, such as assigning an account picture and applying some design tweaks to the program window. The customizing settings you add apply only to your account. Other users who share your program can customize their own accounts. Figure 3.7 points out the customizable areas on Word.

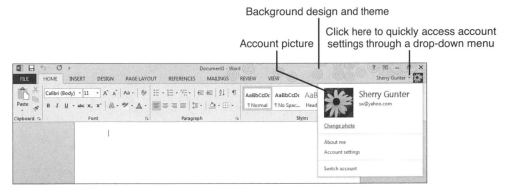

FIGURE 3.7

You can use your Microsoft account's Profile page to change your account picture.

Customizing Your Account Picture

The account picture is shown with all of your Microsoft account activities online as well as in all the Microsoft Office programs you use, such as Word. An account picture can be any graphic file found on your computer, including a photograph or an illustration. To assign a picture, click the **Change photo** link on the **Account** page (refer to Figure 3.5). This opens your Microsoft account **Profile** page, shown in Figure 3.8. Click the **Change picture** link.

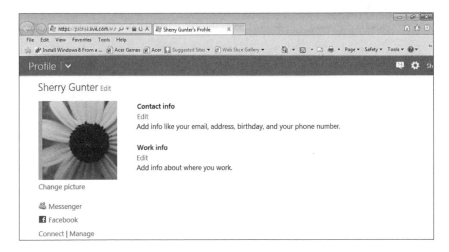

FIGURE 3.8

You can use your Microsoft account's Profile page to change your account picture.

From the **Picture** page, shown in Figure 3.9, click the **Browse** button. This opens the **Choose File to Upload** dialog box, as shown in Figure 3.10.

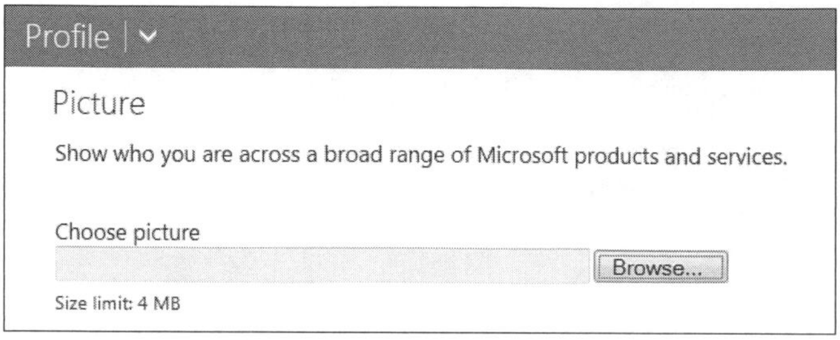

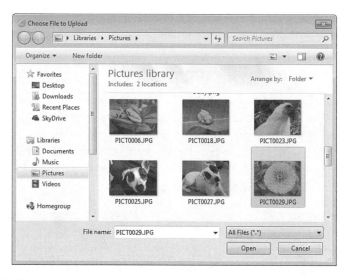

FIGURE 3.9

First you need to find the picture you want to upload, so click the Browse button.

FIGURE 3.10

Next, select the image you want to use.

Navigate to the folder or drive containing the image you want to use, and select the image. Click **Open** to return to the **Picture** page (see Figure 3.11). Per the instructions there, you can drag or resize the picture box to get the best part of your picture to display as the account photo. When you have everything just right, click the **Save** button.

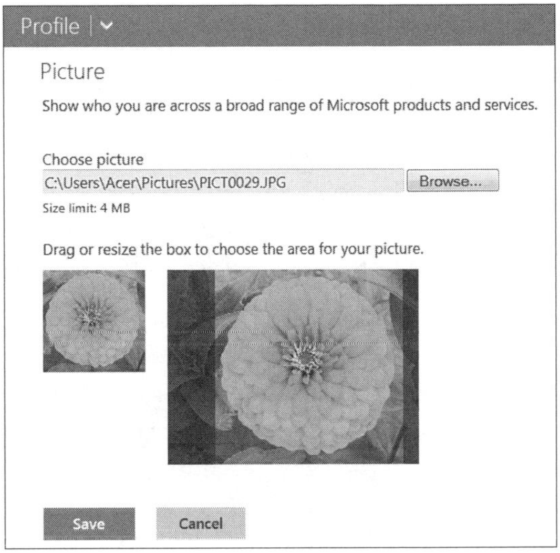

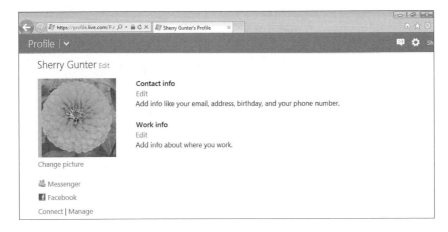

FIGURE 3.11

Position your picture the way you want it.

The **Profile** page now displays the new account picture, as shown in Figure 3.12. You can close out the browser window. The Word window should now sport the new picture. (If not, close the program and open it again.)

FIGURE 3.12

The new account picture now appears with your account name.

Changing the Background and Theme

New to Word 2013 and the other programs in the Microsoft Office suite is the ability to customize the program window background and theme. Changing the background only affects the very top of the program window (title bar and Ribbon tab names), but it does make you feel good choosing a design pattern that suits you. The design you choose doesn't spill over onto your document page, so it's really more of a little extra visual element for personalizing Word.

To change the background, click the **Office Background** drop-down arrow on the **Account** page, as shown in Figure 3.13. Move your mouse pointer over the different selections to preview what each one looks like. Click the one you like, and it's immediately applied. To remove a background, just choose the **No Background** selection.

FIGURE 3.13

Choose a background design from this menu.

The Office theme is a choice between White, Light Gray, or Dark Gray, as shown in Figure 3.14. This color affects the top of the program window, too, including the Ribbon.

Office Theme:

Light Gray ▼
White
Light Gray
Dark Gray

Sherry   Manage

FIGURE 3.14

Choose from three theme colors.

To fully appreciate your new customizing options, click the **Back** navigation arrow (top-left corner) and return to the document window. Now sit back and admire your tweaks.

Adding Services

You can add online services to your Microsoft account to enhance your computing experience and manage them from the **Account** page (see Figure 3.15). You can find services listed under the **Add a service** drop-down menu on the **Account** page. The categories displayed might vary based on whether you are signed in under a personal, organization, or school account.

FIGURE 3.15

Add services such as Facebook or YouTube to access pictures, videos, and more.

The following categories are available with a personal account:

- **Images & Videos**   You can nab images from your favorite sites, including Facebook, Flickr, and YouTube.

- **Storage**   You can store documents on SkyDrive or Office 365 SharePoint.

- **Sharing**   Share documents with other users you know on LinkedIn or Twitter.

To add a service, follow these steps.

1. Open the **Account** page; click the **File** tab and click **Account** or click the user name drop-down arrow and select **Account settings**.

2. Click the **Add a service** button, as shown in Figure 13.16.

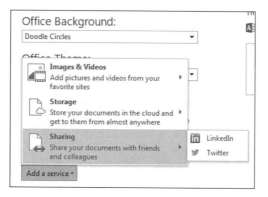

FIGURE 3.16

Click the Add a service button to get started.

3. Click a category.

4. Click a service to add.

5. Depending on which service you add, additional boxes appear and you must log in with the account or give your approval to any apps Microsoft must add; click **Connect** to continue. In this example, shown in Figure 3.17, I'm connecting my Twitter account.

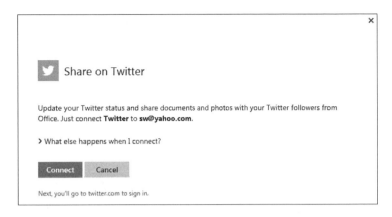

FIGURE 3.17

You'll see a screen like this when you add your Twitter account.

6. Click **Done** when you finish, if applicable.

The new service is listed under the **Connected Services** heading on the **Account** page, similar to what's shown in Figure 3.18. To make changes to the connection, click the **Manage** link and you can change the settings or remove the connection if you no longer want it.

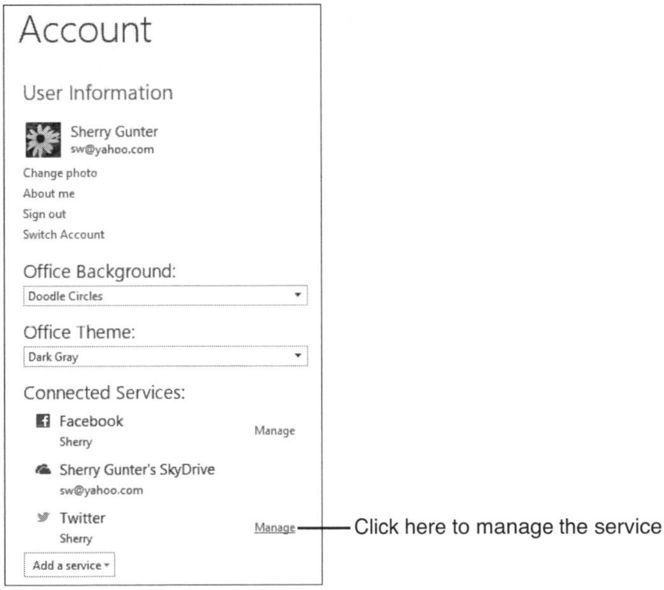

FIGURE 3.18

Manage your connected services through the Account page.

TIP You can also add services through other areas in Word, such as the **Online Pictures** dialog box (you can add Flickr to the mix of picture sources) or the **Online Video** dialog box (you can add YouTube to your selection for video sources).

Adding Apps

Feel up for a little shopping? You can go online and shop for more apps to add to Word and customize the program some more. Apps are small programs that you can add to Word to further enhance your experience, such as adding a dictionary, an additional library of stock photos, or templates for printing labels. The online Office Store, shown in Figure 3.19, is adding apps all the time—some are free and some sell for a small cost—and you can peruse from a variety of apps made specifically for Word. After you find one you like, you can download it and install it into Word.

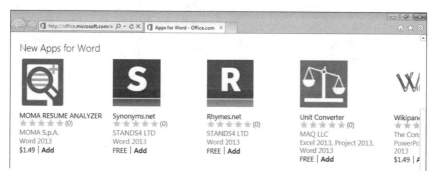

FIGURE 3.19

Visit the Office Store to find apps you can add to Word.

To add apps, begin by clicking the **Insert** tab and clicking the **Apps for Office** button, as shown in Figure 13.20. Click **See All** at the bottom of the menu that appears. This opens the **Apps for Office** dialog box, shown in Figure 13.21. A list of all of your installed apps appears under the **My Apps** tab in the dialog box. But you're looking for new ones, so click the **Find more apps at the Office Store** link at the bottom of the dialog box.

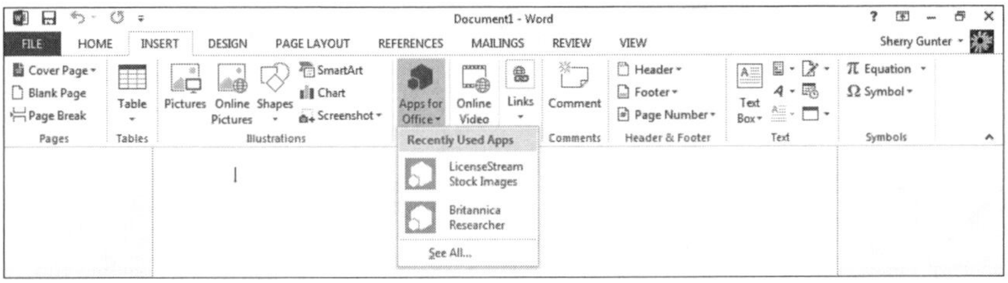

FIGURE 3.20

Find the Apps for Office button to see what's already installed and to look for more apps.

FIGURE 3.21

The Apps for Office dialog box keeps track of all of your apps.

Your web browser opens to the Office Store and displays the Word apps, as shown in Figure 13.22. Start scrolling around the page to see what's available and what you might like or need. When you find something interesting, click it to open another page with additional details, similar to Figure 3.23, and screenshots showing what the app does in Word. If you decide you want the app, click the **Add** button. The website asks you to confirm your purchase; click **Continue** and your app downloads.

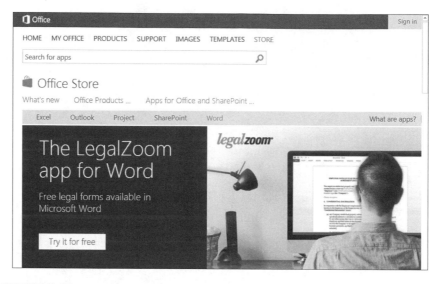

FIGURE 3.22

Visit the Office Store to find apps you can add to Word.

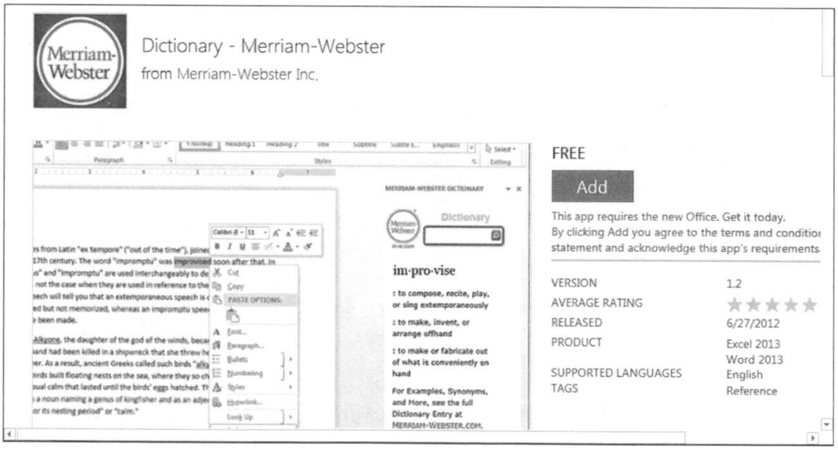

FIGURE 3.23

You can read more about an app before deciding whether you want it.

 TIP To help you decide whether an app is worth your time or not, check out the user reviews to see what others are saying about the app. Scroll around the app's page and click the **Reviews** link to read more.

Lastly, you need to go and find your app and install it. Reopen the **Apps for Office** dialog box you worked with earlier (refer to Figure 3.21). If it's closed, click the **Insert** tab, click the **Apps for Office** button, and click **See All**. Click **My Apps** and look for the icon for the newly downloaded app (see Figure 3.24). Click the app and click **Insert**.

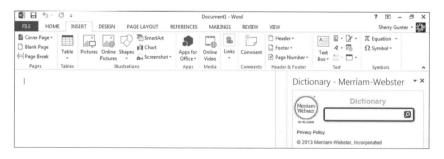

FIGURE 3.24

Ah, look—now there's a new app added to my list.

Word loads the app, which in this case is a dictionary that opens in its own pane off to the side of my document page, as shown in Figure 3.25. Goody—now I can look up words.

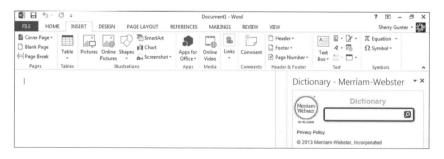

FIGURE 3.25

The new app installs and opens, in this case, a dictionary.

You can revisit the **Apps for Office** dialog box at any time to manage your installed apps, removing ones you don't want or shopping for more.

THE ABSOLUTE MINIMUM

Setting up a Microsoft account is incredibly easy and it gives you access to many new things online. In fact, it seems like all the cool stuff is online, so you'll definitely need an Internet connection to make the most of your Word experience. Here's what else you learned about accounts and services:

- *Cloud storage* refers to storing your files online, whereas *cloud computing* refers to running programs from web servers rather than your own computer.

- As a Word user, you have access to free online storage (SkyDrive) and free Office Web Apps.

- You can use multiple accounts in Word if you share your program with others in your household.

- You can customize your account by assigning a picture and jazzing up the program window with a background and theme.

- Add more connectivity to Word with services like Flickr, YouTube, Facebook, and Twitter (learn more about grabbing content from these sources in Part IV, "Adding Visual Elements with Tables, Charts, and Graphics).

- You can also customize Word by adding apps, small applications designed to help you get more out of your program. Shop for apps at the Office Store, an online site that keeps a growing library of user-rated apps you can download and try for yourself.

IN THIS CHAPTER

- Learn how to open a new document.
- See how to save your work by saving the document file. Also learn about file types and tags.
- Find out how to open recent files, as well as locate files stored on your computer or in the cloud.
- Learn how to switch between open documents.
- Get the scoop about moving and copying items between documents.
- Learn more about document protection options to suit your needs.

4

DOCUMENT BASICS

The term *document* in the non-digital world generally refers to a written or printed paper bearing original, official, or legal information. In the realm of computers, the term *document* refers to a file. Typically, computer documents contain text, but not always. Documents can also include files generated by desktop publishing programs, web pages, and more. Just for the record, the files you create in Word are officially called *documents*.

Because the whole purpose of having a word-processing program is to make documents, you need to learn a variety of basic tasks in order to get things rolling. You need to know how to start new files, open existing documents, juggle multiple open documents, and generally manage how your documents behave. This chapter shows you how to perform such basic document tasks.

Starting a New Document

Every time you open Word, you are presented with the option of starting a new document, opening a recent document, or opening another document stored on your computer, SkyDrive, or other location. The Word Start screen, as it is called, is a launching pad for deciding what you want to do in Word. To open a blank document, choose the **Blank document** option from among the list of templates, as shown in Figure 4.1. Yes, strangely enough, even a blank document is built on a template. You can learn more about using templates in the next chapter.

Click here to start a new document.

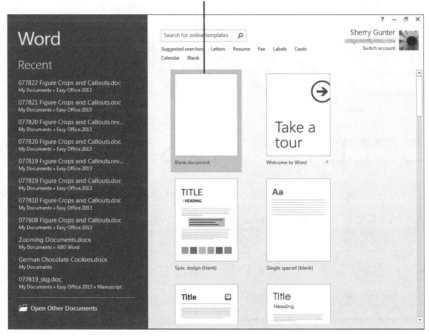

FIGURE 4.1

You can start a new document when you launch Word.

If you're already using Word and want to create a new document, you can summon one by revisiting the launch pad:

1. Click the **File** tab on the Ribbon.

2. Click **New**.

3. Click **Blank document**, shown in Figure 4.2, or any other template you want to use to start a new file.

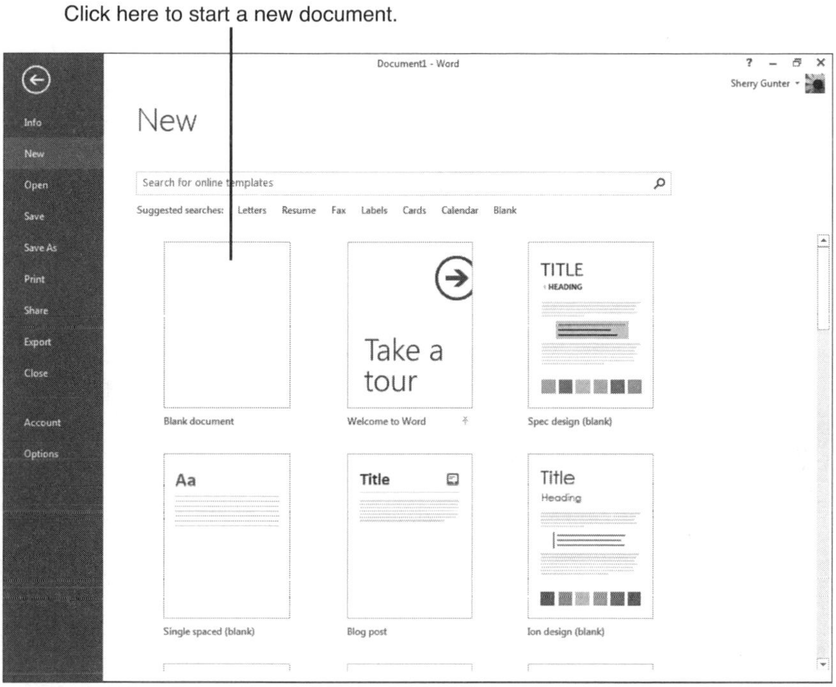

Click here to start a new document.

FIGURE 4.2

Use the New command to start a new document in Word.

Word opens a new, blank document onscreen and you're ready to go.

 NOTE If you prefer a shorter method to create new documents, you can display the **New** command on the Quick Access toolbar—the little line of buttons that appears up at the top of the program window. (We'll look at the Quick Access toolbar in the next section. Jump ahead to Figure 4.3 if you can't stand to wait.) By default, the toolbar starts out with the **Save**, **Undo**, and **Redo** tools, but you can add other tools, such as the **New** command, to the bar for easy access. When you do, you can quickly start a new document without revisiting the launch screen. Follow these steps to add the button to the toolbar.

1. Click the **Customize Quick Access Toolbar** arrow icon at the end of the toolbar.

2. Click **New**.

This adds the button. Just click the **New** button any time you want to start a blank document.

Saving Documents

Another key function of most programs is learning to save your work by activating some sort of **Save** command. In Microsoft Word, that command is conveniently located in the Quick Access toolbar, pointed out in Figure 4.3. You can also find your way to it through the Ribbon's **File** tab by clicking **File**, **Save** or **File**, **Save As** (see Figure 4.4).

The Save command

FIGURE 4.3

The Save command is conveniently located on the Quick Access toolbar.

Save command

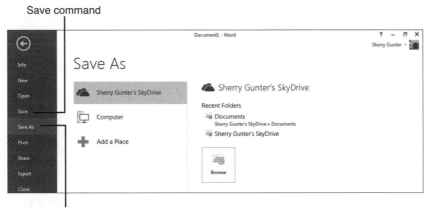

Save As command

FIGURE 4.4

You can also find the Save and Save As commands through the Ribbon's File tab.

Before going any further, let me clarify the difference between the **Save** command and the **Save As** command. Either one of these commands accomplishes the same thing the first time you save a document, which is basically saving your work, assigning a filename, and choosing where you want to save the file. After a file is saved, however, you only need to use the **Save** command to save any subsequent changes you make to the document.

But what if you want to save the same content as a different document, thus creating two different files? That's where the **Save As** command comes into play. You can use it to save an existing document under a new filename. You might do this to create two copies of a report, for example. Perhaps you want to take last year's report and update it to reflect this year's changes. You can start with the original file, save it under a new filename, and then make your changes. This can be a real timesaver, as you can imagine.

Ready to go through the steps for saving a file? Here we go:

1. Click the **File** tab on the Ribbon and click **Save** or **Save As**, or click the **Save** button on the Quick Access toolbar.

2. Click a destination for the saved file.

3. Depending on the selected destination, additional recent folders might appear listed. You can choose one, if needed. If the folder you want isn't listed, you can use the Save As dialog box in the next step to find the folder or drive to which you want to save the file; click **Browse** to get started.

4. Next, the Save As dialog box opens and you can type in a name for the file in the **File name** box, as shown in Figure 4.5. You can also use this dialog box to navigate to a certain folder or drive in which to store the file, if need be.

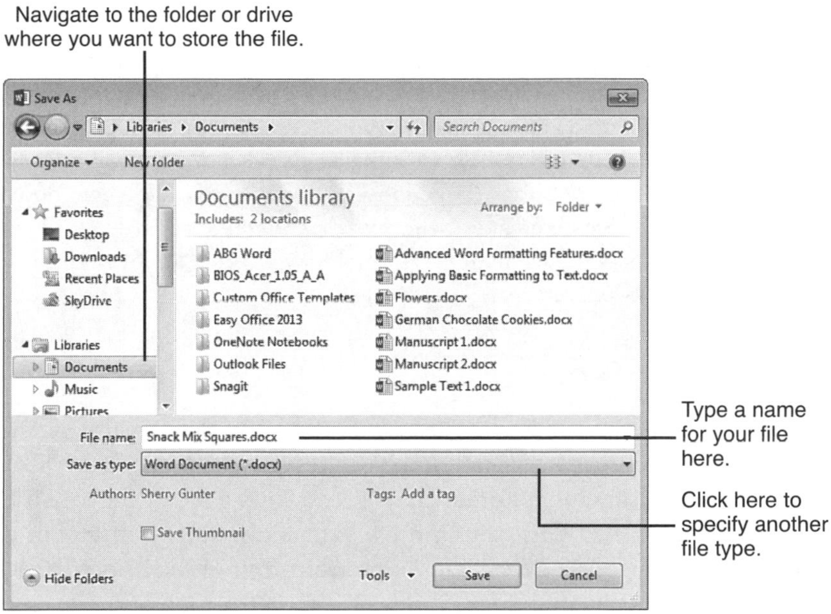

Navigate to the folder or drive
where you want to store the file.

FIGURE 4.5

Use the Save As dialog box to specify a filename, a destination folder, or a particular file type.

5. Optionally, you can use the **Save as type** drop-down menu to assign another file type, such as saving the document as a PDF file or a web page.

6. Click **Save**, and Word saves the file per your directions.

TIP   Use the left pane in the Save As dialog box to scroll up and down to find and select the drive or library folder where you want to store your document, then use the other pane to narrow down your destination to folders within the main library folder or drive.

If you try to exit a document without saving your changes, Word prompts you to do so before closing the file. Click **Save** to save your work, click **Don't Save** to disregard all of your changes, or click **Cancel** to change your mind about closing the document.

NOTE   By default, Word is set up to automatically save temporary copies of your documents as you work. In case of a system crash, you can recover any documents you were working on at the time of the crash. Word's AutoRecover feature is set up to save a file every 10 minutes and keep the last autosave if you close the program without saving. You can adjust these settings, if needed, or turn off AutoRecover. You can find the save options by clicking the **File** tab, and then clicking the **Options** link. This opens the Word Options dialog box; click the **Save** category to find all the AutoRecover settings. You can also find your way to the Word Options dialog box through the Save As dialog box; click the **Tools** drop-down arrow next to the **Save** button and choose **Save Options**. If you ever do need to recover an autosaved file, click the **File** tab, click **Open**, click **Recent Documents**, and scroll down to the **Recover Unsaved Documents** option.

A Word About File Types

Let's talk about file types, also called file formats. By default, the files you create in Word are saved in Word's "document" file type, which adds a .DOCX file extension to the filename automatically. If you save a file and name it **Bob**, its actual full name is **Bob.docx** with the file extension. Most of the time you don't see file extensions in Windows unless you want to, but they determine what sort of program can read the file. Different programs read and create different file types. For example, you normally won't create Word document files in an illustration program, and you can't turn a Word document file into a graphic file—software programs are designed to make certain types of files, hence the distinguishing file extensions.

However, many programs can read and work with a wider variety of file types than just the ones they are designed to create. Microsoft Word lets you open text files of other varieties, web pages, XML documents, OpenDocument Text files, PDF files, XPS files, and files created in older versions of Word. You can also save your documents as these other file types. Take a look at Figure 4.6 to see the **Save as type** drop-down list of available file types. Notice the file extension listed at the end of each file type (I turned my extensions on so you could see what they look like).

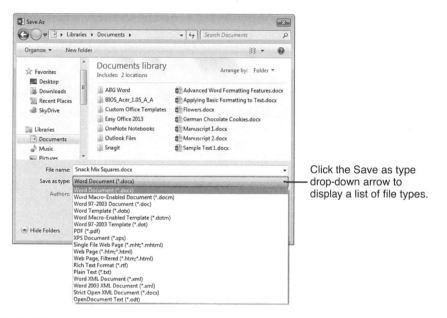

Click the Save as type drop-down arrow to display a list of file types.

FIGURE 4.6

You can choose which file format you want to assign to a document.

The default Word document type is mostly backward compatible, which means you can open your Word 2013 files in older versions of Word.

The more you work with various types of files on your computer, the easier you can distinguish their types and which programs you can use to view the files.

NOTE Ordinarily, you don't see file extensions unless you turn them on. If you want to see them in Windows Explorer or File Explorer (depending on your version of Windows), open the Explorer window (click the **Explorer** icon in the Windows desktop taskbar), click the **Tools** menu and click **Folder Options**. In the Folder Options dialog box, click the **View** tab and deselect the **Hide extensions for known file types** check box. Click **OK** and you can now view file extensions, even in Word's Save As and Open dialog boxes.

Other File-Saving Options to Consider

File *properties* are extra details about a document. The file properties include the behind-the-scenes data saved with a file, such as author name, file creation date, and *tags*—keywords that help you search for the file later. You can use the Save As dialog box to assign tags when you save a document. Just click the **Add a tag** link above the **Save** button in the dialog box and type in your tags, separated by semicolons. Tags are words or phrases that describe or identify, so a document about the declining population of penguins might use tags like "penguin," "population," or "school report,"—anything that might help you look up the document later.

You can also change the author name or add more names to a document's file properties. In the Save As dialog box, click the **Authors** link and make your changes or additions.

 TIP   You can also view a document's properties anytime by clicking the Ribbon's **File** tab and clicking **Info**. To view all the properties, click the **Properties** drop-down arrow and choose **Advanced Properties**. This opens a dialog box with all kinds of file properties, including fields for entering additional information, such as company name, manager name, and so on.

Opening and Closing Documents

What's the point of saving your documents if you can't open them and work on them again? You can open documents using a similar method as saving them. Microsoft Word keeps a list of recently opened files handy for reopening, or you can use the Open dialog box, which looks hauntingly like the Save As dialog box with a different name at the top.

To open a document you have previously saved, the first thing you need to do is to click the Ribbon's **File** tab and click **Open**. You'll see a page similar to Figure 4.7 or Figure 4.8.

Click here to see a list of recent documents.

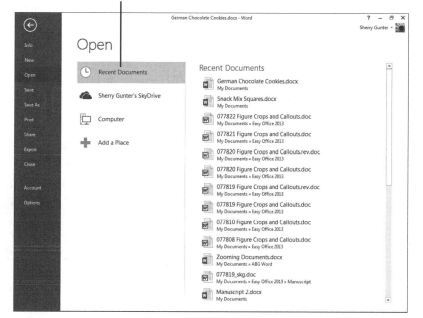

FIGURE 4.7

The Recent Documents option lists recently viewed files.

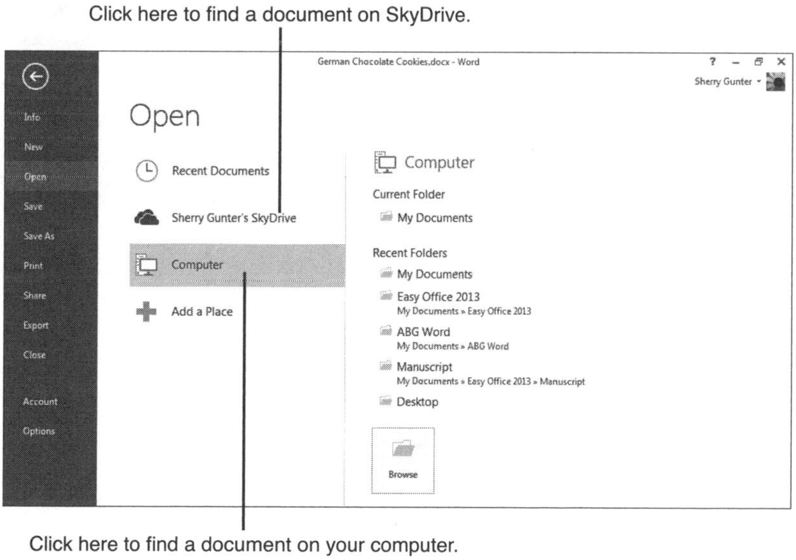

Click here to find a document on SkyDrive.

Click here to find a document on your computer.

FIGURE 4.8

You can look for a document on SkyDrive, your computer, or another storage area or device.

With the Open page displayed, try one of these options:

- Click **Recent Documents** to view a list of recently viewed files, like the one shown earlier in Figure 4.7. You can quickly open a file you previously used simply by clicking its name.

- Click the **SkyDrive** option if you stored the document on the cloud. (For even more cloud storage options, you can use the **Add a Place** option to set up Office 365 access and retrieval.)

- Click **Computer** if you stored your document on the computer, as shown earlier in Figure 4.8. You can then use the Open dialog box to navigate to the file.

- If the file is stored on another device, such as a USB flash drive, plug in the device and click the **Computer** option, then navigate to the device.

Other than the recent files list, the other options all inevitably lead to the Open dialog box, shown in Figure 4.9, where you can navigate to the file you're looking for. The Open dialog box is arranged just like the Save As dialog box. Use the left pane to navigate to a drive or library, then "drill down" to the exact folder containing your document file. After you've located the one you want to open, you can double-click it, or click it and click **Open**.

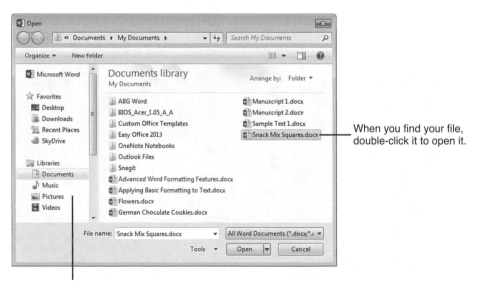

When you find your file, double-click it to open it.

Use this pane to choose the drive or library containing your file.

FIGURE 4.9

The Open dialog box is the place to go to find the document you want to open.

You can close a document without closing the entire program window. Closing a document merely closes the current file, leaving the program window open so you can work on more documents.

To close a document, click the **File** tab, then click **Close**. That's it. (To learn more about closing the program window, revisit Chapter 1, "Getting to Know Microsoft Word).

Viewing Multiple Documents

You can open more than one document at a time and switch between them as you work. This is particularly useful when you want to move text from one to the other, which you'll learn to do in the next section. You can use the Windows taskbar to swap between open documents. Just move the mouse pointer to the taskbar and hover over the Word icon, as shown in Figure 4.10. A list of the open files appears and you can click the one you want to view.

FIGURE 4.10

Use the Windows taskbar to quickly switch between open Word documents.

You can also use Word's **View** tab to switch between document windows, as well as as control the display of two or more windows onscreen at the same time. Click the **View** tab, shown in Figure 4.11, to find all the viewing options.

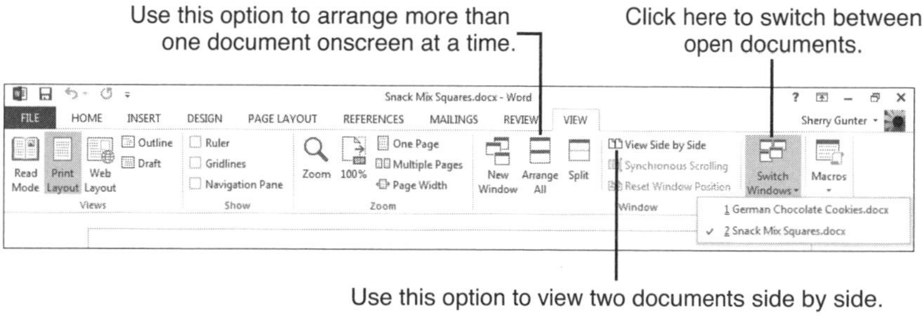

Use this option to arrange more than one document onscreen at a time.　　Click here to switch between open documents.

Use this option to view two documents side by side.

FIGURE 4.11

Find all kinds of viewing options on the View tab.

Here are a few ways to view multiple documents:

- To switch document windows, click the **Switch Windows** button and click the document you want to view.

- To view all open documents onscreen at once, click the **Arrange All** tool. Warning: This can make your screen pretty crowded, as shown in Figure 4.12.

- To view two documents side by side, click the **View Side by Side** tool. Click it again to return to one full document window.

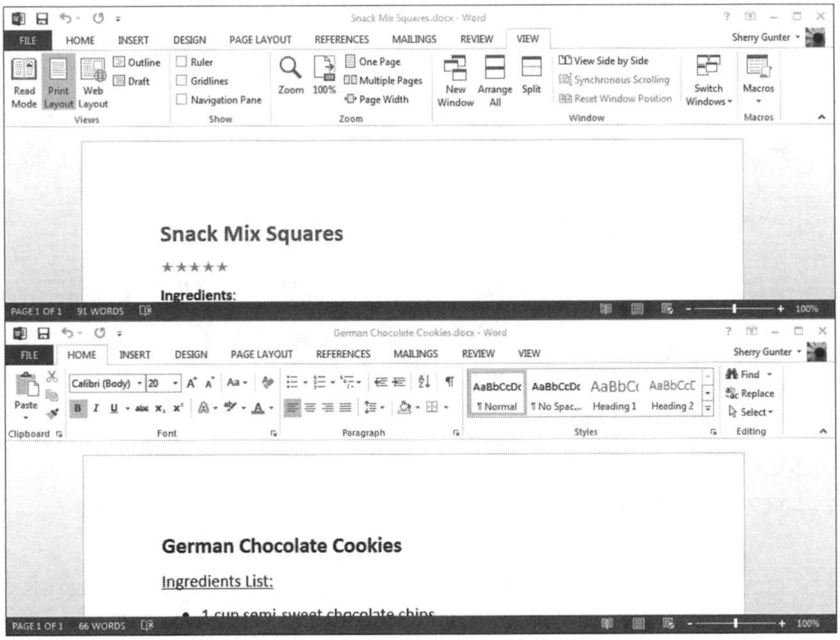

FIGURE 4.12

Use the Arrange All option to view two or more documents onscreen.

Don't forget—you can use the **Minimize**, **Restore**, and **Maximize** tools in the upper-right corner of the document window to control individual windows. See Chapter 1 to learn more.

Moving, Copying, and Pasting Data Between Files

Cut, **Copy**, and **Paste** are the universal go-to commands for moving data around digitally. You can cut data, such as text in Word, and move it to another area in a document, to a completely different document, or to a completely different program and paste it into place. You can use the copy command to do the same thing, but by making a copy of the original item.

The **Cut**, **Copy**, and **Paste** commands have been a crucial part of most software programs since the dawn of personal computing. Chances are, if you've worked with computers before, you most definitely have tapped into the power of cutting and copying items and pasting them where you wanted them to go. Items, whether it's text or pictures, or something else, when cut or copied are placed on the Windows Clipboard, a seemingly magical place where data rests briefly until you paste it somewhere else. It turns out the Clipboard is not so magical, but it does work behind the scenes.

To cut text from one document to place in another, select the text and click the **Cut** tool on the **Home** tab, or press **Ctrl+X** (the keyboard shortcut for the Cut command). Now open the document and click where you want to insert the cut text and click the **Paste** button on the **Home** tab, or press **Ctrl+V** (the keyboard shortcut for Paste). If you want to control whether formatting is carried over along with the cut text, click the **Paste** button's drop-down arrow and choose an option to suit your needs. If you want to copy the text instead of cut it, choose the **Copy** command on the **Home** tab instead (**Ctrl+C**).

Another option for cutting and copying between documents is to simply drag the selected text from one document window to the other and drop it where you want it to go. You'll need both windows displayed onscreen at the same time (use the **Arrange All** button on the **View** tab to accomplish this). To copy selected text instead of just moving it, press and hold the **Ctrl** key while dragging.

You can learn more about using the **Cut**, **Copy**, and **Paste** commands in your Word documents in Chapter 6, "Adding Text."

Assigning Document Protection

Microsoft Word has a variety of protection tools you can use to help keep your documents safe. Let's say you work for a certain intelligence gathering bureau and want to keep your weekly report safe from prying eyes, or you just want to keep your coworker from reading your latest blog entry before it's ready, or you're just super paranoid your cat is secretly reading your computer files while you're sleeping—you can restrict access to your files or encrypt them with passwords. Document protection tools actually aren't just for spies or paranoid people, but they're designed to help you keep your data safe. You can find your way to document protection options through the Info page. Click the **File** tab on the Ribbon, then click **Info**. Click the **Protect Document** button, shown in Figure 4.13, to view a list of options.

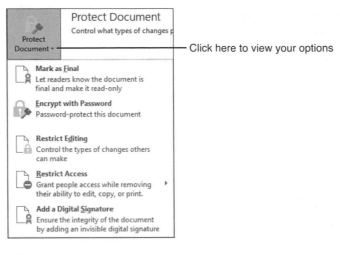

Click here to view your options

FIGURE 4.13

Find protection options through the Info page.

Here's a rundown of ways you can protect your documents:

- **Mark as Final**   This option turns the document into a read-only file, which means no one can make changes to it.

- **Encrypt with Password**   Use this option to assign a password to a document. No one can open the document without the password—including you, so make sure that you'll remember that password or you've recorded it somewhere safe.

- **Restrict Editing**   Use this option to control what sort of changes can be made to a document and who exactly in your network can work with the file.

- **Restrict Access**   If you set up your computer with Information Rights Management (IRM) software, you can restrict access to the file. This is handy for networked computers in an office situation with Windows Rights Management Services Client Service Pack installed. (Did your eyes just glaze over?) Anyway, if this applies to you, go have a chat with your administrator to find out how this works in your scenario.

- **Add a Digital Signature**   If your documents require the added security of authentication, which confirms the information originates from you and has not been altered, you can add a digital signature. Like the restricted access option, digital signatures require some extra setup typically involving a signing certificate to prove identity through a certificate authority. Fees are involved. You can learn more about this feature through Word's Help content.

NOTE Just a word about passwords in Word—they're case sensitive and they're unrecoverable. Be sure to keep them in a safe place. If you lose or forget a password, you can forget about opening the file ever again.

THE ABSOLUTE MINIMUM

This chapter explained several basic document operations. Here's what you should remember:

- You can start a new document through the **File** tab or you can add the **New** button to the Quick Access toolbar for easy access.

- You need to save your work if you ever want to see it again. Although Word is set up to perform automatic saves, those are temporary and gone when you exit the document. Saving your work before closing a file is up to you.

- If you haven't saved your work and attempt to exit a document, Word prompts you to do so, which is very helpful.

- The Save As and the Open dialog box are eerily similar, but do two different tasks. Thankfully, they work the same way so you can easily find your way to folders and drives.

- Use the Open page as the starting point to opening documents, choosing from among recently viewed files, or opening files stored on your computer, SkyDrive, or other storage device.

- You can use the **Cut**, **Copy**, and **Paste** commands to move and copy data between documents.

- You can easily switch between open documents using the Windows taskbar, or the options found on Word's View tab.

- You can add passwords, restrict access, and pursue other document protection options through the Info page.

IN THIS CHAPTER

- Learn the basics of how templates work.
- Find out how to apply a template to create a new document.
- Look for more templates online.
- Create your own template.

5

TEMPLATE BASICS

You might not realize this, but you've already been working with templates as soon as you opened Word and started typing in text. Turns out every document in Word, including blank ones, are built with templates. If you've never worked directly with templates before, this chapter is just for you. Not only does this chapter define them and introduce you to all the ones available in Word, but you'll also learn how to create your own. Templates might sound a little intimidating at first, but after you know how they work and what to do with them, you'll soon be using them like a pro.

Understanding Templates

A *template* is a pattern or boilerplate document that gives you a starting point for building documents. Most templates offer preset formatting and placeholder text which you can replace with your own text. The placeholder text is there to give you an idea of the type of text you can use in the document, as well as an idea of what the preassigned formatting looks like.

Think of a template as a sort of overlay or design guide you place on a document that acts as a pattern as to what goes where. You can use all kinds of templates for all kinds of purposes. For example, you can find templates for creating invoices that have built-in columns and rows for typing in purchase orders, prices, and totals. A fax template, as another example, might include fields for typing in fax numbers, the company name, contact information, and a logo that you can replace with your own company logo.

With an online connection, you can find templates for faxes, cover letters, résumés, calendars, brochures, newsletters, photo albums, award certificates, flyers, and more on the Microsoft Office website. Plus, new ones are added to Microsoft's online content all the time.

So what's the difference between a template and a regular document, you might ask? Template files utilize a special file format and extension. If you turn on the file extension display in Windows Explorer, you can see Word template files listed with the .DOTX, .DOTM, or .DOT extensions. (See Chapter 4, "Document Basics," to learn more about file types.) Don't let the special file format confuse you, however. When you assign a template, you're just placing a style overlay onto a regular Word document file, so the document remains a regular .DOC file type. It doesn't suddenly become a template itself. It merely utilizes the design guide.

The beauty of templates is you can customize them to suit your own needs. You're not stuck using all the placeholder elements a template offers. You can pick which ones you want to use and discard the rest. You can even make a new template out of an existing template or create your own new template that's more tailored to future documents you want to build.

Applying a Template

You can apply a template to an existing document, or you can start a new document based on a template of your choice. To start a new document based on a template, click the Ribbon's **File** tab and click **New**. This displays a screen similar to Figure 5.1 listing templates you can peruse.

The blank document, even though it's blank, is still a template.

Use the search box to look for more templates online.

Use the scroll bar to peruse the full selection of suggested templates.

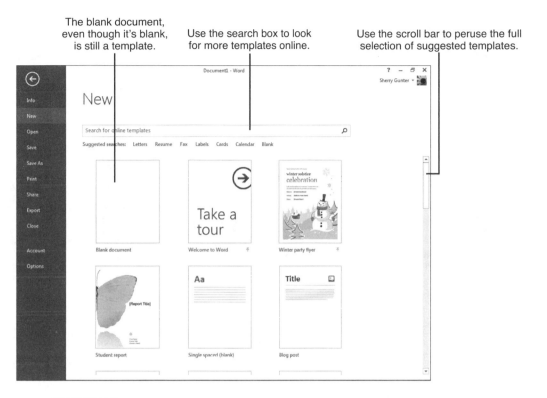

FIGURE 5.1

You can find templates listed on the New page.

The top of the page offers a search box you can use to look for a particular kind of template, and lists some search categories you can inspect with a simple click. Or you can use the scroll bar to scroll along and view various templates displayed in the window. When you find something you actually want to use, just click it to select it. A smaller screen pops up, similar to Figure 5.2, with details about the template, its popularity rating, and a button you can click to download and apply the template. If the template suits you, click the **Create** button. If not, click the **Close** button (X) or use the navigation arrows to view more template descriptions.

Click here to close without adding the template.

You can use the arrow buttons to look through more template descriptions and ratings.

Click here to download and apply the template.

FIGURE 5.2

Read more about the template and decide whether you want to download and apply it or not.

TIP If you find yourself using the same template over and over again, you can pin it so it's always on the top of the list of templates on the New page. To do so, move the mouse over the template you want to pin and click the pushpin icon in the bottom-right corner of the highlighted template. The pushpin icon toggles on and off; a vertical pushpin indicates the template is pinned, a horizontal pushpin means the template is not pinned.

As soon as you download a template, Word applies it to a new document. You'll need to save the file when you finish adding your own text and fixing it the way you want (see Chapter 4 to learn more about saving files). The template you downloaded is automatically added to your template library. Check out the template I added, shown in Figure 5.3. Word created a new document file for me and slapped the template right on it. The file is not saved yet, so it's still sporting the Document2 filename at the top.

FIGURE 5.3

Here's a newly applied template.

To start filling in a template, click the placeholder box and type away. Any placeholder text is replaced with the new text you add, as shown in Figure 5.4. Text blocks are easily moved around and formatted in Word. As soon as you click a box, it's selected and surrounded by *selection handles*, which you can drag to resize the box.

Placeholder boxes and fields can be replaced with your own text.

FIGURE 5.4

You can add your own text as needed to make the document your own.

NOTE   You can apply templates from older versions of Word, or templates you have created and stored elsewhere. Click the Ribbon's **File** tab, then click **Options** in the left pane. This opens the Word Options dialog box. Click **Add-Ins**. Click the **Manage** drop-down arrow at the bottom of the dialog box and select **Templates**, and then click the **Go** button. This opens the Templates and Add-ins dialog box. You can click the **Attach** button to navigate to the folder or drive where your template file is stored, then open the template and attach it to your document.

Finding More Templates

You can use the search box on the New page to look for more templates online. Tapping into the vast resources of the Microsoft Office website, you can look for specific types of templates based on the keyword(s) you enter. With the New page displayed (click the Ribbon's **File** tab and click **New** to display it), click in the search box and type in your search word. Press **Enter** or click the **Search** button and a page opens displaying any matching results (see Figure 5.5). Naturally you'll need an online connection to utilize this feature.

Click here to return
to the main page

Type keyword(s) here.

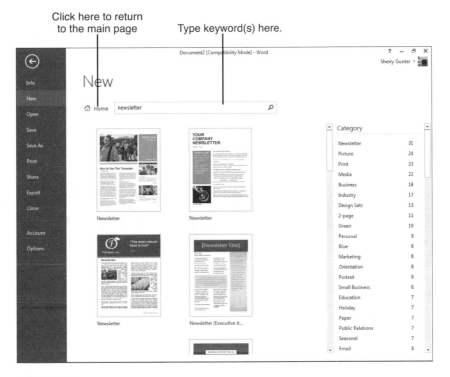

FIGURE 5.5

Use the Search feature to look for more templates online.

Click the **Home** button to return to the main New page. Also on the New page, just below the search box, is a list of suggested search categories. You can click a category to view a list of corresponding templates.

 NOTE   By default, Word 2013 saves templates in the following folder path: **%appdata%\Microsoft\Templates**. If you type this path into the Explorer window's Address bar, you can view all the template files stored within the default folder.

You can also use your web browser to check the Office website for more templates. Browse to **office.microsoft.com** and click the **Templates** link, and then click the link for **Word**. The web page displays all kinds of templates, categories, and links. When you find a template you want, you can click the **Download** button and make it yours. You'll be prompted to save the file to a folder you designate, or you can choose the default Templates folder as its home.

TIP Finding downloaded templates can sometimes be a bit frustrating, especially if you don't remember to specify a folder. You can use Explorer to search for templates (.dotx file extensions). In the Explorer search box, type ***.dot** or ***.dotx** to search for all templates, or if you know the exact name, you can type it in instead.

Saving Templates

You can turn any document into a template file to reuse, or after customizing a template, you can turn it into a new template to apply again and again. When you have finished making the document look just the way you want and are ready to save it as a template file, follow these steps:

1. Click **File**.

2. Click **Save As**.

3. Click **Browse**.

4. Navigate to the folder or drive where you want to store the file; for best results, save your templates in the Custom Office Templates folder in the Documents library.

5. Click the **Save as type** drop-down arrow (see Figure 5.6).

6. Click **Word Template (*.dotx)**.

7. Type in a name for the template.

8. Click **Save**.

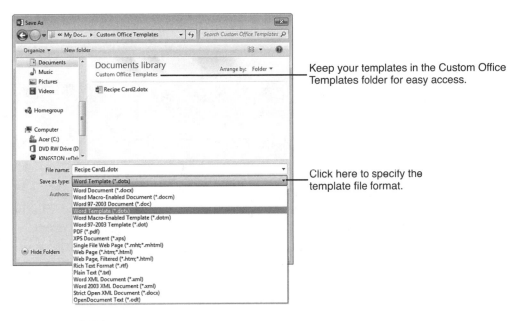

Keep your templates in the Custom Office Templates folder for easy access.

Click here to specify the template file format.

FIGURE 5.6

You can save any file as a template using the Save as type drop-down arrow.

When you save new templates, Word lists them in a new category on the New page. As shown in Figure 5.7, you can click the **Personal** category to view the templates stored in your Custom Office Templates folder.

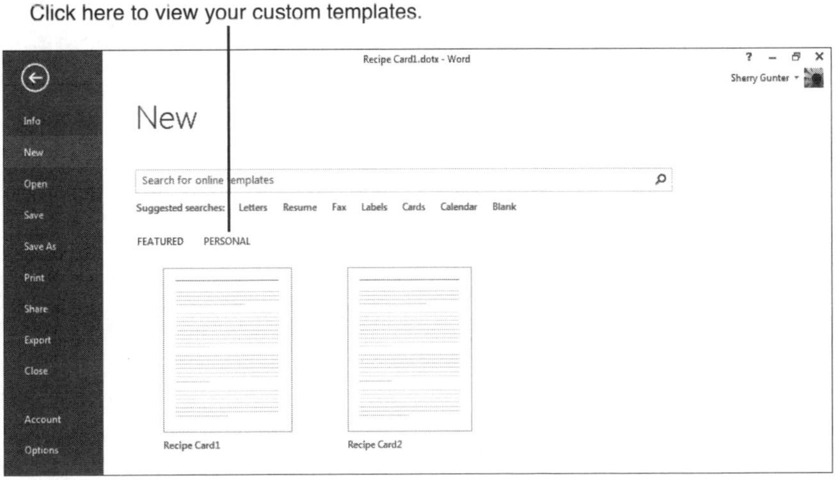

FIGURE 5.7

The Personal category lists your custom template files.

THE ABSOLUTE MINIMUM

By now, you should be feeling much more template-savvy than before you began. Here's a rundown of what you learned in this chapter:

- Templates can help you whip up great-looking documents in a jiffy.

- With an online connection, you can peruse a vast library of Word templates from the Office website.

- You can customize any template to suit your own needs, or you can turn a document into a template to use again and again.

- To make things easy, store your templates in the Custom Office Templates folder found in the Documents library.

6

IN THIS CHAPTER

- Find out how easy it is to start adding text to build documents.
- Learn various methods for selecting text.
- Acquaint yourself with the tried-and-true techniques for moving and copying text.
- See how to tap into Word's Quick Parts—premade text content to help you speed up document creation.
- Explore the mysterious world of symbols and special characters.

ADDING TEXT

We can't really call Microsoft Word a *word processing program* without actually processing words, so it's about time you learned how to start adding text to your documents. Whether you're adding text to a blank document, replacing placeholder text in a template, or editing text someone else entered—working with text is fairly straightforward and easy. It's just you and your keyboard and the wide open space that is your document.

Typing and Editing Text

When you first open a blank Word document, the *cursor* awaits you at the top of the page. The cursor is the blinking vertical line that marks your spot in the document, as pointed out in Figure 6.1. It's also sometimes referred to as the *insertion point*, but that's not nearly as clever sounding as *cursor*. Wherever the cursor sits, that's where your text will appear when you start typing. As you type, the cursor moves along to mark the end of your text, as shown in Figure 6.2. You can double-click anywhere on a page and start typing to add text.

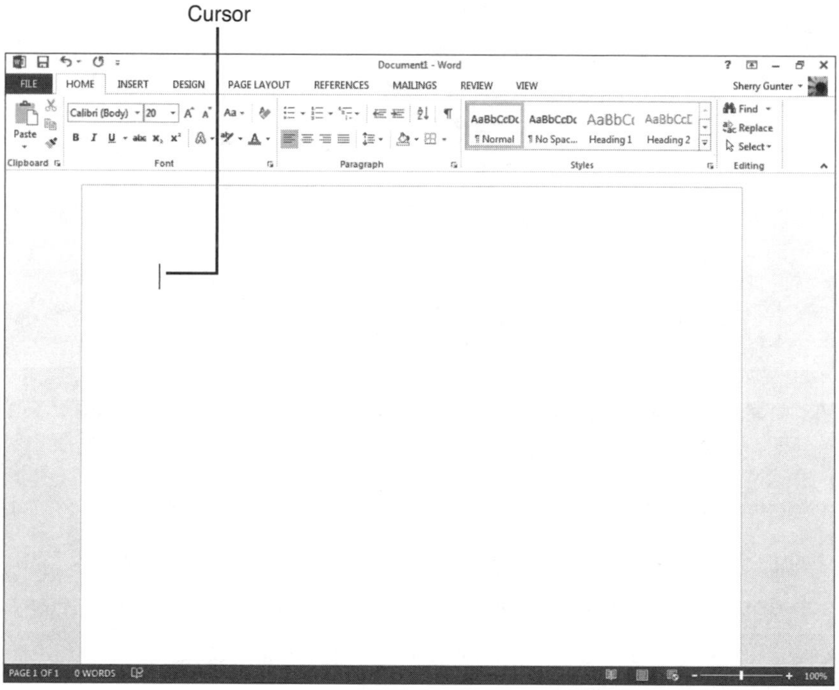

Cursor

FIGURE 6.1

The cursor marks the spot where you're working.

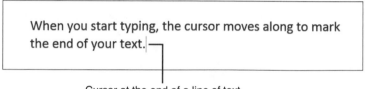

When you start typing, the cursor moves along to mark the end of your text.

Cursor at the end of a line of text

FIGURE 6.2

When you start typing, the cursor moves along to mark the end spot.

As you're typing along, here are a few tips you might find useful:

- You can use the **Backspace** key to back up a character, which is handy to delete the text to the left of the cursor and fix a mistake.
- You can use the **Delete** key to delete a character to the right of the cursor's current location.
- When you reach the end of a line of text, Word automatically wraps it to the next line for you so you can keep typing.
- To start a new paragraph, press **Enter**.
- If you want some extra space between paragraphs, press **Enter** twice.
- If you want an instant indent, press the **Tab** key when you start a new paragraph or line.
- To move the cursor to the end of a line of text, press the keyboard's **End** button.
- To move the cursor to the front of a line of text, press the **Home** button.
- Use the keyboard's **PageUp** and **PageDown** (or **PgUp** and **PgDn**, depending on how they're labeled) buttons to navigate longer documents.
- The scroll bars let you move up and down pages as well as side to side (depending on the page widths and depths). You can click and drag the middle bar, called the scroll box, or you can click arrow buttons to move around.

 NOTE   You can switch between two modes of text entry when working on a document: *Insert* and *Overtype*. Insert mode is the default mode; anywhere you click the cursor you can start typing, and any existing text moves over to make room for the new text. When Overtype mode is turned on, existing text is replaced by whatever you type. For many computers, the Insert key on the keyboard toggles Insert and Overtype modes on and off. You can also control this through the Word Options dialog box: Click **File**, **Options**, **Advanced**, and then click the **Use the Insert key to control overtype mode** check box.

You can learn how to make your text look attractive in Part III, "Making Documents Look Impressive."

 TIP   If you see red wavy lines under a word you typed, Word's spell checker tool is trying to tell you the word might be misspelled. If you see a green wavy line, that's the grammar checker alerting you to a possible grammar issue. You can learn more about Word's proofing tools in Chapter 18, "Using Proofreading Tools."

Selecting Text

To perform edits on your text, whether it's a single word, a paragraph, or an entire page, you'll need to learn how to select text. When you select text, it's highlighted on the page, as shown in Figure 6.3, and you can apply all kinds of commands and features, such as changing the font, moving the text, or applying an indent.

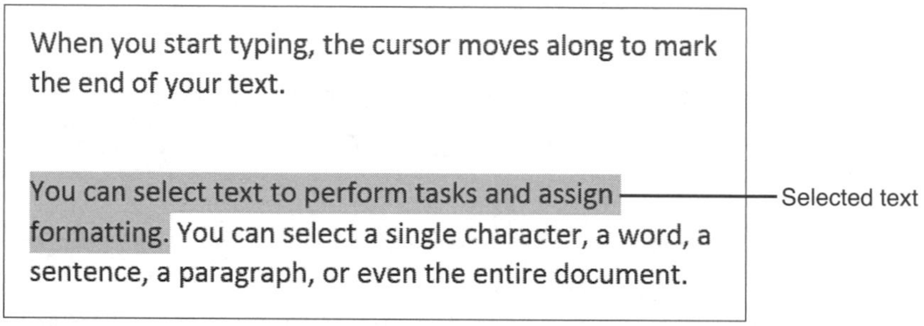

When you start typing, the cursor moves along to mark the end of your text.

You can select text to perform tasks and assign ————— Selected text
formatting. You can select a single character, a word, a sentence, a paragraph, or even the entire document.

FIGURE 6.3

Selected text appears highlighted in the document.

As with most things computer-related, you have a myriad of ways to tackle the same task. The technique you use might just be a matter of preference or just what's easiest at the moment. Here's a variety of selection techniques you can apply:

- Double-click the word you want to select.

- Triple-click to select the entire sentence.

- Press and hold the **Ctrl** key while clicking anywhere in a sentence to select it.

- You can also drag across text to select it. Press and hold the left mouse button and drag across a character to select a single character, or click and drag across a group of words to select them.

- To select text that's not adjacent, select the first bit of text (such as a word or sentence), then click and hold the **Ctrl** key while selecting the next bit of text.

- To select a large chunk of text, click at the beginning of the selection, then press and hold the **Shift** key and click the end of the selection.

- The left-hand margin area is a great place to click and select sentences, paragraphs, and even the entire page. Click to the left of a line of text to select the whole line. Double-click to the left of a paragraph to select the entire paragraph. Triple-click to the left of the text to select the entire page.

- To select everything in a document, click the **Home** tab, click the **Select** drop-down arrow in the **Editing** tool group, and then click **Select All**.

To deselect selected text, click anywhere outside of the selection.

 TIP The mini toolbar often pops up next to your selected text. It's there to offer you quick access to formatting commands and other tools pertinent to the task at hand. You can ignore the toolbar and it goes away if you move the mouse. If you find it bothersome, turn it off. Click the Ribbon's **File** tab, click **Options** to open the Word Options dialog box, click the **General** category, and then deselect the **Show Mini Toolbar on selection** check box. It will still show up with other tasks, but not when you select text anymore.

 NOTE Here's a sneaky fact. Word is set up to automatically select an entire word for you when it thinks you're in the process of selecting. If this annoys you, you can make it stop. Click **File** and click **Options** to open the Word Options dialog box. Click the **Advanced** category, and under the **Editing Options** group of tools, deselect the **When selecting, automatically select entire word** check box. Click **OK** to exit the dialog box and apply your change.

Moving and Copying Text

You can easily move and copy text in a document. Moving text simply takes it from its current location and puts it where you want it to go. Copying does essentially the same thing, but places a copy of the original text in the new location instead of displacing the original. For example, you might want to move a paragraph from the top of the document to the bottom, or copy a heading from one area to another to reuse the text. You can employ the **Cut**, **Copy**, and **Paste** commands to move and copy text in Word.

Any text you move or copy is temporarily placed on the Windows Clipboard where it waits for pasting. The Clipboard acts as a holding area for cut or copied items. When you paste text, you have the option of pasting it without any formatting previously assigned, merging the formatting with that of the new spot in the document, or pasting the text along with any applied formatting.

 TIP Cutting, copying, and pasting isn't just for text. You can move and copy other elements on a page, including artwork, pictures, text boxes (which are special containers for text elements), tables, graphs, and so on, using the same techniques outlined here.

Cutting and Pasting Text

To move text, use one of these techniques on the selected text you want to move:

- Click and drag the selected text and drop it where you want it to go. Try it, it's fun! Figures 6.4 and 6.5 demonstrate how this technique works.

- Click the **Home** tab, click **Cut**. Click where you want to insert the moved text and click **Paste**.

- Prefer a keyboard shortcut? Press **Ctrl+X** to cut text, then when you're ready to paste it press **Ctrl+V**.

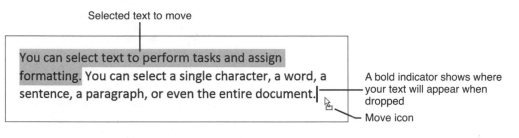

FIGURE 6.4

Moving text is as simple as dragging it where you want it to go.

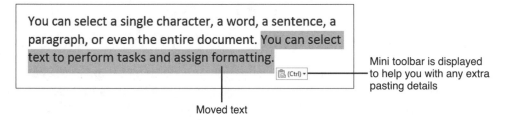

FIGURE 6.5

Drop your moved text, and it's immediately pasted.

Copying and Pasting Text

To copy and paste text, try one of these methods:

- Press and hold the **Ctrl** key, and then drag the selected text and drop it where you want it to go. This little movement is nearly as fun as cutting text.

- Click the **Home** tab, click **Copy**. Click where you want to insert the copied text and click **Paste**.

- For a keyboard shortcut, press **Ctrl+C** to copy text, then when you're ready to paste it press **Ctrl+V**.

Using the Mini Toolbar

As you are cutting, copying, and pasting text, you might encounter the mini toolbar popping up onscreen, as shown in Figure 6.6. You can use this toolbar to quickly access commands related to the task at hand, which in this case is pasting text. Presenting commands so close to what you're doing can save time, so take advantage of them if they help. For example, you might find clicking the **Paste** option on the mini toolbar to be quicker than moving the mouse up to the **Home** tab to access the same commands.

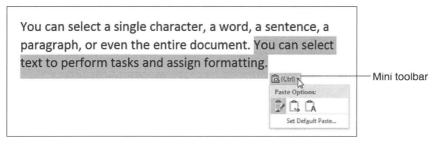

FIGURE 6.6

The mini toolbar is there to help you access the Paste command—fast.

Working with the Clipboard Pane

Let's talk a little more about this Clipboard thing. The **Cut**, **Copy**, and **Paste** commands are conveniently located on the Ribbon's **Home** tab. As you cut and copy data, you can actually view it in the Clipboard pane and choose which items to paste. To view the pane, click the **Clipboard** icon in the corner of the Clipboard group of commands on the **Home** tab, as shown in Figure 6.7. This opens the Clipboard pane, which lists any items you recently cut or copied.

Click here to display the pane
Click here to close the pane

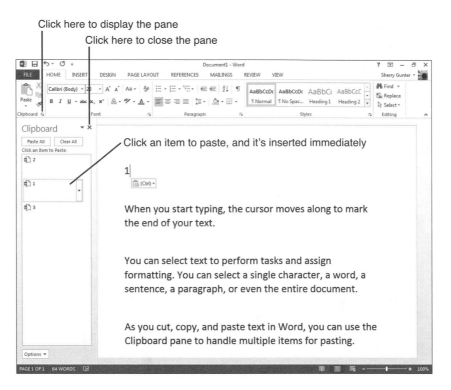

FIGURE 6.7

Display the Clipboard pane when you're juggling a lot of items you want to paste.

Here's what you can do with the Clipboard pane:

- To paste an item from the list, first click in the document where you want the item to go, and then click the item from the list. Word immediately inserts it.

- To paste everything listed, you can click the **Paste All** button at the top of the pane.

- To clear out the pane and start with a clean slate, click the **Clear All** button.

- To exit the pane, click its **Close** button or click the **Clipboard** icon on the **Home** tab.

Adding Text with Quick Parts

To help you build better documents faster, Microsoft Word offers a library of pre-made content you can insert, called *Quick Parts* or building blocks (because you can use them to build onto your document). These building blocks include all kinds of elements, such as headers and footers for the tops and bottoms of your pages, salutations for letters, page numbers, special formatting for quote inserts, tables, cover pages, and more. In fact, you can turn any piece of text you use over and over again into a building block and keep it in the Quick Part library ready to use at a moment's notice.

Acting just like parts of a template, Quick Parts offer preformatted text and designs, which often include more than placeholder text. You can customize the placeholder text with your own text. For example, a quote box (shown in Figure 6.8) includes placeholder text for a quote. Just type in your own quote text and it's good to go.

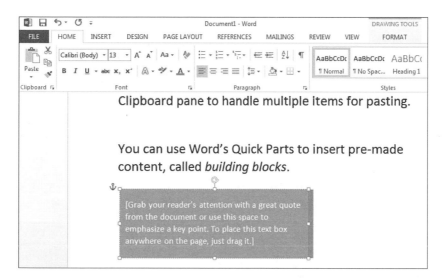

FIGURE 6.8

Here's an example of a quote box, a premade building block you can insert and use, substituting your own text in place of the placeholder text.

  TIP Quick Parts are perfect for smaller bits of preformatted text elements, but if you're looking to create a whole document, then templates are the thing to use. See Chapter 5, "Template Basics," to learn more about using Word's versatile templates—premade documents.

Inserting a Quick Part

To use any of Word's premade building blocks, follow these steps:

1. Click the **Insert** tab.

2. Click the **Quick Parts** drop-down arrow (see Figure 6.9).

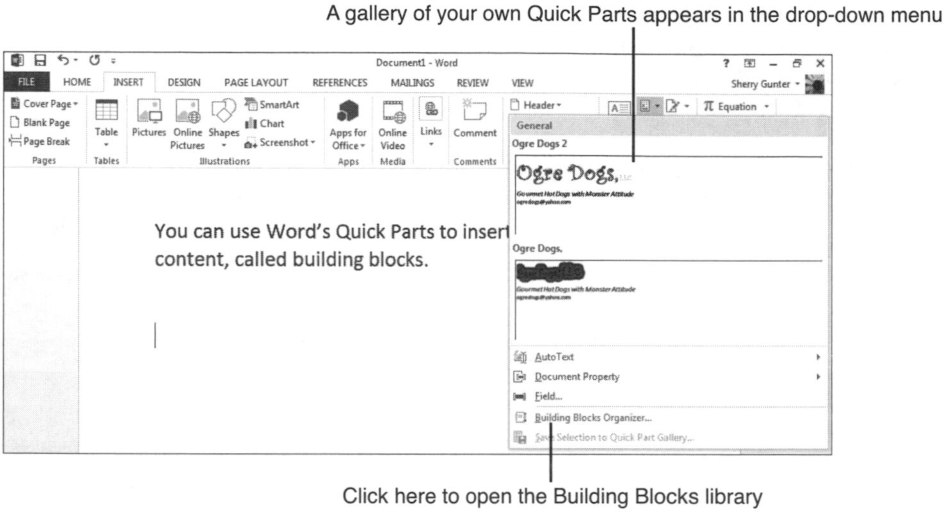

A gallery of your own Quick Parts appears in the drop-down menu

You can use Word's Quick Parts to insert content, called building blocks.

Click here to open the Building Blocks library

FIGURE 6.9

Use the Quick Parts drop-down menu to access your own Quick Parts as well as the building blocks library.

3. Click **Building Blocks Organizer** to open the Building Blocks Organizer dialog box (see Figure 6.10).

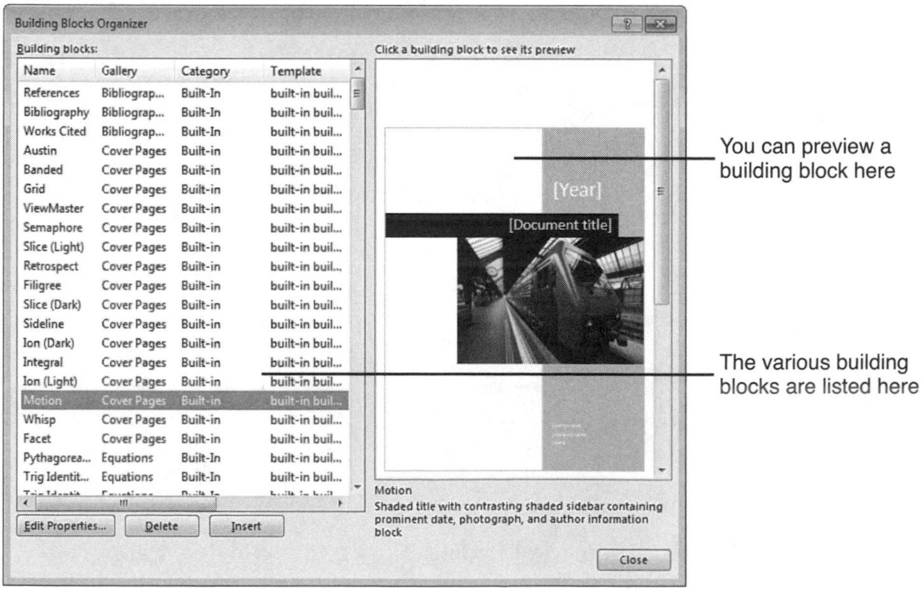

You can preview a building block here

The various building blocks are listed here

FIGURE 6.10

The Building Blocks Organizer.

4. Click the building block you want to preview.

5. When you find one you want to use, click **Insert** and Word adds it to the document.

Creating Your Own Quick Parts

As you might already suspect, creating building blocks for text elements you use a lot in your documents can be a real time saver. For example, if you use a company logo, motto, and contact information at the bottom of every letter document you create in Word, you can turn the information into a building block and reuse it again and again. Saving an item as a building block automatically adds it to the Quick Part Gallery for easy access.

To turn text into a building block, follow these steps:

1. Select the text you want to turn into a Quick Part.

2. Click the **Insert** tab.

3. Click the **Quick Parts** drop-down arrow.

4. Click **Save Selection to Quick Part Gallery**. This opens the Create New Building Block dialog box, as shown in Figure 6.11.

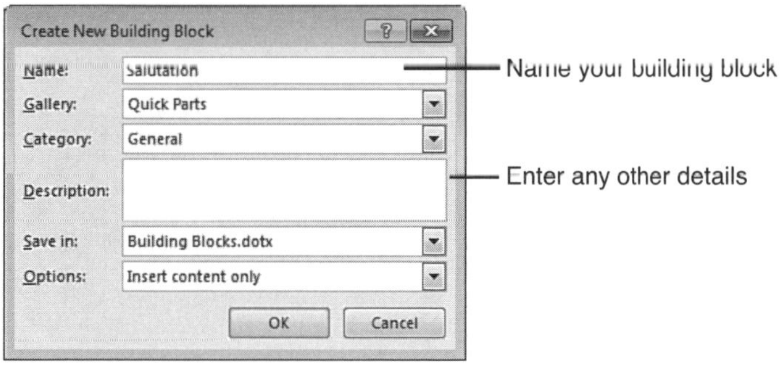

FIGURE 6.11

Create your own Quick Parts using this dialog box.

5. Type a name for your building block.

6. Fill out any additional details you want to save along with the text element.

7. Click **OK** to save the building block.

Any time you want to add your building block to a document, click the **Quick Parts** drop-down menu on the **Insert** tab and choose your item from the Gallery.

Inserting Symbols

Although the typical computer keyboard is jam-packed with plenty of characters, numbers, and symbols, some special symbols cannot be found on a keyboard. These include symbols such as a copyright or registered trademark. You can use Word's Symbol dialog box to find special characters and other symbols to insert into your documents, including mathematical symbols, special quote marks, and wingdings (tiny graphics).

To insert a symbol or special character, use these steps:

1. Click the **Insert** tab on the Ribbon.

2. Click **Symbol**.

3. If the list already shows your symbol (see Figure 6.12), you can click it. If not, click **More Symbols** to open the Symbols dialog box (see Figure 6.13).

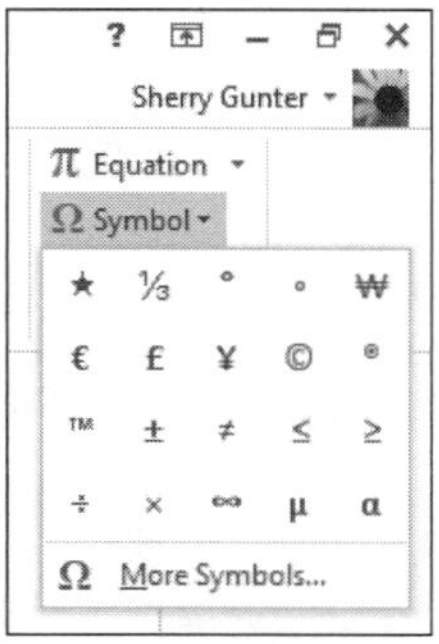

FIGURE 6.12

The drop-down menu displays recently used or common symbols you can insert.

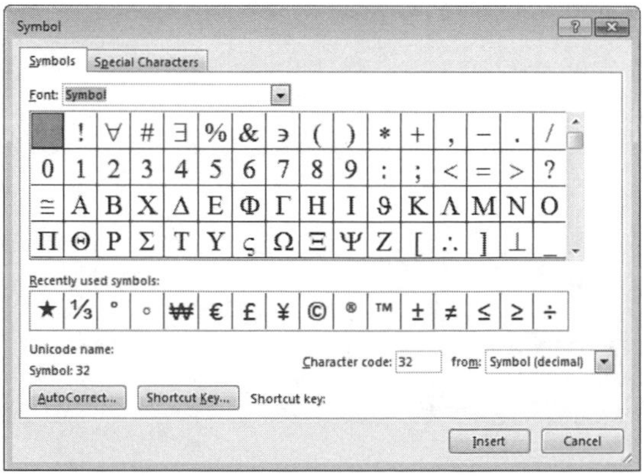

FIGURE 6.13

Use the Symbols dialog box to insert special characters and symbols. The Symbols tab lets you choose from a variety of fonts and subsets.

4. Click the **Symbols** tab to view available symbols.

5. Click the **Special Characters** tab (see Figure 6.14) to view characters.

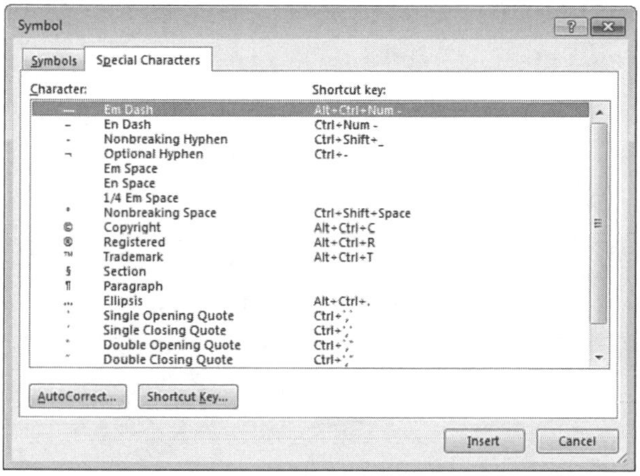

FIGURE 6.14

The Special Characters tab lists special characters, such as dashes and quotes.

6. Click the symbol or character you want to use.

7. Click **Insert** to insert it into your document.

8. The dialog box remains open in case you want to insert more symbols. Click **Close** when you're finished.

Special characters and symbols are actually part of *font sets*, styles of type you can use to change the appearance of your text. If you don't find the symbol or character you are looking for, try searching another font set or symbol subset in the Symbol dialog box.

TIP If you look over on the **Special Characters** tab of the Symbol dialog box, you'll notice some characters offer shortcut keys you can use to insert the symbol. For example, if you press **Alt+Ctrl+C** you can quickly insert a copyright symbol. You can memorize the shortcut key combination for your favorite character.

THE ABSOLUTE MINIMUM

It turns out adding text is pretty easy in Word, and in this chapter you learned how to start typing into your documents. You also learned the following key points:

- The blinking cursor marks your current location in a document.

- You can double-click anywhere in a document and start typing.

- You need to select text to perform certain tasks on it, such as assigning formatting, moving or copying, and other tasks.

- Moving and copying text is a breeze using the Cut, Copy, and Paste commands.

- You can use the Clipboard pane when you want to paste a bunch of items.

- You can use Quick Parts to insert premade content, such as quotes, corporate salutations, page numbers, and other repetitive text.

- The Symbols dialog box can help you insert special characters and other symbols, such as copyrights, mathematical symbols, and quotation marks for smart quotes (unlike the quote marks available on your keyboard).

- Find out what formatting is and how you can use it to make your documents look pretty.
- Learn how to apply basic formatting to your text.
- See how to change fonts and font sizes to give your documents pizzazz.
- Learn how to find your way to the elusive Font dialog box.
- Acquaint yourself with the drop-down Font Color palette.
- Save yourself some formatting time by employing the Format Painter tool.

7

FORMATTING TEXT

Anyone can type in some text and call it a day, but can you make the text look compelling, polished, and easy to read? As it turns out, anyone can with a little formatting. *Text formatting*, also called *attributes*, refers to the ways in which you can change the appearance of document text. For example, to add emphasis to a word, you might apply bold formatting, or italicize the text. Perhaps you want to make a page title stand out, so you assign a different font style or make the title text appear bigger or in another color. Formatting is all about making your document look good.

In this chapter, we'll focus on applying basic formatting commands to text. Most of Word's text formatting tools hang out on the Ribbon's **Home** tab under the heading Font. You can apply text formatting to a word, sentence, paragraph, or the entire document. You can even format a single character. Of course, you'll need to select the text first, so if you haven't learned that skill yet, back up to Chapter 6, "Adding Text," and read all about text selection techniques.

Although the idea of sprucing up your text might appeal to your inner designer, try not to get too carried away—a little formatting goes a long way. The general idea is to make your text legible, appealing, and professional looking. Too much formatting, like a different font for every paragraph, can just as easily confuse your intended audience and circumvent the importance of what the text is trying to say.

Applying Boldface, Italics, and Underline

The three most basic ways you can change the appearance of your text is to apply bold, italics, or underlining. Or you can really go out on a limb and apply all three, but depending on the circumstances that might be gilding the lily. Bold formatting adds some "thickening" to the text, making it stand out from the rest of the text. Italics slants the characters to the right for some subtle emphasis. Underlining adds a line under the text, which is pretty in-your-face as far as drawing attention to something. Check out all three at work in Figure 7.1.

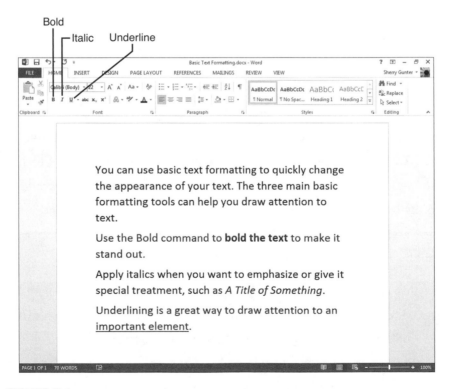

FIGURE 7.1

Use bold, italics, and underlining to add emphasis to your text.

You can find buttons for these three basic formatting attributes on the Ribbon's **Home** tab. Each one is fairly self-explanatory, plus the little icons that appear on the command buttons represent what the command does—the **Bold** button has a bold "B" on it, the **Italic** button has an italicized "I" on it, and the **Underline** button has an underlined "U" on it.

Select the text and then click the button for the formatting you want to apply. The feature toggles on or off. Click the button once to apply the formatting, and click it again to remove the formatting from the same selected text.

Because bold, italics, and underline formatting is so commonly used, you might find that memorizing some keyboard shortcuts to apply each in a flash is helpful:

Ctrl+B	Bolds the text
Ctrl+I	Italicizes the text
Ctrl+U	Underlines the text

 TIP   If you click the **Underline** button's drop-down arrow, you can choose an underline style to apply other than the default style.

Another way you can apply quick formatting to text is to take advantage of the mini toolbar. Word's mini toolbar pops up as you work with selected text and offers you shortcut commands to basic formatting tasks, as shown in Figure 7.2. For example, if you select a word, the toolbar appears with many of the tools found under the Font heading on the Ribbon's **Home** tab. You can click any of the buttons on the mini toolbar to apply the feature to the selected text.

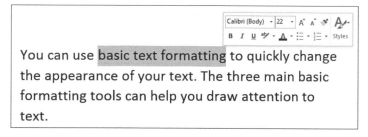

FIGURE 7.2

The mini toolbar offers a subset of formatting commands you can apply.

You don't have to engage the mini toolbar if you don't want to. You can choose to ignore it and keep working and the toolbar goes away. As soon as you move the mouse pointer, the toolbar disappears.

TIP You can turn off the mini toolbar if you do not find it useful for the way you work with selected text. To do so, click the **File** tab and click **Options**. This opens the **Word Options** dialog box. Click the **General** category and deselect the **Show Mini Toolbar on selection** check box.

NOTE Though not really considered basic formatting commands, the **Strikethrough**, **Subscript**, and **Superscript** tools are located next to the **Bold**, **Italic**, and **Underline** commands on the **Home** tab, and you might find them useful from time to time. All three have special uses pertaining to documents, but aren't necessarily essential to making things look good. The **Strikethrough** command puts a line through the text like a proofreader's deletion mark (~~example~~). The **Subscript** and **Superscript** tools make the text smaller in size and set it above or below the text baseline, respectively. You might need to assign subscript to a chemical compound (H_2O) or superscript to a mathematical expression (42^2).

Changing the Font

Another way to change the appearance of your text is to change the font. A *font* is the style of characters applied to your text, also called a *typeface*. Word features a wide variety of fonts to choose from, ranging from sleek and simple to frilly and fanciful. You might think of fonts as design sets that give a unifying appearance to all the text characters (from A to Z) and numbers. Computer fonts trace their history back to the days of typesetting when printing shops used moveable type to make pages for books, magazines, and newspapers. (Learn all about it on the Web!) Back then, styles were limited to just a few fonts. Thousands of digital fonts are available today, and Word installs with quite a few as well. Figure 7.3 shows an example of several different fonts in use.

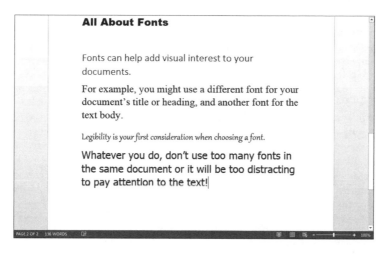

All About Fonts
Fonts can help add visual interest to your documents.
For example, you might use a different font for your document's title or heading, and another font for the text body.
Legibility is your first consideration when choosing a font.
Whatever you do, don't use too many fonts in the same document or it will be too distracting to pay attention to the text!

FIGURE 7.3

Fonts are an important part of formatting your document text and making it attractive or easy to read.

With Word's Live Preview, you can preview a font before applying it. The **Font** drop-down menu, available on the **Home** tab or on the mini toolbar, lets you scroll through your library of fonts, as shown in Figure 7.4. As you move the mouse pointer over a style, any selected text in your document appears in the font style.

Calibri
Theme Fonts
Calibri Light (Headings)
Calibri (Body)
Recently Used Fonts
Tahoma
Arial Black
ALGERIAN
Aharoni
Franklin Gothic Heavy
Times New Roman
Bodoni MT Condensed
Bodoni MT Black
All Fonts
Agency FB
Aharoni
ALGERIAN

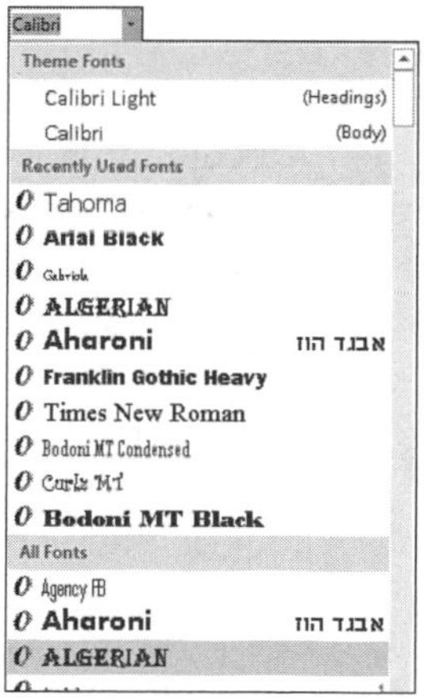

FIGURE 7.4

The scrollable Font menu lets you choose from a vast number of font styles.

To change the font, follow these steps:

1. Select the text.

2. Click the **Home** tab.

3. Click the **Font** drop-down arrow.

4. Click a font and Word immediately applies it to the selected text.

If the mini toolbar is available, you can click the **Font** drop-down arrow on the toolbar and choose a font. You can also use the Font dialog box to assign fonts. Learn more about this method later in this chapter.

TIP   You can set a font before you type in any text, and Word applies the font to any new text you type from the current cursor position onward.

NOTE   When you create a blank document, Word starts you out with a default font and size. Calibri is the default font, but you can apply other fonts as needed. You can also change the default to something else. Click the **Font** icon in the corner of the **Font** group of tools on the **Home** tab to open the Font dialog box. Use the **Font** drop-down menu to choose a font, and then click the **Set As Default** button. You can choose whether to set the font as the default for the current document or all documents based on the template.

Changing the Point Size

You can control the size of your document text by changing the font size. All blank documents you create in Word use a default font size of 11 points unless you specify something else. Font sizes are always measured in points, a remnant measurement system from the bygone days of typesetting. You can assign other sizes to your text as needed. For example, you might want a page title to appear much larger than the rest of the text on the page, say 20-point or 36-point, as shown in Figure 7.5. Font size is an integral part of ensuring your document is legible and easy to read for its intended audience. Plus, if you pick a font size that's too small or too big for your particular printer to handle, you may run into some issues and have to choose another font, too. Using the **Font Size** drop-down menu, shown in Figure 7.6, you can specify a size to suit your own document needs.

Font Size menu

Increase Font Size button

Decrease Font Size button

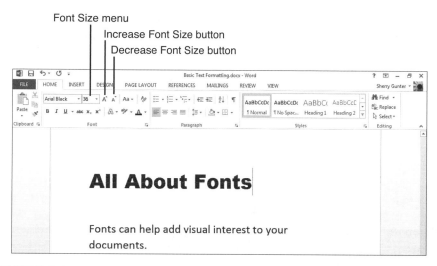

FIGURE 7.5

Controlling font sizes is another important way you can format your document text.

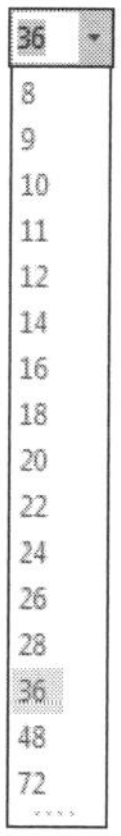

FIGURE 7.6

You can adjust the size of text using the Font Size menu.

To change the font size, follow these steps:

1. Select the text.

2. Click the **Home** tab.

3. Click the **Font** Size drop-down arrow.

4. Click a size and Word immediately applies it to the selected text.

You can also click the **Font Size** drop-down arrow on the mini toolbar and choose a size, or you can use the **Font** dialog box.

If you're not sure what exact size you might need for a situation, you can make incremental adjustments to size using the **Increase Font Size** and **Decrease Font Size** buttons on the **Home** tab. Each click of either button adjusts the size of the selected text up or down in point increments. These buttons are perfect for when you need a quick bump up or down in font size.

 TIP Another way to add flair to your text is using the Text Effects tools. Learn more about these in Chapter 10, "Advanced Formatting."

Using the Font Dialog Box

If you're looking for some additional font controls, open the **Font** dialog box, shown in Figure 7.7. The **Font** dialog box is your one-stop shop for all things font related; it consists of two tabs, one for regular font controls such as size and basic formatting, and another for advanced controls, such as character spacing. The Preview area lets you see what all of your selections will look like when applied to your text.

To open the dialog box, you must click the **Font** icon in the corner of the Font group of tools on the **Home** tab. As it turns out, each group of tools on the Ribbon's tabs have icons for opening dialog boxes associated with the type of commands in the group, and this particular one is for font commands. To apply any changes you make in the **Font** dialog box, click **OK**.

FIGURE 7.7

The Font dialog box.

Adding Color to Text

Let's talk color. Do you need to paint the town red, or at least the word *town* in the color red? You can use the **Font Color** tool to add color to your document text. You can apply color to your text using a color palette, sort of like a drop-down menu but with color squares to choose from. If you find the palette too restrictive, you can open an additional dialog box with even more color choices.

To apply color to text, follow these steps:

1. Select the text.
2. Click the **Home** tab.
3. Click the **Font Color** drop-down arrow, as shown in Figure 7.8.
4. Choose a color, and Word immediately applies it to the selected text.

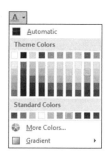

FIGURE 7.8

Use the Font Color palette to assign color to text.

 TIP When choosing colors, be mindful that sometimes what you see onscreen doesn't turn out as well when printed, especially with grayscale tones. You can preview how everything looks if you click the File tab and click Print.

To open the **Colors** dialog box, shown in Figure 7.9, click the **More Colors** option in the Font Color palette. From this dialog box, you can choose additional shades, or create a custom color. Click a color and click **OK** to apply it.

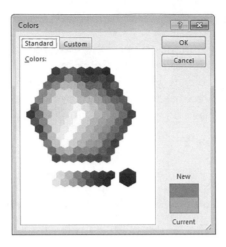

FIGURE 7.9

The Colors dialog box.

 TIP   You can use the **Text Highlighter** tool (located next to the **Font Color** tool on the Ribbon's **Home** tab) to apply color highlighting to your text. Just like a real highlighter pen you might use to mark sections of a textbook, you can use Word's Highlighter pen to mark up a document. You can choose from several highlighter colors and click and drag across the text you want to highlight.

In addition to color, you can also apply a gradient effect. Gradient effects are two or more shades blending from one to another. Click the **Gradient** option on the drop-down color palette and choose a gradient variation to apply it.

Copying Formatting from One Place to Another

Let's say you've spent a great deal of time perfecting formatting for a particular paragraph or title text. What if you need to use the same attributes on the next page—what do you do? Reapply all the same formatting controls again? No, break out the **Format Painter** tool instead. It copies formatting from one spot to another, thus saving you some tedious work.

First select the text containing the formatting you want to copy. Next, click the **Format Painter** button located on the **Home** tab, tucked in with the Clipboard group of tools (see Figure 7.10). The mouse pointer changes to a paint brush icon, and you can now drag across the text you want to copy the formatting to; Word immediately applies the formatting. To copy the same formatting attributes repeatedly, double-click the **Format Painter** button and then start painting.

Format Painter tool

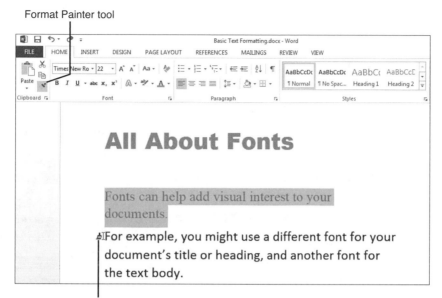

Format Painter icon

FIGURE 7.10

Use the Format Painter to copy formatting.

TIP Removing formatting is easy—just select the text and then click the **Clear All Formatting** button found in the Font group of tools on the **Home** tab.

THE ABSOLUTE MINIMUM

Making your documents look great requires learning to apply text formatting. In this chapter, you learned the following formatting techniques:

- To apply basic formatting, use the **Bold**, **Italic**, and **Underline** tools found on the **Home** tab or on the mini toolbar.

- You can use fonts to change the design of your document text. Click the **Font** drop-down menu to choose another font.

- Along with fonts, you can also control text size. Click the **Font Size** drop-down menu to change the size of text or use the **Increase Font Size** and **Decrease Font Size** to make incremental changes in text size.

- Display the **Font** dialog box when you want to set a bunch of text formatting all at once.

- To instantly apply color to your text, click the **Font Color** drop-down menu and choose a color from the palette.

- You can use the **Format Painter** tool to copy formatting from one spot to another.

IN THIS CHAPTER

- Learn how to align text across the document page.
- Find out how to use indents to shift paragraphs between the left and right margins.
- Create columns of text using Word's tab controls.
- Control spacing between lines of text, paragraphs, and characters.

8

FORMATTING PARAGRAPHS

Another key part of making your documents look impressive is formatting paragraphs. *Paragraph formatting* refers to the commands you can apply to control how text is positioned on a page as well as features for enhancing blocks of text, such as indents, alignment, bulleted lists, and other spacing options. For example, you may want to center a page title or add some extra space between lines of text. You can find Word's many positioning and paragraph commands grouped under the heading of Paragraph on the Ribbon's **Home** tab.

Controlling Alignment

You can align your spine, your car, and your text, but the least painful of the three is text alignment. Granted, a car alignment isn't actually physically painful, unless you count the pain to your pocketbook, and a good chiropractor can produce some pain-free results with your spine, but text alignment is super easy, fast, and you won't feel a thing. *Document alignment* is all about changing how text aligns on a page. Word's paragraph alignment commands control the position of text across the page. You can choose from the following alignments:

- **Align Left** Lines up text flush with the left margin. Align Left is the default alignment unless you specify otherwise.

- **Align Right** Lines up text against the right margin.

- **Center** Centers text in the middle of the page, between the left and right margins.

- **Justify** Lines up text with both the right and left margins, spacing out words in each line of text as needed (except the last line of text in a paragraph).

To assign any of these alignments, simply click the corresponding button on the **Home** tab. You can assign an alignment option to selected text or specify an alignment before you begin typing in new text. Each of the alignment commands have an icon representing what the command does; Align Left shows lines lining up to the left edge of the button, for example. Figure 8.1 shows an example of all four alignments.

 TIP If you're into keyboard shortcuts, you can use the following to align text: **Ctrl+L** to align left, **Ctrl+E** to center, **Ctrl+R** to align right, and **Ctrl+J** to justify.

You can also find paragraph alignment options in the Paragraph dialog box, shown in Figure 8.2. Click the **Paragraph Settings** icon, the small icon in the corner of the Paragraph group of tools on the **Home** tab. Within the dialog box, alignment commands are located on the **Indents and Spacing** tab under the **General** options. Click the **Alignment** drop-down arrow to view the settings.

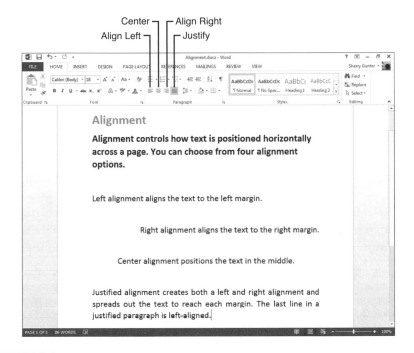

FIGURE 8.1

Alignment controls positioning of text across the page.

FIGURE 8.2

The Paragraph dialog box offers all the paragraph formatting controls in one spot.

TIP You can also control vertical alignment using Word's Page Setup dialog box. Learn more about vertical alignment in Chapter 9, "Formatting Pages."

Indenting Text

Similar to text alignment, *indents* move text horizontally across a page and are useful for setting text apart from other text in a document or for creating uniform, crisp paragraph placement. You can use indents to nudge text over away from a margin, either the left or right margin, or both. Indents are commonly used for the first line of text in a paragraph, but you can use them in all kinds of other ways. You might indent text quoted from another source, for example, thus setting it apart from the document's main text. Figure 8.3 shows several indents at work.

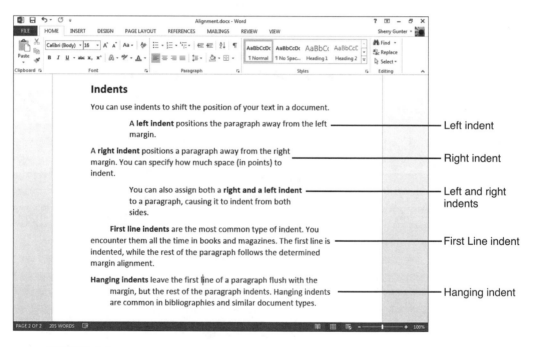

FIGURE 8.3

Here are a few examples of indents on a page.

Indents come in several flavors:

- **Left Indent** Use this indent to shift text away from the left margin.
- **Right Indent** This indent positions text away from the right margin.

- **First Line Indent**   Indent just the first line of text in a paragraph.

- **Hanging Indent**   This indent positions all the text in the paragraph away from the left margin except for the first line of text, which sort of hangs out to the left.

Simple Indents

If simple indents are what you're looking for, you can use the **Increase Indent** and **Decrease Indent** buttons found among the Paragraph tools on the **Home** tab, shown in Figure 8.4. You can click either of these buttons to assign a quick indent at half-inch increments.

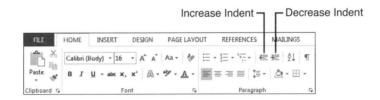

FIGURE 8.4

*You can quickly indent a paragraph using the indent buttons on the **Home** tab.*

Custom Indents

If you want custom indents—which are simply indents you control by defining your own measurements—you can use the **Left** and **Right** indent commands on the **Page Layout** tab, pointed out in Figure 8.5. Here you can specify an exact measurement for the left and right indents, measured in points. You can use the spin arrows to adjust the settings up or down, or you can type a number (in points) directly into the text box.

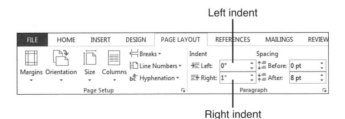

FIGURE 8.5

Use the Page Layout's Indent commands to set exact indents for your paragraphs.

Special Indents

What about special indents, like a hanging indent? If you want to set a hanging or first line indent, you can use the Paragraph dialog box introduced back in Figure 8.2. Click the **Paragraph Settings** icon (located in the corner of the Paragraph group of tools on either the **Home** tab or the **Page Layout** tab), then click the **Indents and Spacing** tab within the dialog box, as shown in Figure 8.6. Click the **Special** drop-down arrow to specify a special indent. You can click the **By** spinner arrows if you want to set a specific measurement for the special indent.

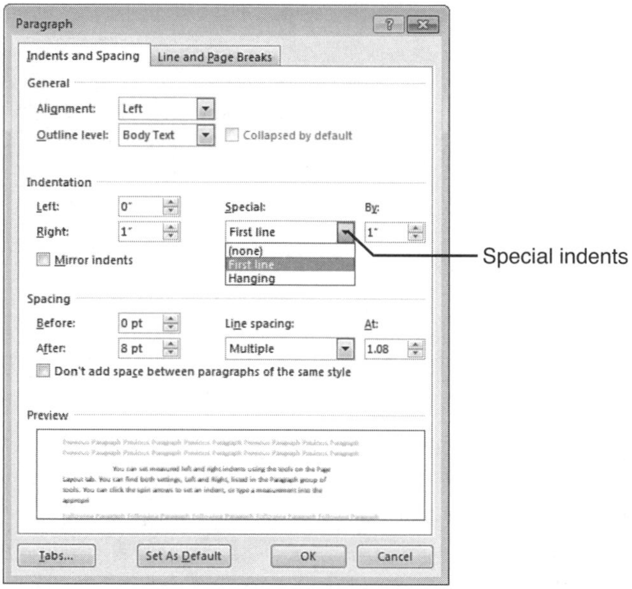

FIGURE 8.6

*You can find all of Word's indent settings in the Paragraph dialog box on the **Indents and Spacing** tab.*

You can also set **Left** and **Right** indents using the Paragraph dialog box. After you've set your indent measurements, click **OK** to apply them to the current paragraph or any selected text.

Setting Indents with the Ruler

As if the previous indent options weren't enough, you can also set indents in your documents using Word's ruler. That's right, Word has a ruler—but it's not visible unless you turn it on. To do so, click the **View** tab and click the **Ruler** check box. Check it out in Figure 8.7. When the ruler is activated, you can view both a horizontal ruler at the top of the document and a vertical ruler running along the left side. Measuring in inches (by default), you can use the rulers to help you design your documents and position items on a page when needed.

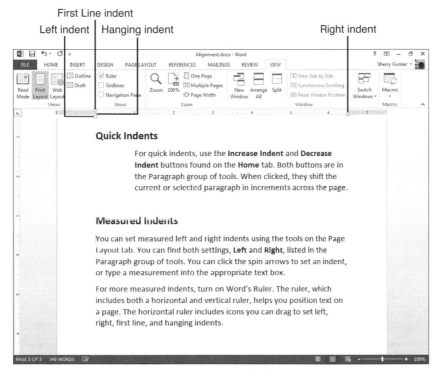

FIGURE 8.7

If you turn on Word's ruler, you can use it to set indents, too.

For the topic at hand, the horizontal ruler is our tool for indents. If you look closely on the horizontal ruler, you'll see some strange-looking icons. The left end of the ruler has three, two of which together look like an hourglass. Those are indent icons. You can drag them on the ruler to set indents. If you hover your mouse pointer over any of the icons, a Screen Tip appears identifying the type of indent it controls. The top icon of the hourglass creates a first line indent. You can click and drag it on the ruler where you want it. The setting controls the current paragraph and any new paragraphs you type after it, as shown in Figure 8.8.

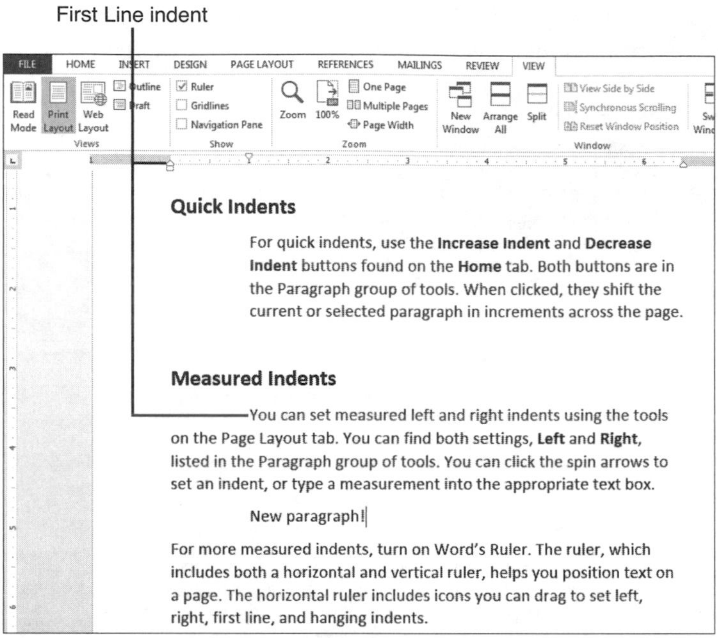

First Line indent
FILE
HOME
INSERT
DESIGN
PAGE LAYOUT
REFERENCES
MAILINGS
REVIEW
VIEW
Read Mode
Print Layout
Web Layout
Outline
Draft
Views
Ruler
Gridlines
Navigation Pane
Show
Zoom
100%
One Page
Multiple Pages
Page Width
Zoom
New Window
Arrange All
Split
View Side by Side
Synchronous Scrolling
Reset Window Position
Window
Quick Indents
For quick indents, use the Increase Indent and Decrease Indent buttons found on the Home tab. Both buttons are in the Paragraph group of tools. When clicked, they shift the current or selected paragraph in increments across the page.
Measured Indents
You can set measured left and right indents using the tools on the Page Layout tab. You can find both settings, Left and Right, listed in the Paragraph group of tools. You can click the spin arrows to set an indent, or type a measurement into the appropriate text box.
New paragraph!
For more measured indents, turn on Word's Ruler. The ruler, which includes both a horizontal and vertical ruler, helps you position text on a page. The horizontal ruler includes icons you can drag to set left, right, first line, and hanging indents.

FIGURE 8.8

Here, a first line indent is set.

The second icon (bottom part of the hourglass) creates a hanging indent. Drag it to set a hanging indent for the current paragraph.

The third icon, which is a rectangle shape sitting under the hourglass, is the **Left Indent** marker. You can drag it on the ruler to set the left indent.

Over on the right side of the ruler sits the **Right Indent** marker. You can drag it, as well, to specify the right indent for the current paragraph.

TIP You can also toggle to the Hanging Indent and First Line Indent using the tab stop icons. See the next section to learn more about tab stops.

TIP Tired of the ruler? You can turn off the display by deselecting the **Ruler** check box on the Ribbon's **View** tab.

NOTE By default, Word's Ruler displays inches, but you can customize the measurement to something else. Click the **File** tab and click **Options** to open the Word Options dialog box. Click the **Advanced** category, then scroll down to find the **Display** group of settings. Click the **Show measurements in units of:** drop-down arrow and choose another measurement. You can choose from centimeters, millimeters, points, and picas—all common measurements in the world of typesetting.

To undo any of the indents, you can drag the markers on the ruler back to their respective positions.

Setting Tabs

You can use *tabs* in Word to create columnar text across the page. For example, you might want to use tabs to line up several columns of numbers or names. You can assign *leader* characters, such as dots or dashes, to tabs to display these characters between tab stops, as shown in Figure 8.9. You can use Word's preset tab stops or set your own tab stop measurements.

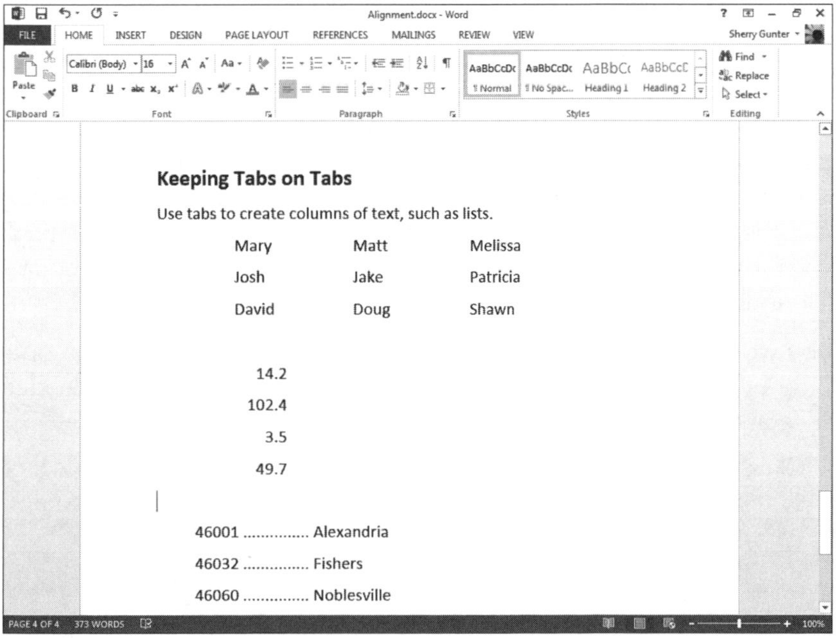

![Screenshot of a Word document titled "Keeping Tabs on Tabs" demonstrating tabbed columns of names, numbers, and leader-dot entries.]

FIGURE 8.9

Here's an example of tabs in a document.

Tabs are a remnant of the old typewriter days in which users had to manually create tab stops to move the typewriter carriage across the page at fixed stops to make columns. Creating columns of text in word processing programs is much easier today, specifically by using the Columns command, tables, or using indents. However, you might still find tab stops useful for your documents for a variety of tasks.

For starters, you can easily indent a line of text with a quick press of the **Tab** key on your keyboard. Some purists ridicule such an action, but what does it matter if you press a **Tab** key or activate an indent command? An indent is an indent on a printed page regardless of how it got there.

The handiest way to create tab stops is to use Word's ruler. Click the **View** tab on the Ribbon, then click the **Ruler** check box to turn the rulers on. To the left of the horizontal ruler is a *tab well*. I know—it's a strange name. Basically it's a stack of tab stop icons. It actually toggles, when clicked, between several kinds of tabs:

- **Left Tab** Aligns tabbed text to the left of the tab column.
- **Center Tab** Centers the tabbed text in the tab column.
- **Right Tab** Aligns tabbed text to the right of the tab column.
- **Decimal Tab** Aligns decimals in the column.
- **Bar Tab** Aligns text to the left of a vertical bar.

The little icons that represent each type of tab stop give you a clue as to what type of tab stop it is. To set a tab stop, click the tab well until the tab you want to use appears. Next, click on the horizontal ruler where you want the tab stop to be set in the document. Word inserts a tiny icon on the ruler representing the tab, as shown in Figure 8.10. You can drag the icon to reposition it, as needed. Or if you no longer want the tab stop, just drag it off the ruler entirely.

If you would rather be more precise about your tab stops, you can open the Tabs dialog box. You must use the Tabs dialog box if you want to set leader characters between tab columns. Follow these steps:

1. Click the **Paragraph Settings** icon in the corner of the Paragraph group of tools (either on the **Home** tab or on the **Page Layout** tab) to open the Paragraph dialog box.

2. Click the **Tabs** button to open the Tabs dialog box, shown in Figure 8.11.

3. Type in the position for the tab (the default measurement is inches). Tab stops are measured from the left margin.

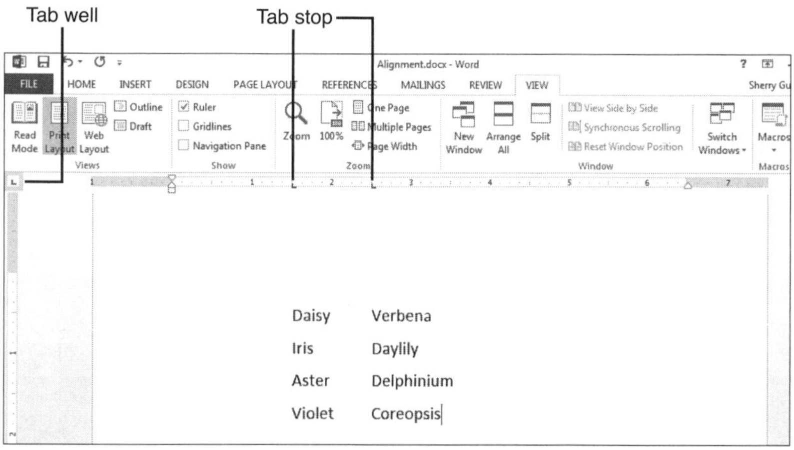

FIGURE 8.10

Tab stops appear as tiny icons on the ruler.

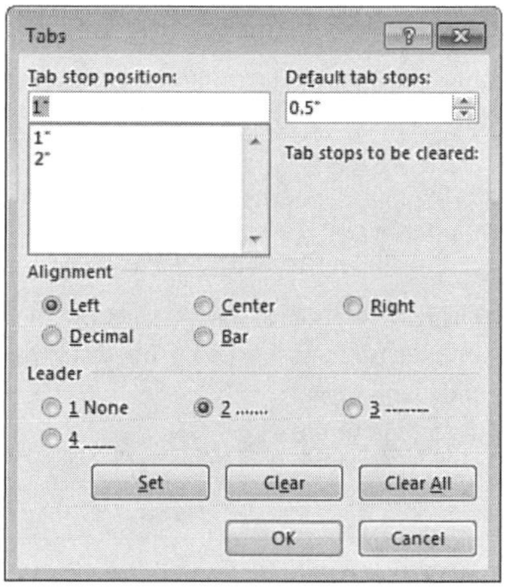

FIGURE 8.11

Use the Tabs dialog box to set custom tabs or add leader characters.

4. Click an alignment option.

5. Optionally, to assign leader characters, specify a leader character to use.

6. Click **Set** and Word adds the custom tab stop to the list. You can add more tab stops, if needed.

7. Click **OK** to exit the dialog box and start using your new tab stops.

You can revisit the Tabs dialog box to remove tabs; just choose the tab to remove and click the **Clear** button, or click **Clear All** to delete all the custom tabs in the list.

Using Bulleted and Numbered Lists

Say you're typing along in a document and decide you need an organized list. Sure, you could create your own and type in numbers or make your own bullets out of asterisks or something, but why not let Word's Bullets and Numbering tools help you out instead? Turning any text into a bulleted or numbered list is incredibly easy, as shown in Figure 8.12. Bullets are simply large dots or other graphics, whereas numbers are, well, numbers. Actually numbers can include Roman numerals and other multilevel listing formats as well.

Crusty Parmesan Chicken

Ingredients:

- 6 chicken breasts (skinned and deboned)
- 3 cups stuffing mix (your flavor choice)
- ¾ cups grated parmesan (canned variety will do nicely)
- 1 ½ cloves of garlic, crushed OR garlic salt
- ¾ cup blanched, slivered almonds
- ¼ teaspoon pepper
- 2 sticks melted butter

Directions:

1. Combine stuffing, parmesan, garlic, almonds, and pepper.
2. Add 2/3 cup melted butter.
3. Mix well.
4. Dip chicken in 1/3 cup melted butter, then roll in coating mixture.
5. Place chicken pieces in uncovered baking dish, topping with leftover crumbs and butter.
6. Bake at 350° for 35 minutes.

FIGURE 8.12

Bulleted and numbered lists can really spruce up a document and turn ordinary lists into something special.

To create a bulleted list, follow these steps:

1. Select the text you want to turn into a bulleted list.

2. Click the **Home** tab.

3. Click the **Bullets** drop-down arrow and click a bullet style, as shown in Figure 8.13, and Word immediately applies the bullets to the list.

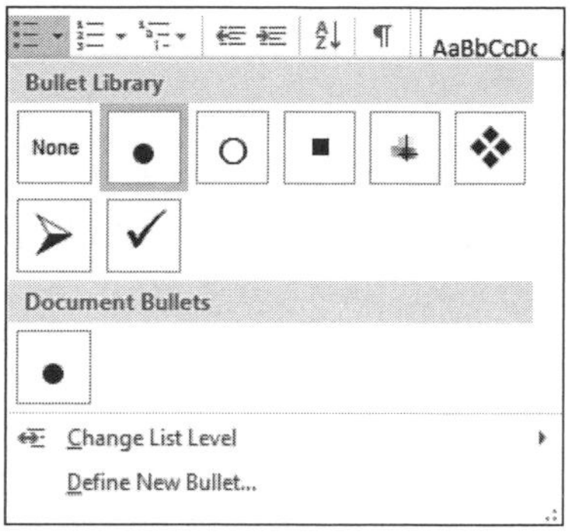

FIGURE 8.13

You can choose from the Bullet Library to assign a particular bullet style.

To create a numbered list, follow these steps:

1. Select the text you want to turn into a numbered list.

2. Click the **Home** tab.

3. Click the **Numbering** drop-down arrow and click a number style, as shown in Figure 8.14, and Word immediately applies the numbers to the list.

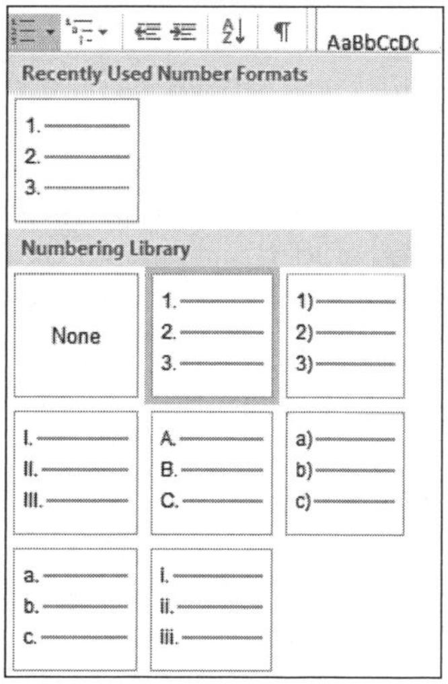

FIGURE 8.14

You can choose a numbering style from the Numbering Library.

TIP You can also use the **Bullets** or **Numbering** buttons on the mini toolbar that appears next to selected text to create quick lists.

To turn off bullets or numbers, just click the **Bullets** or **Numbering** buttons on the **Home** tab to toggle the feature off again. You can also press **Enter** twice at the end of the list to turn off the listing feature and return to regular text.

 NOTE If you want to be a bit more choosy about your bullet or number styles, you can define something else using the Define New Bullet or Define New List dialog boxes. For example, at the bottom of the **Bullets** drop-down menu is a **Define New Bullet** option. Click it to open the Define New Bullet dialog box, and then click the **Symbol** button to choose a different bullet style from the Symbol dialog box.

 TIP You can also utilize multilevel listing in Word, which is like bullets and numbers, but creates hierarchical lists with subsets of indented list text. To activate multilevel listing, just click the **Multilevel List** button on the **Home** tab—it's right next door to the **Numbering** button.

Controlling Spacing

Up until now, we've been discussing horizontal spacing controls. Now let's talk about vertical spacing in a document, particularly in regard to paragraphs and lines of text. When you start typing into a blank document, some default spacing settings are already in place. For starters, *line spacing* controls the space between lines of text. (It's an appropriately named control, don't you think?) Word automatically sets line spacing to **Multiple**, which puts 1.08 points of space between lines of text. This default setting is quite legible and easy to work with, but you might prefer something different. It turns out you can assign other settings. You might want double or triple spacing, or single spacing, or an exact amount of spacing between lines of text in a paragraph. You can control it all, as long as you know where the right commands are located.

In addition to line spacing, Word also automatically assigns some extra spacing between paragraphs, called *paragraph spacing*. (Didn't see that one coming, did you?) By default, Word inserts 8 points of space after every paragraph you type. This might suit you fine, or might not be enough, or might be too much and you want to take it down a notch. You can do that using the paragraph spacing controls.

As if vertical spacing in paragraphs isn't enough to ponder, you can also control the spacing between characters of text. So as you can see, you're really in charge of your own space.

NOTE   If you're curious about what a point measures, let's just stop and satisfy your curiosity right now. A point measures about 1/72 of an inch. The point measuring system comes from the early days of printing when space between lines was called *leading* (pronounced "LED-ing"). Technically speaking, line spacing is the space between two baselines in a paragraph, the baseline being the imaginary line upon which the characters sit. Some characters, such as the letter *t* or the letter *y* (depending on the font style), feature *ascenders* (that rise above the midpoint) or *descenders* (that drop below the baseline), and they need a little extra allowance to make sure they appear legible. Back in the days of manual typesetting, printers used actual strips of lead to add space between lines of text for books and newspaper printing, and inserting the lead was known as *leading*.

Line Spacing

As mentioned previously, you can change the appearance of your document text by controlling the spacing between lines. Take a look at Figure 8.15 to see some examples of line spacing at work. Hopefully, you can see the difference in each paragraph. Depending on your situation, you might need a document with more or less line spacing. In some cases, changing line spacing can help you reduce the page count for a file by reducing the amount of space consumed by your text. In other cases, you might want to adjust line spacing to offer better legibility or to suit project needs.

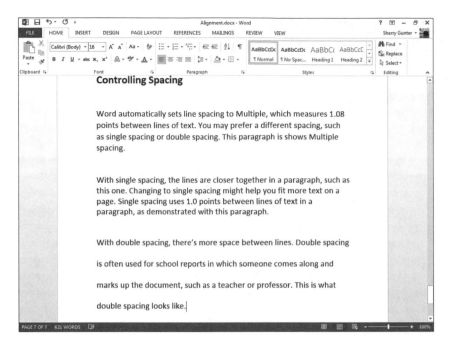

FIGURE 8.15

Here are some examples of line spacing applied to different paragraphs.

To change the line spacing, follow these steps:

1. Select the text you want to change, or click where you want to set a new line spacing.

2. Click the **Home** tab.

3. Click the **Line and Paragraph Spacing** button (see Figure 8.16).

4. Click a spacing setting and Word immediately applies it to the document.

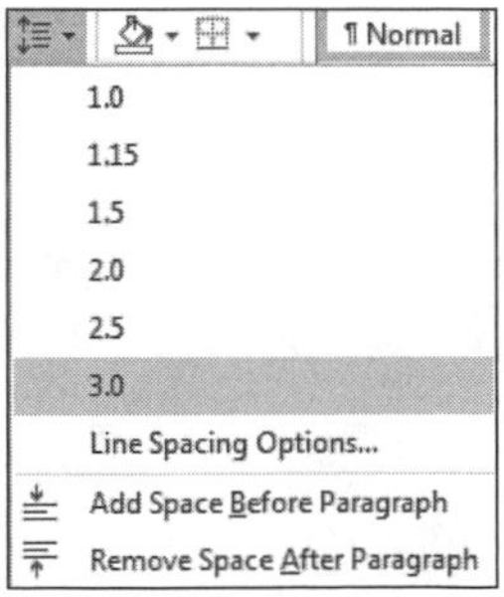

FIGURE 8.16

Use the Line and Paragraph Spacing menu to change line spacing.

You can also open the Paragraph dialog box to control line spacing, as shown in Figure 8.17. Click the **Line Spacing Options** command on the **Line and Paragraph Spacing** menu. With the Paragraph dialog box open, click the **Line spacing** drop-down arrow and make a selection. If you select **Exactly** or **Multiple**, for example, you can use the **At** spinner arrows to set a value for a custom line setting.

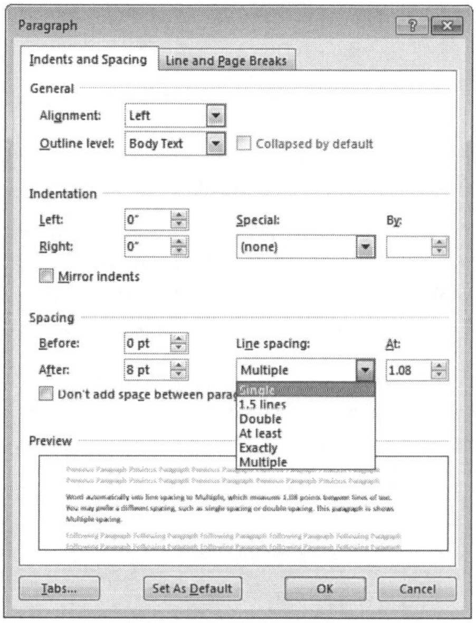

FIGURE 8.17

You can also open the Paragraph dialog box to change line spacing.

Paragraph Spacing

To control the spacing between paragraphs, you can use the same **Line and Paragraph Spacing** drop-down menu on the **Home** tab that you used to control spacing between lines of text. Word is automatically set up to add a little bit of extra space after each paragraph. You can change this value, such as setting it to 0 or specifying another measurement.

To make a quick change, select the text then click the **Line and Spacing** drop-down menu, shown in Figure 8.18. Click **Add Space Before Paragraph** to add extra space, or click **Remove Space After Paragraph** to remove it.

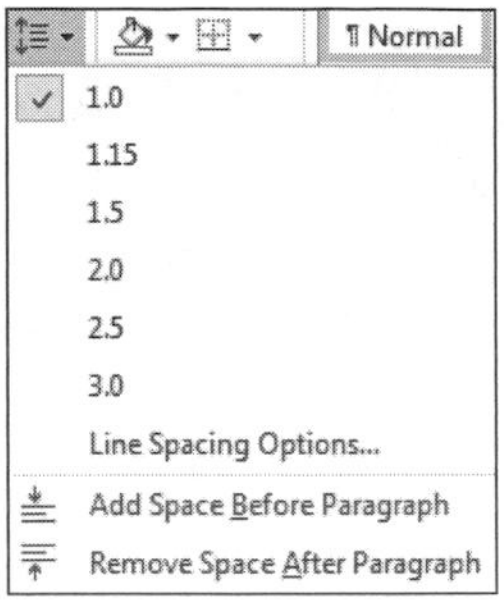

FIGURE 8.18

Use the drop-down menu for quick adjustments.

To specify an exact spacing, open the Paragraph dialog box (see Figure 8.19) and enter a value in the **Before** or **After** boxes. To display the dialog box, click the **Line Spacing Options** command in the drop-down menu, or click the **Paragraph Settings** icon (located in the corner of the Paragraph group of commands). You can use the Spacing **Before** and **After** spinner arrows to set a value, or you can type a value into the box. Remember, spacing is measured in points.

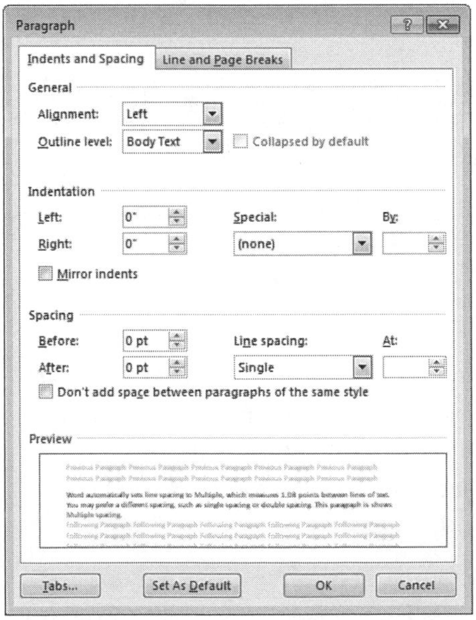

FIGURE 8.19

Or you can open the Paragraph dialog box to change paragraph spacing.

TIP   Does a paragraph need more oomph? Or maybe you want to completely set it apart from the rest of the page? Try assigning a background shade or color, or place a border around the paragraph. To add a background color, click the **Shading** drop-down arrow and pick a color from the palette. You can find the tool right next to the **Line and Paragraph Spacing** tool. If you prefer an actual border instead of a color, click the **Borders** drop-down arrow and choose a border style. (See Chapter 10, "Advanced Formatting," for more on these special features.)

Character Spacing

One more way you can control text spacing is to adjust the amount of spacing that occurs between characters on a line of text, often referred to as *tracking*. You can expand or condense the appearance of characters using *character spacing*. I know this isn't really related to spacing paragraphs *per se*, but it still falls under the umbrella of spacing and it can affect the appearance of your paragraphs. For example, you might want to expand text to fill a particular spot in your document, or you might need to condense it to fit properly in your document layout.

To change character spacing, you must first open the Font dialog box to the **Advanced** tab. Click the **Font** icon in the corner of the Font group of tools on the **Home** tab. Click the **Advanced** tab to view all the character spacing controls. Here you can adjust the scale of the font style, expand or condense characters, or change the baseline for your text. To adjust character spacing, click the **Spacing** drop-down arrow and choose **Expanded** or **Condensed**. You can use the **By** spinner arrows to adjust the value for each.

THE ABSOLUTE MINIMUM

Formatting paragraphs is all about making them look good on a page, which means learning how to fine-tune their positioning. In this chapter you learned that:

- You can assign an alignment to text to control how it sits between the left and right margins.

- You can choose between left, right, center, and justified alignments, and find quick buttons for each on the Ribbon's **Home** tab.

- Indents shift paragraphs around on a page, creating left and right indents, first line indents, and hanging indents.

- You can create tabular columns of text in a document using Word's tab feature.

- You can turn on the ruler display to set quick tabs and indents in your document.

- You can control the spacing between lines of text and paragraphs using the **Line and Paragraph Spacing** drop-down menu on the **Home** tab.

- You can also control the spacing between characters using the spacing commands found in the Font dialog box.

IN THIS CHAPTER

- Learn how to set margins in your documents.
- Turn text into columns that flow up and down your pages.
- Explore ways to control the vertical alignment of text on a page.
- Add header and footer elements to the tops and bottoms of your pages.
- Quickly insert new pages and page breaks.

9

FORMATTING PAGES

Just when your head is about to explode from all the formatting options available in Microsoft Word, it's time to show you some more! This chapter concentrates on formatting you can apply to entire pages to make them look polished and easy on the eyes. Page formatting includes features such as setting page margins, turning text into columns, adding headers and footers, and controlling vertical alignment. Whereas text formatting and paragraph formatting makes your document's content look good, page formatting is all about making your pages look good—and when your documents look good, you look good.

Setting Margins

Margins are the area between the content of your document and the actual edges of the printed or visual page. You can adjust the margins in Word to suit your needs. For example, if you plan on binding your printed pages in some sort of book or binder format, leaving ample right margins is key to making sure users can see everything when turning pages. If you are creating a single-page flyer, you might not want much space in terms of margins around the printed page. In some cases, making slight adjustments to the document's margins can help you cram everything onto one page.

Page margins are also where some special page elements hang out, such as page numbers, headers, and footers (you'll learn more about these features later in this chapter). By default, every blank document in Word starts with 1-inch margins on all four sides. This default margin scheme is affectionately known as the **Normal** margin setting. You can make adjustments to your margins using the **Margins** tool on the **Page Layout** tab, as shown in Figure 9.1. When you click the **Margins** button you can choose from several preset margins or you can create your own custom margin(s). That's right, you can control just one margin on a page, several, or all four. How's that for flexibility?

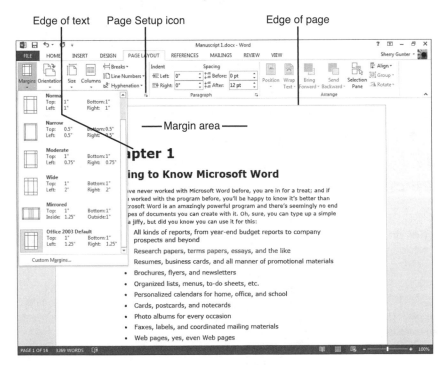

FIGURE 9.1

Find Word's margin controls on the Page Layout tab.

To set your own margins, click the **Custom Margins** option at the bottom of the **Margins** menu. This opens the Page Layout dialog box to the **Margins** tab, as shown in Figure 9.2. You can also access this same dialog box by clicking the **Page Setup** icon—the tiny icon with an arrow on it located in the bottom-right corner of the Page Setup group of tools on the Ribbon's **Page Layout** tab.

In the Page Setup dialog box, you can specify a value—measured in inches—for the top and bottom of the page, and the left and right sides. You can change just one margin, or as many as you want. Click the spinner arrows to adjust the value or type directly into the box you want to change. The **Preview** area at the bottom of the dialog box gives you a thumbnail preview of what the new margin(s) will look like. Click **OK** to exit the dialog and apply the changes.

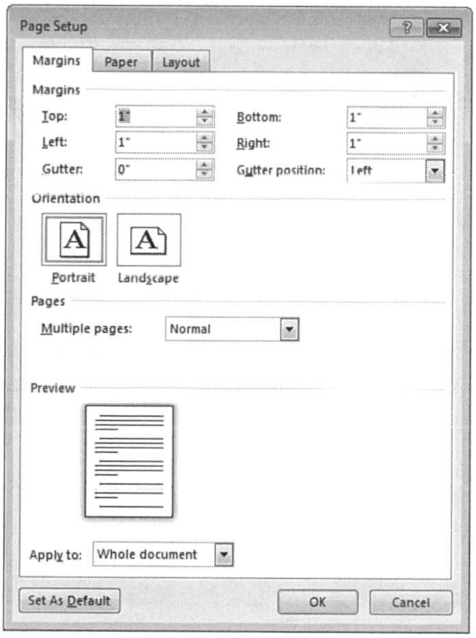

FIGURE 9.2

You can also open the Page Setup dialog box to set your own margins.

TIP When you create a two-page spread, the margins for the adjacent pages are called the *gutter*. You can control the amount of gutter space using the Page Setup dialog box.

NOTE Margins aren't the only setting you can adjust in the Page Setup dialog box. You can also use the settings within to change the page orientation (direction) for printing, choose a paper size for your printer, and control how page elements like headers, footers, and vertical alignment affect the document.

Remember the ruler you learned how to use in Chapter 8, "Formatting Paragraphs," to set indents and tabs? Well, you can use it to set margins, too. Click the Ribbon's **View** tab and click the **Ruler** check box to display the horizontal and vertical rulers. The margin area is marked in a darker shade on the ends of the rulers. Move the mouse pointer over the edge of the margin shading, then click and drag the border to adjust the margin, as shown in Figure 9.3. As you drag the margin, a temporary line appears across the page, helping you to see where the new location for the margin will be when you release the mouse button.

Top margin   Left margin   Right margin

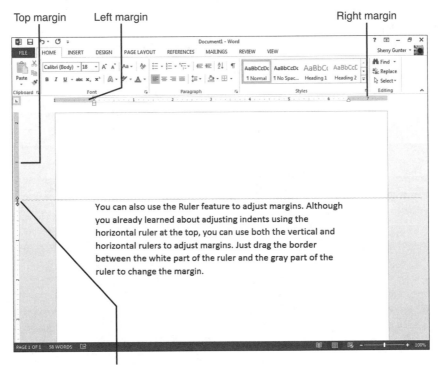

Drag the margin border to adjust the margin

FIGURE 9.3

You can use the rulers to set margins.

If you want to return to the default margins, display the **Margins** drop-down menu and choose **Normal**.

Creating Columns

You can turn your text into columns that run up and down the page, just like columns you find in a magazine or newspaper. The column format is perfect for newsletters, brochures, and other printed publications. You can choose between several preset column formats, including two specialized formats that create a narrower right or left column (appropriately called Left and Right)—in other words, the columns differ in width size. You can also create your own custom columns. Figure 9.4 shows an example of columns at work in a document.

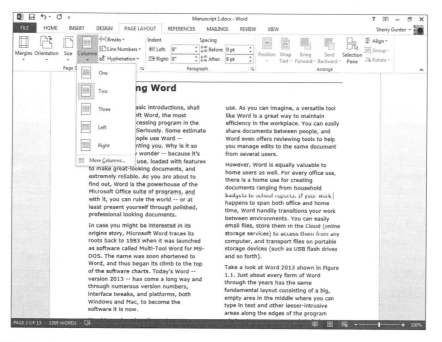

FIGURE 9.4

Use the Columns button to assign column formatting.

To create columns, follow these steps:

1. Select the text you want to turn into columns.

2. Click the **Page Layout** tab.

3. Click the **Columns** button (see Figure 9.4).

4. Click the number of columns you want to create and Word immediately applies the column formatting to the selected text.

If you need to create custom columns, you can open the Columns dialog box, as shown in Figure 9.5. You can use the dialog box to specify the number of columns, their width and spacing, and even include vertical lines to separate the columns. To display the dialog box, click the **More Columns** command at the bottom of the **Columns** menu (shown earlier in Figure 9.4).

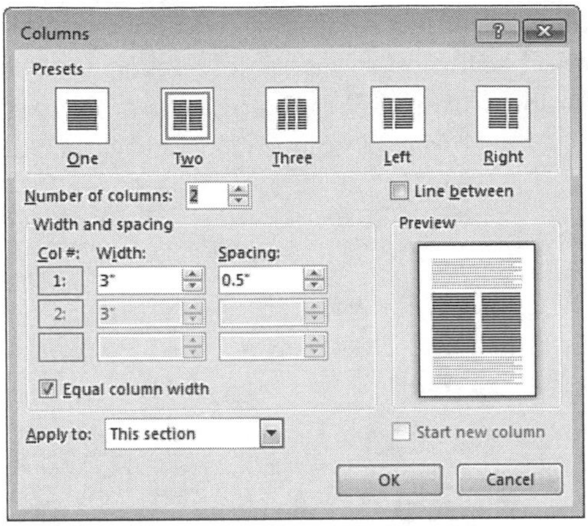

FIGURE 9.5

You can create custom columns using the Columns dialog box.

If you type new text at the bottom of the last column, Word assumes you want to keep using the column formatting. If you do, but need to insert a break of some kind, you can insert a column break. This breaks the column and starts a new column. To do this, click the **Page Layout** tab, click the **Breaks** drop-down arrow, and choose **Column**.

 TIP If you ever need to revert to a no-column format in your document, select the column text or just click anywhere in the column and use the **Columns** drop-down menu to choose **One**. This returns everything to the default page width for the text. You can also do this to turn off the columns and start a regular page again.

Changing Vertical Alignment

Back in Chapter 8, you learned how to control all kinds of horizontal alignment on a page, including aligning text to a margin and setting indents, controlling spacing between lines of text, and using tabs. Did you know you can also control vertical alignment in your document? Well, you can. Word's vertical alignment controls mirror the horizontal ones, which means you can align text to the top, center, and bottom of the page, as well as justify it between the top and bottom margins. By default, the vertical alignment is set to **Top**. This means everything you type in starts out at the top of the page. You can use the other alignments to shift text to align at the center or bottom of the page.

Vertical alignment isn't quite as obvious as horizontal alignment, unless you only have a few lines of text or paragraphs on a page. However, you might find vertical alignment useful when creating title pages or other types of pages where vertical text is important.

 TIP The best way to see vertical alignment happen onscreen is to adjust the zoom setting to see the entire page. Use the **Zoom** slider (in the bottom-right corner of the program window) to zoom out and view more of your document page.

You can find Word's vertical alignment controls tucked away in the Page Setup dialog box, as shown in Figure 9.6. To display the dialog box, click the **Page Setup** icon, the tiny square with an arrow in it located in the bottom corner of the Page Setup group of tools on the **Page Layout** tab. After the dialog box is open, click the **Layout** tab and click the **Vertical** alignment drop-down arrow to choose another alignment. Click **OK** to exit the dialog box and apply the new setting.

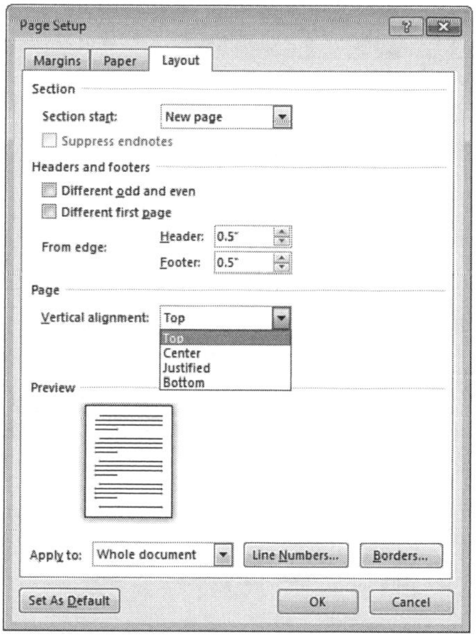

FIGURE 9.6

Control vertical alignment through the Page Setup dialog box.

Take a look at Figure 9.7 to see how vertical alignment affects a title page. In this example, the Bottom alignment is assigned and all the lines of text stack up against the bottom margin.

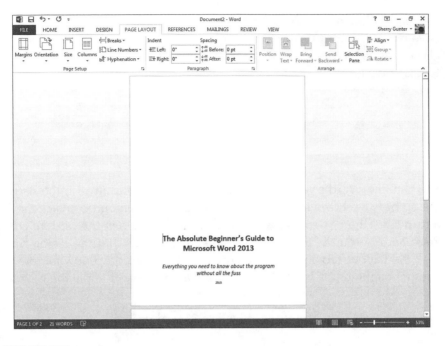

FIGURE 9.7

In this example, vertical alignment is set to Bottom.

 TIP You can choose to apply the vertical alignment setting to the current page rather than the whole document. You might do this for a title page, for example. Click the **Apply to** drop-down arrow at the bottom of the Page Setup dialog box and choose an option. On the next document page, you can reopen the dialog box and choose another alignment to apply for that page onward.

Adding Headers and Footers to a Document

There's an invisible no-man's land that exists between the top and bottom margins and the actual edge of the page—this area is called the *header area* at the top of the page and the *footer area* at the bottom of the page. You can use the header and footer areas to add extra elements to your documents such as page numbers, author name, dates, and other pertinent information about the document.

The great thing about this special area is that the information you place here prints on every page, which is quite helpful when organizing your documents.

Longer documents can really benefit from page numbers, and in a busy workplace environment, including the author information, document title, or dates at the top of every page can help other users know where the document came from or when it was created (see Figure 9.8).

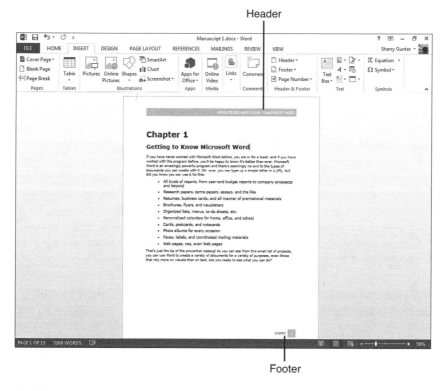

Header

Footer

FIGURE 9.8

Headers and footers appear between the page margins and the actual edge of the page.

Adding Headers and Footers

The Ribbon's **Insert** tab offers access to headers and footers. As with a lot of things in Word, you can choose to create your own header and footer elements, or you can utilize one of the preset designs available. The presets are part of Word's built-in elements, *Quick Parts*, which are preformatted elements sporting a variety of designs and styles. You might remember learning something about Quick Parts in Chapter 6, "Adding Text." Most of the preset headers and footers feature placeholder fields—spots you can fill in with your own text. If you see a "Type Here" spot, that's where you add your own stuff. Take a look at the drop-down menu for **Header** shown in Figure 9.9. You can scroll through the library of built-in headers to find something to suit your document.

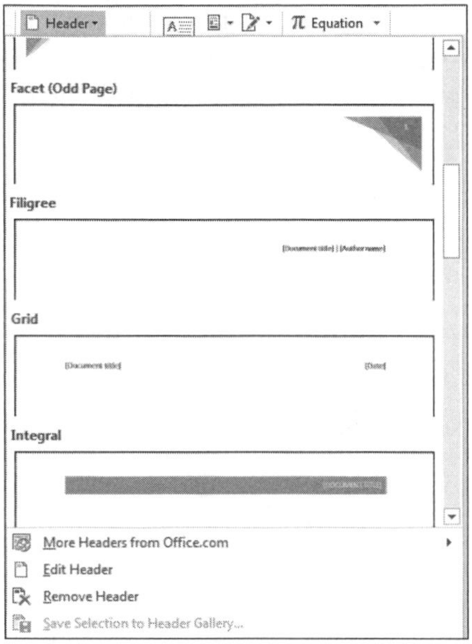

FIGURE 9.9

You can choose from a variety of preset headers.

If you don't see anything you like from the preset elements, you can look for more headers on the Microsoft Office website. You can also choose a header and edit to suit your own needs and then save it to the Header Gallery as a template piece to reuse again.

The **Footer** menu shows a similar setup but with some presets designed for the bottom of pages.

To actually assign a header or footer, just choose it from the appropriate menu. After doing so, you can replace any placeholder text with your own, as shown in Figure 9.10. When you insert a header or footer, Word instantly puts the cursor in the header or footer area and one or more special tabs appear on the Ribbon. You can use the **Header & Footer Tools Design** tab to add more preset fields (such as a date and time or filename) and customize your header or footer text, as well as assign any special options or positioning controls. You can also use the **Design** tab to navigate between the two areas of the page, if your document uses both header and footer information.

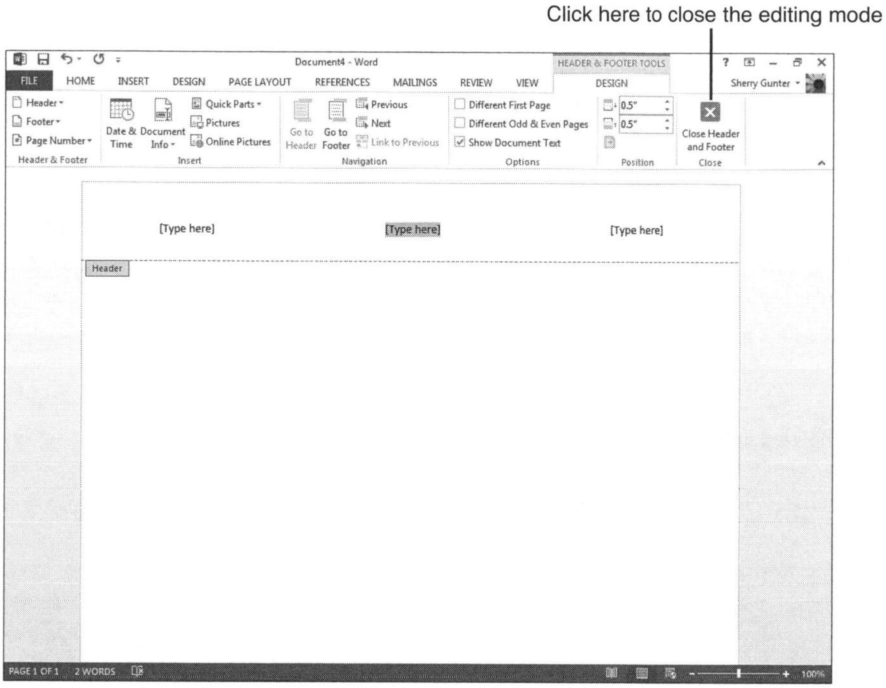

Click here to close the editing mode

FIGURE 9.10

Word switches to a special editing mode to work on headers and footers, and displays special tabs of tools to help you with the task.

If the header or footer you choose utilizes a special design element, the **Table Tools** or **Drawing Tools** tabs might appear offering access to more tools for customizing header or footer appearance.

To start filling in header or footer information, click the placeholder text and type in your own. When you finish creating your header or footer, you can click the **Close Header and Footer** button on the **Header & Footer's Design** tab, or you can double-click anywhere else on the document page.

To return to the header or footer area and make changes, double-click in the header or footer area. To remove a header or footer, click the **Insert** tab, click the **Header** or **Footer** menu and choose **Remove Header** or **Remove Footer**.

TIP   Headers and footers print on every page, unless you specify otherwise. To control printing, open the Page Setup dialog box to the **Layout** tab where you'll find options for placing different odd and even or first page headers and footers. Refer to Figure 9.6 to see the location of these controls.

Adding Page Numbers

You can insert simple page number headers or footers using the **Page Number** drop-down menu on the **Insert** tab. You can choose from a library of preset designs for various locations on the page. You can also format the numbers the way you want.

To assign page numbers, click the **Insert** tab and click the **Page Number** drop-down arrow. Next, choose a position for the numbers and choose a design from the library. Word immediately applies the page numbers to your document (see Figure 9.11).

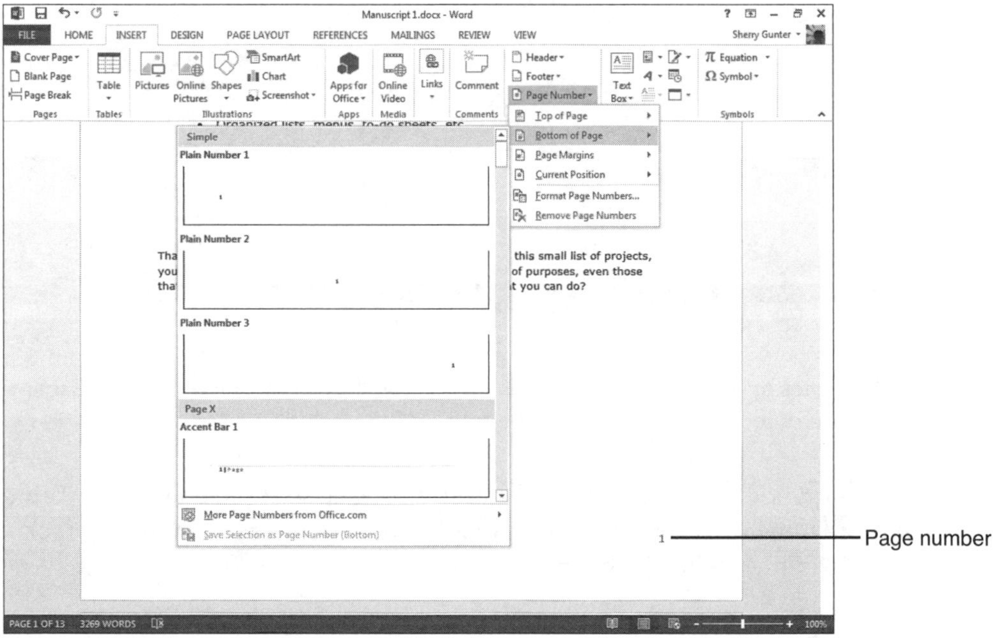

Page number

FIGURE 9.11

Use the Page Numbers feature to insert page numbers as headers or footers on your document pages.

Like regular headers or footers, when you insert page numbers, Word opens the special editing mode for working with header and footer text, depending on where you chose to insert the page numbers. You can double-click anywhere else in the document to exit the special editing mode. To return to the header or footer area and make changes to the numbers or formats, double-click in the header or footer area. To remove the page numbers entirely, click the **Insert** tab, click the **Page Numbers** drop-down menu, and choose **Remove Page Numbers**.

TIP Word keeps a running tally of pages and words down on the status bar.

TIP Need to navigate to a specific page in your document? That's easy; click the **Home** tab and click the **Find** drop-down arrow, then click **Go To** (or press **Ctrl+G**). Type in the page number and press Enter.

Inserting Pages, Breaks, and Sections

When working with documents longer than a single page, Microsoft Word automatically inserts page breaks for you as you type. However, sometimes you need to insert your own new pages or breaks, or divide the document into sections. Not that this comes as a surprise to you by now, but Word has tools for doing all of this. For example, maybe you suddenly need a new page in the middle of your report to add some more information or a graph. You can easily add new pages where you need them. Or maybe you decide to insert a page break and start the next chapter on a new page. You can control page insertions using the **Insert** tab on the Ribbon.

TIP Word can also tally section numbers on the status bar. To turn on section number display, right-click the status bar and choose Section.

TIP Need to navigate to a specific section in your document? Press **Ctrl+G** to summon the Find and Replace dialog box to the Go To tab. Specify sections in the list box, then type in the section number and press **Enter**.

Inserting Pages

Ready for a blank page? Start by clicking in the page you want to appear after the newly inserted page. After you've done this, click the **Insert** tab and click **Blank Page.** Bada-boom, bada-bing, Word inserts a new, empty page for you.

You can also insert instant cover pages for your documents. A cover page typically includes some sort of document title, and information about the author, company, or creation date. You can choose from a variety of cover page *built-ins*—preset designs in which you add your own original content. Click the **Insert** tab and click **Cover Page** to display a drop-down menu of choices. Scroll through and click the one you want, then replace any placeholder text with your own information.

Inserting Breaks

You can also control where a page breaks using, you guessed it, Word's **Page Break** command. When you insert a page break, you're splitting an existing page into two pages. This is handy when you want to turn a paragraph into the start of a new page, or end one chapter and start another. Click where you want to insert a break and click the **Insert** tab and click the **Page Break** command.

As you're typing along, you can also use a keyboard shortcut to insert a page break: Press **Ctrl+Enter**.

If you click the **Page Layout** tab, as shown in Figure 9.12, the **Breaks** drop-down menu lists other page and section breaks you can add. You can use this menu to insert page breaks, column breaks, and several types of section breaks. Figure 9.13 shows an example of a page break.

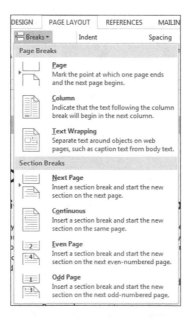

FIGURE 9.12

You can use the Breaks menu to insert page and section breaks.

Page break

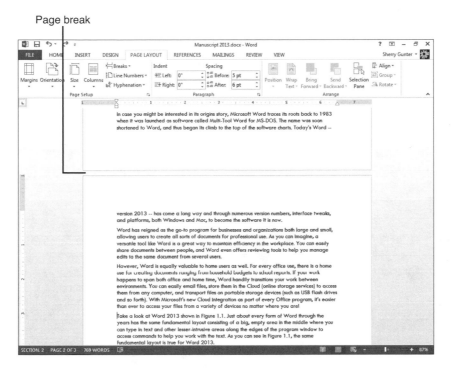

FIGURE 9.13

Here's what a page break looks like in Print Layout view mode.

Section breaks work a bit differently than forcing a new page. You can divide a page into sections and utilize section header and footers for each section. Section breaks are typically used when you want to start a new area with new formatting. For example, maybe you're creating a report that utilizes regular portrait-oriented pages (the page is taller than it is wide), but you need to add a graph that fits on a landscape-oriented page (the page is wider than it is tall). You can do this with a section break. Or maybe your research paper uses regular numbered lists in one part, but Roman numerals in another—a section break can help you format both separately.

With page breaks, the new page retains the same formatting as the previous page, but with section breaks, you can use completely different page formatting, including different margins, columns, or page orientation. You can choose from four different types of section breaks:

- **Next Page** Inserts a new page or continues text on the next consecutive page.

- **Continuous** Starts a new section without adding a page (common for columns).

- **Even Page**   Inserts a new even-numbered page, or continues text on the next even-numbered page.

- **Odd Page**   Inserts a new odd-numbered page, or continues text on the next odd-numbered page.

TIP   To remove a break, turn on the display of paragraph marks (click the **Home** tab and click the **Show/Hide** button in the Paragraph group of tools—this feature toggles on or off). Now navigate to the page break in the file, select it and press the **Delete** key to remove it.

THE ABSOLUTE MINIMUM

You can use Word's page formatting controls to manipulate page margins, vertical alignment, and add extra elements such as headers and footers. You learned the following in this chapter:

- To control page margins, display the **Page Layout** tab and click the **Margins** button or set custom margins using the Page Setup dialog box.

- You can make your text flow nicely on a page using columns and the **Columns** drop-down menu on the **Page Layout** tab.

- You can position text vertically up and down a page using the Page Layout options found in the Page Setup dialog box.

- Headers appear at the top of pages between the margin and the actual edge of the page, while footers appear at the bottom.

- You can insert headers and footers using drop-down menus on the **Insert** tab.

- When working with headers and footers, Word displays special tools and an editing area for working with header or footer text.

- You can also insert page numbers as simple headers or footers using the **Page Numbers** drop-down menu on the **Insert** tab.

- You can insert or remove new pages, page breaks, and section breaks wherever you want in your document.

IN THIS CHAPTER

- Learn how themes and styles can help you create a uniform look throughout a document.
- See how to choose a style set and apply individual styles to your text.
- Find out how to use special text effects to enhance your document.
- Add a little shading or a border to make your text or pages pop.

10

ADVANCED FORMATTING

Just when you thought you had learned all there is to make your Word documents look their loveliest, there are a couple of more tools and features to consider. Let's wrap up our exploration of all things formatting to include the finishing touches you can apply to your documents to make them look extra special and attractive. Some of these extra features can be, quite simply, timesavers and/or lifesavers. If you're looking for quick polish for a document, sort of like a manicure for your text, then look no further than Word's special text effects. They can add instant pizzazz to a document. If uniformity is more your goal, then themes and styles can help you keep your document's major plot points looking groomed. If it's overall background elements you need, then borders and shading can help you out, as well as applying a subtle, yet serious, watermark. This chapter shows you how to make a real show of your text.

Applying a Theme

One of the best ways you can apply an overall consistent look and feel to a document is to utilize one of Word's many themes. A *theme* includes a coordinating set of colors, fonts, and text effects you can apply to make sure your documents share a harmonious appearance. Themes control the primary design aspects of your document, such as colors, fonts, styling of charts and tables, and shapes and diagrams. You can choose from a variety of preset themes, or browse for more themes online. Figure 10.1 shows a document before a theme is applied, and Figure 10.2 shows a document after a theme is applied. It's like a makeover for your file!

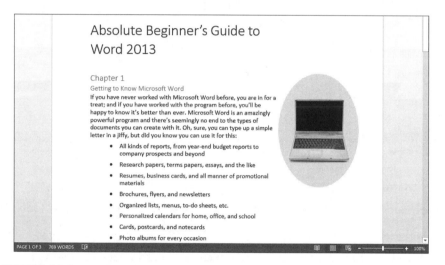

FIGURE 10.1

Before a theme is applied.

Themes work best with *styles* you apply in a document, which you'll learn about in the next section. Themes and styles work hand-in-hand to help ensure design efficiency in your documents. Although at first glance, themes and styles seem a lot alike in Word, they're actually different in their focus. A *theme* defines the overall appearance of your document, whereas *styles* help you control various design options within the document. When you assign a theme, a set of styles is included with the design. Naturally, you can make changes to the various parts of a theme or a style to your liking.

To apply a theme, follow these steps:

1. Click the **Design** tab.

2. Click the **Themes** button.

3. Click a theme from the gallery (see Figure 10.3) to immediately apply it.

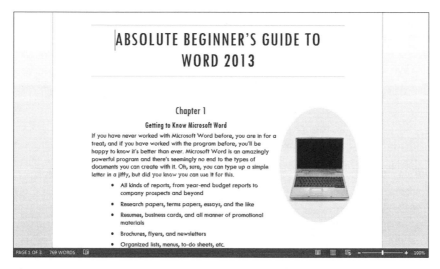

FIGURE 10.2

After applying a theme.

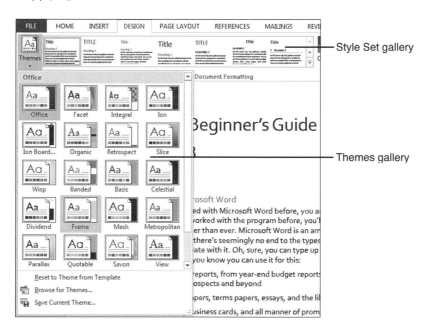

FIGURE 10.3

The Themes gallery lists preset themes you can apply.

You can preview each theme by hovering the mouse pointer over the theme in the gallery menu. Word's Live Preview feature kicks in and also previews the theme on the document page, just to show you what things will look like if you decide to use that particular theme.

NOTE Just a warning: Unless your document already has some styles applied, you might not see much by way of theme elements reflected with Live Preview.

As you can see in the **Themes** gallery, each theme has a color strip of coordinating colors. When you activate a theme, the **Style Set** gallery (see Figure 10.4) displays coordinating styles designed for that particular theme.

TIP If you find yourself using the themes for every document you create, add the **Themes** gallery to Word's Quick Access toolbar—that toolbar in the upper-left corner of the program window where the **Save** and **Undo** buttons sit, ready for action. To add the gallery, right-click over any theme name in the **Themes** drop-down menu, and then click **Add Gallery to Quick Access Toolbar**. This immediately puts a button on the toolbar; click the button to view the gallery of themes. Pretty handy, huh?

To turn off a theme and return to the default Office theme, click the **Themes** button on the **Design** tab and choose the **Office** theme from the gallery.

Themes aren't terribly useful until you start assigning styles, so let's proceed with the rest of the story—learning all about styles.

Applying Styles

Of course you obviously already have your own style going for you—kudos to you—but you might not know your Word text can strut some style as well. When I use the term *style*, I'm not talking about fashion sense, unless you count good-looking fonts as *haute couture*, but rather the term refers to a set of formatting definitions. *Styles* are sets of formatting you can apply to create a uniform look throughout your document. Figure 10.4 shows an example of text without styles, whereas Figure 10.5 shows the same document with styles applied. Notice the change in formatting and text color. That's what styles are all about.

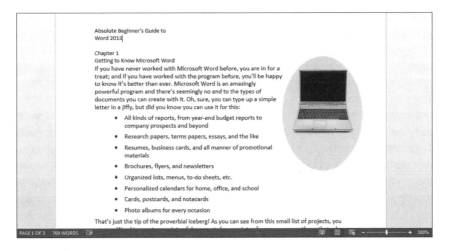

FIGURE 10.4

Before styles.

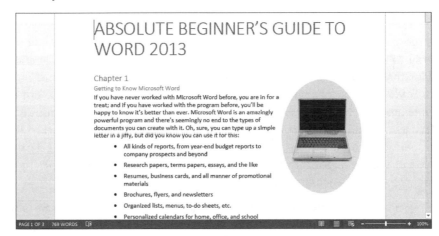

FIGURE 10.5

After styles.

Styles are particularly useful when you need to apply the same formatting to specific types of text in a document, such as headings and subheadings, pull quotes and book titles, references, captions, and all the various parts and pieces that go into building longer documents that require a great deal of consistency. Rather than tediously assign the same formatting manually for each spot in the document where it's needed, you can assign the formatting to a style and apply all the formatting at one time. Wait—that's not all. If you update a style in one spot in the document, the changes are made to all the other text sporting the same assigned style throughout the document—automatically.

For example, let's say your corporate report uses headings throughout the document with the formatting set to Times New Roman font, 16-point size, and bold. Normally, you would have to use three steps to assign the different formatting settings to the selected line of text. With a style, you just perform one step to assign all three formatting commands at once.

Styles can consist of the typical text formatting you might think of, such as fonts, sizes, bold or italics, or paragraph formatting, such as indents and spacing. Just about any formatting you can think of as it applies to your document text can be used with styles. Styles can also include colors, borders and shading, text effects, and anything else you need to apply to create a uniform appearance throughout your document. As you can imagine, styles really come in handy for multilevel, complex documents.

 NOTE   There are technically two types of styles: paragraph and character styles. Paragraph styles contain both text formatting and paragraph formatting, whereas character styles work for single words and characters; that is, text.

As mentioned in the previous section, style sets are part of themes you can apply to a document. Each theme offers different *style sets*—a collection of styles that coordinate nicely with the chosen theme. Style sets hang out over in the **Style Sets** gallery on the **Design** tab, as shown in Figure 10.6. But individual styles are listed in the **Styles** gallery on the **Home** tab. A little confusing, isn't it? Most people who worked with previous versions of Word are used to the styles appearing with the rest of the text-building tools, which are located on the **Home** tab, but the document formatting tools are over on the **Design** tab, hence the placement of themes and style sets over there.

Are you ready to view some style sets? Glance through the **Style Sets** gallery and see what you like. You can click the **More** button in the **Style Sets** gallery to view all the associated sets, as shown in Figure 10.7.

Choose a style set here

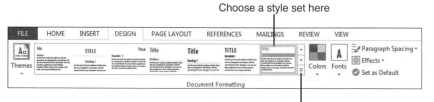

Click here to view all the associated style sets at a glance

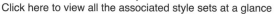

FIGURE 10.6

Use the Design tab's Style Sets gallery to choose a style set.

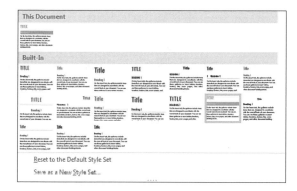

FIGURE 10.7

You might want to expand the gallery to see everything at a glance.

After you designate a style set from the gallery, you can apply individual styles from that set using the **Styles** gallery on the **Home** tab, as shown in Figure 10.8. You can also create your own styles and add them to the style set.

Assign individual styles

Styles button

FIGURE 10.8

Use the Home tab's Styles gallery to assign individual styles to document text.

Choosing Style Sets

By default, Word starts you out with the Office theme and a default Office style set. It includes some basic styles for heading levels, titles, and a few other items. For example, it assigns the Normal Quick Style to the body text of your documents, unless you change it.

To choose a style set, follow these steps:

1. Click the **Design** tab.

2. Click a style set (refer to Figure 10.6).

You can use the tools located next to the **Style Set** gallery to tweak the overall design, such as changing the color scheme, font, or spacing.

Assigning Styles

You can apply a style to specific text by selecting it first, or you can apply a style to an entire paragraph just by clicking anywhere in the paragraph.

To assign a style, follow these steps:

1. Click or select the text to which you want to assign a style.

2. Click the **Home** tab.

3. Click a style (refer to Figure 10.8).

The **Styles** gallery on the **Home** tab is a bit limiting in what styles appear (unless the one you want is always shown first). To see more, click the **Styles** button— the tiny icon with an arrow in it displayed in the corner of the **Styles** group of tools (see Figure 10.8). When clicked, this feature opens the **Styles** pane, shown in Figure 10.9. This pane lists all the styles for the style set currently applied to the document. You can choose a style from the list to apply it to text in your document. You can keep the pane open to assign more styles throughout your document.

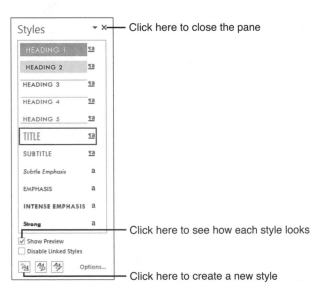

FIGURE 10.9

The Styles pane.

TIP If you don't see all of your styles listed, then click the **Options** link at the bottom of the **Styles** pane and change the **Select styles to show** option to **All Styles**.

Creating New Styles

You can modify an existing style and save it as a new style in the list. You can also create a new style from scratch. Start by applying all the necessary formatting, then click the **New Style** button at the bottom of the **Style** pane (refer to Figure 10.9). This opens the **Create New Style from Formatting** dialog box, as shown in Figure 10.10. You can type in a name for the style, and change any other settings as needed. Click **OK** when you finish, and Word adds the style to the Styles gallery. Now it's ready to go the next time you need it.

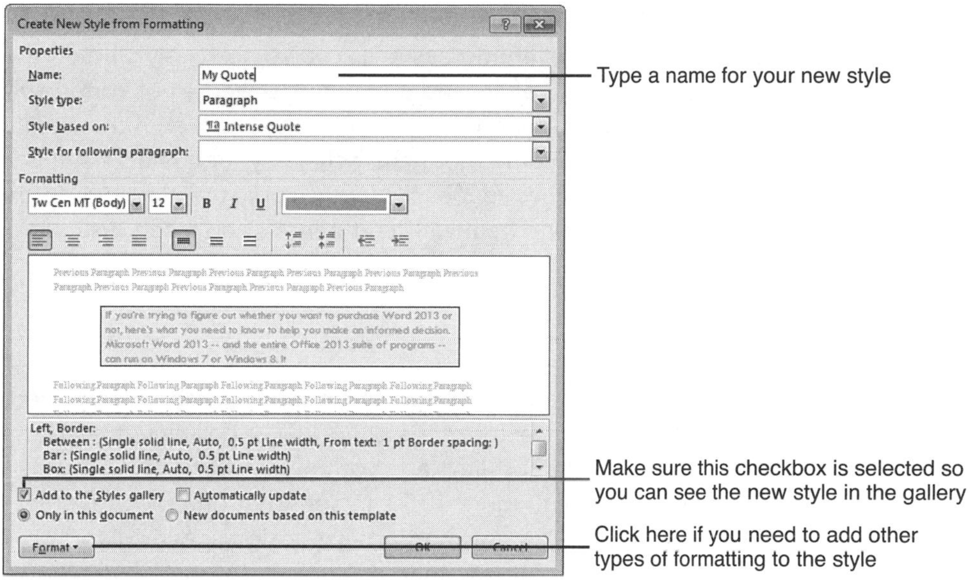

Type a name for your new style

Make sure this checkbox is selected so you can see the new style in the gallery

Click here if you need to add other types of formatting to the style

FIGURE 10.10

Use this dialog box to create a new style.

If you want the new style available in other documents as well as the current one, you need to select the **New documents based on this template** option in the dialog box.

If you want to update all the uses of the new style throughout the document (in case you tweak the formatting or something), select the **Automatically update** check box in the dialog box.

TIP If you notice unexpected formatting changes keep happening to your paragraphs, you probably have the Automatically Update option on and need to change the setting. To turn this off, right-click the style name in the Styles pane and choose **Modify**. This opens the Modify Style dialog box. Uncheck the **Automatically update** check box to turn the feature off.

Adding Special Effects

I certainly don't want to leave you with the impression that your document text isn't special and glamorous enough as it is. You've obviously studied the previous formatting chapters carefully and diligently applied all of your newfound knowledge to make your document a thing of beauty. However, if the situation warrants it, you can easily add some more character to your characters, if you know what I mean. In this section, you learn how to apply the classic drop caps technique, turn up the formatting heat with text effects, and insert a subtle behind-the-scenes watermark.

Inserting Drop Caps

Drop caps have long been a part of the publishing industry, commonly used in books to present the first character of the chapter in a prominent fashion. Typically, a drop cap is an enlarged first letter of the first word of the first paragraph, an initial—check out Figure 10.11 to see what one looks like. European monks used to painstakingly and artfully design spectacular drop caps for manuscripts. We're not going to do that in Word, but we can make some nice drop caps.

FIGURE 10.11

Here's an example of a drop cap, plus a peek at the Drop Cap menu.

Drop caps can appear below or above the text baseline (the invisible horizontal line that characters sit on). They work best with a longer paragraph that has more than three lines of text.

To create your own drop cap, follow these steps:

1. Select the text character you want to turn into a drop cap.

2. Click the **Insert** tab.

3. Click the **Add a Drop Cap** drop-down arrow to display the menu shown in Figure 10.11.

4. Click **Dropped**, and Word turns the character into a drop cap.

You can edit a drop cap using the **Drop Cap** dialog box, shown in Figure 10.12. To open this box, either click the **Drop Cap** drop-down arrow and choose **Drop Cap Options**, or right-click over a selected drop cap's border and choose **Drop Cap**. You can use the tools in the dialog box to adjust the font style, how many lines to drop, and distance from the rest of the text. If you decide you need to remove the drop cap, select it and activate the **None** command.

FIGURE 10.12

The Drop Cap dialog box.

Applying Text Effects

Word's text effect tools can add some serious flair and style to your text. Utilizing such techniques as outlining, shadows, glow, and reflection, you can create a variety of artsy looks. To use the feature, click the **Home** tab, then click the **Text Effects** drop-down arrow. A menu of effects categories appears, and each one offers a submenu of choices presented in a gallery. Figure 10.13 shows the **Glow** gallery, and the text displays a preview of the highlighted effect. To assign an effect, just click it.

To turn off an effect, select the text, reopen the gallery, and choose the **No** command offered, such as **No Glow**.

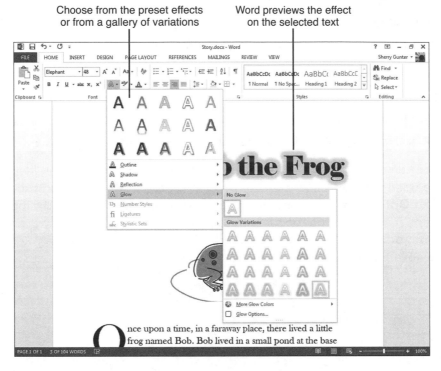

FIGURE 10.13

You can add text effects to turn text into fancy-looking typography.

Adding a Watermark

It sounds like a fancy term for something involving liquid, which is never a good idea near a computer, but a *watermark* is actually text or an image that appears faded in the background of a page. Take a look at Figure 10.14. Can you make out the DRAFT watermark, printed on an angle?

Watermarks are commonly used in corporate and industrial settings; for example, to identify documents as confidential or drafts, or in the case of government agencies, top secret. Watermarks appear behind the document text as a background element. You can use text or pictures as watermarks, including photos. Word's Watermark tool includes several default choices presented in the Watermark gallery (see Figure 10.15).

FIGURE 10.14

Watermarks appear behind text on a page.

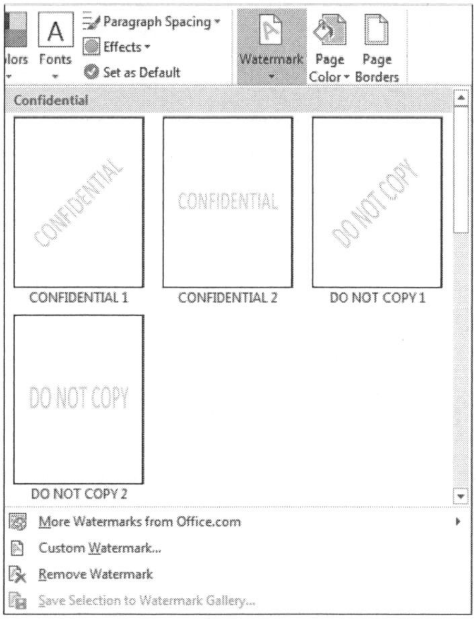

FIGURE 10.15

You can use the Watermark tool to add a watermark from the scrollable gallery.

To insert a simple watermark, follow these steps:

1. Click the **Design** tab.

2. Click the **Watermark** drop-down arrow.

3. Scroll through the gallery and choose a watermark design (see Figure 10.15).

To create a custom design, you can open the **Printed Watermark** dialog box. Click the **Custom Watermark** command at the bottom of the **Watermark** menu. This opens the Printed Watermark dialog box, as shown in Figure 10.16. To use a picture as a watermark, click the **Picture watermark** option and navigate to the file. To use a different word or phrase than the gallery offers, click the **Text** drop-down menu and make a selection. You can also use the settings to control the font, size, color, and layout of the watermark.

FIGURE 10.16

Use this dialog box to add a picture as a watermark or create custom text.

To remove a watermark, click the **Watermark** drop-down arrow and choose **Remove Watermark**.

Adding Borders and Shading

You can add borders and background shading to text, paragraphs, or entire pages. Borders are a great way to section off parts of your document or draw attention to special areas. The use of color as a background can do the same. This section shows you how to utilize the borders and shading tools, and the skills you learn here can help you as you continue to work with other document elements you add, such as tables and clip art.

TIP Colors, borders, and all manner of formatting are great, but always keep legibility in mind. If any of the extra formatting makes reading your text too difficult, then you've defeated the purpose.

Adding Text Borders

You can create custom borders in Word and control the color and thickness of the lines. You can also customize the line style and even choose which sides you want bordered. Options, options, options—so many options!

To add a border around text, whether it's a single word or paragraph, follow these steps:

1. Select the text you want to add a border to.

2. Click the **Home** tab.

3. Click the **Borders** drop-down arrow (see Figure 10.17).

4. Choose a border option.

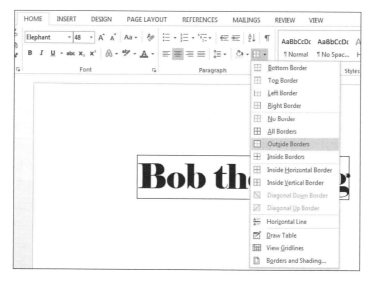

FIGURE 10.17

Use the Borders tool to add borders to your text.

You can customize a border using the **Borders and Shading** dialog box, shown in Figure 10.18. To find your way to this feature, click the **Borders and Shading** command at the bottom of the **Borders** drop-down menu. With the **Borders** tab displayed, you can choose a border setting, line style, color, and line width. When you've set all the options you want, click **OK** to apply them to the selected text.

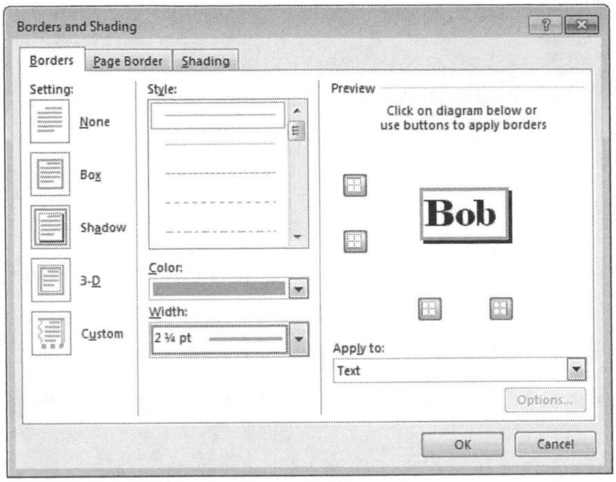

FIGURE 10.18

The Borders and Shading dialog box.

Adding Page Borders

You can add a border to the entire page using Word's **Page Borders** tool. You'll find this feature on the **Design** tab. Click the **Page Borders** button to open the **Borders and Shading** dialog box to the **Page Border** tab, as shown in Figure 10.19. This tab shows the exact same tools as the **Borders** tab shown in Figure 10.18, but anything you set here applies to the page instead of selected text. You can set a custom border and specify sides, or choose from a regular box, shadow, or 3-D border. You can also control the line style, line width, and color.

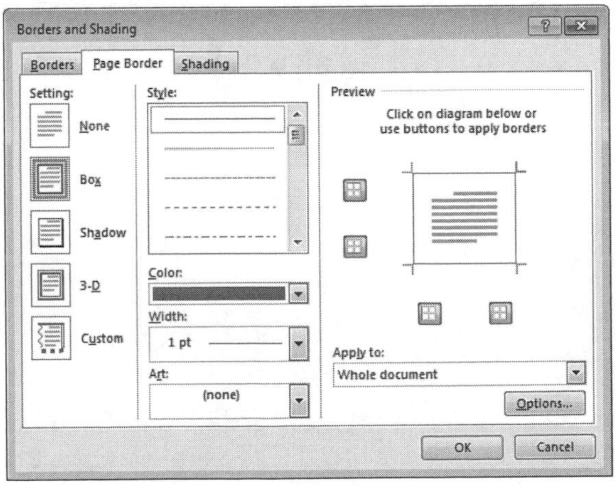

FIGURE 10.19

The Borders and Shading dialog box, again.

Adding Shading

Word's **Shading** tool adds a background color behind the selected text or the entire page.

1. Select the text you want to be shaded.
2. Click the **Home** tab.
3. Click the **Shading** drop-down arrow (see Figure 10.20).
4. Choose a color option. You can choose from the palette of standard colors or theme colors.

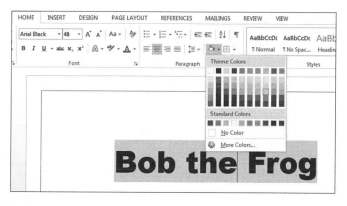

FIGURE 10.20

Use the Shading tool to add background color to your text.

You can use the same technique to add shading to the entire page, but the command for this is on the **Design** tab. Click the **Page Color** button to display the exact same drop-down palette of colors.

 TIP You can open the **Colors** dialog box to find more customized colors than what the color palette presents. Click the **More Colors** command below the color palette to open the dialog box and explore more choices.

THE ABSOLUTE MINIMUM

You are now a formatting master and must carefully guard the secrets of making documents look spectacular. Here's a summary of your vast new knowledge:

- Themes control the primary design aspects of your document, such as colors, fonts, styling of charts and tables, and shapes and diagrams, and you can change themes using the **Themes** tool on the **Design** tab.

- Styles help you control various design options within the document.

- Every theme includes a set of styles, also found on the **Design** tab listed in the **Style Set** gallery.

- Individual styles are applied from the **Styles** gallery on the **Home** tab.

- A drop cap is a large initial at the beginning of a paragraph; you can use the **Drop Cap** tool on the **Insert** tab to create one.

- Text effects add artsy typography techniques to your text, such as glows and shadows; click the **Text Effects** button on the **Home** tab to assign them.

- A watermark is large text or a picture that appears faded in the background of a page, typically used to mark documents with special meaning, such as DRAFT or CONFIDENTIAL.

- You can use Word's borders and shading tools to add borders and shading to text or entire pages.

11

IN THIS CHAPTER

- Learn how to insert a simple table.

- Add a preset, preformatted table using Word's Quick Tables gallery.

- Draw your own tables just like Picasso used to do— or would have done if he had Microsoft Word.

- Create tables using Microsoft Excel's spreadsheet tools—without leaving Word.

ADDING TABLES TO WORD DOCUMENTS

Prepare yourself to learn about one of Word's most versatile features— *tables*. At the outset, tables might seem like just a bunch of simple columns and rows, but in truth, they are so much more than that. Tables are structural beauty in the midst of a page. They are vehicles for the presentation of data, they create graphic interest (particularly with the borders turned on), and are designed to help you bring order and organization to ungainly text.

Tables in their simplest form are a grid of interconnecting rows and columns. The areas made by this interconnectivity are called *cells*. You can fill cells with text, numbers, artwork and pictures, or even with other tables. You can choose to create tables with or without borders, or add borders around certain cells, add background shading, and a gazillion other options.

You can use tables to present data in an easy-to-read fashion. For example, you might need to present side-by-side lists in a document, or type up a household budget, create a form, or even design a web page. Because a table's columns and rows are so easy to resize the way you want, there's no limit to the things you can do with tables. Tables are ideal for making invoices, catalogs, newsletters, or any kind of situation in which text requires defined structure. If this is your first time using tables, don't be intimidated by their power, and whatever you do, don't let Word's Table tools go under-utilized in your document-building tasks. Let's start by learning the various ways to insert tables into a Word document.

Inserting a Basic Table

Word makes inserting a table so incredibly easy, you'll wonder why you don't start every document with one. Okay, maybe not *every* document, but you certainly can't deny how easy it is. Located conveniently on the **Insert** tab, you can click the **Table** drop-down palette and specify how many columns and rows you want simply by dragging the mouse across the grid, as shown in Figure 11.1. As soon as you release the mouse button, your new table instantly appears in the document at the current cursor location, as shown in Figure 11.2.

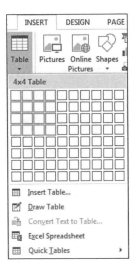

FIGURE 11.1

For an instant table, look for the Table tool on the Insert tab.

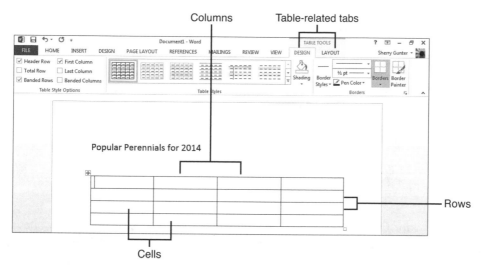

FIGURE 11.2

A newly inserted Word table, measuring 4 × 4 (rows and columns).

Anytime you add a table or click anywhere in one, the Ribbon immediately displays the **Table Tools** group of tabs, which include the **Design** tab filled with various table style options and design features, and the **Layout** tab, which includes tools for changing the table's columns, rows, cell size, alignment, and so on.

Microsoft Word assumes you want to begin filling your table starting with the first cell, so the cursor sits in the first table cell ready for you to type in text. At this point, you might be wondering how to navigate your tables. Here are a few methods to help you move around in them:

- You can press the **Tab** key on your keyboard to navigate from cell to cell.

- Press **Shift+Tab** to move back to the previous cell.

- You can use the arrow buttons on your keyboard to navigate up and down, right and left in a table. Each click of the button moves the cursor to the next cell.

- Press **Ctrl+Home** to move to the first cell in the table.

- Press **Alt+Page Up** to move to the top cell in the current column.

- Press **Alt+Page Down** to move to the last cell in the current column.

Of course, you can always use the mouse to navigate between cells, clicking which cell you want to work in. Take a look at Figure 11.3 to see the table with text added.

Popular Perennials for 2014			
Poppy	Salvia	Iris	Sedum
Astilbe	Hosta	Bee Balm	Coralbells
Daylily	Coreopsis	Daisy	Foxglove
Russian Sage	Phlox	Lavender	Dianthus

FIGURE 11.3

Here's a table filled with text.

If you want to control not only columns and rows, but also how text behaves within the table cells, you can create a table using the **Insert Table** dialog box, shown in Figure 11.4, and choose from the AutoFit options available. To do so, follow these steps:

1. Click the **Insert** tab.

2. Click the **Table** button.

3. Click **Insert Table**.

4. Specify the number of columns and rows (see Figure 11.4); click the spinner arrows or just type in a value in the appropriate box.

5. Select an AutoFit behavior; you can choose a particular column width, fit the contents to the table (which means the columns expand to fit whatever you type), or fit the table to the window (which means the table fits the size of your document).

6. Click **OK**, and Word creates your table.

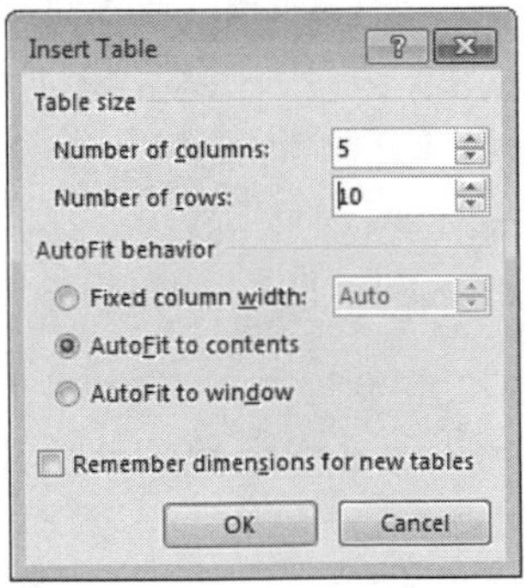

FIGURE 11.4

You can also use the Insert Table dialog box to insert tables.

NOTE   Learn how to modify and format tables in Chapter 12, "Editing Tables."

TIP   You can convert existing text into a table using Word's **Convert Text to Table** command. First select the text you want to turn into a table, click the **Table** button, and then choose **Convert Text to Table** from the menu. You can then specify the number of columns you want or let Word determine the amount for you, and instruct Word how you want the text separated (such as paragraphs or commas). Click **OK**, and Word carries out your instructions.

Inserting and Creating Quick Tables

Although design-it-yourself tables are fun, you might prefer to speed up your table creation using one of Word's built-in Quick Tables. Part of Word's library collection of Quick Parts and built-in *building blocks*, you can use the Quick Tables gallery to insert calendars, tabular lists, and preformatted tables with preset subheadings. Basically, building blocks are tiny templates you can reuse to base new content on. To access the gallery, click the **Table** button on the **Insert** tab, and click the **Quick Tables** command to view the gallery, shown in Figure 11.5.

FIGURE 11.5

You can choose from several preset tables to insert into your document.

When you see a Quick Table you like, click it in the gallery to insert it into your document. You can add your own text to make the table your own. All the built-in tables include placeholder text for things such as column headings or calendar months. Figure 11.6 shows an example of a Quick Table with subheadings. Notice everything is preformatted, so I don't have to change anything unless I really want to. All I need to do is fill in the table with my own text.

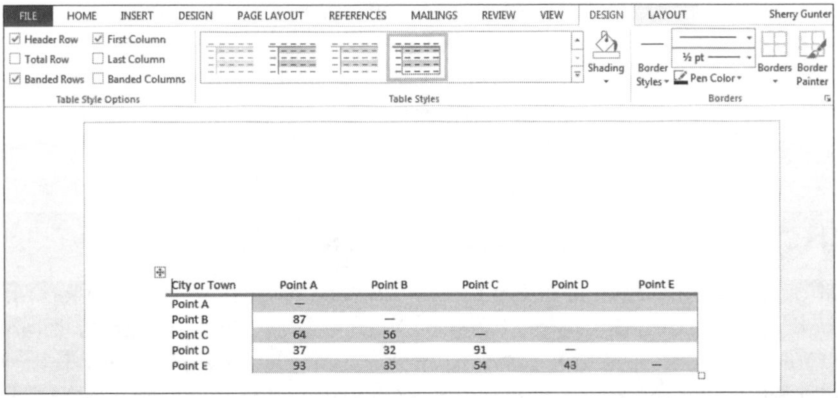

City or Town	Point A	Point B	Point C	Point D	Point E
Point A	—				
Point B	87	—			
Point C	64	56	—		
Point D	37	32	91	—	
Point E	93	35	54	43	—

FIGURE 11.6

Here's one of Word's Quick Tables.

TIP To learn more about using building blocks or Quick Parts, see Chapter 6, "Adding Text."

When you customize a Quick Table, or any table for that matter, you can turn it into a Quick Part and use it again. To do so, click the finished table's upper-left corner icon to select the table, click the **Table** button and choose the **Quick Tables** command, then click **Save Selection to Quick Tables Gallery**. This opens the **Create New Building Block** dialog box (see Figure 11.7) where you can name the table and add a description. By default, the table you save becomes part of the building blocks library and appears in the Quick Tables gallery along with the other table templates.

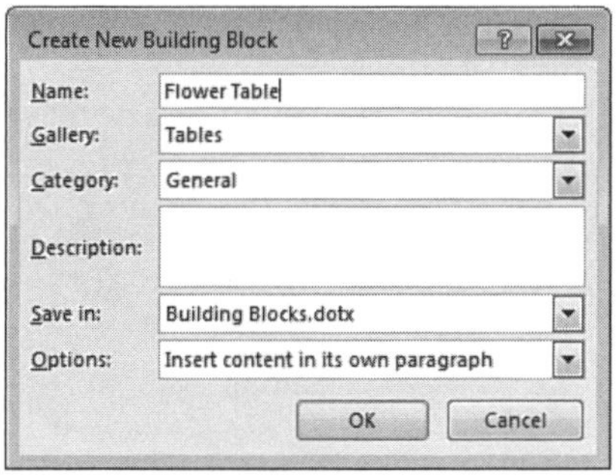

FIGURE 11.7

Save a table to the Quick Table gallery to reuse it.

Drawing a Custom Table

There's one more way to insert a table into your document—you can draw it yourself. Sounds like a strange thing to do, doesn't it? It's actually rather handy, especially if your table is a bit more complex in its layout and content. For example, you might have a plan for a particular layout for your table that includes one really wide column and several smaller ones, or perhaps your content needs both small and large cells in the same table. Rather than try to move column and row borders to adjust cells, why not draw them just the way you want them? With Word's Draw Table feature, you can control how big the table is, how many columns and rows it contains, and the size and spacing of those columns and rows.

To draw a table, follow these steps:

1. Click the **Insert** tab.

2. Click **Table**.

3. Click **Draw Table**. The mouse pointer turns into a pencil icon.

4. Click and drag the size of the table you want to create, as shown in Figure 11.8.

5. Click and drag each row and column you want to appear inside the table, as shown in Figure 11.9.

6. When the table is finished, click the **Draw Table** button on the Table Tools **Layout** tab to turn off drawing mode.

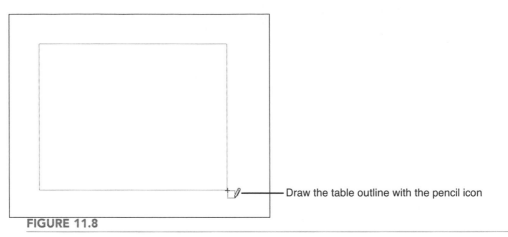

Draw the table outline with the pencil icon

FIGURE 11.8

When drawing a table, start by establishing the outer perimeters.

Click here to turn off
table drawing mode

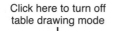

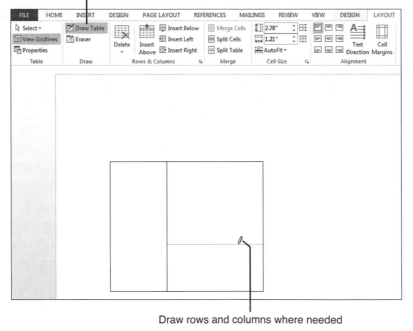

Draw rows and columns where needed

FIGURE 11.9

Customize the table by drawing in the columns and rows.

You can edit your table by drawing new lines, erasing existing lines, or dragging lines to resize cell borders. Try some of these techniques to fine-tune your newly drawn table:

- To erase a line, click the **Eraser** tool on the **Layout** tab and drag across the line you want to erase.
- To add a new line to create a new column or row, click the **Draw Table** button on the **Layout** tab and draw the line. The button toggles the drawing mode on or off.
- To reposition a row or column border, drag the border line.

You can learn more table formatting skills in the next chapter.

Inserting Excel Spreadsheets as Tables

What if you need a table that acts more like a spreadsheet, rather than Word content? Word has a tool for that—the Excel Spreadsheet command inserts a spreadsheet right into your document. Best of all, when you activate this feature, you can tap into tools for adding formulas and functions, sorting and filtering, and more, thus putting powerful spreadsheet features at your fingertips.

When you insert a spreadsheet, you might suddenly think you've opened the Excel program window. As you can see in Figure 11.10, Word's Ribbon immediately switches over to reveal Excel tabs and tools. Don't worry; as soon as you click outside the Excel spreadsheet table, you're back in the familiar Word environment again.

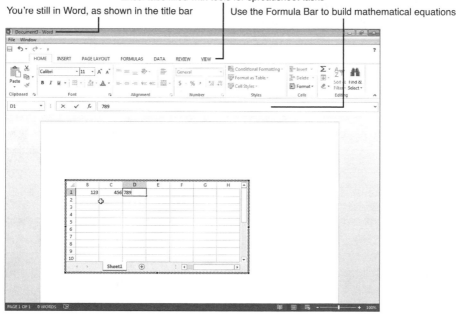

FIGURE 11.10

You can insert an Excel-style table into Word and use Excel tools to populate the table.

TIP Microsoft Excel is a powerful spreadsheet program designed to help users juggle all kinds of data, particularly numbers.

To insert an Excel spreadsheet as a table, follow these steps:

1. Click the **Insert** tab.

2. Click **Table**.

3. Click **Excel Spreadsheet**.

Word opens a blank spreadsheet for you, as shown in Figure 11.10. Excel spreadsheets act a lot like a regular Word table; you can type in text or numbers, resize columns and rows, add pictures, and so on. The row and column labels (numbers for rows and letters for columns) don't print with your table; rather, they are used with formulas and functions you might add to the table. The table gridlines appear in printouts, but you can format them to your liking.

THE ABSOLUTE MINIMUM

You can use tables to organize and present text in a structured fashion. Here's what you learned about inserting tables:

- The quickest way to create a table on the fly is to use the Tables palette and drag across the grid of columns and rows.

- For more precise control when inserting a table, open the **Insert Table** dialog box.

- If you need a custom table, use the **Draw Table** tool.

- Whenever you insert a table, regardless of the technique, Word automatically displays the Table Tools, two extra tabs of tools (Design and Layout) for working with tables (learn more about these tools in the next chapter).

- You can also insert an Excel spreadsheet as a table in Word, tapping into Excel's many tools for crunching data.

12

IN THIS CHAPTER

- Learn a lot of ways to resize your table's columns and rows.
- Fine-tune your table structure by adding and deleting columns, rows, and cells.
- Examine the magical Merge Cells and Split Cells commands.
- Control your cell's margins and alignment to suit your table contents.
- Learn how to reposition and resize your table.
- Apply styles to make your tables look spiffy.

EDITING TABLES

You can do all kinds of things to make your table and its data look good. Sometimes you might need to nudge a row or column size to add a little space around the cell contents, or add and subtract cells, columns, and rows. Other times, your table might require a complete makeover with new fonts and styles. Or how about changing the table border style and color to really add some pizzazz? In this chapter, we'll delve into the many ways you can make adjustments to your table's appearance and structure.

For starters, any of the regular formatting tools you use to change the appearance of your document text can be applied to your table data, too. You can change the fonts, sizes, positioning, color, and so forth using the **Home** tab to access basic formatting tools. In addition to the basics, Word adds two new tabs to the Ribbon when working with tables: **Design** and **Layout**. Grouped under the heading of **Table Tools**, these tabs offer an array of tools for working specifically with tables and table elements. You're about to learn how to apply these tools, so get your table ready for company.

Selecting Table Parts

Before you can apply formatting or other changes to your table data, you need to learn how to select the various parts of your table. Selecting table parts is akin to selecting regular document text: Much clicking and dragging is involved. Figure 12.1 shows an example of a selected row; notice all the row cells are highlighted in gray signifying selection.

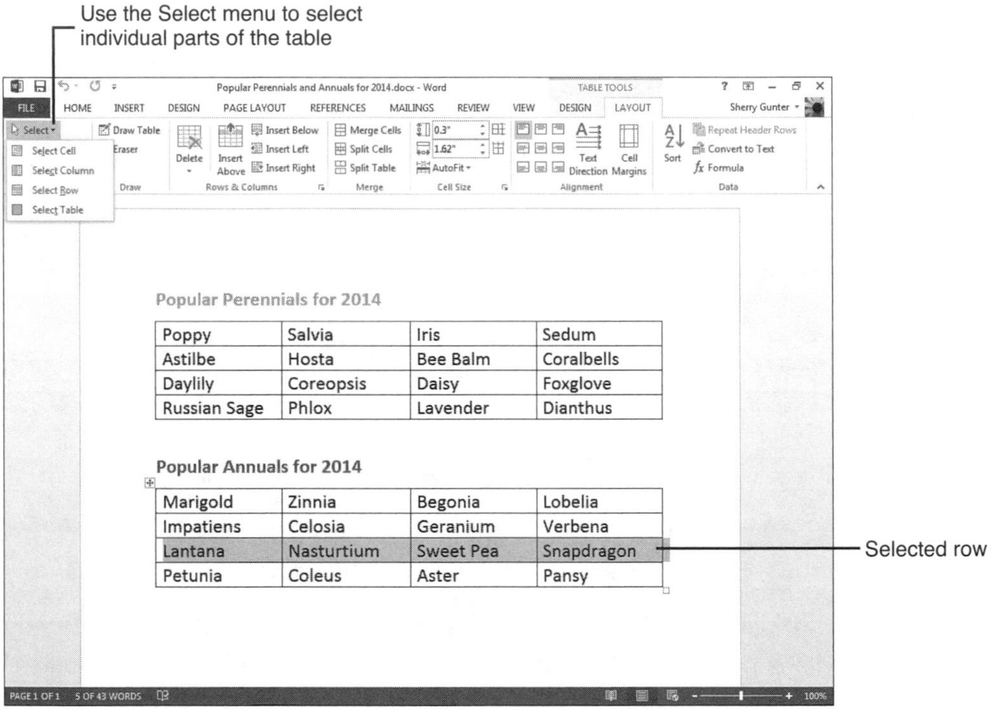

FIGURE 12.1

You can easily select parts of the table in order to apply formatting or make other modifications.

Use these selection techniques to select parts of the table:

- To select a single word or number, double-click the data.

- You can also select a cell by moving the mouse pointer to the left border of the cell until the pointer looks like a thick arrow icon, then click.

- You can also triple-click to select a cell.

- Drag across multiple cells to select them.

- To select an entire row, move the mouse pointer to the left border of the row until it takes the shape of a thick arrow pointer, then double-click.

- To select an entire column, click the top border of the column (the mouse pointer turns into a thick downward-pointing icon when you're hovering over the column border).

- To select the whole table, click the tiny square in the upper-left corner of the table.

- You can also use the **Layout** tab's **Select** drop-down menu to select parts of your table.

To deselect any selected area or item in a table, just click anywhere outside the selected element.

Changing Column Widths and Row Heights

Every column and row is resizable in a table. You can expand and contract columns and rows to modify the appearance of your table. For example, if the cell contents look too tight, adjust the column width, or if you need to insert more lines of text in a cell, you can adjust the row height to fit more text. Many scenarios arise that require some tweaking of table columns and rows, so let me show you how to manage them when they happen.

Resizing by Dragging

One of the most direct ways to change the column width or row height is to just move the border yourself. You can do this by dragging the row or column border. Move your mouse pointer over the border you want to adjust until the icon changes to a double-sided arrow pointer, as shown in Figure 12.2. Next, click and drag the line to the size you need. When you drag a row or column border, it affects the entire row or column. Depending on what line you're dragging and which direction, the column width grows or shrinks, or the row height gets taller or smaller.

Drag here to adjust the border

Popular Perennials for 2014			
Poppy	Salvia	Iris	Sedum
Astilbe	Hosta	Bee Balm	Coralbells
Daylily	Coreopsis	Daisy	Foxglove
Russian Sage	Phlox	Lavender	Dianthus

FIGURE 12.2

Manually dragging a column or row border is an easy way to adjust your table.

Using the Tab Tools

You can also adjust the cell size using the controls found on the **Layout** tab, one of the two **Table Tools** tabs displayed whenever you work with a table. Grouped under the heading of **Cell Size**, shown in Figure 12.3, you can see and set measurements for columns and rows. The first measurement (**Table Row Height**) shows row height, and you can adjust it using the spinner arrows or you can type in a precise measurement (based on inches). The second measurement (**Table Column Width**) shows column width, and again, you can click the spinner arrows or type in a value to change the setting. Simply click in a cell in the row or column you want to change, then specify another value on the **Layout** tab.

Adjust row height
Adjust column width

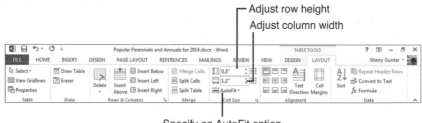

Specify an AutoFit option

FIGURE 12.3

You can also use the tools on the Layout tab to adjust your table.

Under the **Table Row Height** and **Table Column Width** controls on the **Layout** tab sits the **AutoFit** command, shown in Figure 12.3. AutoFit does exactly as its name suggests—it automatically adjusts the row or column to fit the content, resizes to fit the page, or lets you set a fixed width. Click the **AutoFit** drop-down arrow and make your selection. **AutoFit Contents** is the default setting unless you specify something else.

Using the Table Properties Dialog Box

Yet another way to set column width and row height is through the **Table Properties** dialog box, shown in Figure 12.4. You might use this route if you want to set a few additional options along with resizing your columns and rows, such as controlling how a row or column breaks across pages, or specify a minimum width or height, or change the measurement from inches to percentage.

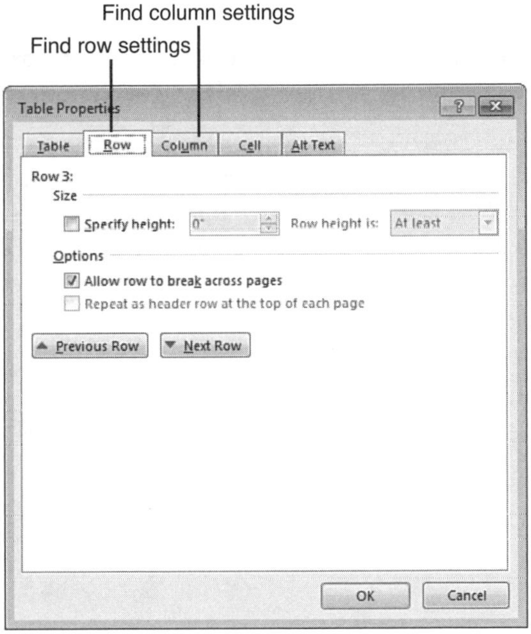

FIGURE 12.4

You can also use the Table Properties dialog box to adjust rows and columns.

To open the dialog box:

- Click the tiny **Table Properties** icon in the corner of the **Cell Size** group of tools on the **Layout** tab.

- Or right-click the table and choose **Table Properties** from the pop-up menu.

- Or click the **Properties** button on the **Layout** tab.

Next, click either the **Row** tab or the **Column** tab within the dialog box to view the associated settings.

Here's something interesting about the **Table Properties** dialog box: The **Row** and **Column** tabs both offer two buttons labeled **Previous** and **Next** that you can use to set different row height or column width values for each row or column in your table. Set a value for the current row or column, then click the **Previous** or **Next** button (depending on which direction in the table you're going) and set another value for the next row or column.

Adding and Deleting Columns and Rows

An essential part of working with tables is the ability to add and subtract columns and rows. For example, you might need to add some columns to include more data in a table, or you might want to remove rows you no longer need. As usual, you have several ways to add and delete columns and rows. I'm going to show you all the major methods; you can pick the one that you like the best.

Let's start with adding rows and columns. One technique that's quick and easy is to just move your mouse pointer over to the left of a row line, as shown in Figure 12.5, and click. Word inserts a new row immediately. If it's a new column you want, move the mouse pointer over the top of a column border line, as shown in Figure 12.6, until it becomes a plus icon, then click to instantly insert a column.

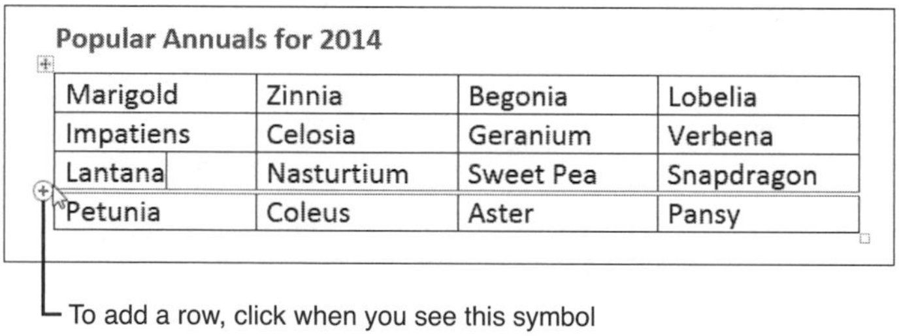

FIGURE 12.5

You can instantly insert a row by hovering to the left of the row border.

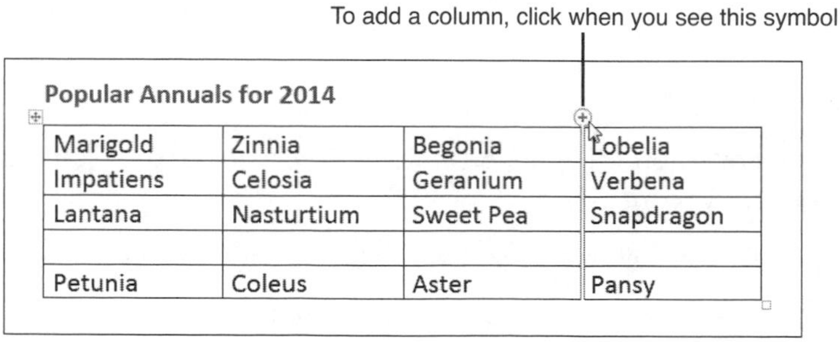

FIGURE 12.6

You can instantly insert a column just by hovering over the column border.

My favorite method is the right-click technique. Right-click a cell in the column or row to display the pop-up shortcut menu, click the **Insert** command, and then click an **Insert** option (see Figure 12.7). You can insert a column to the left or right of the current location in the table, or insert a row above or below the current location.

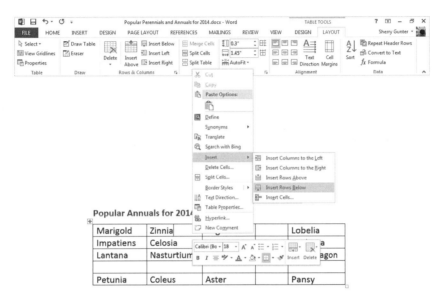

FIGURE 12.7

Right-click a row or column and choose an Insert option from the pop-up menu.

Just as easy as the right-click method is to click what you want to do using the tools on the **Layout** tab, shown in Figure 12.8. Grouped under the Rows & Column heading of tools on the tab are four **Insert** commands. Here's what each one accomplishes with a simple click:

- **Insert Above**   Adds a new row directly above the current row.

- **Insert Below**   Adds a new row directly below the current row.

- **Insert Left**   Adds a new column directly to the left of the current column.

- **Insert Right**   Adds a new column directly to the right of the current column.

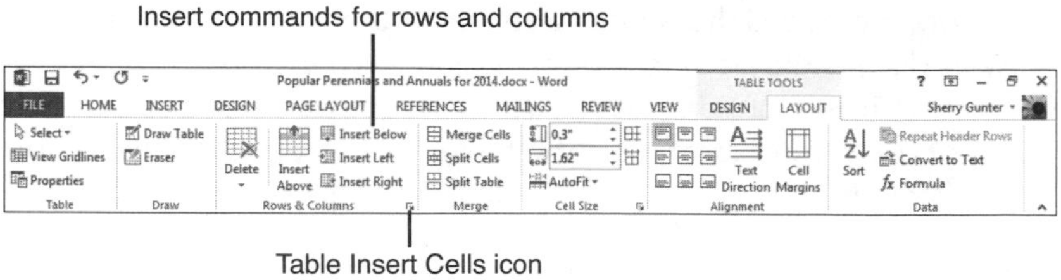

Insert commands for rows and columns

Table Insert Cells icon

FIGURE 12.8

You can also use the tools on the Layout tab to add and remove columns and rows.

If it's removal you want, you can click the **Delete** button on the **Layout** tab, shown in Figure 12.9, and remove columns and rows using the **Delete Columns** or **Delete Rows** commands. To remove multiple columns or rows, first select them, then activate the appropriate command.

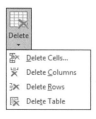

FIGURE 12.9

Use the Delete command to remove columns and rows.

Do you want to add multiple rows and columns? That's easy—first select the number of columns or rows adjacent to the spot where new columns and rows are to be inserted. Now when you activate the **Insert** command, Word inserts the same number of new rows and columns. (Repeat, if necessary; for example, if you want to insert four columns but can't select that many because you have only three columns, select two of the columns and then choose **Insert** twice.)

You can also remove multiple rows or columns by selecting them before applying a deletion technique.

You can also use Word's mini toolbar to add rows and columns. The toolbar often appears when you're performing various tasks, and if you're performing tasks in a table, the **Insert** and **Delete** buttons are added so you can quickly add or remove a row or column you're currently working with in the table. To use the toolbar, click the **Insert** or **Delete** button and choose an option.

Another method for adding and deleting cells involves a dialog box. You can use the **Insert Cells** or **Delete Cells** dialog boxes to change your table. Both dialog boxes look the same, but one is obviously for adding to the table, and the other is for deleting. To open the **Insert Cells** dialog box, shown in Figure 12.10, click the **Table Insert Cells** icon (the tiny icon in the bottom-right corner of the **Rows & Columns** group of commands on the **Layout** tab, pointed out in Figure 12.8). You can also access the dialog box by right-clicking and choosing **Insert**, **Insert Cells**. From the dialog box, click the **Insert entire row** or **Insert entire column** option and click **OK** to activate the change.

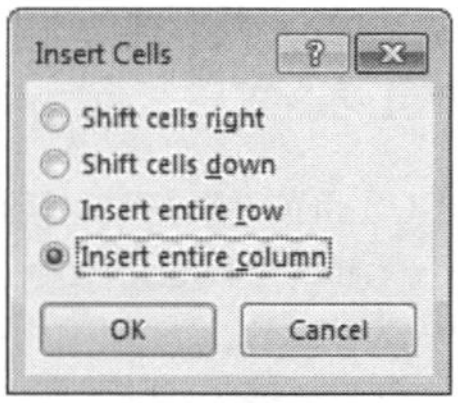

FIGURE 12.10

The Insert Cells dialog box.

To open the **Delete Cells** dialog box, shown in Figure 12.11, click the **Delete** button and chose **Delete Cells**. You can also right-click the row or column and choose **Delete Cells** from the pop-up menu. From the dialog box, click **Delete entire row** or **Delete entire column** and click **OK**.

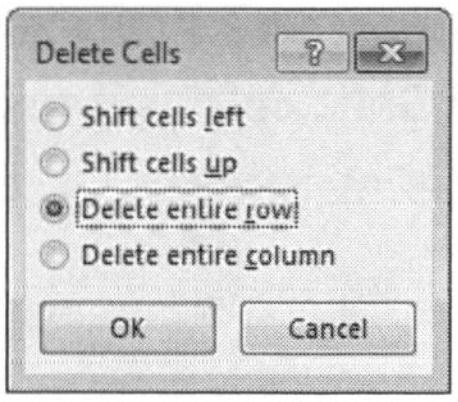

FIGURE 12.11

The Delete Cells dialog box.

You can learn more about deleting individual cells in the next section.

 TIP   Did you make a mistake and delete the wrong column or row? No problem; just click the **Undo** button on the **Quick Access** toolbar (upper-left corner of the program window, above the Ribbon's tabs).

NOTE   Did you draw a custom table using the **Draw Table** command? You can draw more lines in the table using the same drawing mode to create more columns, rows, and split cells. Just click the **Draw Table** button on the **Layout** tab and start drawing in new lines. You can use the **Eraser** tool to erase lines and remove columns and rows. Learn more about drawing your own tables in Chapter 11, "Adding Tables to Word Documents."

Adding and Deleting Cells

Adding and removing columns and rows might seem like a no-brainer, but adding and removing individual cells might require a little more thinking. When you insert a new row, you're inserting new cells spanning the entire table. However, some table structures you work with might only require an additional cell, not a bunch of cells. You can choose to add and delete individual cells in a table.

The **Delete Cells** dialog box, which you were introduced to in the previous section, lets you remove a cell and specify how you want the other cells to adjust. For example, if you remove a cell in a column, you might want the cells below the deleted cell to shift up, filling the hole created by the removal process.

To access the **Delete Cells** dialog box, right-click over the cell you want to remove and choose **Delete Cells**. You can also click the **Delete** button on the **Layout** tab and choose **Delete Cells**. Either method opens the dialog box shown in Figure 12.12. Click either **Shift cells left** or **Shift cells up**, and then click **OK** to apply the changes to your table.

FIGURE 12.12

The Delete Cells dialog box is useful for removing individual cells in a table.

The **Insert Cells** dialog box, shown in Figure 12.13, works in a similar fashion, except your table cells are making room for the new cell you add. Start by clicking where you want to insert a new cell, then right-click and choose **Insert**, **Insert Cells**, or just click the **Table Insert Cells** icon (see Figure 12.8 to identify this icon). Next, click either **Shift cells right** or **Shift cells down**; click **OK** to apply the changes.

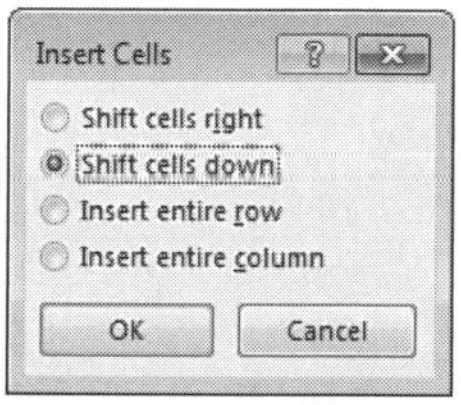

FIGURE 12.13

The Insert Cells dialog box is useful for adding individual cells in a table.

NOTE Naturally, you might assume the **Delete** key on your keyboard deletes table elements, such as cells, but that's not the case. Pressing **Delete** only deletes the cell contents. Pressing **Insert** also doesn't insert table elements.

TIP Do you need to delete the whole table? Click the **Layout** tab and click the **Delete** button, then click **Delete Table**.

Merging and Splitting Table Cells

Two of the coolest table commands, in my humble opinion, are **Merging Cells** and **Splitting Cells**. You can use the **Merge Cells** command to turn two or more separate table cells into one big cell. For example, you might combine two side-by-side cells to create a large cell for a title across the top of your table, or combine two cells vertically to insert a large logo or picture. Figures 12.14 and 12.15 show a before and after merge effect.

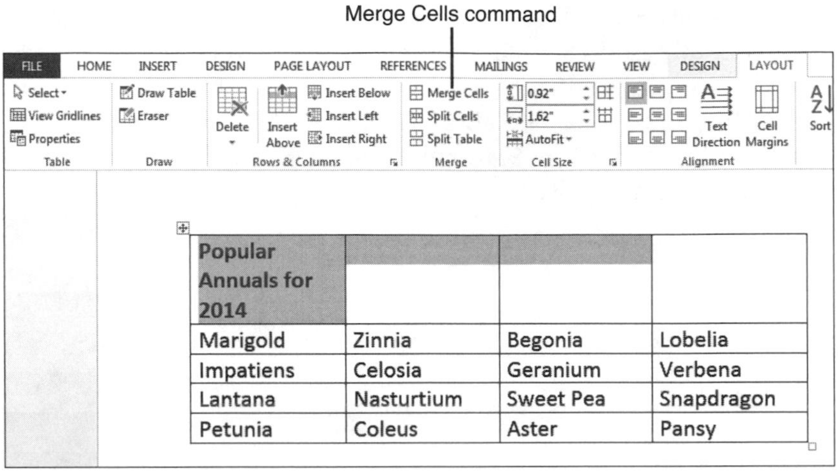

Merge Cells command

FIGURE 12.14

Before a merge.

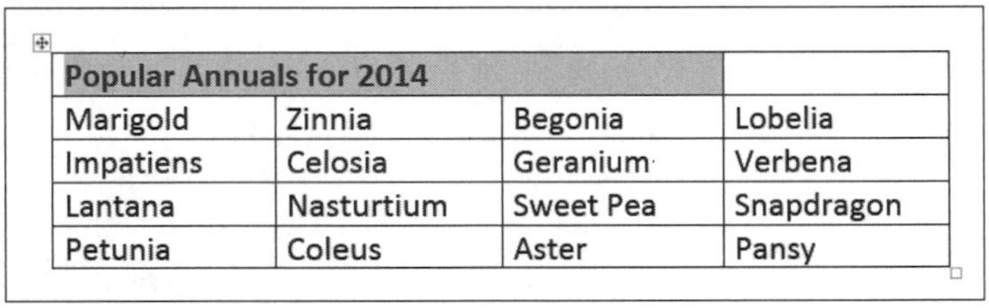

FIGURE 12.15

After a merge.

To merge cells, follow these steps:

1. Select the cells you want to merge.

2. Click the **Layout** tab.

3. Click **Merge Cells** (see Figure 12.14).

Word immediately merges the cells, including any content each might have held.

Splitting cells is the reverse of merging them. When you split a cell, you are creating two new separate cells out of one cell. Figures 12.16 and 12.17 show the before and after results of splitting cells.

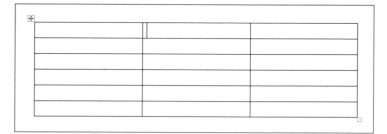

FIGURE 12.16

Before a split.

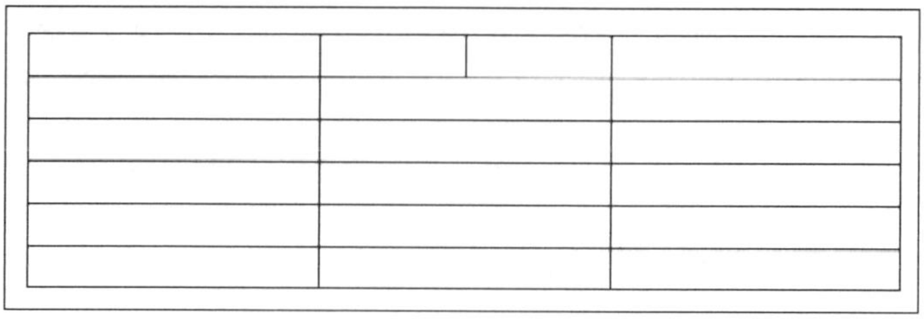

FIGURE 12.17

After a split.

To split cells, follow these steps:

1. Select the cells you want to split.

2. Click the **Layout** tab.

3. Click **Split Cells** and the **Split Cells** dialog box opens, as shown in Figure 12.18.

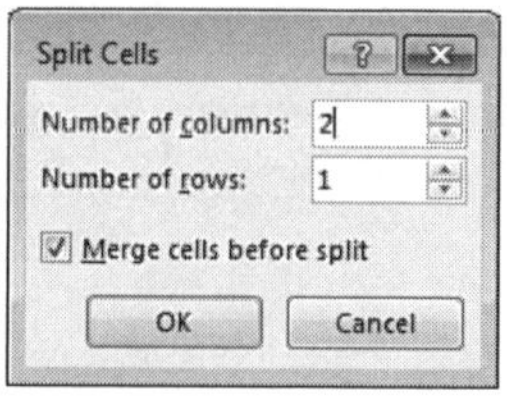

FIGURE 12.18

Specify how you want to split a cell using the Split Cells dialog box.

4. Specify the number of columns or rows you want to create; type in a number or click the spinner arrows to set a number.

5. Click **OK**.

Word immediately splits the cells.

 TIP You can also split a table into two separate tables using the **Split Table** command on the **Layout** tab. When activated, this command splits the table at the current cursor location.

Changing Cell Alignment and Margins

Don't forget you can use any of Word's formatting tools to make your table data look nice, such as changing the font, size, color, and so forth. You can also change the way in which text is positioned within a cell, or as we like to say in the table business—*alignment*. The **Layout** tab (one of the two specialty **Table Tools** tabs) offers all the alignment options as buttons listed under the **Alignment** group of tools (see Figure 12.19). Not only do these commands pertain to horizontal positioning of text (left, center, and right), but also the vertical positioning (top, center, bottom). To assign an alignment to a cell, click in the cell or select the group of cells and activate an alignment setting.

Alignment buttons

Popular Annuals for 2014			
Marigold	Zinnia	Begonia	Lobelia
Impatiens	Celosia	Geranium	Verbena
Lantana	Nasturtium	Sweet Pea	Snapdragon
Petunia	Coleus	Aster	Pansy

FIGURE 12.19

Control cell alignment using the alignment buttons on the Layout tab.

Here are the alignments you can apply:

- **Align Top Left** Aligns cell text to the top-left corner.

- **Align Top Center** Centers cell text and aligns it to the top of the cell.

- **Align Top Right** Aligns cell text to the top-right corner.

- **Align Center Left**   Centers text and aligns it to the left side of the cell.

- **Align Center**   Centers text vertically and horizontally in the cell.

- **Align Center Right**   Centers text and aligns it to the right side of the cell.

- **Align Bottom Left**   Aligns cell text to the bottom-left corner.

- **Align Bottom Center**   Centers cell text and aligns it at the bottom of the cell.

- **Align Bottom Right**   Aligns cell text to the bottom-right corner.

Word automatically assigns some default margins to your table cells, giving them a little bit of breathing space between the text and the sides of the cell. You can make adjustments to these inner margins using the **Table Options** dialog box, shown in Figure 12.20. Click the **Cell Margins** tool on the **Layout** tab to open the dialog box.

You can change the margin settings by clicking the spinner arrows or by typing in a value (measured in inches). Click **OK** to exit the dialog box and apply the changes to the current cell. Be sure to select the entire table if you want to apply the margins to all the cells.

Table Options		?	X
Default cell margins			
Top: 0"		Left: 0.08"	
Bottom: 0"		Right: 0.08"	
Default cell spacing			
☐ Allow spacing between cells	0"		
Options			
☑ Automatically resize to fit contents			
	OK	Cancel	

FIGURE 12.20

You can control cell margins using the Table Options dialog box.

NOTE   You can use the **Text Direction** button on the **Layout** tab to change the direction of text in a cell, thus creating text that reads vertically in the cell. Each click of the button rotates the cell's text.

Repositioning and Resizing Tables

When you insert a table into your document, some default settings are in play regarding its positioning on the page. Mainly, the table is automatically left-aligned on the page itself, and no text wrapping is applied. *Text wrapping* refers to how text flows around an object you add to a page, such as a picture, logo, drawn shape, or in this case, a table. You can fine-tune the positioning aspects of your table, as well as resize it on the page, as I am about to show you.

To find positioning controls for the entire table, open the **Table Properties** dialog box to its **Table** tab, shown in Figure 12.21. You can use the options on this tab to set a different alignment and turn on text wrapping, which is helpful for a smaller table that you want paragraphs to flow around. You can even use the **Table Properties** dialog box to indent the table's position from the left margin or set a preferred width for the table.

To open the **Table Properties** dialog box, click the **Layout** tab and click the **Properties** command.

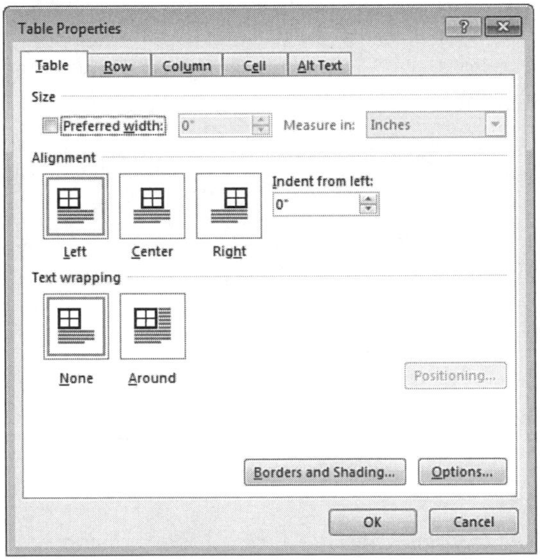

FIGURE 12.21

The Table Properties dialog box offers positioning settings for the table.

If the **Table** tab is not displayed, click it to view its contents. After you make changes to the settings, click **OK** to exit the dialog box and apply them to the current table.

You can move a table and drop it anywhere you want it to appear in your document. When you click inside a table, the table icon appears in the upper-left corner of the table, as shown in Figure 12.22. You can click and drag the icon to move the table.

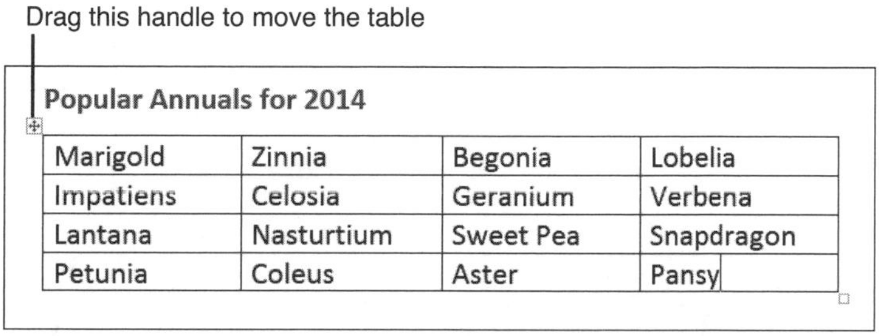

Drag this handle to move the table

Popular Annuals for 2014			
Marigold	Zinnia	Begonia	Lobelia
Impatiens	Celosia	Geranium	Verbena
Lantana	Nasturtium	Sweet Pea	Snapdragon
Petunia	Coleus	Aster	Pansy

FIGURE 12.22

Use the table's selection handle to drag the table to a new location.

You can also resize a table by dragging the bottom-right corner of the table, shown in Figure 12.23. Resizing a table automatically resizes all the rows and columns in the table to fit.

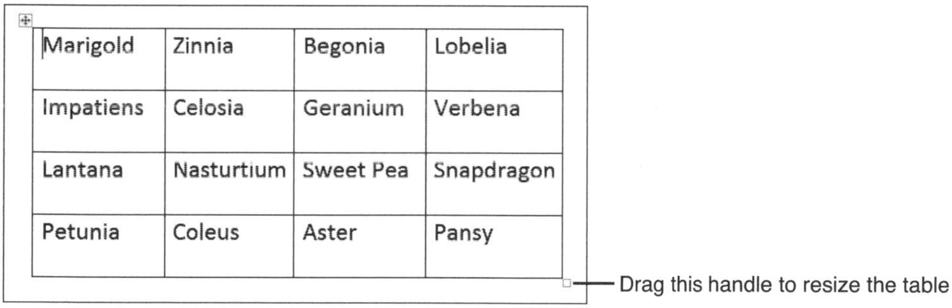

Marigold	Zinnia	Begonia	Lobelia
Impatiens	Celosia	Geranium	Verbena
Lantana	Nasturtium	Sweet Pea	Snapdragon
Petunia	Coleus	Aster	Pansy

Drag this handle to resize the table

FIGURE 12.23

Resize a table using its bottom-right handle.

Dressing Up a Table with Table Styles and Borders

If you need to speed up your table design work without all the effort of applying various formatting, consider assigning a style instead. Table styles let you dress up a table using one of Word's built-in table designs that include colors, borders, background cell shading, fonts, and more. You can find the **Table Styles** gallery on the **Design** tab (the other specialty tab under the **Table Tools** options). Take a look at a full view of the gallery, shown in Figure 12.24.

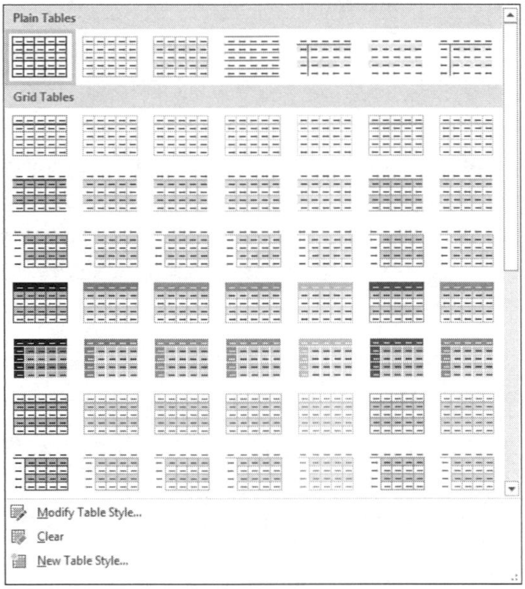

FIGURE 12.24

The Table Styles gallery offers a variety of preset table formatting.

A style gives your table an instant makeover. For example, Figure 12.25 shows a simple table, and Figure 12.26 shows the same table with a style applied. As you can see, a style adds immediate impact and gives the table visual depth and emphasis in the document. Styles are a great way to make your table stand out, plus you can tweak the style after you assign it to make the table look the way you want. As part of Word's Quick Parts, templates, and built-ins, table styles are easily modified.

2014

Quarterly Sales

	Quarter 1	Quarter 2	Quarter 3	Quarter 4
Ralph	8,905	9,975	10,425	8,700
Lulu	7,800	10,680	12,250	10,200
Eddie	9,100	9,900	10,700	9,300
Bob	5,750	8,890	11,050	11,500

FIGURE 12.25

Before a table style.

2014

Quarterly Sales

	Quarter 1	Quarter 2	Quarter 3	Quarter 4
Ralph	8,905	9,975	10,425	8,700
Lulu	7,800	10,680	12,250	10,200
Eddie	9,100	9,900	10,700	9,300
Bob	5,750	8,890	11,050	11,500

FIGURE 12.26

After a table style.

To assign a preset style, follow these steps:

1. Click anywhere in the table you want to format.

2. Click the **Design** tab (see Figure 12.27).

3. Click a style.

Word immediately applies the chosen style. You can preview all the styles from the **Table Styles** gallery simply by moving your mouse pointer over each style. Word previews the effect on the current table.

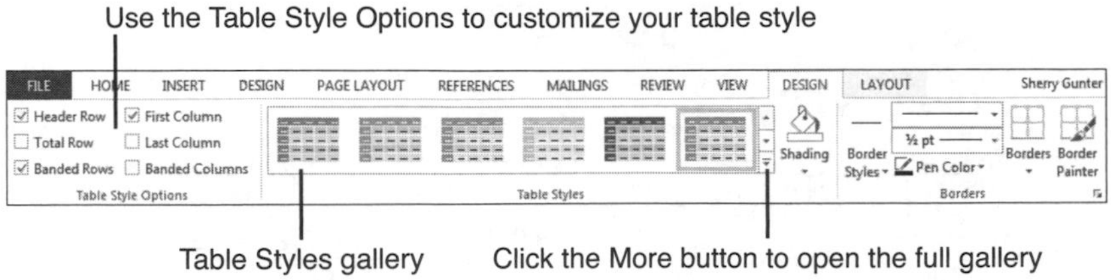

Use the Table Style Options to customize your table style

Table Styles gallery   Click the More button to open the full gallery

FIGURE 12.27

Use the Design tab to make changes to your table's design and style.

 NOTE You can modify an existing table style and save it as a new style in the gallery. Start by applying all the necessary formatting to the table, then click the **New Table Style** button at the bottom of the full **Table Styles** gallery. This opens the **Create New Style from Formatting** dialog box where you can type in a name for the style, and change any other settings as needed. Click **OK** when you finish, and Word adds the style to the gallery. Now it's ready to go the next time you need it.

To the left of the **Table Styles** gallery sit the **Table Style Options**. You can turn these on or off to customize your table style. For example, if you choose a style with banded rows, you can turn off the shading for the bands to change the appearance of the style. You can experiment with the options to see what looks best on your particular table.

To the right of the Table Styles gallery is a **Shading** drop-down menu, shown in Figure 12.28. Click the button to display a palette of background shading you can add to your table cells. You can apply shading to a selected cell or the entire table.

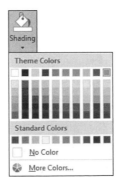

FIGURE 12.28

Add background shading to your table with the Shading drop-down palette.

The far-right side of the **Design** tab offers a variety of tools to create borders in your tables (see Figure 12.29). You can change the border style, line thickness, and color, and create custom borders for certain sides of a cell. For example, to change the border style, click the **Border Styles** drop-down arrow and choose from the **Theme Borders** gallery. You can experiment with the various formatting features here to create just the right framework for your table or table cells.

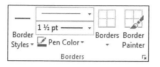

FIGURE 12.29

Use these tools to experiment with different borders for your table.

   NOTE   There's plenty more you can do with your tables than just decorate them. You can use the Data group of tools on the far-right side of the **Layout** tab to sort table data, repeat header rows across multiple page-spanning tables, add formulas to perform mathematical equations (such as summing a column of numbers), or convert a table back into regular document text. But don't get too carried away. There's a point at which a table can become so complicated that you would save time by creating the table in Microsoft Excel and embedding it into your Word document.

THE ABSOLUTE MINIMUM

To help you make your tables look their best, Word offers two specialized tabs of tools and multiple techniques you can apply to design, fine-tune, and polish tables. In this chapter, you learned the following table editing skills:

- To edit and format parts of the table, you need to learn a few selection techniques.

- Find commands and tools for adjusting table structure and positioning on the **Layout** tab.

- Find commands and tools for styling and designing tables on the **Design** tab.

- Resizing columns and rows can add or subtract space within your table to help the cell contents look better.

- You can grow or shrink your table by inserting or deleting columns and rows. Use the **Insert** commands on the **Layout** tab to add to the table structure, or the **Delete** command to remove columns or rows.

- You can also add or subtract individual cells within your table, split single cells into two, or merge two or more cells into one.

- To adjust the alignment of content within cells, use the alignment buttons on the **Layout** tab.

- To adjust the margins within a cell, use the **Cell Margins** tool to open the **Table Options** dialog box and change inner cell margins.

- All it takes to move or resize a table is some simple clicking and dragging.

- Speed up table design by assigning a preset style on the **Design** tab.

- You can fine-tune a table's design by tweaking background shading and borders.

IN THIS CHAPTER

- Learn how to build your own diagrams using Word's SmartArt feature.
- See how easy it is to format a diagram with styles, colors, shapes, and more.
- Plot out a graph using Word's charting tools.
- Find out how to use a datasheet to enter chart data.
- Make your charts look pretty with formatting techniques.

13

ADDING CHARTS, GRAPHS, AND DIAGRAMS

Charts, graphs, and diagrams are a great way to add visual impact to data and explain an important concept or procedure. Most of us are quite visual by nature, and seeing any kind of message presented in a visual way makes it much more engaging. You can use charts, graphs, and diagrams with great success in your Word files, and this chapter demonstrates how you can get started.

Exactly what's the difference between a chart, a graph, and a diagram? Well, if you want to get technical about it, *chart* is really more of an umbrella term for all kinds of information graphics, such as maps, pie and bar graphs, and tables. *Graphs* traditionally show mathematical relationships, such as income and expenses, or population growth over time. *Diagrams* present data more pictorially and abstractly using shapes and connecting lines. Typically, diagrams are geared more toward showing relationships or processes. Unless you're a purist in the world of informational graphics, however, the distinctions between charts, graphs, and diagrams are really quite murky. They're all related in some fashion, and the bottom line is they illustrate data in a visual way. You're free to call them charts, graphs, or diagrams, but the best part is you can build them all in Microsoft Word.

Working with SmartArt

One of the quickest ways to insert an illustration into your document is to use Word's SmartArt graphics to represent information. Basically, *SmartArt* is pre-drawn artwork you can use to build graphics to illustrate or explain relationships, such as a visual layout of your corporate structure or the workflow for a manufactured product. You can use SmartArt to illustrate lists, processes, procedures, hierarchies, organization charts, and more. Figure 13.1 shows an example of a SmartArt illustration. As you can see, it illustrates a process. Most SmartArt graphics consist of shapes, text boxes, and connecting arrows or lines, but not all.

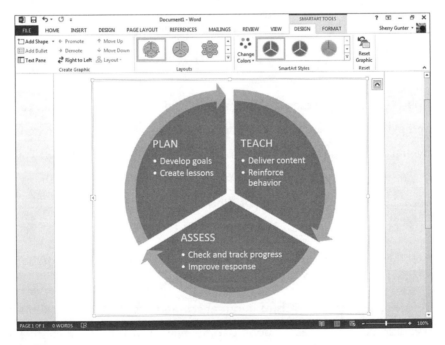

FIGURE 13.1

Graphics are easy to insert into a document using the SmartArt tools.

When planning out your own illustrations, think about what type of data you want to include and what sort of layout best communicates your information. If you find your first choice in a SmartArt layout isn't working out, you can easily swap it out for another layout that does a better job. This is just one way the SmartArt tools are so flexible. You can also fine-tune a layout by changing the shapes and colors used in the illustration, changing fonts and sizes of any text, and even assigning a different style. As you work with SmartArt, Word displays two specialized **SmartArt Tools** tabs on the Ribbon to help you format and design the graphic. These tabs are chock-full of tools for controlling the appearance and structure of the illustration.

You can access the library of layouts through the **Choose a SmartArt Graphic** dialog box, shown in Figure 13.2. You can choose graphical layouts from several categories, and preview a layout and its intended purpose before inserting it into your document. The SmartArt library features a wide variety of illustration types and variations of each type. You can choose from the following SmartArt categories:

- **List** Turn list data, such as a bulleted list, into shapes for added emphasis. List layouts do not include connecting arrows or demonstrate a sequence.

- **Process** Use to illustrate a directional flow, such as steps or stages.

- **Cycle** This type of graphic illustrates a circular or repetitive process.

- **Hierarchy** Use to illustrate a hierarchy, such as a family tree, company organization, or product family.

- **Relationship** Illustrate interlocking or overlapping concepts and relationships with this type of graphic. The famous Venn diagram is a Relationship style chart.

- **Matrix** Use this type of graphic to visually show the relationship of parts to a whole.

- **Pyramid** Just as its name suggests, this illustration style shows proportional or hierarchical relationships that build from top to bottom or bottom to top.

- **Picture** Good for showing non-sequential information or groups of blocks in a list diagram.

- **All** Choose this category if you want to see all the diagram layouts.

- **Office.com** Go online with this choice and find new diagram layouts from Microsoft's Office website.

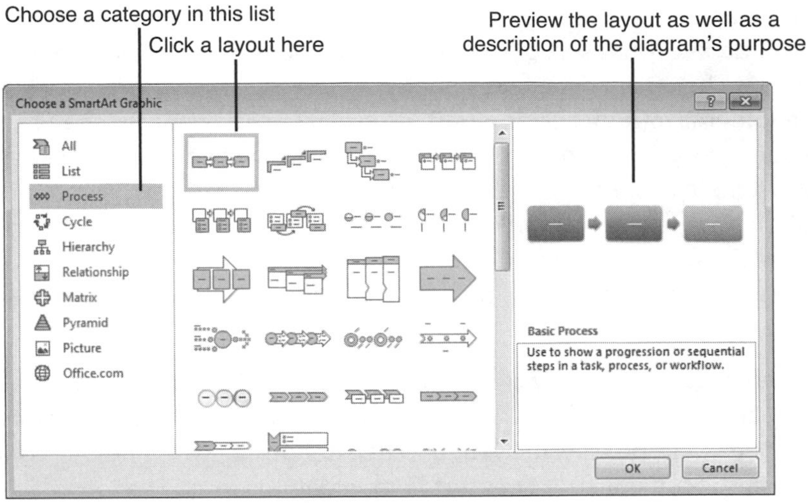

Choose a category in this list
Click a layout here
Preview the layout as well as a description of the diagram's purpose

FIGURE 13.2

Choose the category of illustration you want to make, then choose a style.

 NOTE The SmartArt feature is also available in the other Microsoft Office programs, including Excel, PowerPoint, and Outlook.

 TIP You're not limited to building your own illustrations. You can also utilize the **Copy** and **Paste** commands to copy and paste illustrations from other places and insert them onto a document page. You won't be able to edit them like SmartArt, per se, but with a finished graphic you might not want to.

Inserting SmartArt

Inserting a graphic is the easy part. Before you get started, though, make sure you have a pretty good idea of how you want your illustration to look. This helps you narrow down your choice of graphic type and layout. When you're ready to insert a SmartArt graphic, follow these steps:

1. Click the **Insert** tab.

2. Click **SmartArt** to open the Choose a SmartArt Graphic dialog box, shown in Figure 13.2.

3. Click a category.

4. Click a graphic style.

5. Click **OK**.

Word adds a SmartArt graphic to your document with placeholder text, as shown in Figure 13.3.

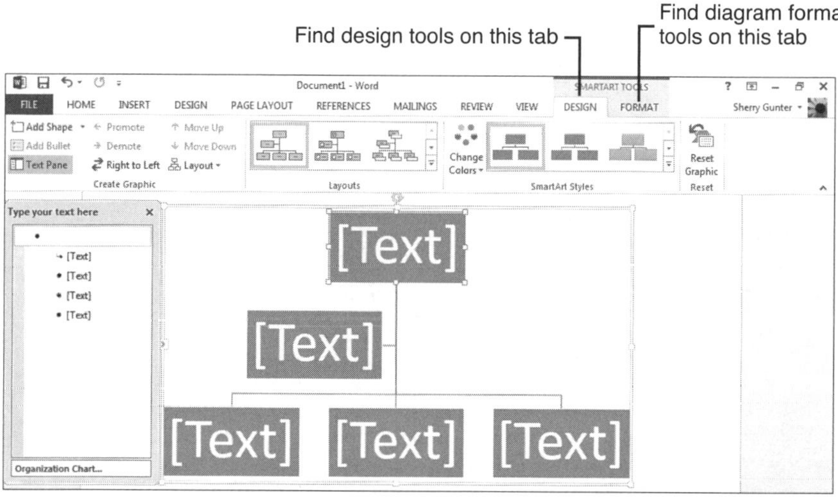

FIGURE 13.3

Here's an example of a snazzy SmartArt illustration.

As you can see in Figure 13.3, two new tabs appear on the Ribbon when a SmartArt object is active: **Design** and **Format**. You can use the tools on these tabs to work with and edit the graphic, as explained in the next section.

Customizing SmartArt Graphics

After you insert a SmartArt graphic, you can immediately start filling it with your own information or modifying it to work with your document. As you've seen in other template-type features in Word, your SmartArt graphic layout includes placeholders. A *placeholder* is a stand-in for where your own content is added. SmartArt placeholders are pretty obvious; they say **[Text]** everywhere your text is supposed to go.

When you insert a new graphic, a **Text** pane appears next to it by default to help you build your illustration (see Figure 13.4), with directions at the top of the pane telling you where to type your text. To start working with text in this pane, just click the text element you want to edit and start typing. When you're ready to move on to another text element, click the next one and type in more text. Don't press **Enter** unless you want to add another shape to the illustration. You can also click a shape to type text directly onto the shape (see Figure 13.5). Choose whichever method works best for you.

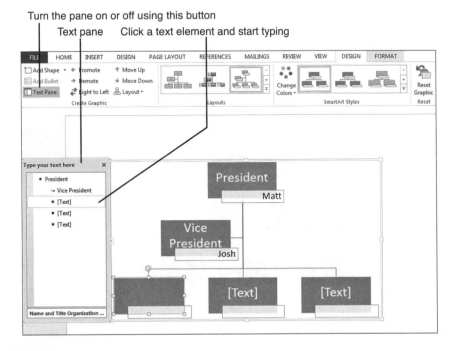

FIGURE 13.4

You can enter text using the Text pane.

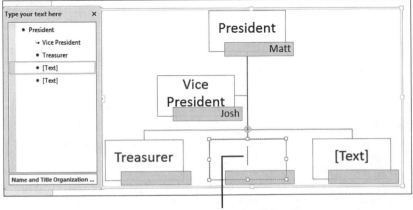

FIGURE 13.5

Another option is to enter text directly into a shape in the illustration.

As you're building your illustration, the **Design** tab on the Ribbon offers all the tools you need to adjust the layout, add more shapes, and assign a different style. For example, click the **Text Pane** button to turn the pane on or off, or click the **Add Shape** button to add another element to the illustration. Let's go over a few of the ways you can build your illustration and adjust the layout.

To modify your layout, check out the tools listed under the **Create Graphic** group on the **Design** tab, shown in Figure 13.6. Depending on the type of layout you're working with, you can move text elements around to change their position in the illustration. For example, you might want to promote a shape or move it up in the hierarchy. You can apply any of these commands to a selected shape in the diagram or the current text item selected in the Text pane. Here are a few rearrangement options you can apply:

- Click the **Promote** button to move a text element up in superiority.

- Click the **Demote** button to make a text element subordinate to the text above or adjacent to it.

- Click the **Right to Left** button to reorder the diagram in the opposite direction.

- Click the **Move Up** button to move a text element up in the order.

- Click the **Move Down** button to move a text element down in the order.

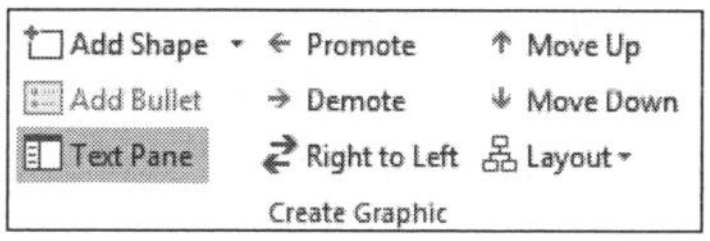

FIGURE 13.6

You can use the Create Graphic group of tools to rearrange illustration text order.

To add a shape to your illustration, click the **Add Shape** drop-down arrow on the **Design** tab, shown in Figure 13.7, and choose one of the following:

- Click the **Add Shape After** command to add a new shape directly after the current (selected) shape.

- Click the **Add Shape Before** command to add a new shape directly before the current shape.

- Click the **Add Shape Above** command to add a new shape directly above the current shape.

- Click the **Add Shape Below** command to add a new shape directly below the current shape.

- Click the **Add Assistant** command to add an assistant shape to an organizational chart.

A grayed-out **Add Shape** command means that it doesn't apply to the particular layout you chose. Not all the diagrams are built the same way; some allow for shapes before and after elements, others allow for shapes above and below existing elements.

FIGURE 13.7

Use the Add Shape button to add shapes to your diagram.

 TIP After you select a particular **Add Shape** command, it's in effect until you choose another, so to continue adding the same shape throughout, just click the **Add Shape** button rather than the drop-down arrow.

If your shape needs some subordinate bullet items, just click the **Add Bullet** command. As you can see in both the **Text** pane and illustration shown in Figure 13.8, the new bullet appears below the main text.

One more command under the **Create Graphic** group you might want to know about is the **Layout** drop-down menu, shown in Figure 13.9. The layouts offered in this menu are only available to an organizational chart created under the Hierarchy category. You can change the direction of a shape in the organization layout by choosing an option from the **Layout** menu.

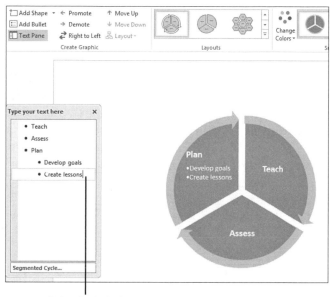

Subordinate text

FIGURE 13.8

Use the Add Bullet button to create subordinate text.

FIGURE 13.9

If you're building an organization layout, you can use the Layout menu to change the illustration's direction.

Inexplicably, no removal button is available to delete a shape from the diagram. However, you can press the **Delete** key to remove a selected shape, or you can employ the **Cut** command. The remainder of the diagram's shapes shift to make up for the deletion.

 NOTE If you choose a layout with pictures, you can insert digital pictures, such as photos of the various people in your corporate hierarchy, into the diagram. Like the placeholder text elements, placeholder picture elements are marked with an icon that looks like a tiny photograph. Click it to open the **Insert Pictures** dialog box and navigate to the file you want to insert. To learn more about using pictures in Word, see Chapter 14, "Adding Simple Graphic Elements."

Changing Layouts, Colors, and Styles

As you're working with your illustration, you might find that the layout you originally chose is not working out. Rather than delete everything and redo the steps for adding graphics, you can use the **Layouts** gallery on the **Design** tab (see Figure 13.10) to switch to another layout. Click another layout to immediately apply it to the current illustration. If you would rather view all the choices at a glance, click the **More** button in the corner of the **Layouts** gallery to open a full view of the available layouts. The layouts shown in the gallery pertain to the particular illustration category you selected at the beginning of the process.

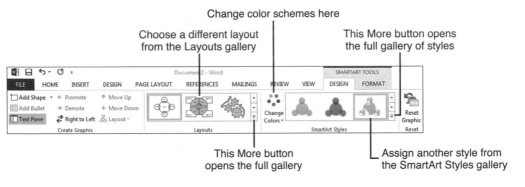

Change color schemes here

Choose a different layout
from the Layouts gallery

This More button opens
the full gallery of styles

This More button
opens the full gallery

Assign another style from
the SmartArt Styles gallery

FIGURE 13.10

Change the layout, style, or color scheme using the other Design tab features.

SmartArt graphics also include a wide variety of styles you can apply to adjust the appearance of the shapes. Styles include 3-D effects that add shadows and depth to shapes, and lots of blending, lines, and other subtle design flourishes. To see what's available for your illustration's layout, choose a style from the **SmartArt Styles** gallery. To view all the styles at a glance, click the gallery's **More** button.

To change the illustration's coloring, click the **Change Colors** button and choose another scheme from the palette, as shown in Figure 13.11.

TIP You can undo any of your edits using the **Undo** button on the Quick Access toolbar.

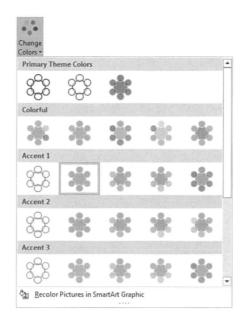

FIGURE 13.11

Use the Change Colors palette to assign another color scheme.

Formatting SmartArt

Flip over to the Ribbon's **Format** tab to view all kinds of tools to format your SmartArt graphic. You can find tools for changing the shapes, assigning styles to shapes, and changing text styles. As shown in Figure 13.12, you can use these tools to further refine your illustration. For example, you might want to increase the size of the shapes within it, or change their fill color. You can apply such changes to a select part of the illustration, or to all of it at once.

FIGURE 13.12

The Format tab offers tools for changing the various attributes of the graphic's shapes and text.

The tools on the **Format** tab are grouped into commands for working with shapes and commands for working with text. In the Shapes group, for example, you can click the **Change Shape** button and choose another shape to use from Word's

Shapes gallery. The gallery offers basic shapes, arrows, stars, and more.

Here are a few more formatting techniques you can apply to a selected shape:

- Click the **Larger** button to increase the shape size.
- Click the **Smaller** button to decrease the shape size.
- Click the **Size** drop-down button if you want to set an exact height and width measurement for the shape.
- Click the **Shape Fill** button to choose a fill color for the shape.
- Click the **Shape Outline** button to set an outline color or line thickness.
- Click the **Shape Effects** button to assign a special effect, such as a shadow, glow, or 3-D look.
- Use the **Shape Styles** gallery to assign a different style to the shape.

Meanwhile, over in the WordArt Styles group of tools, you can format the text within the illustration's shape. You can apply a WordArt effect to text, giving it an artistic appearance, then use the text tools to adjust the style, fill color, outline, or choose a special effect (shadows, glows, and so on). Here's what you can do:

- Use the **WordArt Styles** gallery to assign a specific WordArt effect.
- Click the **Text Fill** button to choose a fill color for the text.
- Click the **Text Outline** button to set an outline color or line thickness.
- Click the **Text Effects** button to choose a special effect, such as a shadow, glow, or 3-D look.

As if those aren't enough formatting options, you can also make adjustments to the arrangement of elements in your illustration, specifically the shape and the text. Click the **Arrange** button to view a variety of tools for positioning, controlling text wrapping, rotating and aligning elements, and grouping and arranging shapes and text on top of each other. These same controls are used in working with other graphics you add to a document, such as shapes you draw or artwork you import. You can learn more about utilizing these commands to change the appearance of graphic objects in Chapter 16, "Fine-Tuning Your Graphics."

 NOTE   To remove a SmartArt graphic you no longer want, select it and press the **Delete** key.

TIP   If you click the border that surrounds the selected SmartArt graphic, a **Layout Options** icon appears at the top-right corner. You can click the icon to view a menu of layout options that control text wrapping around the graphic.

Inserting Charts

Microsoft Word's charting feature taps into the power of spreadsheets and helps you create visuals to illustrate quantitative and qualitative data. For example, your boss might say, "Put a graph showing the department's sales figures for last month in your report" or your spouse says, "Let's see a pie chart of our expenses." Don't panic. You can access charting tools directly in Word without ever having to open Excel or another spreadsheet program. You can whip up an excellent chart in no time at all. Figure 13.13 shows an example of a pie chart.

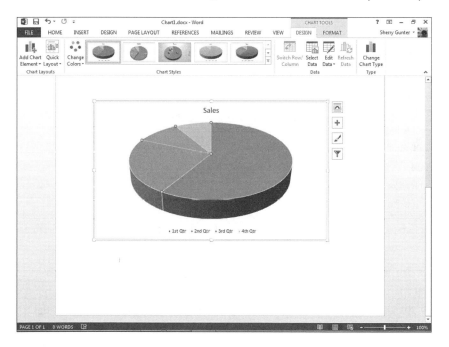

FIGURE 13.13

My freshly made pie chart looks quite delicious.

If you're new to charts in general, reviewing what types are available and making sure you have a broad understanding of the lingo used in making charts might help. After you have that under your belt, you can start inserting charts and learning how to tweak them with a little formatting.

Understanding the Chart Types

First things first—you need to figure out what sort of chart you want to create. You can choose from 10 different chart categories, and each one has a specific purpose. Within each category you can find a variety of styles to depict the data. For example, if you go with a bar chart, the bars measure something of quantity, such as dollar amounts, and you can choose stacked or clustered bars, or bars rendered in 3-D style. So many choices! Before you get tangled in styles, decide on a chart type. To help you out, take a look at this list describing the categories:

- **Column** Shows changes in data over a period of time or compares data.

- **Line** Shows trends in intervals, such as time.

- **Pie** Shows how individual values are proportional to the sum of the whole.

- **Bar** Compares data using rectangular horizontal bars.

- **Area** Shows trends or amounts of change over time or across categories.

- **X Y (Scatter)** Illustrates relationships between numerical values or trends across uneven time periods.

- **Stock** Illustrates fluctuating stock prices.

- **Surface** Looking like topographical maps, this chart type illustrates combinations between data values.

- **Radar** Shows changes in values relative to a center point. This chart type looks like a spider web.

- **Combo** Uses a combination of chart types to illustrate up to three data series.

You don't have to memorize any of these types. Choose Insert, Chart to open the **Insert Chart** dialog box, which does a pretty good job of explaining each one and gives you a chance to preview any chart type before attempting to build it. Figure 13.14 shows the dialog box and what you can expect.

 NOTE Two more categories are listed in the **Insert Chart** dialog box: Recent and Templates. The Recent category keeps track of recently used charts so you can quickly insert them again without wading through the chart types. The Templates category lists any charts you've saved as templates to reuse in more chart creation.

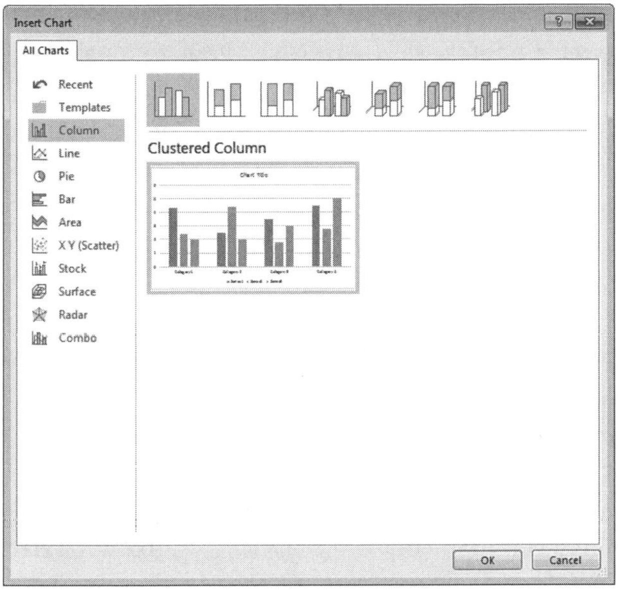

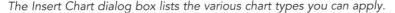

FIGURE 13.14

The Insert Chart dialog box lists the various chart types you can apply.

Understanding Chart Parts

Just by naming chart types, we're already getting into the charting vernacular. Not all charts look the same, but the general elements are fairly common. Charts are typically composed of several key parts, and naturally those parts have distinct names:

- **Data points**   The individual values you plot in a chart. For example, if you're creating a chart that tracks monthly sales, the total for each salesperson is a *data point* on the chart.

- **Data series**   A group of related values in a chart. Back to the monthly sales total example used previously, if you're charting three months' worth of sales for each salesperson, you're using a *data series*—three totals for the same person makes it a series, you see.

- **Data categories**   When you organize data for a chart, such as the three months you're tracking for sales, the name of each month becomes a *data category* in your chart.

- **Axes**   The display of horizontal and vertical scale upon which the data is plotted. The X axis, also called the *category axis*, is the horizontal scale, and the Y axis, also called the *value axis*, is the vertical scale. In our monthly sales example, the X axis would list the individual salespeople by name and the Y axis lists the monetary values by which you are measuring their success, such as increments of $1,000 or $10,000.

- **Axis labels**   These identify what data is being plotted out on the chart, such as time intervals, categories, or monetary scale.
- **Plot area**   Shows the measurement for the given values in the chart, such as how much money each salesperson generated displayed in bars or lines, and so on.
- **Legend**   A summary or key indicating what the chart is mapping out. Depending on the type of chart, the legend identifies the data series or differentiates between the series.
- **Chart area**   Refers to the entire chart and all of its parts, including any borders you assign.
- **Gridlines**   Also called *tick marks*, these are the lines that appear in the plot area to help you read your chart and line up the chart data with the scale it's illustrating.
- **Data table**   The chunk of worksheet cells you use to enter the chart data. You can include the cells in the final chart, if you want, if you need to show how you built the chart.
- **Chart text**   You can add chart titles, subtitles, and other information text to a chart. You can also format the text to correspond with the rest of the document.

Figure 13.15 shows some of these chart terms pointed out on an actual chart.

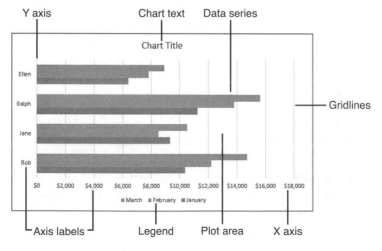

FIGURE 13.15

See if you can identify several of the chart parts; then try it blindfolded for added fun.

Inserting a Chart

If phase 1 is deciding on the type of chart you want, then phase 2 is inserting a chart into your document. Decide where you want it to appear with a click on the page, and then follow these steps:

1. Click the **Insert** tab.

2. Click **Chart** to open the Insert Chart dialog box (refer to Figure 13.14).

3. Click a chart type.

4. Click the chart you want to create.

5. Click **OK** and Word creates the chart, similar to Figure 13.16.

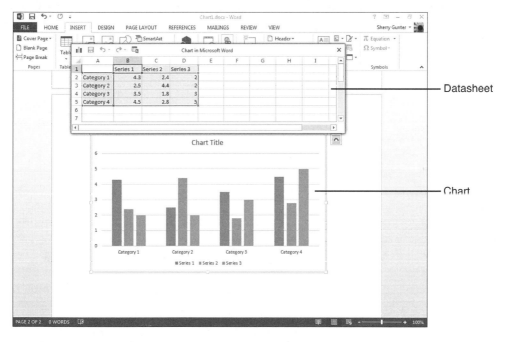

FIGURE 13.16

Look at the sweet newborn chart. Isn't it adorable, and empty?

Suddenly, the Word program window is overtaken by a worksheet grid, a large chart area filled with placeholder chart elements, and two new tabs on the Ribbon. Yikes! Now what? Time to start adding your own chart data.

Entering Chart Data

Phase 3 is inputting chart data. If you've worked with Microsoft Excel before, then you're already familiar with the worksheet columns, rows, and cells upon which charting data is recorded. If not, you're in for a treat. Everything is neatly organized in a worksheet, so jumping in and assembling your chart material is pretty easy. The grid of columns and rows is the datasheet, the spot where you record all the data you want to turn into a chart. The datasheet window even presents some helpful placeholder data to help you get started, and names it appropriately to give you a clue as to what might go where.

To begin, click in a cell and type your own data. As soon as you type something, Word updates the chart with the new data. Let's reuse that monthly sales totals example we've been talking about so far. For this example, we'll use a Column chart. To plot three salespeople's totals across three months, you can type the month names in as your column headings, as shown in Figure 13.17.

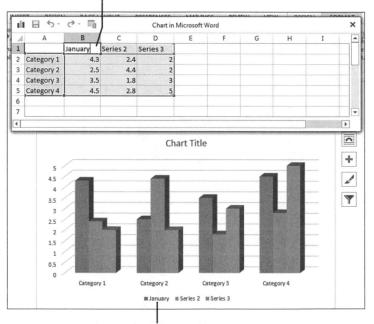

I'm typing my sales months starting here

The chart immediately reflects my edits

FIGURE 13.17

This example shows months as column headings.

Next, add the individual names of your sales force in the row headings, shown in Figure 13.18.

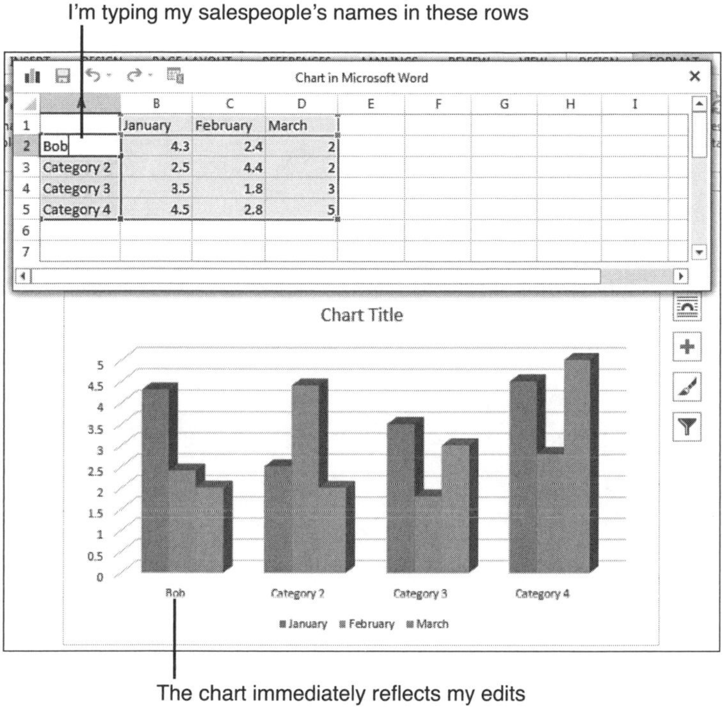

I'm typing my salespeople's names in these rows

The chart immediately reflects my edits

FIGURE 13.18

Type in each salesperson's name in the row headings.

The intersecting cells hold all the sales figures for each person, as shown in Figure 13.19. Type in the sales amounts for each person in their corresponding columns and rows.

When you finish typing in all the chart data, you can close the datasheet by clicking the little window's **Close** button. You can also drag it by its title bar to move it out of the way, or minimize it. If you do close it and want to open it again, right-click the chart and click **Edit Data** or click the **Edit Data** button on the **Design** tab.

I start typing my sales figures in the cells

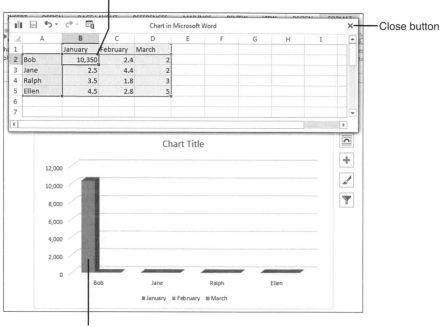

Close button

The chart immediately reflects my edits

FIGURE 13.19

Type in all the sales figures.

Editing Charts

Remember those two specialized tabs of tools I told you about when we started talking about charts? Well, you'll use those tabs and tools to work on your chart, such as adding chart elements, changing the layout or style, or formatting parts of your chart. As soon as you click anywhere on a chart, the **Chart Tools** appear: **Design** and **Format**. The **Design** tab offers tools for fiddling with the design elements of the chart, and the **Format** tab has tools for changing the appearance of chart shapes, text, and arrangement.

Shall we discuss some ways to add items to your chart? Click the **Design** tab, shown in Figure 13.20, and we'll get going. If you click the first button on the tab, the **Add Chart Elements** button, a drop-down menu appears listing various elements you can add. Click a category to open a submenu and then click the item you want to insert. For example, if you want to include a legend—a key to what all the colors or data series stand for—click the **Legend** category and click a location for the item. You can easily experiment with each of the items listed to see what they look like in your chart. As you move the mouse pointer over each, the chart reflects the addition.

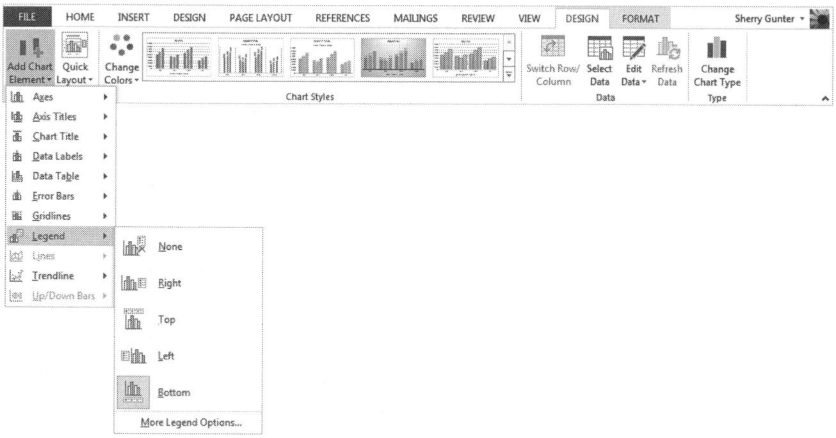

FIGURE 13.20

You can add elements to enhance your chart using the Add Chart Elements menu.

The Design tab offers other chart-changing tools you can apply:

- Don't like the original layout you chose? You can change it using the **Quick Layout** drop-down list. Click the **Quick Layout** button on the **Design** tab and click another layout. (These are the same layouts you viewed in the **Insert Chart** dialog box.)

- Don't like the chart color scheme? Change it with the **Change Colors** drop-down list. Click the button and choose another color set to apply.

- Don't like the chart's overall style? Swap it out with something different from the available styles listed in the **Chart Styles** gallery. Chart styles include colors, fonts, and backgrounds.

- Don't like your chart type? Click the **Change Chart Type** button to open the appropriately named **Change Chart Type** dialog box and select another chart type.

If you need to edit your chart's data, you can click the **Edit Data** button and click **Edit Data** from the drop-down menu. This opens the datasheet window you used to enter all the chart data. If you would rather do your editing over in the Excel program window instead, click the **Edit Data in Excel 2013** option.

The **Format** tab, shown in Figure 13.21, displays tools for changing the formatting attributes of your chart parts and controlling the position of the chart. Most of the tools are the same tools used to format SmartArt, shapes, and pictures, so we won't go over them again here, except to talk about a few unique to charts.

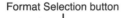

FIGURE 13.21

Use the tools on the Format tab to change the appearance of various chart elements.

Over on the left side of the tab is a group of tools labeled **Current Selection**. You can use these tools to format a particular selection in your chart, such as the legend or data series. When you click the **Format Selection** button, a pane opens with additional options you can apply to format the selection, as shown in Figure 13.22. The pane changes based on what item you're formatting and you can click the tools within the pane to make different types of changes, such as changing a fill color or plotting the series on another axis. Many of the tools duplicate what's already offered on the **Format** tab, such as the **Shape Fill** or **Shape Effects** tools. But the pane handily groups tools related to the task at hand in one spot so you can easily change the settings for the selected item in one fell swoop. When you finish using the pane, click its **Close** button.

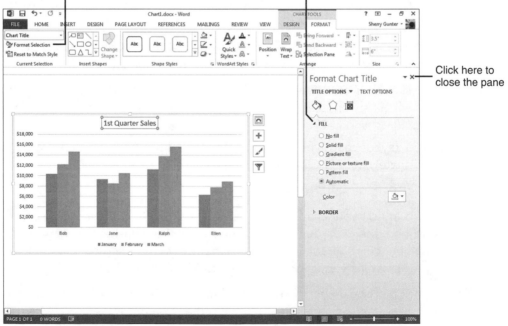

FIGURE 13.22

Formatting panes help you quickly assign attributes to a selected chart element.

TIP You can also double-click a chart to open the pane of formatting tools.

In addition to Ribbon tabs, you can also jump right to task-related chart editing features using some special shortcuts, shown in Figure 13.23. When you work with a chart, four icons appear to the right of the chart:

- **Layout Options** Displays text wrapping settings to control how the chart interacts with the rest of the document page.
- **Chart Elements** Add or subtract chart elements using this pop-up list.
- **Chart Styles** Gives you quick access to the Chart Styles gallery to change the chart appearance.
- **Chart Filters** Edit data points and names on the chart using this pop-up list.

Click an icon to view its related information.

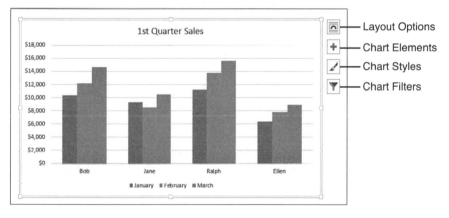

FIGURE 13.23

Use the task-related editing features as shortcuts to chart commands and tools.

 TIP You can right-click on a chart to view a shortcut menu of commands to help you edit and format chart elements.

THE ABSOLUTE MINIMUM

When they say a picture's worth a thousand words, they mean it—graphics can really help you convey a lot in an eyeful. Whether you call them graphics, charts, or diagrams, you can use them to visually present a concept, process, and quantitative data. You learned:

- You can use the **SmartArt** feature on the **Insert** tab to build diagrams in your document to illustrate processes, organizations, or relationships.

- You can choose from multiple types of diagrams.

- SmartArt includes placeholder text and shapes already formatted and ready to go. All you have to do is add your own content.

- When working with a SmartArt diagram, two specialized SmartArt Tools tabs appear: **Design** and **Format**. These tabs are loaded with tools for designing and formatting the graph to make it look the way you want.

- If you need to plot out some number data, use Word's charting features to create your own chart. Click the **Chart** tool on the **Insert** tab to get started.

- Word offers nine different chart types you can choose from, and each type includes a variety of layouts.

- Like the SmartArt tools, two special tabs appear on the Ribbon when you work with charts: **Design** and **Format**. You can use the tools found on each to modify a chart's appearance.

- In addition to the tabs, you can use specialized formatting panes to help you change the attributes of different chart elements.

14

IN THIS CHAPTER

- Learn how to draw shapes using Word's Shapes tools.

- Turn text into artwork with the amazing WordArt feature.

- Add text boxes to create quotes and sidebars in your documents.

ADDING SIMPLE GRAPHIC ELEMENTS

Now it's time for some graphic talk. The term *graphic* refers to artwork you add to your documents. Artwork can include pictures (digital or scanned), clip art (pre-drawn artwork), shapes you draw using your software's drawing tools, even charts and graphs (which you learned about in Chapter 13, "Adding Charts, Graphs, and Diagrams"). You can use graphics as another way to add visual interest to your files. Graphics can enhance a report, illustrate a point, tie-in a theme, or generally just dress up an ordinary page.

In this chapter, I'll show you how to make use of Word's simple graphic elements. These include shapes, text boxes, and WordArt objects. In the next chapter, you can learn how to insert pictures, clip art, and videos.

Drawing Shapes

There are times when you're working in a document and you think to yourself, "Hey, I wish I could put a big arrow next to this paragraph" or "My title really needs a colorful oval behind it." It turns out that you can add a wide variety of visual shapes to your documents using Word's **Shapes** tool. Formerly called AutoShapes in previous renditions of Microsoft Office, you can use the **Shapes** tool to quickly draw all manner of basic shapes, lines, rectangles, block arrows, equation shapes, flowchart shapes, stars and banners, and callouts. In fact, the **Shapes** library (or as some like to call it, *Shapes gallery*) gives you quite a range with which to work. The great thing about shapes is you can layer them with other shapes and graphics, put text on them, resize them, and pretty much use them any way you want. Take a look at Figure 14.1 to see an example of how you can put a shape into use. This is the title page of my upcoming great American novel. Obviously, the heart shape really dresses it up, right? The point is that you can use shapes in all kinds of novel ways (pun intended) in your own document tasks.

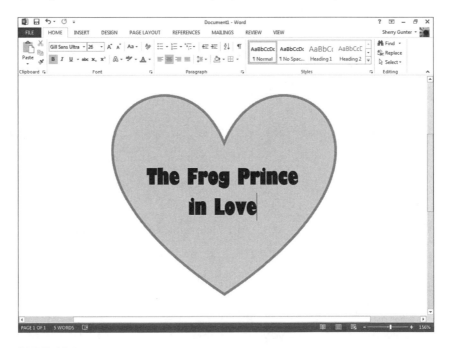

FIGURE 14.1

You draw shapes to add visual interest to documents.

GRAPHIC FORMATTING LINGO YOU NEED TO KNOW

As you start working with graphics, there are a few terms you will run across repeatedly with formatting attributes. One of those terms is *fill color*. A fill color is the shading that appears within a shape or WordArt text. You can swap out the fill color with another color selection to change the graphic object's appearance.

Another common term is *outline*. This refers to the border around the shape or the outline of the text letters of a WordArt object. Like a fill color, you can control the color of an outline's line. In addition to color, you can also control an outline's line style, such as turning a solid line into dashes, or making a thin line thicker in appearance.

Lastly, the term *effects* is another part of the formatting options you can apply to shapes and other graphic objects. Effects are the special formatting attributes you can assign to create artistic looks, such as shadows and glows.

You're bound to encounter this lingo over and over again, and not just for shapes, so don't let it throw you when you see the terms *fills*, *outlines*, and *effects* tossed about casually in upcoming conversations.

To insert a shape, follow these steps:

1. Click the **Insert** tab.
2. Click the **Shapes** button.
3. Click a shape from the library, as shown in Figure 14.2.

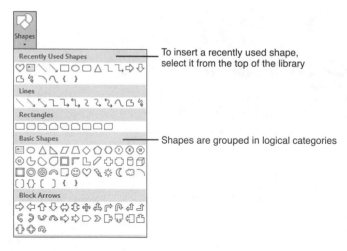

To insert a recently used shape, select it from the top of the library

Shapes are grouped in logical categories

FIGURE 14.2

Check out all the shapes available in the Shapes library!

4. Click and drag on the page where you want the shape to appear; Word draws the shape as you drag, as shown in Figure 14.3.

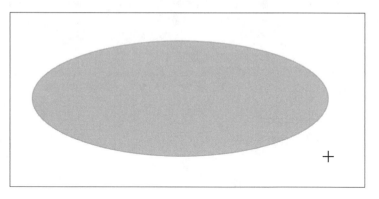

FIGURE 14.3

Click and drag to start drawing.

5. When you release the mouse button, Word inserts the shape (see Figure 14.4).

You can resize and reposition a shape any way you want. Plus, you can format the shape, changing its fill color, border, or even assign special effects. You can also control how text flows around the shape (called *text wrapping*). You can access the text flow options simply by clicking the **Layout Options** icon that appears in the upper-right corner of the selected shape, shown in Figure 14.4. When activated, this option offers you quick access to text wrapping controls, as shown in Figure 14.5, or you can choose to open a **Layout** dialog box to view more options. To activate a command from the Layout Options list, just click it.

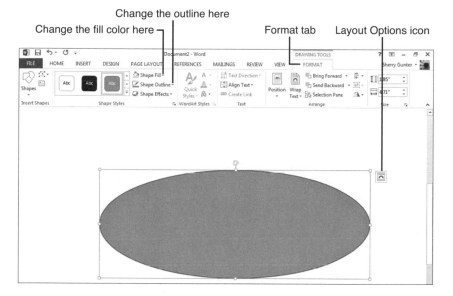

FIGURE 14.4

Release the mouse button when you finish drawing, and the shape appears in full.

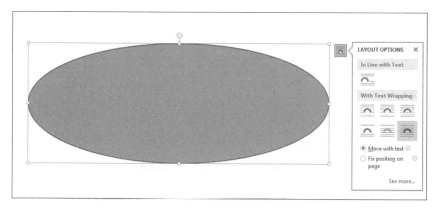

FIGURE 14.5

You can use the shortcut icons to quickly access commands related to the task at hand.

Word automatically applies some default formatting to the shapes you draw, including a preassigned fill color and outline color. Sure, it would have been nice if Word asked you what color you wanted before you got started, but alas, it didn't. To change either the fill color or outline, or both, click the **Shape Fill** button or **Shape Outline** button (refer to Figure 14.4) on the **Format** tab and make your selections.

TIP You can activate Word's drawing canvas feature and draw as many shapes as you like to create your own original artwork. The drawing canvas gives you a special drawing area separate from the rest of the page. To use this feature, click the **Insert** tab and click **Shapes**, and then click the **New Drawing Canvas** command at the bottom of the **Shapes** library. You can draw multiple shapes on the canvas, and utilize all the shape tools on the Format tab to add new shapes, freeform shapes, fill colors, and more. You might use the drawing canvas to draw your own diagram from scratch or design a simple company logo. You can also group the objects you draw with the Group Objects command. Press the **Esc** key to exit the canvas and return to the document. Basically, this just takes you out of edit mode. To revisit the canvas again to make changes, just click on the shape.

Repositioning and Resizing Shapes

Repositioning and resizing shapes is pretty easy. The same technique is used for just about everything you insert that displays selection handles. *Selection handles* are the tiny squares that surround a selected object, as shown in Figure 14.6. You can drag a middle handle to increase the graphic size up or down, or right or left. If you drag a corner handle, you can resize the entire object.

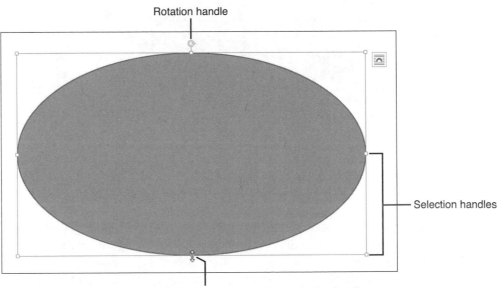

Rotation handle

Selection handles

The mouse pointer changes when you hover over a selection handle

FIGURE 14.6

Look for selection handles when you want to resize a graphic.

TIP The funny-looking circle icon with an arrow in it is the rotation handle. You can use it to rotate the object. Learn more about this technique in Chapter 16, "Fine-Tuning Your Graphics."

As for repositioning a shape, first hover your mouse pointer over the border until the pointer becomes a four-sided arrow icon, as shown in Figure 14.7. Now drag the graphic and drop it where you want it to appear. Depending on what text wrapping option is applied, the rest of the document text might or might not flow around the object. You can learn more about text wrapping controls in Chapter 16.

Four-sided arrow icon

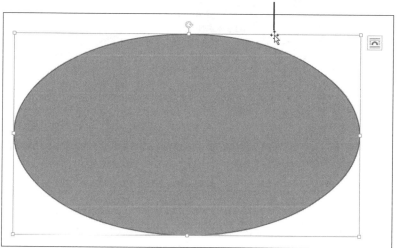

FIGURE 14.7

You can drag and drop a selected object to move it around the document.

 TIP You can always break out your trusty **Cut** and **Paste** commands to move a graphic around in a document. See Chapter 4, "Document Basics," to learn more.

Formatting Shapes

Shape formatting boils down to a few key attributes: style, fill color, outline color, and special effects. When you're ready to apply any of this formatting to a shape, the Ribbon's **Format** tab is the place to go because it's sitting right up at the top of your screen. The bulk of the shape formatting falls under the group of tools labeled **Shape Styles** on the tab, as shown in Figure 14.8.

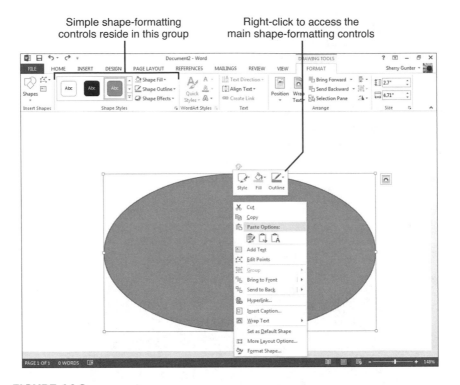

FIGURE 14.8

Access formatting controls through the Format tab or summon the shortcut menu.

However, there are some other ways to access formatting fast. The handy little shortcut menu, for example, is just a click away. A right-click on the shape displays a menu similar to what you see in Figure 14.8. The top of the menu offers shortcuts to changing the shape style, fill color, or outline. Just click the attribute you want to change and make your selection. What could be easier than that?

There's also a task pane you can use to format graphics, shown in Figure 14.9. You can use the pane to access all the detailed settings normally found in a dialog box. The **Format Shape** pane offers commands and tools grouped under collapsible/expandable headings in the pane; click an arrow next to the group name to view more or fewer tools. The **Format Shape** pane is the way to go when you want to fine-tune the shape's attributes and try out different features as you work. As you can see, there's a lot to play around with and each category icon at the top of the pane displays different settings.

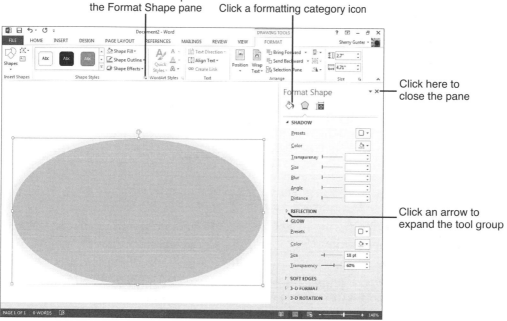

FIGURE 14.9

Whoa! A task pane dedicated to detailed formatting!

To display the pane, click the **Format Shape** icon on the **Format** tab in the corner of the **Shape Styles** group of tools. You can also right-click the shape and choose **Format Shape**.

After the pane appears, you can make adjustments to various settings. The tools you see listed work the same way as the other commands you've used so far on the Ribbon and in Word's many dialog boxes. To start fiddling with the settings, you can use the usual techniques: dragging slider bars, typing in a value, clicking spinner arrows, choosing from drop-down menus, clicking radio buttons and check boxes, and so on.

This is just the tip of the formatting iceberg. We'll go over some of the more complex formatting features in Chapter 16, such as layering shapes and text to create logos. In the meantime, this should be enough to give your shapes a quick makeover.

TIP   Do you need to change one shape into another? Click the **Format** tab and then look for the **Insert Shapes** group of tools on the left end of the tab. Click the **Edit Shape** drop-down arrow, click **Change Shape**, then choose another shape from the library.

NOTE You can make your own unique shapes out of any existing shape by making modifications to the shape's edit points. *Edit points* are draggable handles you can use to adjust the shape's perimeters. To turn them on, click the **Edit Shape** drop-down arrow found in the **Insert Shapes** group of tools on the left end of the **Format** tab. Click **Edit Points** from the drop-down menu and Word displays all the edit points for the corners or connecting spots on the shape. You can click and drag an edit point to modify the shape. You can also click the edge of the shape to add a new edit point.

Inserting WordArt Objects

Word has a cool feature you can use to turn text into graphic objects. Called *WordArt*, it's been around for quite some time in all the Office programs. You can use it to create logos or turn text into visual works of art like a modern-day Picasso. The great thing about turning text into art is that you can then treat it as a graphic, resizing it, recoloring it, layering it with other shapes and artwork, and so on. Take a gander at an example of WordArt in Figure 14.10.

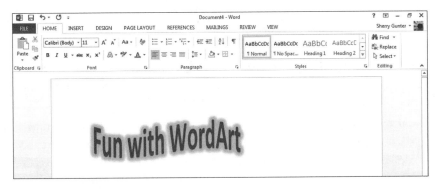

FIGURE 14.10

Is it text or is it art? It's WordArt!

In previous versions of Word, the WordArt tool included a library of various artistic variations you could apply to the graphic. In this version of Word, you can choose from a small library of Quick Styles to get started, but then you can assign all kinds of different formatting effects to customize the artwork. The effects are where all the excitement is.

To insert a WordArt object, begin by clicking the **Insert** tab and clicking the **Insert WordArt** drop-down arrow. Word displays the gallery, shown in Figure 14.11. Click a style and Word inserts a text box into your document with some placeholder text, similar to Figure 14.12. As with the **Shapes** tool you learned about in the previous section, the selected WordArt object also displays the **Layout Options** icon in the corner so you can quickly control text wrapping, if needed. Word also opens a special tab on the Ribbon you can use to format the object, called, strangely enough, the **Format** tab.

WordArt tool

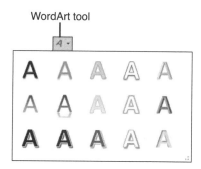

FIGURE 14.11

Start a WordArt object by choosing a style from the Quick Styles gallery.

Layout Options icon

![Screenshot showing the Format tab in Word with "Your text here" placeholder]

FIGURE 14.12

Word displays placeholder text you must replace with your own.

The next part of creating WordArt is typing in your text. As soon as you start typing, Word assigns the style you applied, as you can see in Figure 14.13.

To make changes to your WordArt object, check out all the options available on the **Format** tab. Specifically pay attention to the group of tools under the heading **WordArt Styles** (see Figure 14.13). Here's what you can do with the tools you find there:

- Change the WordArt style by clicking the **Quick Styles** button and choosing another style.

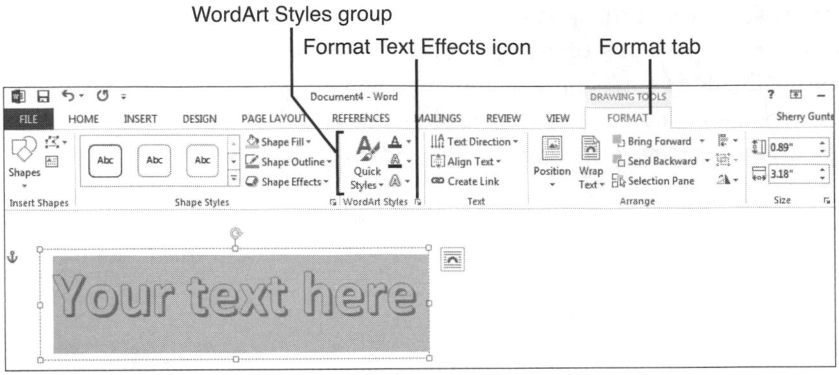

WordArt Styles group

Format Text Effects icon

Format tab

FIGURE 14.13

Replace the placeholder text with your own.

- To change the fill color, click the **Text Fill** drop-down arrow and choose another color.

- Don't see the color you want? Click the **Text Fill** drop-down arrow and choose **More Fill Colors** to open the **Colors** dialog box where you can choose from a larger palette.

- To change the outline color of the text, click the **Text Outline** drop-down arrow and choose another color.

- To change the line style for the outline, click the **Text Outline** drop-down arrow, click the **Weight** command, and choose a line style.

- What? Not enough line styles for you? Then click the **Text Outline** drop-down arrow, click the **Weight** command, then click **More Lines**. This opens the **Format Shape** pane where you can adjust all kinds of line options, such as transparency, thickness, or no line at all.

- To change the text effect, click the **Text Effects** drop-down arrow, click an effect category, and then click an effect from the gallery.

- Need more customizing options for your effect? Then activate the **Options** command at the bottom of the effects gallery to open additional settings via the **Format** pane or a separate dialog box (depending on the type of effect you choose).

 TIP If you don't want a text fill color or a text outline border around your WordArt, you can turn the feature off. Click the **Text Fill** drop-down arrow and choose **No Fill**, or click the **Text Outline** drop-down arrow and choose **No Outline**.

Speaking of formatting, have you checked out the **Format** pane yet? It's bursting at the seams with settings you can use to further fine-tune your WordArt object. Granted, some of the tools on the pane are just duplicates of what's on the Ribbon's **Format** tab, but others offer greater details. To display the pane, click the **Format Text Effects** icon in the corner of the **WordArt Styles** group of tools (see Figure 14.13), or right-click your WordArt object and choose **Format Shape** from the pop-up menu.

The **Format Shape** pane, shown in Figure 14.14, is just like the one used for shapes (see the previous section), but this time the tools offered include text tools. You can switch between shape tools and text tools by clicking the **Shape Options** or **Text Options** labels at the top of the pane. The **Text Options** include the three main attribute groups you can format with: **Text Fill & Outline**, **Text Effects**, and **Layout & Properties**. Click a category icon to view the related tools. Be sure to note the **Text Effects** category where you can play around with all kinds of different effects, such as adding different types and directions of shadows, applying glowing edges to the object, trying out 3-D styles, and more. Just like with shapes, you can drag slider bars, type in values, click spinner arrows, select from drop-down menus, and click radio buttons and check boxes to make adjustments to the settings for your WordArt object.

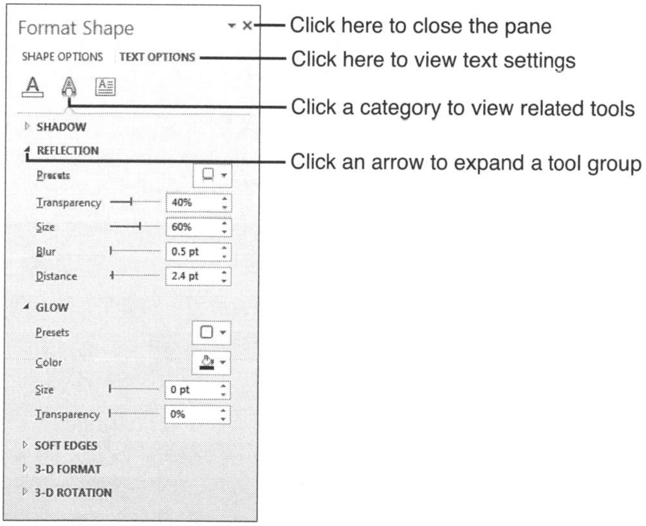

FIGURE 14.14

You can also open the Format Shape pane to the Text Options to adjust your WordArt formatting.

My all-time favorite WordArt formatting is the ability to transform the text into waves, arches, and full-on circles of words. You can do all of this using the Transform category of text effects. To find your way to this riveting feature, click the **Text Effects** drop-down arrow on the **Format** tab, and then click the **Transform** category. From the palette that appears, as shown in Figure 14.15, you can choose from curving text, waving text, circular text, and more. Click the one you want to immediately apply it.

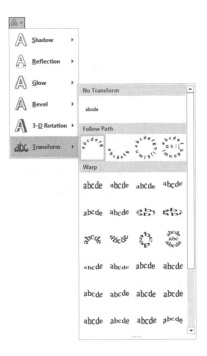

FIGURE 14.15

Visit the Transform category on the Text Effects palette to view all kinds of transformations for your WordArt.

TIP If you ever need to turn off a WordArt text effect, or even a text effect applied to a shape or normal text, you need to reopen the Effects palette and choose the **No** option for the particular effect type you applied. For example, if you applied a glow, click the **Glow** category and choose **No Glow**.

Inserting Text Box Objects

Did you know you can put text in a box and treat it like a graphic? You can. Using Word's **Text Box** tool, you can place text in a special "container" (that is, a box) and move it about the document separately from the regular document text. You might do this to create a quote that floats on its own on a page, or to insert a sidebar of information related to the main topic of the document. Figure 14.16 shows an example of a text box in a document. Text boxes are useful for adding captions, labels, or basically adding extra emphasis to a specific bit of text. You can use them to group text and graphics together, like a picture or a shape along with text, and you can even link text boxes to each other to flow text from one to another just like the technique used in desktop publishing software. Oh, and the text box doesn't even have to have an actual border around it to be a box. Intrigued? Then let's learn how to make them.

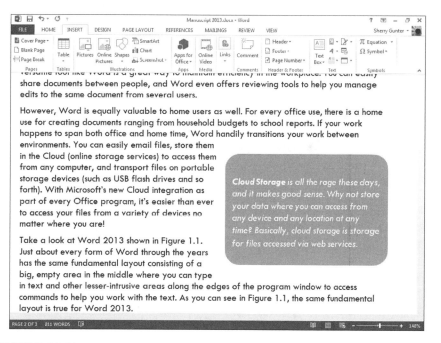

FIGURE 14.16

Text boxes are the perfect tool for setting text apart from the rest of the page.

Essentially, a text box acts just like any other graphic object, similar to a shape or WordArt object. You can move it around, resize it, and format it using all the same tools used for formatting shapes and WordArt. In fact, when you work with a text box, the Ribbon displays the same **Format** tab. This means you can add a fill color to the text box, set a border color and line thickness, and apply special styles. The

Text group of tools found on the **Format** tab can help you do a few things with your text boxes.

As it turns out, Word installs with a library of preset text boxes already formatted and ready to go. Part of the collection of built-ins and Quick Parts, the **Text Box** gallery includes boxes for quotes and sidebars featuring a variety of artistic stylings. You can insert one of these and modify it any way you like, or you can go with a basic no-thrills text box and work from there. Plus, there's a third option—you can draw your own text box to just the right size. With the preset text boxes, including the simple text box, Word includes placeholder text; of course, you can replace this with your own content. If you opt to draw your own box, it's completely empty.

To insert a built-in text box, follow these steps:

1. Click where you want to insert a text box.

2. Click the **Insert** tab.

3. Click the **Text Box** button.

4. Click a text box from the gallery, as shown in Figure 14.17. Choose the **Simple Text Box** option to start with a plain text box.

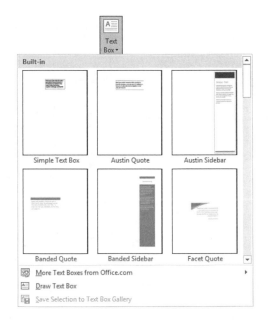

FIGURE 14.17

Scroll through and choose a built-in text box.

Word immediately inserts the box into your document (see Figure 14.18). Replace any placeholder text with your own and format it any way you want.

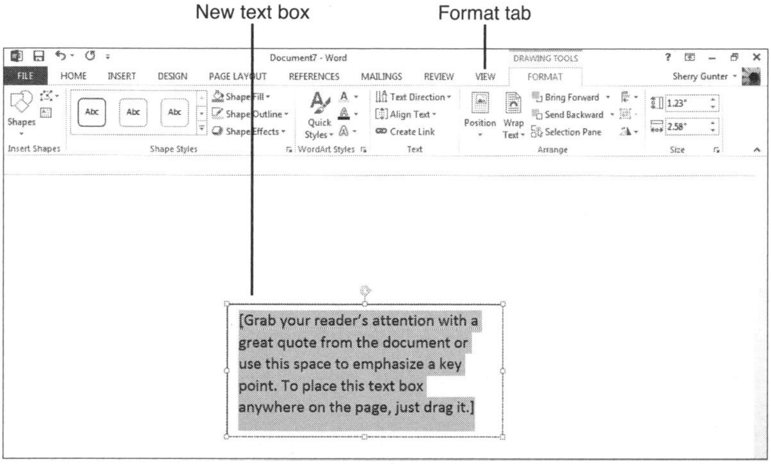

New text box   Format tab

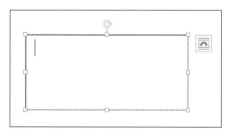

FIGURE 14.18

Type in your own text and format the box however you want.

Would you rather draw your own text box? Okay, first click the **Insert** tab, click **Text Box**, and click **Draw Text Box**. Next, click and drag on the page making the box as big or little as you want. When you stop dragging, the box is inserted and ready for text, similar to Figure 14.19. Notice the box is empty and you don't have to replace any placeholder text.

FIGURE 14.19

Draw your own text box if you want to create a certain size.

TIP   If the **Format** tab is already displayed, you can click the **Draw Text Box** button located at the far left end of the tab and draw your own box. This route is handy if you're drawing both shapes and text boxes to create a logo or something.

TIP You can create a custom text box and save it to the Text Box gallery to reuse in other documents. Simply select the entire box, click the **Insert** tab, click the **Text Box** drop-down arrow and choose **Save Selection to Text Box Gallery**. Give the graphic a unique name and click **OK** to save it.

After you add a text box, here are a few things you can do with it:

- To adjust the alignment of text within the text box, click the **Align Text** drop-down arrow on the **Format** tab and choose another alignment setting.

- You can change the direction of the text in a text box. Click the **Format** tab and click the **Text Direction** drop-down arrow and make a selection.

- The **Layout Options** icon that appears in the corner of an active text box lets you control the text wrapping for a text box. Click the **Layout Options** icon to display the menu of text wrapping controls and choose the one you want.

- You can use the text formatting tools on the **Home** tab to change the font and size of the text.

- You can use the Shape Styles group of tools on the **Format** tab to change the fill color, box border, and assign a special effect to the box.

- You can also right-click the box and access the **Style**, **Fill**, and **Outline** buttons to assign formatting.

- Text boxes use the same **Format Shape** task pane that WordArt objects use if you would rather set options from the pane instead of the Ribbon. Right-click the box and click **Format Shape** to open the task pane.

- You can use edit points to make irregular text boxes. Right-click the box and click **Edit Points**. Click on the box edge to add an edit point, which you can then drag to reshape the box.

- To link two text boxes, click the **Create Link** button on the **Format** tab and then click an empty text box to link to. When applied, any extra text you add to the first box flows into the second no matter where it is located in the document. You might use this feature to create custom columns for a particular project.

TIP If you format a box just right and want to save it as the new default text box style, right-click the box and click **Set as Default Text Box**.

Learn about layering text boxes, applying text wrapping, grouping boxes with other shapes and boxes, and several other graphic arrangement features in Chapter 16.

THE ABSOLUTE MINIMUM

Simple graphic elements go a long way toward adding visual interest to your documents. With a little imagination and ingenuity, you can insert shapes, WordArt objects, and text boxes to help convey a message or illustrate a point, or just make a good document look even better. In this chapter, you learned the following:

- The Ribbon's **Insert** tab is the place to go to add shapes, WordArt, or text boxes.

- After you add a graphic element, the **Format** tab offers tools to help you modify the object.

- For more detailed formatting controls, open the **Format Shape** task pane and fine-tune the settings for any shape, WordArt object, or text box.

- Word's **Shapes** library includes a vast array of shapes ranging from arrows and stars to callouts and flowchart blocks.

- The WordArt tool takes ordinary text and turns it into graphics utilizing a variety of styles and configurations.

- Text boxes are handy for setting apart text for special functions, such as quotes and sidebars. You can also use them to group graphic elements together.

INSERTING PICTURES AND VIDEOS

Time to kick your graphics knowledge up a notch and start illustrating your documents with visuals that are a bit more complex in nature than the shapes and WordArt images covered in Chapter 14, "Adding Simple Graphic Elements." I'm talking about *digital pictures*. Although they offer a great deal more in pixels, they aren't any more difficult to add than simple graphic elements, such as shapes. However, the impact they bring to your documents is considerable. Pictures have the power to provoke, inspire, explain, and communicate in a glance. In this chapter, you learn how to tap into the vast collections of images available on the Microsoft Office website, as well as insert your own photographic images stored on your computer or memory device.

Pictures fall under the broad umbrella of graphic elements you can add to spruce up and complement your text. The term *picture* loosely covers any sort of detailed image, whether it's computer-generated artwork from a drawing program or a photograph taken with a digital camera or scanned in using a scanner device. Whether you like to call them pictures, illustrations, images, or artwork, we're still talking about the same type of visuals you can put to use in your own word-processing tasks.

Understanding Picture File Types

Before you dive head first into inserting pictures, I thought I would give you the scoop about picture file types. At first glance, this might not be anything you're interested in, but knowing a few things about file formats for pictures might help you out when you're searching for artwork to insert into your documents. The devices and programs used to make pictures determine what sort of file format is assigned to the picture file. Just as Microsoft Word makes document files (which utilize the .DOCX file extension), programs and devices that create pictures make different kinds of picture file formats. For example, my digital camera typically spits out JPEG files when I import them into a photo viewer program. Yours might assign another format, such as TIFF. A piece of clip art you download from the Office website might use the WMF format. Knowing the file type can help you as you organize and search for picture files on your computer and on the Web.

Figure 15.1 shows examples of four different picture file types. Your naked eye might not distinguish a great deal of difference between them, but behind the scenes in the coding, things become very different.

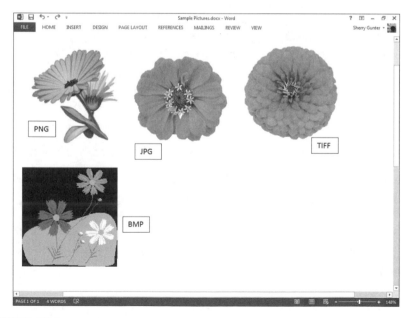

FIGURE 15.1

Picture files use different file formats. You had better know this for the quiz later.

Obviously, different graphic file types are used with different scenarios. For example, graphics for Web use don't require the same quality settings as those used in professional printing. With everyone sharing picture files these days, though, either directly or over the Internet, file size and quality is an issue regardless of the scenario. Picture files are notoriously large in size because of all the colors and details needed to make them. Because of this, data compression techniques are employed to help keep picture file sizes down. Lossy compression and lossless compression are two such methods. *Lossy compression* reduces the file size by eliminating certain data, such as redundant information; but when uncompressed, some of the original data is gone. With *lossless compression*, everything in the file can be recovered when the file is uncompressed. Image file formats, like those described in the following list, apply these types of data compression methods to reduce the overall file size.

The most common picture formats you'll encounter today are

- **JPEG** or **JPG**   Stands for Joint Photographics Expert Group. JPG is commonly used on photos and similar types of illustration files. Its flexible compression levels let you control the file size. JPG is a good choice when you want a smaller file size for an image, but that means the quality is lower due to its lossy compression method. However, the quality loss might not be noticeable.

- **TIFF** or **TIF**   Stands for Tagged Image File Format. TIFF is great for high-color, high-depth digital images, and its lossless compression format retains image quality no matter how many times you open and resave the file. TIF is the highest quality for commercial work.

- **PNG**   Stands for Portable Network Graphics. PNG is a bitmap file format designed specifically for use with web pages. It was originally designed to replace the GIF format to save color information more efficiently. Although not as popular as JPEG and TIFF, it's a good choice for lossless quality images.

- **GIF**   Stands for Graphics Interchange Format. GIF is an older file format commonly used with simple graphics, such as logos, shapes, and icons. It also supports animation. It's a bit limiting for today's digital technology (it only supports 8-bit, 256 color at the maximum), but it still has its place on the Web for simple graphics.

- **BMP**   Stands for Windows Bitmap. This file format is commonly used with Windows graphics. Also called raster or paint format, it's not compressed, which results in a larger file size. BMP files aren't very popular as web graphics.

- **RAW**   This is uncompressed digital image data straight from your camera. It's not been fiddled with or compressed in any way. You must convert RAW files to another file format in order to open them in a photo-viewing program.

If you hand someone a RAW file, chances are they can't read it; it has to be converted first. With Windows 7 and later, the Camera Codec Pack helps with reading RAW file types.

- **DNG**   Stands for Digital Negative. DNG is a new open standard RAW format developed by Adobe, and just about every digital photo program can read DNG file types.

Hey, don't think I didn't notice your eyes glazing over after reading about all those file types. Just remember to flip back to the list if you ever need to identify one as you encounter different graphic files on your computer journey.

NOTE   A picture's file format can tell you a lot about the compression, which in turn can tell you about the picture's quality. Other file formats can tell you about the program from which it originates. You will run into other formats, such as Windows Metafile Format (WMF) for things such as clip art illustrations, but don't let the formats throw you off. Lots of programs, like Adobe Illustrator, save artwork in a native file format (AI for Adobe Illustrator), so you'll run across all kinds of different formats as you work with different graphic elements.

Inserting Images from the Internet

In the prehistoric days of early computing, digital artwork was quite rudimentary, jaggedy-edged and limited in color scope. It often looked like a caveman drew it rather than a highly qualified computer programmer. As time progressed, predrawn clip art began to proliferate among software manufacturers as clip art collections, allowing users to easily illustrate their files with cartoony-like graphics. The collections themselves used to install with software programs, such as Microsoft Word, and included a small variety of themes related to business, desktop publishing, and computer technologies. Eventually, full-blown photographic images—also called stock photography—made their way into clip art collections, too.

NOTE   *Clip art* got its name from the practice of clipping the artwork from existing printed art. Long before computers, printing people clipped artwork from other printed material and pasted it onto new publications. Now most publications are produced through desktop publishing software.

Today, most of the image collections offered with software programs are available online. Rather than clog up your computer's hard drive with lots of images you might not ever use, you can access pictures on the Web instead and find just the right ones you want. With an Internet connection, you can peruse vast libraries of pictures, from drawings and illustrations to photographs and video clips.

You need an online connection and a Microsoft account to tap into the Office. com site and search for artwork. The **Insert Pictures** feature, shown in Figure 15.2, lets you search for pictures in the following sources:

- **Office.com**   Search through Microsoft's own collection of royalty-free pictures.

- **Bing Image Search**   Use this option to search for pictures on the Web using Microsoft's Bing search engine.

- **SkyDrive**   If you store pictures on your cloud account, you can use this option to look for picture files among your SkyDrive content.

That's not all: If you use a Flickr photo sharing account, you can add it to the mix and search for digital pictures from it as well.

Insert Pictures

Office.com Clip Art
Royalty-free photos and illustrations   Search Office.com

Bing Image Search
Search the web   Search Bing

Sherry Gunter's SkyDrive
swkgunter@yahoo.com   Browse ▸

Also insert from:

FIGURE 15.2

The new Insert Pictures box lets you search for online pictures from several sources.

Thumbnails are miniatures of images. Rather than take up a lot of space with full-size images, most photo displays used in galleries, photo viewers, and search engines show smaller versions of the images. The term *thumbnail* also applies to files you view using Windows Explorer. For example, you can choose to view folder contents as thumbnails. This sort of gives you a glance at what the files contain without the inconvenience of a full-on screen-hogging view.

 NOTE   Pictures offered through the Office.com site are royalty-free, which means you can use them for free. That's not always the case with other web content. Be careful about randomly copying artwork from other sources or you might be in copyright violation.

TIP You can always use the good old **Copy** and **Paste** commands to copy pictures into your documents from other sources.

Using Pictures from Office.com

To insert a picture from Microsoft's online collection, follow these steps:

1. Click the **Insert** tab.

2. Click **Online Pictures** to open the **Insert Pictures** tool (see Figure 15.2).

3. Click in the **Office.com Clip Art** search field and type in a keyword or words for the type of picture you're looking for.

4. Press **Enter** or click the **Search** icon.

5. A search results page lists any matches, similar to Figure 15.3. Use the scrollbar to look through the thumbnails.

Click the picture you want

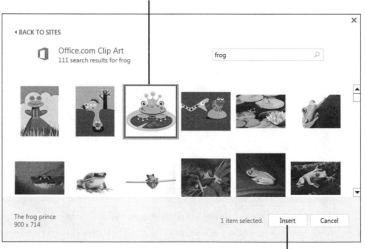

Click here when you're ready to download the image

FIGURE 15.3

Look through the search results to find the picture you want to use.

6. When you find one you want, click it. If you find more than one, press and hold the **Ctrl** key while clicking each image.

7. To download the picture, click **Insert**.

When the download is complete, Word inserts the picture into your document, much like what you see in Figure 15.4, and displays a new **Format** tab for working with the image. You might need to resize the picture right away to make it fit. More often than not, you'll find yourself having to do this with any artwork you bring into Word. Drag a picture's corner selection handle to resize the image. To move the picture around in the document, click and drag it.

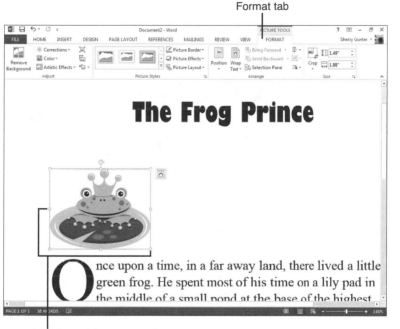

FIGURE 15.4

Word downloads the picture and inserts it for you. In this example, I inserted a clip art illustration.

If your initial search doesn't result in any good matches on Office.com, try typing in another keyword or phrase in the **Search** box. Finding the right picture for an occasion might take a few tries. If you give up on searching, click the **Back to Sites** link in the upper-left corner to return to the main **Insert Pictures** screen and try another source.

 TIP In Chapter 16, "Fine-Tuning Your Graphics," you can learn how to apply some formatting techniques to your pictures, such as how to add shadows, 3-D effects, borders, and more.

LEISURELY PICTURE SHOPPING

The new **Insert Pictures** tool forces you to type in keywords and then perform a search to look for images on the Office.com website. You might prefer a more leisurely approach to looking for just the right picture. You can use your browser window to navigate to the Microsoft Office website and peruse to your heart's content. Open the main page (www.office.com) and click the **Images** link at the top. This takes you to the Clip art, photos, and animations page. You can scroll around and click different categories and look through the selections, and if you see something you want, you can download it or copy it. Just hover the mouse pointer over the picture and click either **Copy** or **Download**.

If you click **Copy**, you can return to your Word document and activate the **Paste** command to immediately add the picture to your document.

If you click **Download**, you can save the picture file to a designated folder or drive on your computer. By default, downloaded pictures are automatically saved to the Windows Downloads folder, unless you specify somewhere else. Here's a tip: To make the picture easier to find later, you might want to give it a name you'll recognize. The Office.com pictures typically have cryptic names that never really signify what the image is.

Searching for Pictures Using Bing

Now let's try searching for pictures using the **Bing Image Search** feature. As you might or might not know, the Bing search engine is part of Microsoft's world domination plan, so all the Microsoft Office programs point you toward Bing any time you want to conduct a web search from within the programs.

To search the Web for pictures using Bing, follow these steps:

1. Click the **Insert** tab.

2. Click **Online Pictures**.

3. Click in the **Bing Image Search** field and type in a keyword or words for the type of picture you're looking for, as shown in Figure 15.5.

4. Press **Enter** or click the **Search** icon.

5. A search results page lists any matches, similar to what you see in Figure 15.6. Use the scrollbar to look through the thumbnails. Notice this time there's a big warning in the box about copyright material. Unlike the Office.com site, the items you search for using Bing are not necessarily royalty-free.

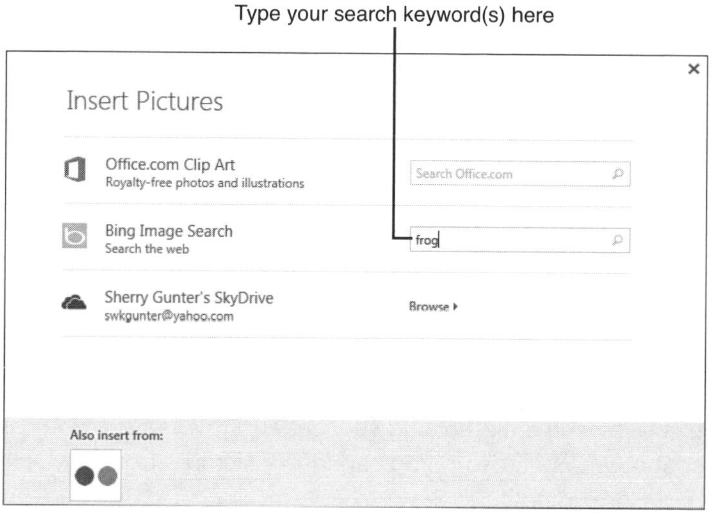

Type your search keyword(s) here

FIGURE 15.5

This time, let's search with Bing.

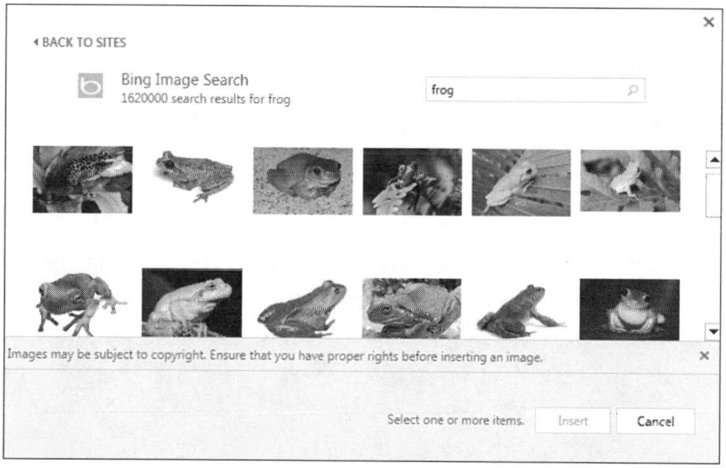

FIGURE 15.6

The results are images gathered from all over the Web that match your search criteria.

6. When you find a picture, click it to view its details, as well as a link to its web address you can use to learn more about the image.

7. Click **Insert**.

NOTE You can click a picture in your Bing search results to view a link to the source's website. Look in the bottom-left corner to view the link. Click it and you can learn more about where the picture comes from and how to contact the owner to ask for permission to use it. It never hurts to contact the source and ask. If you notice you are not able to copy, download, or use the PrintScreen capture to nab an image, then it's probably not supposed to be used by anyone else; stay away from protected images.

Searching for Pictures on SkyDrive

SkyDrive is Microsoft's file-hosting service, and if you store your photos on your cloud account with Microsoft, you can insert pictures from SkyDrive and place them in your documents.

To search your SkyDrive account for pictures, follow these steps:

1. Click the **Insert** tab.

2. Click **Online Pictures**.

3. Click the **Browse** link under the **SkyDrive** option (see Figure 15.7).

4. Open the folder containing your pictures and click the picture you want to insert (see Figure 15.8).

5. Click **Insert**.

As soon as you click the **Insert** button, Word downloads the picture and inserts it into your document. You will probably need to resize the picture to fit; just drag a corner selection handle, pointed out in Figure 15.9, to resize the image.

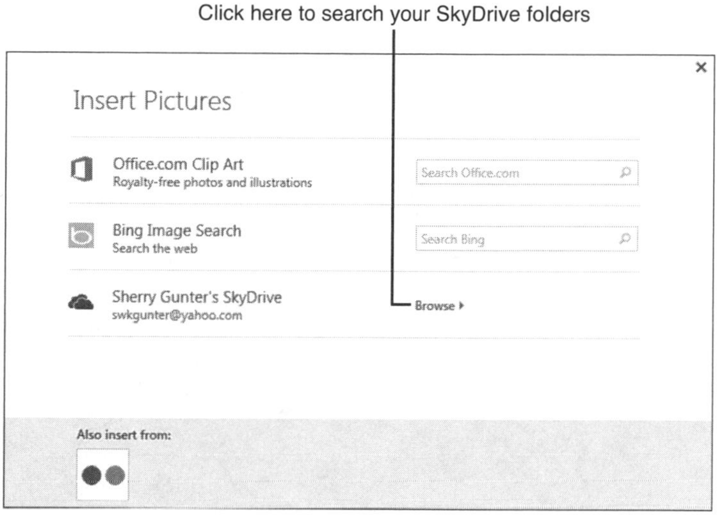

Click here to search your SkyDrive folders

Insert Pictures

Office.com Clip Art
Royalty-free photos and illustrations

Search Office.com 🔎

Bing Image Search
Search the web

Search Bing 🔎

Sherry Gunter's SkyDrive
swkgunter@yahoo.com

Browse ▸

Also insert from:

FIGURE 15.7

Now let's try searching your SkyDrive storage for pictures.

◂ BACK TO SITES

Sherry Gunter's SkyDrive
All folders

Documents   Random Photos

MINOLTA DIGITAL CAMERA
2048 x 1536

1 item selected.   Insert   Cancel

FIGURE 15.8

I'm looking for a frog picture, and I think this is the one.

You can resize a picture using a selection handle

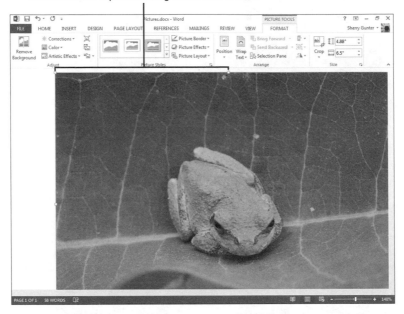

FIGURE 15.9

It's a tree frog resting on a zinnia flower leaf, if you must know.

 NOTE Are you new to SkyDrive? If so, you might be wondering how to store pictures on the cloud. It's easy. First use your favorite web browser to navigate to **www.skydrive.com** and log on to your account. Next, look for an **Upload** link at the top of the page and follow the onscreen directions to upload pictures from your computer to the cloud storage site. If you've activated the Windows SkyDrive folder on your computer (look for it listed under **Favorites** in the Explorer window), you can also drag files to it to store them in the cloud without having to open the browser.

If you have a Flickr account, click the **Flickr** icon at the bottom of the **Insert Pictures** window and follow the instructions to connect your account. If you don't have a Flickr account, you can use the link to make one.

Inserting Your Own Pictures

You can access any image stored on your computer and insert it into a Word file. If you have a digital camera, you might end up being the only illustrator your documents need. Digital cameras make adding your own visual content easier than ever. You can transfer files from the camera to your computer's hard drive, or you can store photos on a flash drive or memory card and access them from your PC.

To insert a picture stored on your computer or other plug-in devices, follow these steps:

1. Click the **Insert** tab.

2. Click **Pictures** to open the **Insert Picture** dialog box (see Figure 15.10).

3. Navigate to the folder or drive containing the picture you want to use and click the filename.

4. Click **Insert**.

FIGURE 15.10

Use the Insert Picture dialog box to add pictures found on your computer.

After you add a picture, you can easily resize it by dragging its selection handles. You can also drag it around to move it to a new location in the document. Look for the familiar **Layout Options** icon that appears in the upper-right corner of a selected picture; you can use it to control text flow around a picture.

As soon as you insert a picture, the **Picture Tools Format** tab is added to the Ribbon. This specialized tab displays tools you can use to edit your picture. You can learn more about ways to modify an image in the next chapter.

NOTE You can store data, including pictures, on a wide variety of devices these days. Most digital cameras utilize *memory cards*, for example, that pop in and out of the camera as well as any card reader slots on a computer. *Flash drives* (also called *thumb drives*, *stick drives*, or *key drives*) are compact stick-like storage you can use by plugging into a USB port. Flash drives are incredibly handy for storing files and transferring them between computers and other devices. Writable *CDs* and *DVDs* let you save files using an optical disk drive. Lastly, if you have an *external hard drive*, you can plug it into your computer and store picture files. When you're inserting pictures with the **Insert Picture** dialog box, you can navigate to any of these types of storage devices to retrieve a picture file. Just specify the appropriate drive listed in the left pane to view the contents.

TIP To remove any picture or video clip you insert, select it and press **Delete**.

Capturing Screenshots

You can use Word's **Screenshot** tool to add a snapshot of any open window on your desktop and immediately insert it into a document. You can also use it to take a clipping of a portion of anything open on the desktop, such as a sticky note or a game screen.

For example, maybe you're assembling a department budget in Excel and you want to grab a picture of your progress to include in a memo document you're creating in Word. You can capture the Excel window as a screenshot and tuck it away in your Word document as an illustration of how things are going. Or how about this: You're working on a report about a newly discovered iguana and want to grab a picture of the news story from your web browser window so you can read and reference it later. You can do this with the **Screenshot** tool. Pretty nifty, eh?

The feature keeps track of the current windows you have open, even though you're busy working in Word. It also keeps track of multiple Word documents you have open, so you can use it to snap screenshots from one document to insert into another. The key to using the feature is to make sure the window you want to capture is not minimized on the Windows Taskbar, but open onscreen.

Ready to give this a whirl? Start by opening a program window or Windows feature you want to capture. Remember, it can be any kind of window—a game, a sticky note, the Windows calculator, a photo viewer, web browser, and so on.

Display the Word window and click the **Insert** tab. Now click the **Screenshot** drop-down arrow, as shown in Figure 15.11, and click the window you want to insert. Boom, that was fast—the captured window is immediately inserted! Figure 15.12 shows an example of a screenshot.

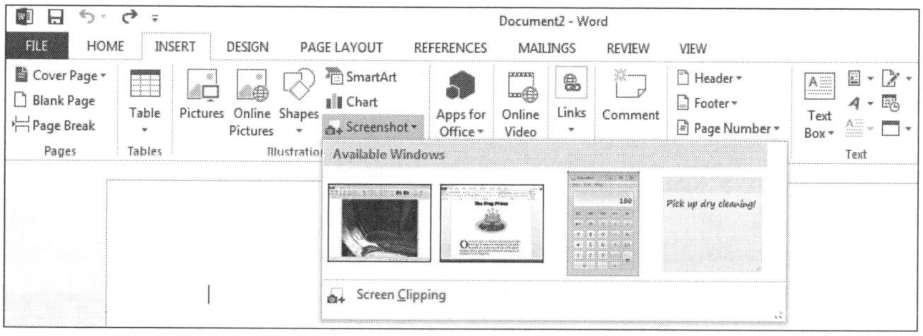

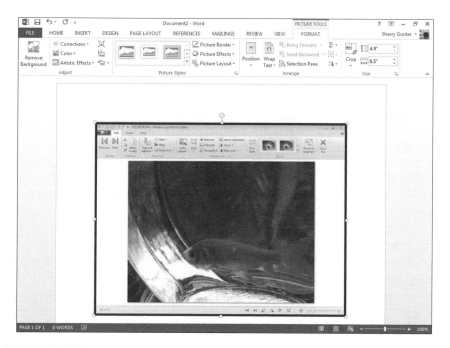

FIGURE 15.11

Use the Screenshot tool to add a screenshot of any open window or Windows feature.

FIGURE 15.12

The screenshot is immediately added to your document, complete with a border.

TIP Capture the wrong screen? Just click the **Undo** button on the Quick Access toolbar or press **Ctrl+Z** to remove the pasted screenshot or clipping right away and try again with the right one.

Now let's try out a screen clipping. Again, start by having the window open that you want to clip from, such as a photo album, web page, or game. Next, click the **Insert** tab and click the **Screenshot** drop-down arrow. Click **Screen Clipping** (see Figure 15.11 to locate this command). The first time you use the screen clipping tool, it's a little odd because your screen turns a foggy white color and the mouse pointer turns into a crosshair icon, like you see in Figure 15.13, but that's just your cue to drag across the clipping you want to capture. So, drag across the part of the screen you want to clip, as shown in Figure 15.14. The part you're clipping becomes clear as you drag. As soon as you release the mouse button, the area you dragged over is inserted into your Word document, much like what you see in Figure 15.15. Don't wait too long to drag over the clipping area or the function times out and you have to start all over again.

Move the crosshair icon to the upper-left corner where you want to clip

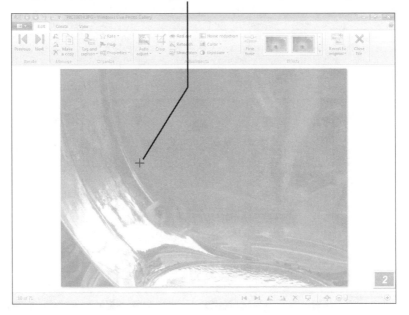

FIGURE 15.13

The first phase of the screen clip turns your screen foggy.

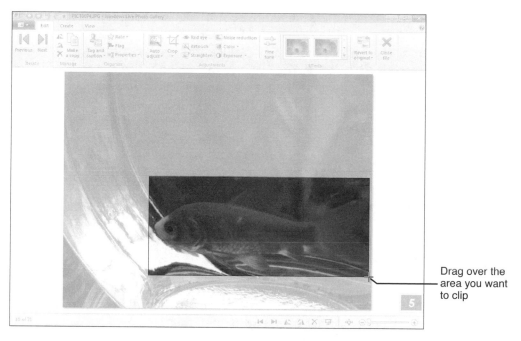

Drag over the
area you want
to clip

FIGURE 15.14

The second part of the process is to drag over the area you want to clip.

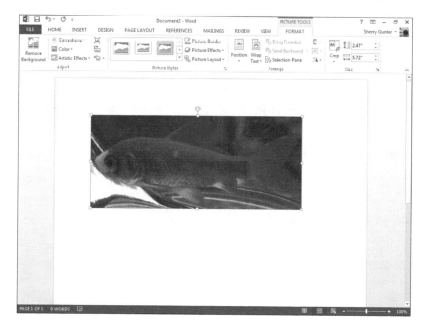

FIGURE 15.15

The screenshot is immediately added to your document.

I'll bet you're starting to see the future potential of this tool, right? Like any other graphic element you add to Word, the **Format** tab opens with your selected screenshot or clip, and you can apply picture attributes to the image. We'll cover more on those in Chapter 16. You can also move and resize any screenshot or clipping in your document, treating it just like any other graphic element.

TIP　Here's something interesting—you can save an inserted screenshot or clipping as a new picture file to reuse again. Right-click over the image and choose **Save as Picture**. This opens the **File Save** dialog box and you can give the file a unique name and store it where you like. You can also specify a particular file format for the picture using the **Save as type** drop-down menu.

Embedding Videos

Adding dynamic content to your documents is easier than ever, and by *dynamic*, I mean video clips. You can watch the clips without having to exit the Word document. This means other people who open the document file can watch the clip as well. Let's use that example about the iguana report again—say you want to include a video clip of the newly discovered lizard to show your readers what it looks like climbing a rock. You can insert the clip and treat it as a graphic element, which means you can move it, resize it, and apply some stylistic attributes (such as a border). The clip automatically displays a **Play** button that you, or another user, can click to play the clip.

Inserting a video embeds within the document. This means its information is included as part of the file when you save the document. Prior to this new feature, you could only insert links to videos. Of course, you can still insert links to videos stored elsewhere, but it's just a link and not an actual embedded clip.

You can insert video from the following sources:

- **Bing Video Search**　Use this option to search for videos on the Web using Microsoft's Bing search engine.

- **From a Video Embed Code**　Use this option if you know the specific embed code for the clip from its website.

- **YouTube**　Use this option to look for clips on the YouTube site. This option isn't set up by default; you'll have to click the **YouTube** icon at the bottom of the window to include the service in your video options list.

To insert a video from an online source, follow these steps:

1. Click the **Insert** tab.

2. Click **Online Video** to open the **Insert Video** tool (see Figure 15.16).

FIGURE 15.16

Start by choosing a source and typing in a keyword or words.

3. Click in the **Bing Video Search** field and type in a keyword or words for the type of video you're looking for.

4. Press **Enter** or click the **Search** icon.

5. A search results page lists any matches, similar to what's shown in Figure 15.17. Use the scrollbar to look through the thumbnails.

6. When you find one you want, click it.

7. To download and embed the video, click **Insert**.

Click the clip you want to add

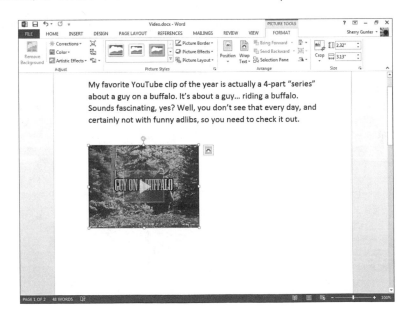

FIGURE 15.17

Look through the search results to find the video you want to use.

When the download is complete, Word inserts the video clip as a picture in your document, much like Figure 15.18, and displays the **Format** tab for working with the image. As always, you can resize and reposition the clip image area, if needed, or control the flow of text around the clip box.

FIGURE 15.18

Word downloads the clip and inserts it for you.

To play the clip, click the giant **Play** button in the center of the clip (see Figure 15.18). Another window opens, as shown in Figure 15.19, along with additional playback controls. Click the **Play** button again to start the clip. You can click the **Pause** button to pause the playback, or click the **Volume** button to adjust the sound. To exit the clip, click anywhere outside the window.

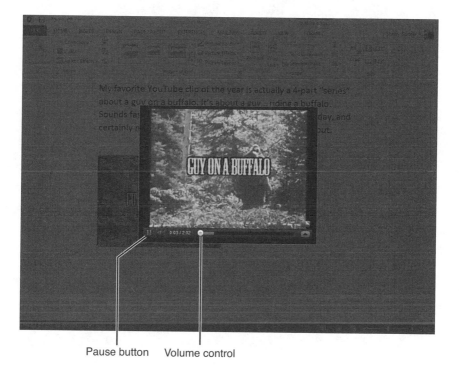

Pause button   Volume control

FIGURE 15.19

An embedded clip plays in its own special window.

To remove a clip you no longer want, select it and press **Delete**.

THE ABSOLUTE MINIMUM

Now you know enough about illustrating your documents with pictures and video clips to make your head spin. We covered a lot of information in this chapter, but it boils down to this:

- You can use your online connection to tap into a vast library of pictures on the Office.com site, including clip art and stock photos. To get things rolling, click the **Online Pictures** tool on the **Insert** tab.

- You can also use the **Online Pictures** tool to search for pictures on the Internet.

- Wait, there's more—you can also use the **Online Pictures** tool to download pictures from your SkyDrive account.

- You can insert pictures from any of your storage devices, including your hard drive, flash drive, memory card, or CD/DVD. Just click the **Pictures** button and locate the file.

- You can use the **Screenshot** tool to capture open program windows or take clippings from a screen.

- You can now embed video clips directly in your document and play them back without leaving Word.

IN THIS CHAPTER

- Control how text flows around your graphics.
- Give your graphics new direction by rotating and flipping them.
- Layer and group graphics.
- Add styles and borders to make graphics stand out.
- Discover an overwhelming number of special effects that you can assign to pictures.
- Edit your photos with Word's Adjust tools.

FINE-TUNING YOUR GRAPHICS

Now that you have some amazing graphics placed in your document—or at least you do if you read Chapters 14, "Adding Simple Graphic Elements," and 15, "Inserting Pictures and Videos"—it's time to fiddle with them a bit and make them even more amazing. Word has a plethora of formatting attributes you can assign to any of your visual elements. Whether it's a simple graphic or WordArt object, a clip art picture or photograph, you can add formatting such as borders, styles, and effects to give some added pizzazz. Not only that, but you can perform a variety of other techniques to change your artwork and give it a completely new look.

In this chapter, I show you a variety of techniques and attributes that might, in fact, knock your socks off—assuming you are wearing socks. For example, did you know you can layer graphic objects or crop and recolor a picture, or even remove its background? Ha—I didn't think so, but by the end of this chapter, you will know for sure. Get your graphics ready and follow along.

NOTE The term *graphic object* refers to any type of artwork you place in a document, including any shapes you draw (circles, lines, triangles, arrows, and so on), or WordArt object you insert, or text box you add. The term also covers picture files, photos, clip art, screenshots, and even the image of an embedded video clip. Graphic is an overarching term for all the visual, artsy-oriented things you add to a file. So when we talk about formatting graphic objects, now you know what it means.

Resizing, Positioning, and Wrapping Text Around Graphics

I realize you probably remember this from the previous two chapters, but in case you've slept since then, let's briefly go over how to position and resize your artwork again. Besides, you're going to need this information at your fingertips to do other things with the graphics coming up.

Anytime you click on a graphic object, it's selected and you can start performing edits on it. A few more things happen automatically when you click a graphic element:

- A new tab or set of tabs appears on the Ribbon, offering formatting controls and tools.
- A **Layout Options** icon appears next to the selected graphic.
- Selection handles surround the graphic.

Take a gander at Figure 16.1 to see all of these things in play.

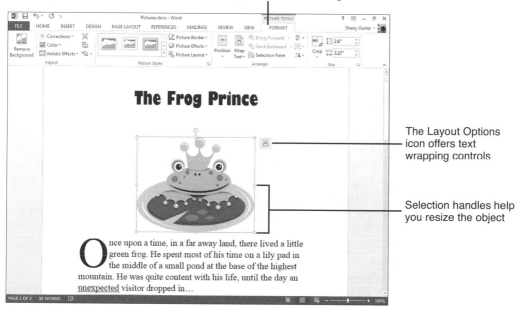

FIGURE 16.1

You can count on several things to happen onscreen every time you select a graphic, regardless of what type of graphic object it is.

Out of all of these things that happen when you select an object, you can use each of them to do something with positioning and resizing. Let's start with the most obvious one—the *selection handles*. Here's what you can do with them:

- Drag a corner handle—any corner—to resize the graphic in any direction you drag.

- Drag a top or bottom middle handle to increase or decrease the object's height, up or down.

- Drag a side middle handle to increase or decrease the object's width, left or right.

- The circular icon that sits at the top of a graphic is the rotation handle, and you can use it to rotate the graphic—more about this technique coming up later.

Figure 16.2 maps out what each of these handles can do for you.

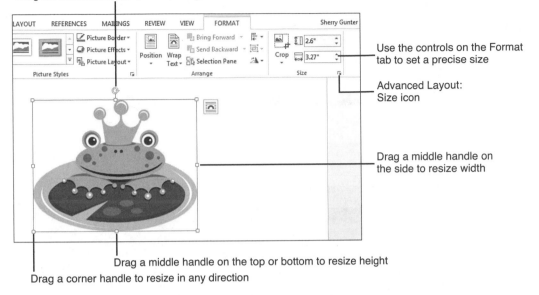

Drag the rotation handle to turn the object

Use the controls on the Format tab to set a precise size

Advanced Layout: Size icon

Drag a middle handle on the side to resize width

Drag a middle handle on the top or bottom to resize height

Drag a corner handle to resize in any direction

FIGURE 16.2

The easiest way to resize a graphic is to use the selection handles and drag it to a new size.

Word offers other sizing controls you can apply. If you click the Ribbon's Format tab (which appears only when you select a graphic object), you can find some exact sizing commands. Under the group of tools labeled **Size** sits a control for adjusting height and another for adjusting width (see Figure 16.2). You can click the spinner arrows to reset a value, or you can type a value directly into the appropriate box. The size settings are measured in inches, by the way.

If you would like to access some additional sizing controls, open the Layout dialog box to its **Size** tab, as shown in Figure 16.3. To find your way to this dialog box, click the **Advanced Layout: Size** icon in the bottom-right corner of the **Size** group of tools on the **Format** tab. You can also right-click the object and choose **Size and Position** from the pop-up menu, or click the **Layout Options** icon and choose **See more** command. All of these routes lead to the Layout dialog box.

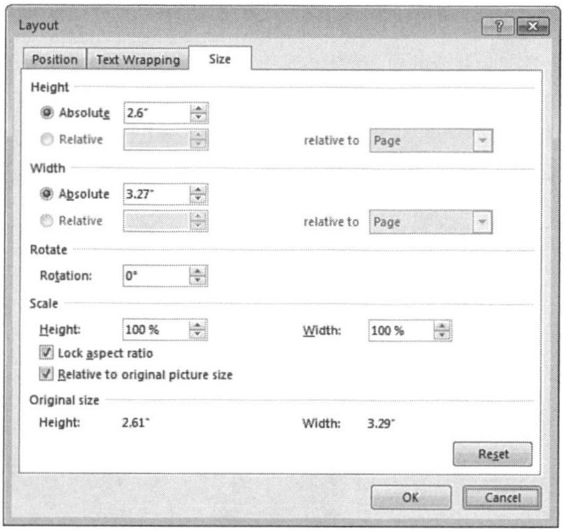

FIGURE 16.3

The Layout dialog box has controls for positioning, text wrapping, and size.

The Layout dialog box has some extra controls for resizing, such as unlocking the aspect ratio or scaling the size by a certain percentage. You can utilize this dialog box any time you need some precision in your sizing tasks.

Let's move on to positioning. Most of the time when you insert an object, it appears where the cursor was last located in the document. Often you'll need to adjust the position, especially to make the object work well with the document layout. The natural thing to do is just drag the object where you want it. When you move the mouse pointer over a selected graphic, a four-sided arrow pointer appears. When you see this icon, you know it's safe to start dragging (see Figure 16.4).

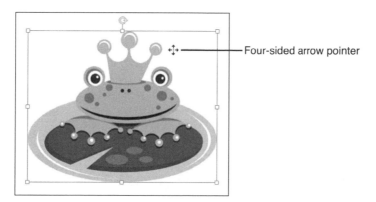

Four-sided arrow pointer

FIGURE 16.4

One way to move a graphic is to just drag it and drop it.

Word's new *alignment guides* can help you position objects on a page. As you drag, the green horizontal or vertical lines show you how the object lines up with other page elements, as shown in Figure 16.5, as well as margins. The alignment guides can really help you line up elements fast, so keep an eye out for them as you drag things around your page.

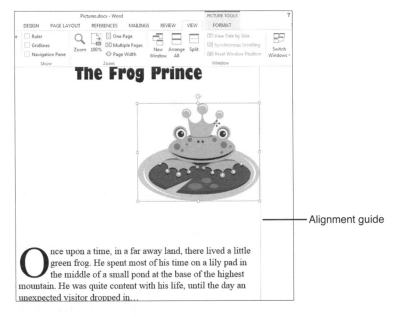

Alignment guide

FIGURE 16.5

Use the alignment guides to help you position objects on a page.

When you reposition a graphic, the next thing you have to contend with is the way in which text flows around the object. Called *text wrapping*, you can choose between several options:

- **In Line with Text**   The graphic sits on the same baseline as the adjacent text. This is typically the default setting.

- **Square**   Text flows around the object and treats it as a square, with a little breathing room between the text and the object on all four sides.

- **Tight**   The text flow with this option hugs the object on all sides, nice and tight, with little space between the text and the object.

- **Through**   This option flows the text directly "through" the object, from one side to the next. The lines of text only break the flow to accommodate the object, then pick up again on the other side of the object as if nothing had impeded it.

- **Top and Bottom**   Text flows at the top and bottom of the object, but not left or right of the object. (Note that text might appear beside the object if you're using a multi-column layout.)

- **Behind Text**   Flows text directly behind the object; looks like you just plopped the graphic right on top of the text.

- **In Front of Text**   Flows text directly on top of the object, thus making the object more of a background behind the text.

 TIP   If you ever run into trouble trying to move a graphic object around on a page, try changing its text wrapping setting. Swapping to **Tight** text wrapping, for example, allows the object to move around more freely.

Figure 16.6 shows an example of wrapping that flows behind the text. Notice how legibility is going to be a big issue with this setting. But if my graphic was nearly transparent or faded out, it might work. You can click the **Layout Options** icon (upper-right corner of the selected object) to access a quick menu of text wrapping options, as shown in Figure 16.6. Just click the wrapping option you want to assign. To close the options menu, click its **Close** button. Changing text color can also make it more readable; white text on a faded print can sometimes look better than black, for example.

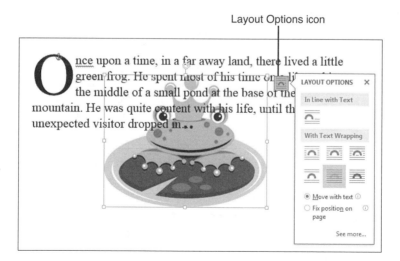

FIGURE 16.6

The Layout Options icon is a quick way to assign a text wrapping option.

You can also find a drop-down menu of text wrapping options on the **Picture Tools Format** tab, shown in Figure 16.7. Click the **Format** tab and click the **Wrap Text** button to display the menu. Figure 16.7 shows text wrapping at the top and bottom of the graphic object.

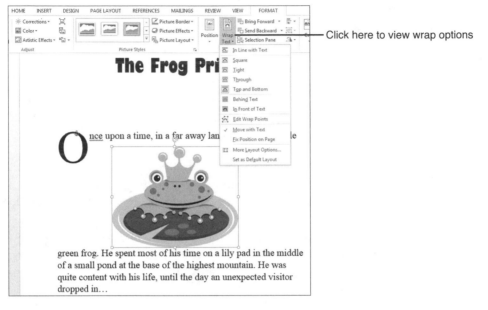

Click here to view wrap options

FIGURE 16.7

Or you can use the Format tab to set a wrap option.

 TIP Thankfully, the icons associated with each wrap text command give a visual clue about the effect they assign to the text flow, so look carefully at the icon graphic to see what the effect on your text will be when applied.

If you're looking for some additional controls for text wrapping, then look no further than the **Layout** dialog box's **Text Wrapping** tab, shown in Figure 16.8. You can use the settings in this box to control the exact distance of text from the graphic object (measured in inches). You can also find a few more wrapping options, such as flowing text only on certain sides of the selected object.

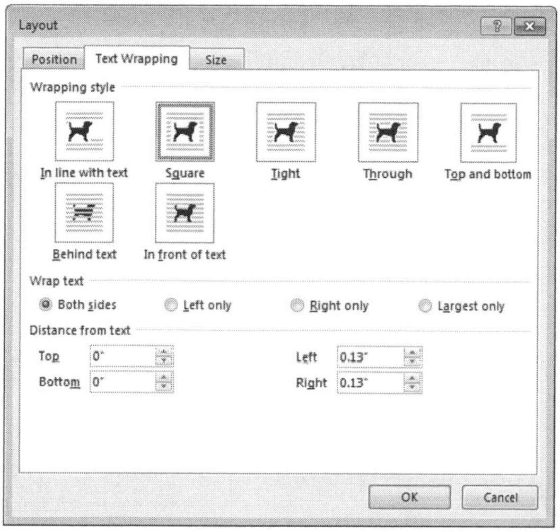

FIGURE 16.8

Open the Layout dialog box for more text wrapping controls.

To display the dialog box, click the **More Layout Options** command at the bottom of the **Wrap Text drop**-down menu (refer to Figure 16.7), or click the **See more** command at the bottom of the **Layout Options** menu (refer to Figure 16.6).

Oh, and one more method to use, you can always count on a shortcut menu to offer a route to common commands; right-click the object and click **Wrap Text** and choose a text wrap option to apply.

 TIP As long as we're talking about positioning, don't forget about the alignment commands. You can align objects on the page just like you align text. You can actually use the text alignment controls (found on the **Home** tab), to assign an alignment setting to an object or you can click the **Align Objects** drop-down arrow on the **Format** tab. The **Align Objects** menu offers all the alignment options in one convenient spot.

Rotating and Flipping Objects

Sometimes you just need to make a different kind of positioning adjustment to a graphic—like flipping it to face the other direction or rotating it slightly to fit your document layout better. You can both flip and rotate graphic elements, and doing either takes little effort.

To flip a selected object, click the **Format** tab and click the **Rotate Objects** drop-down arrow, shown in Figure 16.9. Click either **Flip Vertical** or **Flip Horizontal**.

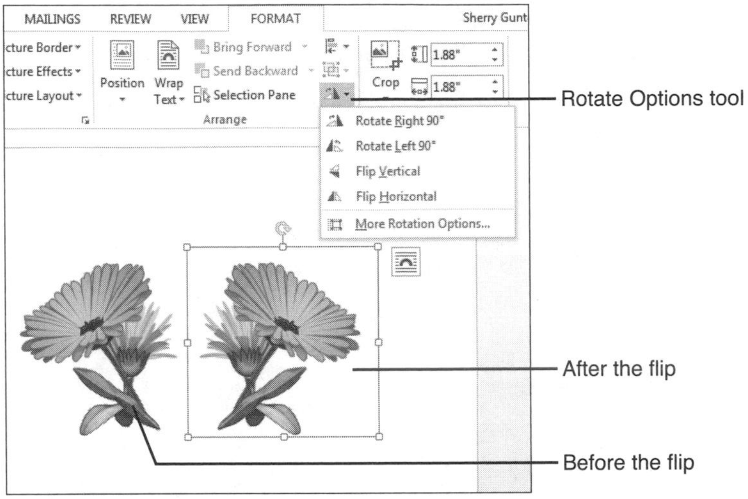

FIGURE 16.9

Flip an object with a click of a Flip command.

 TIP You don't have enough energy to display the **Rotate Objects** menu? Then just drag a middle side selection handle to the opposite edge of the object to flip the graphic. To flip it the other direction, drag the middle top or bottom selection handle and drag it to the opposite edge.

If you thought flipping was cool, you might even flip out over the rotation tool, or maybe turn head over heels? Never mind the puns, just keep reading. You can rotate a graphic in either direction and control how much it rotates. For a quick rotation, use the selected graphic's rotation handle, pointed out in Figure 16.10. Simply drag the handle in either direction to start rotating the object.

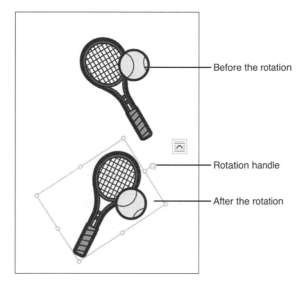

FIGURE 16.10

Drag the rotation handle to rotate an object.

You can also summon the **Rotate Objects** menu on the **Format** tab and choose a rotation setting, as shown in Figure 16.11. Click the **Rotate Objects** drop-down arrow and choose to rotate the object left or right.

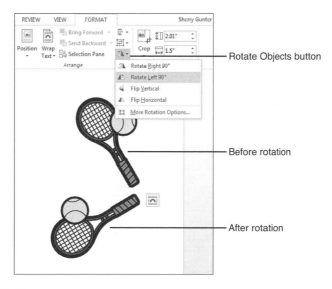

FIGURE 16.11

You can also use the Format tab to assign a quick left or right rotation.

For even more rotation controls, you can open the **Layout** dialog box, shown in Figure 16.12. To open the dialog box, click the **More Rotation Options** command on the **Rotate Object** menu (see Figure 16.11) or right-click the object and click **Size and Position**. Using the **Rotation** setting in the dialog box, you can click the spinner arrows to set an exact value, or type it directly into the box. Negative values rotate to the left, positive values rotate to the right. When you've set the rotation the way you want, click **OK** to apply it.

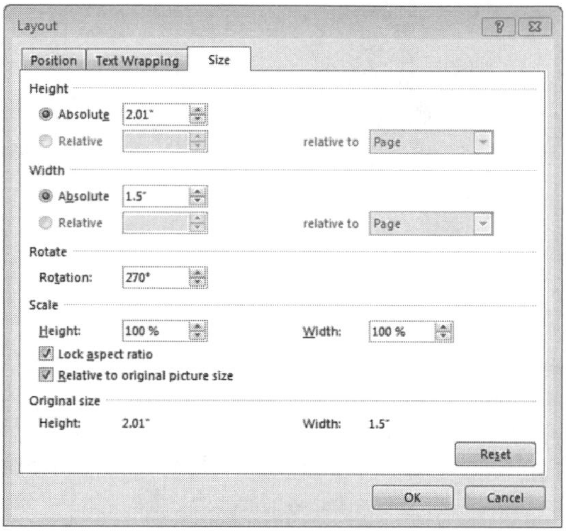

FIGURE 16.12

The Layout dialog box also has a rotation setting.

> **TIP** If you don't like all the formatting you've applied to a graphic, you can reset it to its original state. Click the **Reset Picture** drop-down arrow on the **Format** tab and click **Reset Picture & Size**.

Layering and Grouping Objects

You can create different arrangements of graphic elements in a document, and you can group different objects together to move them or apply formatting to all of them at once. Using these techniques, you can create new objects out of existing graphics. For example, you might layer a WordArt object over a shape object to create a logo, then group the two elements together as one. You might place a text box on top of a photo to use as a special caption, or layer one picture over another to start building a collage. There's all kinds of ways you can stack objects on top of each other in a layering effect. Figure 16.13 shows an example of a WordArt object stacked on top of a shape.

FIGURE 16.13

Stacking shapes, text boxes, and pictures can create some interesting artwork in your documents.

I can easily turn the two layered objects shown in Figure 16.13 into a single graphic using Word's grouping feature. Rather than move each object independently, I can group them and move them about the document as one object. This technique can really come in handy when you work with multiple objects in a document. First things first, though—let's start with layering.

Layering Objects

Layering involves changing an object's position backward or forward in a stack. Depending on how many objects you use, several positions can be in the stack: back of the layer, middle of the layer, top of the layer, and so on. To layer an object, drag it on top of another object. To see what I mean by stacking, take a look at Figure 16.14—I've drawn three shapes and stacked them on top of each other. The hexagon is on the top of the stack, which is called the *front* in layering lingo, and the triangle is on the bottom of the stack, which is called the *back* in layering lingo. The circle is between the two.

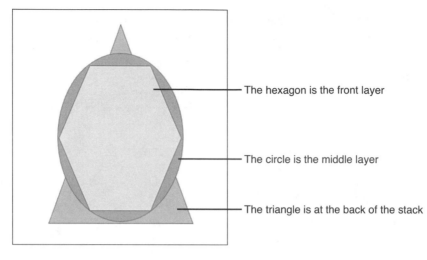

The hexagon is the front layer

The circle is the middle layer

The triangle is at the back of the stack

FIGURE 16.14

Here's an example of three layered shapes.

Now take a look at Figure 16.15 to see what happened when I changed the layering order. The triangle is now at the front, the circle is in the back, and the hexagon is in the middle. This should give you some idea how you can control positioning of objects to make them interact with each other in your document.

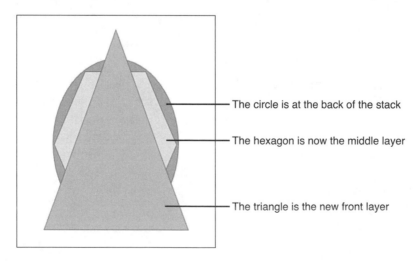

The circle is at the back of the stack

The hexagon is now the middle layer

The triangle is the new front layer

FIGURE 16.15

Here's how the shapes look when I change the order of layers.

One of the easiest ways to change an object's layer order is to use the right-click shortcut menu, shown in Figure 16.16. To change an object's placement in a stack, try one of these methods:

- To move the object to the front layer, right-click the object and choose **Bring to Front**, **Bring to Front**. (This command's so nice, they used it twice.)

- To move the object to the back layer, right-click the object and choose **Send to Back**, **Send to Back**.

- To bring the object forward one level, right-click the object, click the **Bring to Front** arrow, and then click **Bring Forward**.

- To send the object back a level, right-click the object, click the **Send to Back** arrow, and then click **Send Backward**.

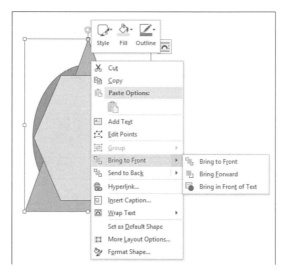

FIGURE 16.16

For quick reordering, use the right-click method and choose layering commands from the shortcut menu.

You can also find the layering commands on the Ribbon's **Format** tab. Click the **Bring Forward** drop-down arrow to specify a forward action. Click the **Send Backward** drop-down arrow to specify a backward action (see Figure 16.17).

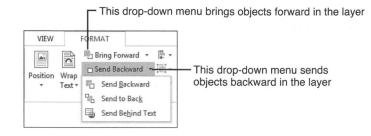

FIGURE 16.17

Look for layering controls in the Arrange group of tools on the Format tab.

If you ever run into trouble selecting items in the stack, you can display the **Selection Pane** to help you. Click the **Selection Pane** button on the **Format** tab, then click the object you want to select (see Figure 16.18). Word immediately surrounds it with selection handles and you can specify another layer for the object or apply any other formatting attributes.

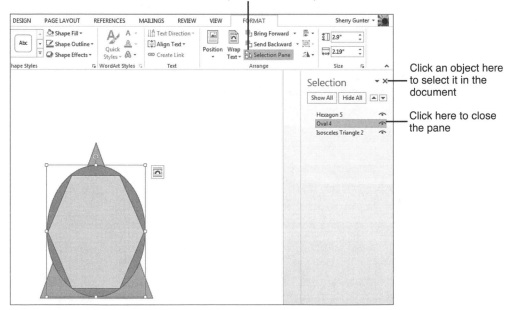

FIGURE 16.18

When working with several different objects in a layer, the Selection pane can help you select items in a stack.

You can close the **Selection** pane when you no longer need it. Click its **Close** button or click the **Selection Pane** button on the **Format** tab again.

Grouping Objects

You can use Word's grouping feature to gather multiple objects into one moveable, formattable unit. You might, for example, group several shapes together to apply the same formatting attributes to all of them at once to save yourself some steps. Or you might want to group two pictures together to move them to the end of a document in one fell swoop. Grouping is a real timesaver for working with multiple elements in Word.

You can choose to group objects for just one task and then ungroup them again, or you can keep them grouped together, such as components you combine to make a logo. To group objects, you first have to select them. After you've selected what you want, you can apply the **Group** command. Follow these steps:

1. Click the first object you want to select, then press and hold the **Ctrl** key while clicking the remaining objects you want to group (notice each selected object has its own selection border and handles, as shown in Figure 16.19).

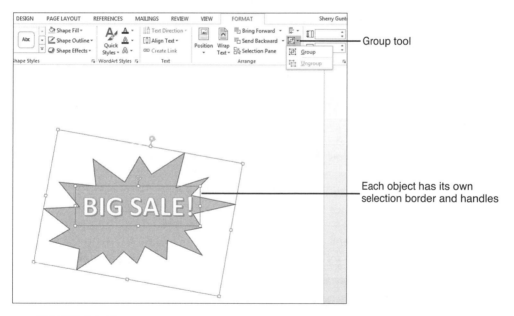

FIGURE 16.19

To group objects, start by selecting which ones you want to include in the group.

2. Click the **Format** tab.
3. Click **Group Objects**.
4. Click **Group**.

Word groups your objects and surrounds them with a selection border and handles, as shown in Figure 16.20.

FIGURE 16.20

After assigning the Group command, all the objects are grouped as a unit.

To ungroup the group, select it and click the **Group Objects** button and choose **Ungroup**.

 TIP You can also right-click the selected objects and click **Group** and **Group** or **Ungroup**.

Adding Picture Styles and Borders

Microsoft Word has a surprising amount of graphic-editing tools for a word-processing program, but that's a good thing. Visuals are often a crucial part of conveying your text's message, so being able to alter them to suit your message is an important aspect of making your document look its best. One such modifying feature well worth checking out is Word's **Picture Styles** gallery.

The gallery, shown in Figure 16.21, displays preset styles you can apply to clip art illustrations and photographs. Picture styles, much like Word's built-in styles for shapes and WordArt objects, offer a variety of looks, such as borders, shading, shadows, and an assortment of combinations. You'll want to sample each one to see what it looks like applied to your selected image.

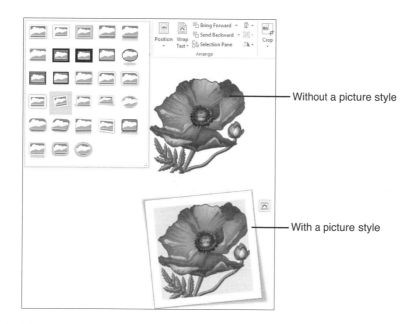

Without a picture style

With a picture style

FIGURE 16.21

Dress up your pictures by applying picture styles.

To assign a picture style, follow these steps:

1. Select the picture you want to edit.
2. Click the **Format** tab.
3. Click a picture style from the **Picture Styles** gallery (see Figure 16.22).

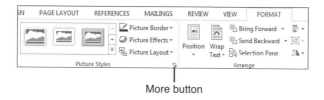

More button

FIGURE 16.22

Find the Picture Styles gallery on the Format tab.

Word immediately assigns the style. To view all the styles at a glance, click the **More** button in the corner of the gallery. To preview a style, move the mouse pointer over the style and check it out as it temporarily transforms your selected image (it helps to move the document page so you can see the full gallery as well as the picture).

NOTE The **Picture Styles** and **Picture Border** tools only work with pictures—clip art illustrations or photos. If you want to add a style to a shape, text box, or WordArt object, they have their own styles to apply. For example, when you select a shape, the **Shape Styles** gallery appears on the **Format** toolbar and you can use it to change the shape's style.

Although the **Picture Styles** gallery has quite a few borders to choose from, you might prefer to add a straight-up, simple border to your picture. You can use the **Picture Border** tool to do this. From the **Format** tab, click the **Picture Border** drop-down arrow and choose a color for the border. If you want to assign a different line thickness or dash style, you can do that, too. Just click the submenu and make your choice. Word immediately applies it to the picture, as shown in Figure 16.23.

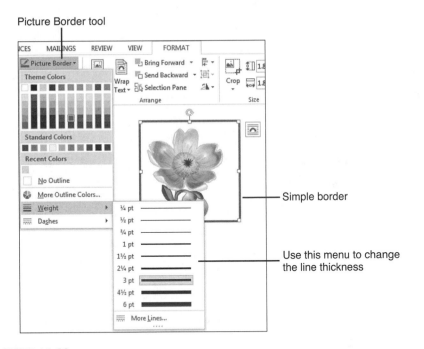

FIGURE 16.23

Add a simple border using the Picture Border tool.

To remove a border, select the picture, reopen the **Picture Border** palette, and choose **No Outline**.

Adding Flourishes with Effects

If you're in an especially artistic mood, consider perusing the two effects groups of formatting attributes in Word. You'll find them geared toward making more of your basic shapes, illustrations, and photos by way of preset design flourishes. One group, called *Artistic Effects*, works only with illustrations and photos. The other group, plain old *Effects*, work with all the graphic elements, including shapes and WordArt. Each different effect you apply changes the appearance of the selected object in one way or another. You'll definitely need to experiment with these to see what kind of transformations you can make to your own graphics.

Assigning Effects

All the shapes, WordArt, photos, and clip art can dip into a group of settings called *Effects* to change the appearance of the object. If you're working with a shape, for example, they're labeled **Shape Effects**. If you're working with WordArt, they're called **Text Effects**. If you're working with other image types, such as illustrations or photographs you inserted, they're called **Picture Effects**. Despite the slight differences in naming, the effects are all the same and they break down into the following categories:

- **Shadow** Adds a shadow to the graphic, including outer and inner shadows as well as perspectives.

- **Reflection** Creates a reflection of the graphic.

- **Glow** Adds a glowing color of your choice around the graphic.

- **Soft Edges** Creates fuzzy edges around the graphic.

- **Bevel** Adds beveled angles or edges to a graphic.

- **3-D Rotation** Assigns a 3-D rotation effect to a graphic, giving it the appearance of depth.

Figure 16.24 shows an example of a glow effect added to a clip art illustration. Within each category are subcategories and variations to choose from. As you can see in Figure 16.24, you can access the effects through the **Picture Effects** button on the **Format** tab for pictures. If you're formatting a shape, look for the **Shape Effects** button, and if you're formatting WordArt, use the **Text Effects** button. All of these tools lead to the same controls.

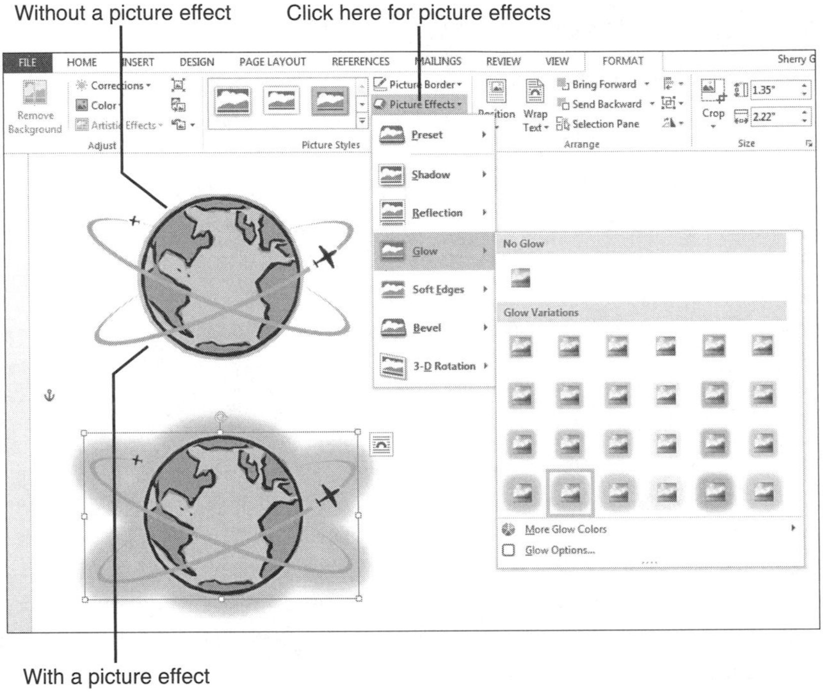

Without a picture effect

Click here for picture effects

With a picture effect

FIGURE 16.24

Look for the effects button on the Format tab for the type of graphic you're editing.

You also have the option of tweaking the effect further using the **Format** pane, shown in Figure 16.25. Again, there's a slight naming difference for this pane depending on what type of graphic you're editing. If it's a picture, it's called the **Format Picture** pane; if it's a shape, it's the **Format Shape** pane. To open the pane, click the **Format** icon in the corner of the **Picture Styles**, **Shape Styles**, or **WordArt Styles** groups of tools. You can also get there via the shortcut menu; right-click over the object and choose **Format Shape** or **Format Picture**. After the pane is open, click the **Effects** icon at the top of the pane (if it's not already selected by default).

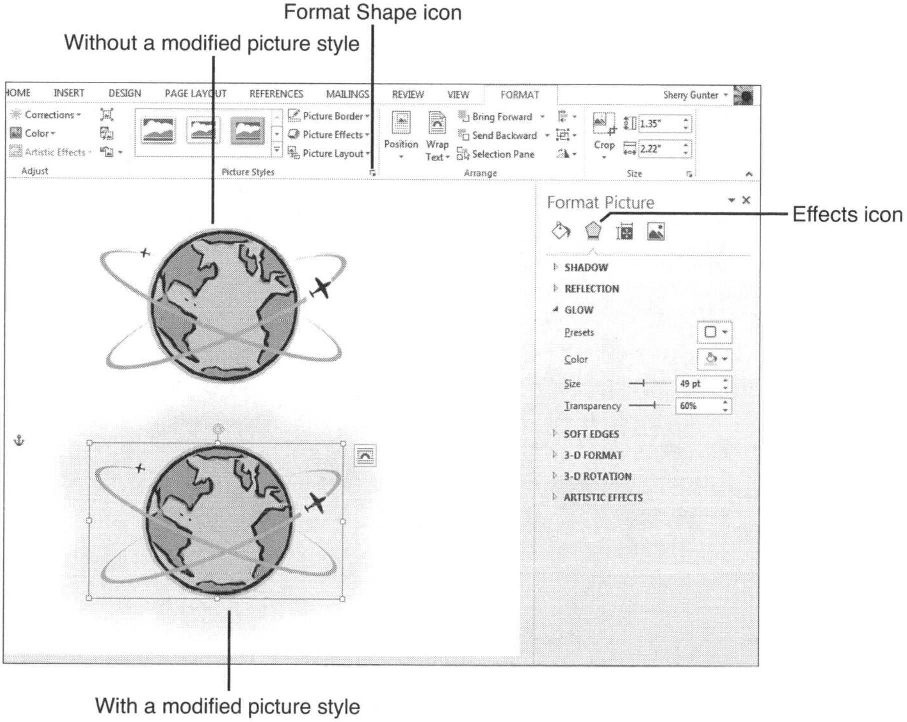

FIGURE 16.25

Use the Format pane to further modify an effect.

Using the **Format** pane, you can make adjustments to individual elements that make up the effect. For example, in Figure 16.25, the glow effect color is changed and the size of the glow increased. Different effects offer different settings, so tweak them to your heart's delight.

Applying Artistic Effects to Pictures

If you liked the regular special effects, wait till you see the artistic ones. You can turn a photo into a mosaic painting, a black and white pencil sketch, or a photocopy. Using the **Artistic Effects** gallery, shown in Figure 16.26, you can pretend you're your own Monet. The only caveat is that they're applicable to pictures, not shapes or WordArt. On the plus side, pictures include any artwork you insert from other sources, such as illustrations, photo files, clip art, and so forth.

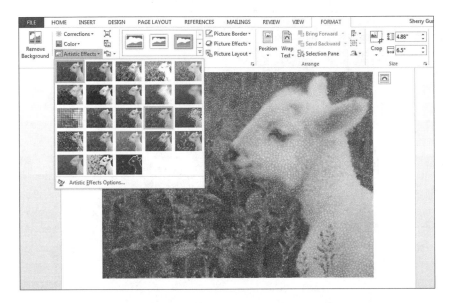

FIGURE 16.26

You can apply some really creative touches using Word's Artistic Effects.

Select your intended artwork and click the **Format** tab's **Artistic Effects** button, then choose an effect from the gallery. Remember, you can preview the effect on the intended graphic simply by moving your mouse over each one in the gallery. When you find the right one, click it and Word assigns it to the picture.

Cropping Pictures

Say you have the perfect picture to illustrate your Word document, but you need to edit out the telephone pole off to the side, or the picture is great but too big for the spot you want to place it. You can employ the cropping tool to trim the picture, removing the distracting telephone pole. Figure 16.27 shows a before and after crop effect, just to give you an idea of how it works.

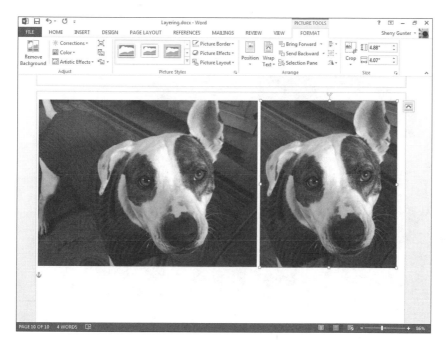

FIGURE 16.27

You can crop pictures using Word's cropping tool.

Ready to try your own cropping? Follow these steps:

1. Select the picture you want to crop.

2. Click the **Format** tab.

3. Click the **Crop** drop-down arrow (see Figure 16.28).

4. Click **Crop**.

5. Drag a crop handle to the desired cropping edge (see Figure 16.29). To crop equally from both sides, press the **Ctrl** key while dragging a center crop handle. To crop all four sides, press **Ctrl** while dragging a corner cropping handle.

6. Continue cropping as many edges as needed.

7. Click the **Crop** button again or press **Esc**, and Word applies the new settings.

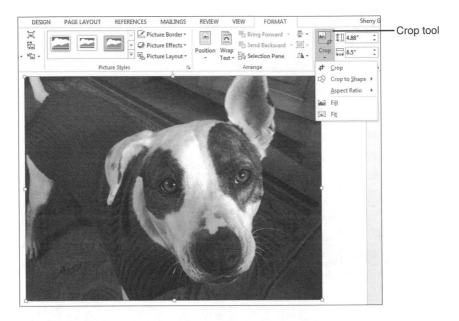

FIGURE 16.28

Find the Crop button on the Format tab.

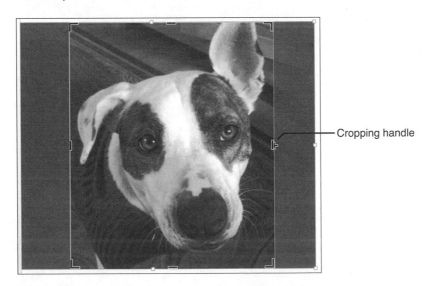

FIGURE 16.29

Drag a cropping handle to crop a side of the picture.

You can also access the cropping tool by right-clicking the picture and clicking the **Crop** button from the pop-up toolbar.

TIP   Here's a cool trick—you can crop out a picture to a shape. Click the **Crop** drop-down arrow and click **Crop to Shape**, then choose the shape from the **Shapes** gallery. Word immediately crops out the picture, and the remainder takes the shape of the shape you picked.

 TIP   If your cropping needs to comply with a certain picture frame dimension, you can apply a common aspect ratio. Click the **Crop** drop-down arrow, click **Aspect Ratio**, and choose a setting. If your picture needs to fill a shape's height or width, apply the **Fill** or **Fit** commands from the same drop-down menu.

Adjusting Pictures

You can find a few more picture editing tools under the **Adjust** group of tools on the **Format** tab. These editing tools work on any type of picture, including photographs. For example, you can make color corrections (helpful for digital photographs), tweak brightness and contrast, compress pictures, and even remove a background.

Correcting Picture Problems

Granted, we're not all professional photographers, but even they need to fix photos from time to time. Word has a few picture correcting tricks you can apply in a pinch. You can sharpen up a not-so-focused photo or make adjustments to the overall brightness and contrast.

With the **Format** tab displayed, click the **Corrections** drop-down arrow to view the gallery (see Figure 16.30). To sharpen a picture, choose from among the **Sharpen/Soften** settings. To adjust the contrast or brightness, try a selection from the **Brightness/Contrast** picks. As always, you can hover over a gallery setting and see what effect it has before actually applying it to the photo. When you find an adjustment you want to apply, click it.

Corrections drop-down arrow

FIGURE 16.30

You can apply a few photo corrections to a picture with a little help from the Corrections gallery.

You can make further adjustments to a correction using the **Format Picture** pane. Using slider bars and spinner arrows, you can make more adjustments as needed. To display the pane, click the **Artistic Effects Options** command at the bottom of the **Corrections** gallery.

Tweaking Colors

Does your photo suffer from dullness, or do you need to turn it into a black-and-white image for your particular publication? You can make adjustments to the color using the **Color** gallery, shown in Figure 16.31. From the **Format** tab, click the **Color** drop-down arrow to open the gallery. You can choose from among the saturation (intensifies or de-intensifies color), color tone (adjusts color temperature), or recolor (changes the image's color scale) settings.

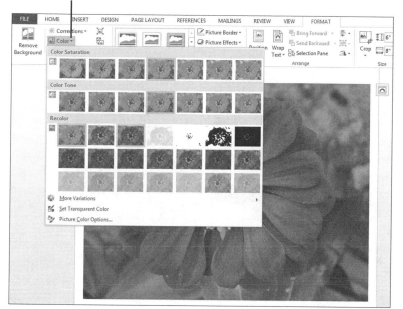

FIGURE 16.31

Tweak picture color with the Color gallery.

As with picture corrections (see the previous section), you can make further adjustments to whatever color setting you applied with the options found in the **Format Picture** pane (click the **Picture Color Options** command at the bottom of the **Color** gallery to open the pane). Using slider bars and spinner arrows, you can make more adjustments as needed.

TIP You can activate the **Compress Pictures** tool to compress a picture and specify the type of output required for the picture quality.

Removing Backgrounds

Okay, I've saved the best for last. I love the tool I'm about to show you. It's the **Remove Background** tool and you can use it to take away the background of a picture. You have to see it to believe it. Figure 16.32 shows a regular picture of a flower, and right next to it is the same picture with the background removed. Cool, right?

Remove Background tool

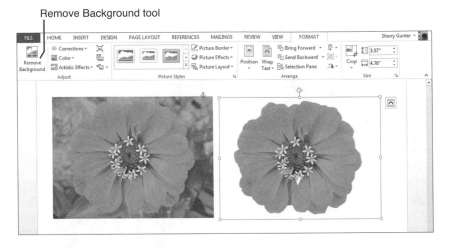

FIGURE 16.32

You can remove a picture's background and end up with just the subject.

This works best on photos in which it's pretty easy to see the main subject. Want to try it yourself? Select your picture, click the **Format** tab, and click the **Remove Background** button (see Figure 16.33). The picture turns purple around the edges, and Word tries to guess what the subject is, leaving it clear. You can help it out by dragging the handles to include any parts of the subject that might appear cut off, yet you want to include in the picture.

Next, click the **Mark Areas to Remove** button on the **Background Removal** tab. Depending on your picture, you might prefer to mark the areas to keep instead of the parts to remove, and if so, click the **Mark Areas to Keep** button.

The mouse pointer becomes a pencil icon. Click the areas on the picture you want to remove. You might need to click in several spots, such as corners. When you finish, click the **Keep Changes** button to return to the document and see your results.

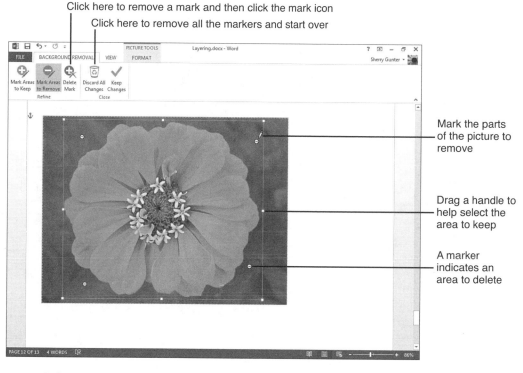

FIGURE 16.33

You can control exactly what parts of the picture are removed.

It might take a little practice to get it right, but the **Background Removal** tool might prove useful in helping you create artwork to flow with and around the document text.

THE ABSOLUTE MINIMUM

Did you ever imagine so many graphic-editing tools were available in a word-processing program? Now you know what to do with them all. Everything you need is on the **Format** tab or the **Format** pane. In this chapter, you learned the following points about fine-tuning graphic objects:

- The easiest way to resize and position a picture is to interact with it directly on the page; drag selection handles to resize, and drag the whole graphic to move it.

- You can rotate and flip graphic objects to change their appearance ever so slightly.

- You can layer objects to create new objects, such as a logo, and then you can group objects to move them as one unit.

- Styles and borders are a great way to instantly set off a picture.

- You can add general effects to shapes, WordArt, clip art, and photos, such as shadows, glows, and reflections.

- You can add picture effects, such as painterly styles, to photos and clip art.

- You can crop pictures to remove unwanted areas.

- Word even has some more complex photo-editing controls you can assign to improve your pictures.

IN THIS CHAPTER

- Learn how to plot out your document structure using Word's Outline view.

- Make yourself look scholarly by adding footnotes and endnotes, cross-references, and captions.

- See how to instantly insert a table of contents at the front of your document and an index at the back.

- Take advantage of the Navigation pane to move around your long document.

TOOLS FOR LONGER DOCUMENTS

Word's versatility kicks into high gear when you create long documents. Unless you're a professional blurb writer and your documents are destined to always be one-page in length or less, then you might be interested to know about all the features Word offers for longer types of documents. If you use Microsoft Word to write research papers, term papers, legal contracts, manuscripts, and other lengthy tomes, you can take advantage of a wide variety of tools for outlining, inserting footnotes, endnotes, captions, indexes, cross-references, and so on. The **References** tab is the place to look for most of these features, and in this chapter, how to put several of these tools to work.

Structuring Documents with Outline View

Often an overlooked feature in Word, Outline view can help you construct documents based on a hierarchy of headings, subheadings, and body content. Use Outline view when you want to focus on the document's structure rather than its formatting. When you're crafting any type of document that requires you to group ideas or arrange thoughts in a hierarchical fashion (which means top to bottom with levels of importance), switch over to Outline view and get busy organizing your thoughts. You can assign and change heading levels (such as Heading 1, Heading 2, and so on) as needed as your document develops. This hierarchical framework is incredibly practical for planning out elements that go into your document, whether you're formulating a letter or list or plotting a full-blown script for the next big television series (good luck with that, by the way).

Let's say you're working on a particularly lengthy document, like a thesis, report, or dissertation. Chances are you're going to use headings and subheadings throughout to plan and develop your topic and coverage. You might start with a rough outline of all the main points you want to make, so your outline might look like Figure 17.1. Then within each of those main points you'll add subtopics, much like you see in Figure 17.2. Within each subheading, you'll start adding content. You can do all of this in Word using Outline view.

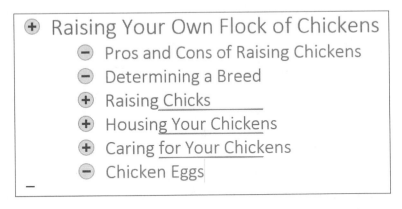

FIGURE 17.1

An outline in Outline view showing the headings I plan on writing about for my report.

FIGURE 17.2

Here's the same outline, but with subheadings developing under each main topic point.

At first glance you might think "Hey, I can do that in Word without using a special view," in which case you would be right. But you're overlooking something. When you use Outline view, you're tapping into some powerful tools to help you work with your outline—namely the **Outlining** tab, shown in Figure 17.3. This tab offers tools to help you promote and demote items in the hierarchy with a click, and expand and collapse groups so you can focus on important points. It also offers a menu of heading levels you can select from as you build the document.

To turn on the Outline view, click the **View** tab on the Ribbon, then click the **Outline** button (located in the **Views** group of tools). Word displays the **Outlining** tab, and the text you type into the document is organized into levels, starting with a default level until you specify another. Notice in Figure 17.3 that the headings and subheadings have icons in front of the text. A plus sign indicates subheadings exist within that heading level, and a minus sign indicates no subheadings.

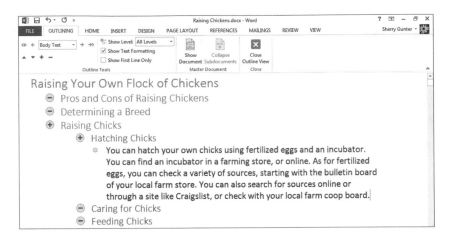

FIGURE 17.3

The Outlining tab offers a variety of tools to help you build and work with your outline.

You can click in the document and start typing; press the **Enter** key to start a new topic. You can use the following tools to make changes to the outline:

- To assign a heading level, click the line of text, click the **Outline Level** drop-down menu, shown in Figure 17.4, and choose a level.

- To promote text one level, click the **Promote** button.

- To promote text to heading 1, click the **Promote to Heading 1** button.

- To demote text one level, click the **Demote** button.

- To demote text to body text, click the **Demote to Body Text** button.

- To move a topic up in the hierarchy, click the **Move Up** button (see Figure 17.5).

- To move a topic downward in the hierarchy, click the **Move Down** button.

- To expand a group to view all the subpoints and body content, click the **Expand** button.

- To collapse a group and just view its main heading level, click the **Collapse** button.

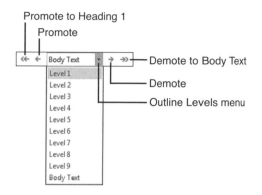

FIGURE 17.4

Assign levels with the Outline Levels menu.

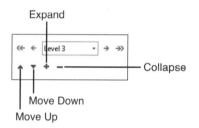

FIGURE 17.5

Use the Outlining tools to move your document points around.

 TIP Many people are confused by Word's heading styles and the idea of promoting/demoting levels, but it's a simple system: The lower the heading *number*, the higher the *ranking* of that heading. So Heading 1 style is applied to the most important topics you address in your document. (Think of them as "number one points to get across to my audience.") Apply Heading 2 styles to subtopics within your Heading 1 topics, Heading 3 styles to issues that are subordinate to your Heading 2 topics, and so on. Word has nine heading levels you can apply to the various topics and sections in your document to organize its structure.

You can drag and drop lines of text in your document to change their positioning in the hierarchy. You can also choose to view only certain levels in your document, which simplifies reviewing the overall structure and organizing the outline. For example, maybe you need to print out a copy of the main points of your report without all the subheadings and body content. You can use the **Show Levels** drop-down menu, shown in Figure 17.6, to choose to view all the Level 2 text, for example.

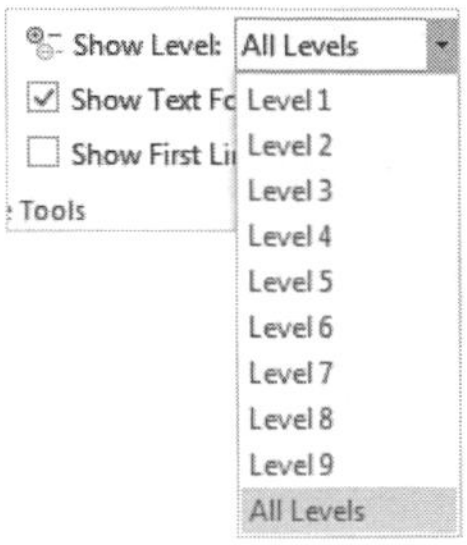

FIGURE 17.6

Control what levels appear in the document view using this menu.

You can use the **Show Text Formatting** check box to show or hide formatting. Click the **Show First Line Only** check box to reveal only the first line of body text and not the whole paragraph of body text. This might come in handy when reviewing a longer outline.

After you've finalized your document's structure in Outline view, you can switch over to Print Layout view and make it look nice with formatting attributes. To close Outline view, click the **Close Outline View** button. This returns you to Word and the outline appears as normal text—with all the proper headings and levels assigned, of course.

WHO'S THE MASTER OF THIS DOCUMENT?

Did you notice the group of tools on the **Outlining** tab labeled **Master Document**? These tools are designed to help you work with really long documents that are composed of multiple parts, such as chapters. For example, if you are working on a multi-chapter book that's hundreds of pages long, you can break out each chapter on its own; when you're ready to combine all the chapters again, use the **Master Document** tool to bring all the parts together for a final product.

To utilize this tool, you'll need to start with a master document, which is sort of the home base for all the parts you're going to assemble. Then using the **Outlining** tab in Outline view, click the **Show Document** button to reveal more of the associated commands. You can use the **Create** button to start a brand-new subdocument, or you can use the **Insert** button to insert an existing document as a subdocument. Word automatically assigns filenames to your subdocuments based on their headings and saves them as separate files that you can open from the master document.

That's pretty much the gist of the feature, but if it sounds like something that fits one of your Word projects, you can read more about it through Word's help files.

Inserting Footnotes and Endnotes

If you're working with the type of document that requires resource notations—extra explanations or comments in addition to the text, or other references—you can insert footnotes and endnotes. A *footnote* is an explanatory flagged note inserted at the bottom of a page to cite a source. *Endnotes* appear at the end of a section or at the end of a document rather than at the bottom of a page. You can find buttons for adding footnotes, endnotes, and other reference features on the Ribbon's **References** tab, shown in Figure 17.7.

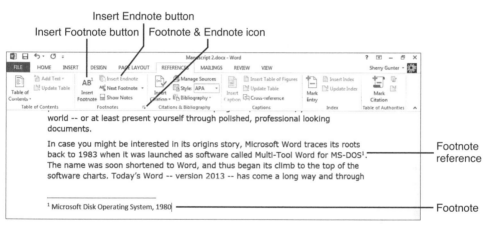

FIGURE 17.7

Find footnote and endnote tools on the References tab.

To insert a footnote or endnote, use these steps:

1. Click where you want to add the numeral or symbol indicating a footnote or endnote.

2. Click the **References** tab on the Ribbon.

3. Click **Insert Footnote** or **Insert Endnote**.

4. Word inserts a superscripted reference mark to flag the note.

5. Type your footnote or endnote text at the bottom of the page or section. As you keep adding footnotes or endnotes throughout your document, Word keeps track of the sequencing for you and continues the numbering automatically. To customize how the footnotes and endnotes appear, including what type of numbering format is used (such as Arabic numbers or Roman numerals), open the **Footnote and Endnote** dialog box shown in Figure 17.8. To display the dialog box, click the **Footnote & Endnote** icon in the corner of the **Footnotes** group of tools on the **References** tab. You can also right-click a footnote or endnote and choose **Note Options** to open the dialog box.

FIGURE 17.8

The Footnote and Endnote dialog box has customizing options you can apply.

The dialog box offers several ways to customize your notes. For example, to control where on the page the footnote or endnote should appear, click the corresponding location drop-down arrow and choose a placement. To change the number format, click the **Number** format drop-down arrow and choose the format you want. To control the sequence of numbering, such as continuing the sequence throughout the whole document or just within a particular section, click the **Numbering** drop-down arrow and choose an option. You can also insert a custom mark or symbol to use in place of a superscripted number. After you make your changes to the customizing options, click **Apply**.

 TIP The cool thing about using Word's automatic footnote/endnote numbering is that if you move the text containing the note, Word automatically fixes the numbering for you.

To work with footnotes or endnotes, you can use these options:

- You can move your mouse pointer over a note's superscripted character to view a ScreenTip with the footnote or endnote text.

- To edit a footnote or endnote, click in the footnote or endnote text and make your changes.

- To move between footnotes, click the **Next Footnote** drop-down arrow on the **References** tab and choose which direction to move in the document.

- To remove a footnote or endnote, select the superscripted numeral or symbol that flags the note, then press the **Delete** key.

USING CITATIONS AND BIBLIOGRAPHY

If you need to compile all of your notations into a bibliography page at the end of your document, you can use Word's citation and bibliography tools (located in the **Citations & Bibliography** group of tools on the **References** tab). The **Citation** tool helps you organize and enter precise source information using a special form. You can enter bibliography fields for the author, title, year, city, and publisher. You can also specify the type of source, like a book or article. After you enter your citation information, Word inserts a reference in parentheses in the designated spot in the document. You can even manage your sources from one convenient dialog box (click the **Manage Sources** button).

When you are ready to create a bibliography of all the citations you noted in the document, click the end of your document and activate the **Bibliography** tool and choose a style. Word offers several presets you can choose from for your bibliography page. Click the one you want and Word adds a page to the end of the document listing all the sources you cited. You can adjust the page's formatting to suit your needs.

As with the footnote/endnote feature, if you move a section of text containing a reference, Word automatically adjusts the bibliography to match the new positioning of the references.

Adding Captions

You can add captions to pictures, charts, tables, text boxes, and other graphic objects you place in a document. A caption is basically a numbered label. In fact, I've been using them throughout this book to alert you to screen captures that go along with whatever topic we're discussing. Every time I refer to a figure, the text reads Figure 17.1 or 17.2, and so forth—those numbers refer to caption numbers assigned to each figure in the book (in this example, we're in Chapter 17 and the figure numbers start at 1, so 17.1 is the first figure reference in the sequence).

Word's captioning feature includes preset labels to use: Figures, Equation, or Table. If those preset labels won't work for you, you can create your own custom label.

Word also handles the caption numbering for you, such as Figure 1, Figure 2, and so forth. As with footnote/endnote numbering, Word keeps your captions in order even if you move everything around in the document. Another bonus to captioning using the official caption styles is you can use the captions in cross-references (see the next section to learn more about this concept).

To add a caption, use these steps:

1. Select the object to which you want to add a caption.

2. Click the **References** tab on the Ribbon.

3. Click **Insert Caption**.

4. The **Caption** dialog box opens, as shown in Figure 17.9. Click the **Label** drop-down arrow and choose your label type.

FIGURE 17.9

The Caption dialog box.

5. You can position the caption above or below the object; below is the default setting. Click the **Position** drop-down arrow to change the position.

6. Click **OK**.

7. Word inserts the caption, similar to Figure 17.10. Type in any additional text you want the caption to include.

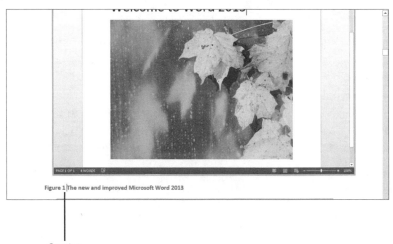

Caption

FIGURE 17.10

Captions can appear above or below the figure, table, or equation.

You can apply formatting to your captions to make them look good. Look for text formatting tools on the **Home** tab.

Inserting Cross-References

You can use cross-references in your documents to refer readers to another section of the document or to additional information. You can insert cross-references to refer readers to existing text that is styled as a heading, to footnotes or endnotes, to captions and bookmarks, figures, and even to numbered paragraphs. The key to make them work properly is to make sure your document has that reference type somewhere within the document. For example, if you want to refer the reader to another section, make sure you assign the section title a heading level using Word's styles (see Chapter 10, "Advanced Formatting," to learn more about styles), or if you want to refer the reader to a figure located elsewhere, make sure the document has captioned figures to refer to. So before you attempt to insert a cross-reference, first make sure you include the reference types in the document. After you have the reference types in place, follow these steps to insert a cross-reference:

1. Click in the document where you want to insert a cross-reference.

2. Click the **References** tab on the Ribbon.

3. Click **Cross-reference**.

4. The **Cross-reference** dialog box opens, as shown in Figure 17.11. Click the **Reference type** drop-down arrow and choose the type of document element to which the cross-reference refers.

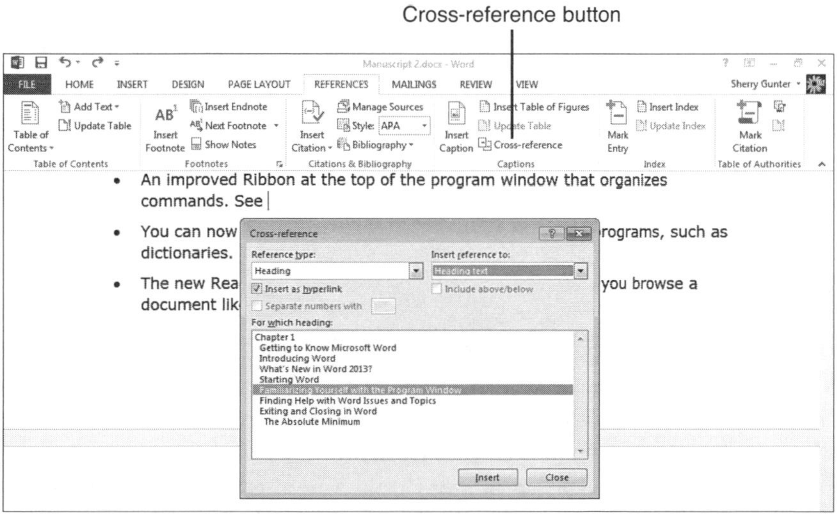

Cross-reference button

FIGURE 17.11

The Cross-reference dialog box.

5. Click the **Insert reference to** drop-down arrow and select what type of information the cross-reference will contain.

6. Select the specific item to which the cross-reference should refer.

7. Leave the **Insert as hyperlink** check box selected if you want readers to be able to navigate directly to the cross-reference item.

8. Click **Insert** and Word inserts the cross-reference, as shown in Figure 17.12.

9. Click **Close**.

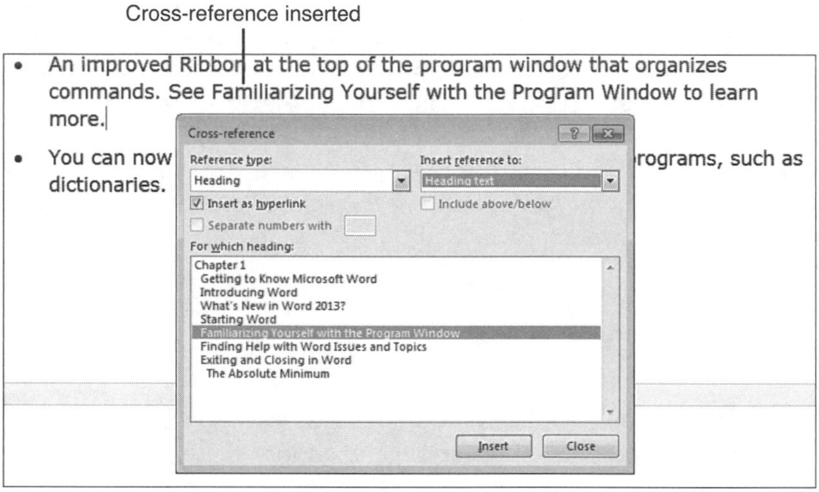

FIGURE 17.12

You can pick which reference to insert from the list of choices.

After you insert a cross-reference, you can tweak it with additional text and punctuation as needed. To remove a cross-reference you no longer want, select it and press the **Delete** key.

Creating an Index

Would your lengthy document benefit from an index? An *index* is a list of important terms that appear in the document along with the page numbers on which they appear. Indexes are used to help readers look up content and topics, and typically appear at the end of a document. You've probably encountered plenty of indexes in various types of books, such as reference books or even how-to manuals. It turns out that adding an index in Word is fairly easy, as long as you're not frightened by paragraph marks and indexing fields. Don't worry, there's nothing scary about either of these.

To start the process, you have to mark your index words using a special field. After you've marked all the important words you want to include in the index, you can turn them into a tabbed columnar list that Word automatically updates for you. Word's indexing feature allows you to customize your index to include leader characters and preset index designs.

To start building an index, begin marking words you want to designate as index terms. Select the word or phrase in the document, click the **References** tab, and then click the **Mark Entry** button. Word opens the **Mark Index Entry** dialog box, shown in Figure 17.13. Click the **Mark** button to create an entry for the word or phrase on this page only, or click **Mark All** to create entries for all occurrences in the document.

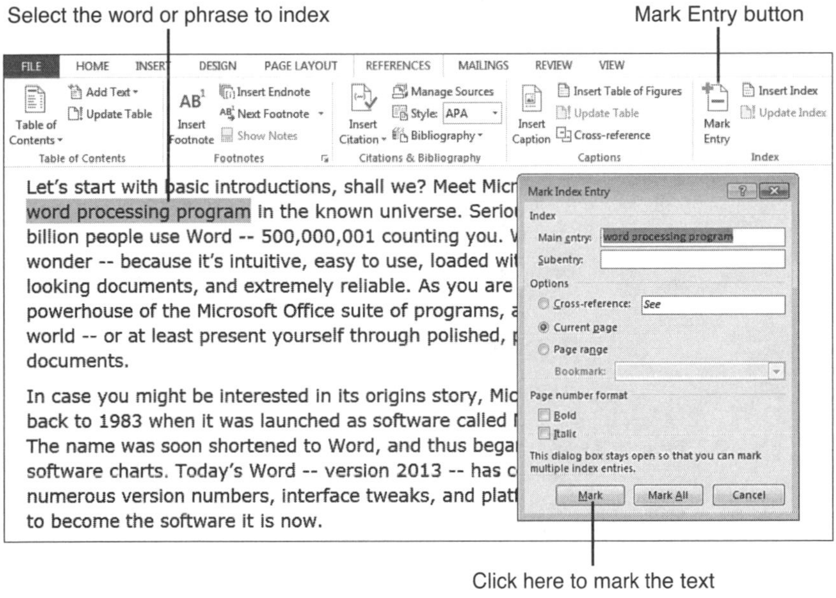

FIGURE 17.13

You can use the Mark Index Entry dialog box to mark words and phrases for indexing.

When you mark the entry, Word adds a special XE indexing field to your document and turns on paragraph marks, as shown in Figure 17.14. The indexing field is enclosed in braces ({ }) and marked with an XE tag (for "index entry"). You can continue adding more indexing markers; just keep selecting words and clicking the **Mark** button in the dialog box to mark them as you read through the document. The dialog box stays open while you work. When you finish, click **Cancel** to close the dialog box.

TIP You don't have to mark all of your document's index entries in a single session. You might prefer to mark entries in multiple sessions, refreshing the index as you go along.

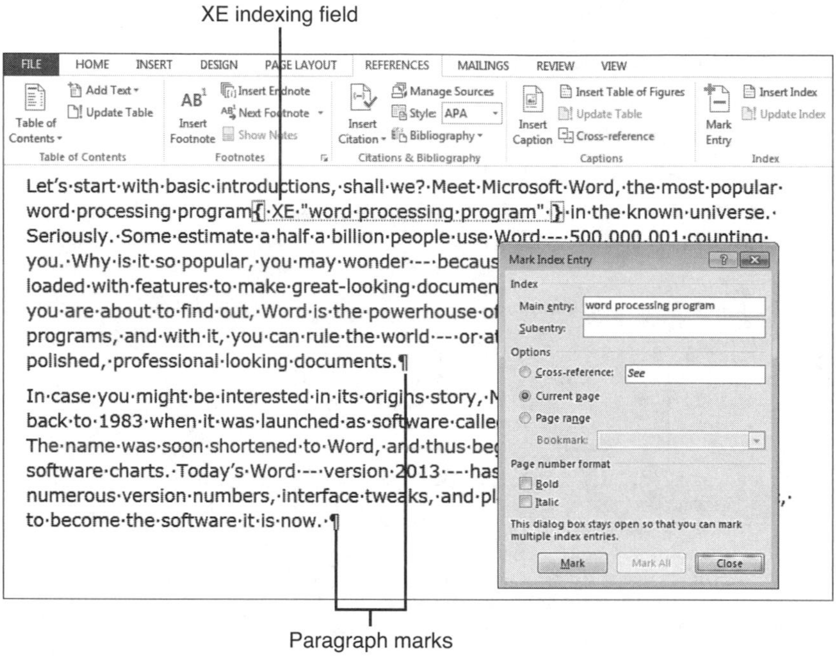

XE indexing field

Paragraph marks

FIGURE 17.14

Word turns on the display of paragraph marks and adds an indexing field to the document.

TIP You can drag the dialog box around on the screen to move it out of the way while you mark words and phrases. Drag it by its title bar and drop it somewhere out of the way.

The next part of making an index is clicking at the end of the document, or wherever you want the index to appear. From the **References** tab, click **Insert Index**. This opens the **Index** dialog box, shown in Figure 17.15.

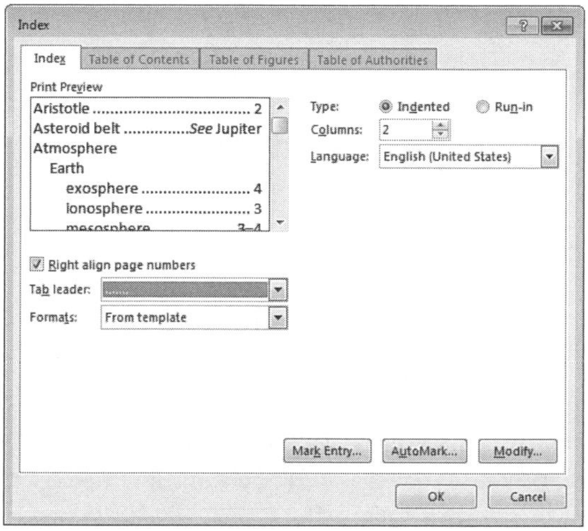

FIGURE 17.15

The Index dialog box.

Click the **Right align page numbers** check box, then click the **Tab** leader drop-down arrow and choose a design. Click **OK** and Word inserts an alphabetical index, similar to Figure 17.16. That's all there is to it.

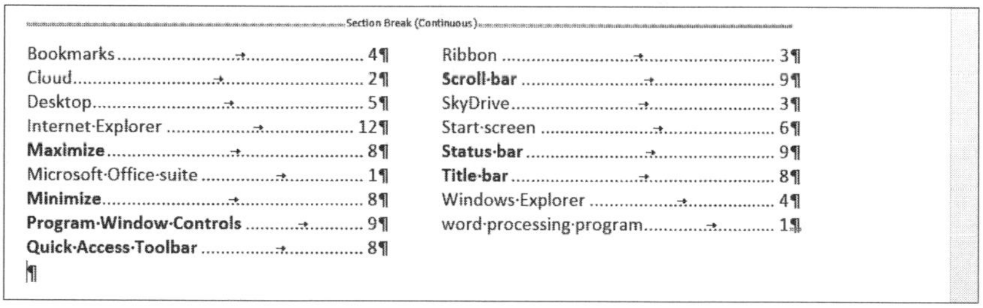
Section Break (Continuous)
Bookmarks .... 4¶
Cloud .... 2¶
Desktop .... 5¶
Internet·Explorer .... 12¶
Maximize .... 8¶
Microsoft·Office·suite .... 1¶
Minimize .... 8¶
Program·Window·Controls .... 9¶
Quick·Access·Toolbar .... 8¶
¶
Ribbon .... 3¶
Scroll·bar .... 9¶
SkyDrive .... 3¶
Start·screen .... 6¶
Status·bar .... 9¶
Title·bar .... 8¶
Windows·Explorer .... 4¶
word·processing·program .... 1¶

FIGURE 17.16

Here's an example of an index.

TIP You can turn off paragraph marks by clicking the **Show/Hide ¶** button on the **Home** tab. Look for it in the corner of the **Paragraph** group of tools.

To remove an XE field, select the entire field and press the **Delete** key, and then update the index. Click the **References** tab and click the **Update Index** button.

NOTE Fields are special containers you add into your Word documents to hold data that often requires updating, such as dates or page numbers. Word updates fields automatically when the reference changes. However, sometimes you need to update a field manually. To quickly update a single field, click it and press **F9**.

Creating a Table of Contents

The front end of your long document might benefit from a *table of contents*—a quick reference of where to find what content within your document. You can instruct Word to generate a table of contents, or TOC for short, based on the predefined heading styles you assigned throughout the document. Of course, first assigning the headings is up to you. (You can find headings listed in the **Styles** gallery found on the **Home** tab.) After your headings are ready to go, you can create a table of contents using these steps:

1. Click where you want to place your table of contents. For best results, place your TOC on a blank page at the front of the document.

2. Click the **References** tab on the Ribbon.

3. Click **Table of Contents**.

4. Click a TOC style from the menu, as shown in Figure 17.17, and Word immediately inserts it, similar to Figure 17.18.

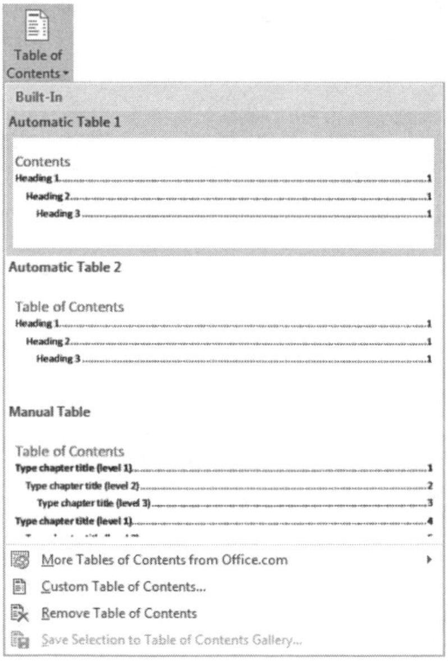

FIGURE 17.17

Use the Table of Contents drop-down menu to choose a TOC style.

Table of Contents

Chapter 1..2

Getting to Know Microsoft Word 2

Introducing Word 2

What's New in Word 2013?..4

Starting Word 5

Familiarizing Yourself with the Program Window 8

Finding Help with Word Issues and Topics 12

Exiting and Closing in Word 13

The Absolute Minimum 14

FIGURE 17.18

Word creates a TOC based on the headings assigned in your document.

Here's what you can do with your table of contents:

- When you click inside the TOC, two special tool buttons appear at the top. These duplicate the TOC tools found on the **References** tab. You can use either the shortcut buttons or the Ribbon buttons to edit your TOC, your choice.

- You can edit your TOC by changing which level headings are listed. Click the **Add Text** button and choose a heading to add.

- To switch to another TOC style, click the **Table of Contents** button again and choose another style.

- If you make changes to your document headings and content, click the **Update Table** button to make your TOC current.

Inserting Bookmarks

You can add *bookmarks* to help you navigate longer documents. Digital bookmarks act a lot like actual bookmarks, allowing you to mark a location in the document for easy access later. For example, you might use a bookmark to quickly navigate to a key word or phrase, or bookmark text you want to revisit after you've researched a few things. You might also use a bookmark to help you quickly jump to another spot in your document, such as a table of contents.

In order for Word to keep track of all the bookmarks in a document, you have to give them individual names. When naming your bookmark, you must follow very strict naming rules. Bookmark names must begin with a letter, and names can include numbers along with letter characters. However, no spaces are allowed in the bookmark name. Instead of a space, use an underscore character, such as in Chapter_3.

Use these steps to add a bookmark:

1. Select the text you want to turn into a bookmark.

2. Click the **Insert** tab on the Ribbon.

3. Click **Links**.

4. Click **Bookmark**, as shown in Figure 17.19.

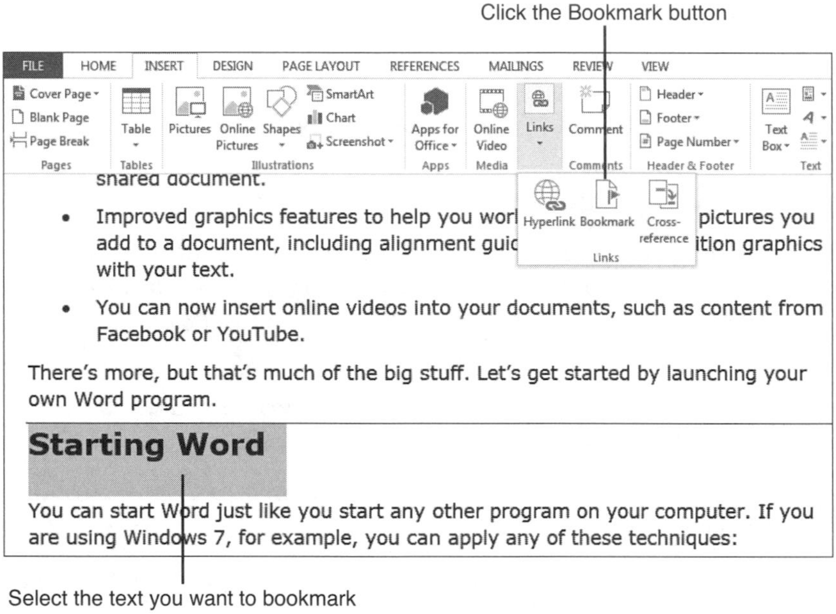

FIGURE 17.19

Find the Bookmark tool on the Insert tab.

5. The **Bookmark** dialog box opens, as shown in Figure 17.20. Type a name for the bookmark.

6. Click **Add**.

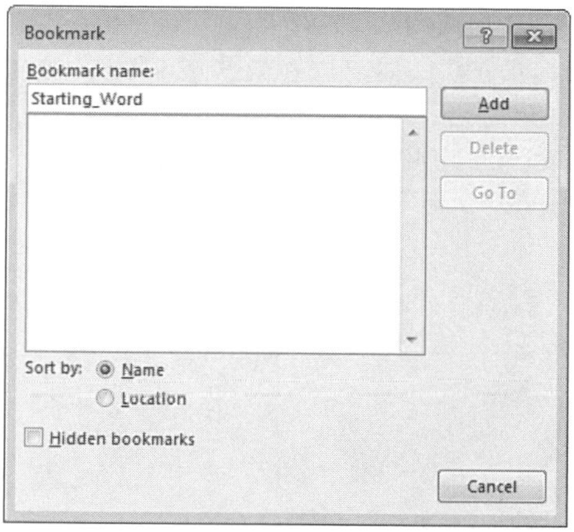

FIGURE 17.20

Give your bookmark a name in the Bookmark dialog box.

To use the bookmark later, click the **Home** tab, click the **Find** drop-down arrow, and choose **Go To**. This opens the **Find and Replace** dialog box (you can learn more about the Find and Replace tools in Chapter 18) to the **Go To** tab, as shown in Figure 17.21. Click the **Bookmark** element and then choose the particular bookmark you want to jump to, then click the **Go To** button to transport yourself to the location in the document. To exit the dialog box when finished jumping around the document, click the **Close** button.

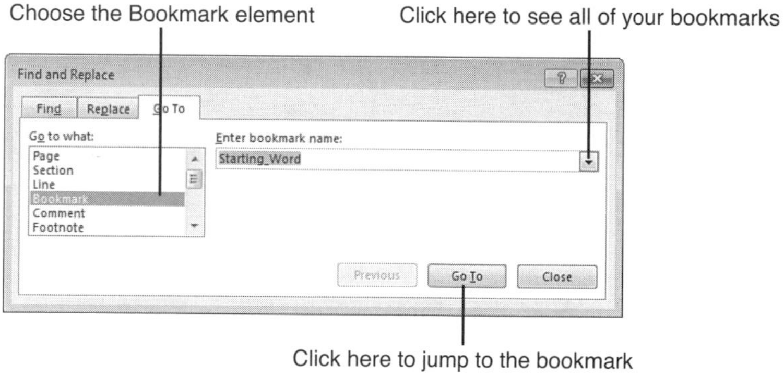

FIGURE 17.21

You can use the Find and Replace dialog box to navigate the document using bookmarks.

 TIP   You can also use the **Go To** tab in the **Find and Replace** dialog box to navigate to other designated elements in your documents, including footnotes, endnotes, and headings.

Word 2013 also bookmarks the last place you were working in a document when you last saved and closed your file, and it offers to jump you right back there when you reopen the file. A bookmark prompt icon appears, as shown in Figure 17.22, which you can click to return to the spot. If you don't want to pick up where you left off, just ignore the icon.

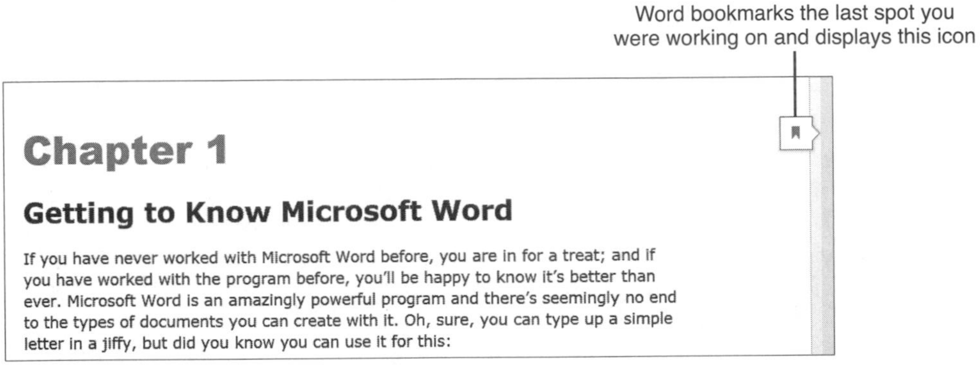

Word bookmarks the last spot you were working on and displays this icon

Chapter 1

Getting to Know Microsoft Word

If you have never worked with Microsoft Word before, you are in for a treat; and if you have worked with the program before, you'll be happy to know it's better than ever. Microsoft Word is an amazingly powerful program and there's seemingly no end to the types of documents you can create with it. Oh, sure, you can type up a simple letter in a jiffy, but did you know you can use it for this:

FIGURE 17.22

Word 2013 automatically bookmarks your last editing location in a document and offers to take you there.

 NOTE Bookmarks are a part of the document, so if you hand off your document to another user, just remember everyone who reads your document reads your bookmarks as well. For that reason, you may want to remove them from a document first, or simply make sure they're acceptable for all audiences.

Navigating Long Documents with the Navigation Pane

The longer your document grows, the more important it is to learn how to move around in it. Word has just the tool for you to zip back and forth to the places you want to view—the **Navigation** pane. This pane, shown in Figure 17.23, displays your document headings as a list, or shows each page as a thumbnail image (small image), and also doubles as a search function. To turn on the **Navigation** pane, click the **View** tab on the Ribbon, and click the **Navigation Pane** check box. (A check mark means the pane is turned on, no check mark means the pane is off.) You can also press **Ctrl+F** to open the pane.

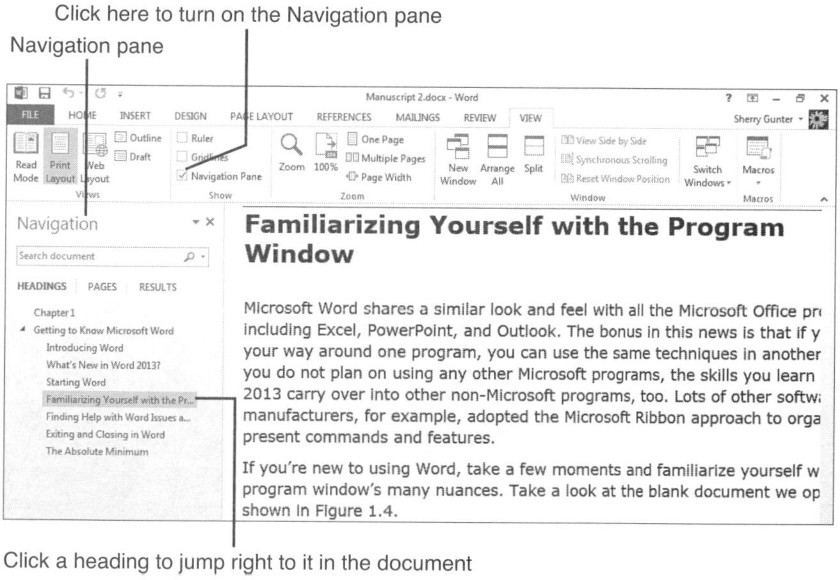

Click here to turn on the Navigation pane

Navigation pane

Click a heading to jump right to it in the document

FIGURE 17.23

You can use the Navigation pane to view all the headings in a document and navigate to a particular one.

Click the **Headings** link at the top of the pane to view all the headings listed in the pane, as demonstrated in Figure 17.23. To jump to a heading, click it in the pane.

Click the **Pages** link to view your pages as thumbnail images, as shown in Figure 17.24. To jump to a page, click it in the list.

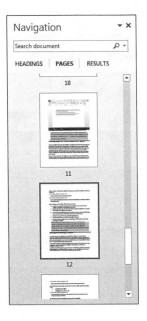

FIGURE 17.24

You can also use the Navigation pane to view all your pages as thumbnails and navigate to a particular one.

To use the pane as a search tool, click the **Results** link, and then click in the **Search** box and type in your keyword or phrase. Press **Enter** or click the **Search** button. Any matching results are listed in the pane, similar to Figure 17.25. Click a result to jump to that spot in the document. You can also use the pane to find objects, like drawings, amongst the text, or figure references and section numbers and the like. You might also use the Navigation pane to scan through pages to spot errors.

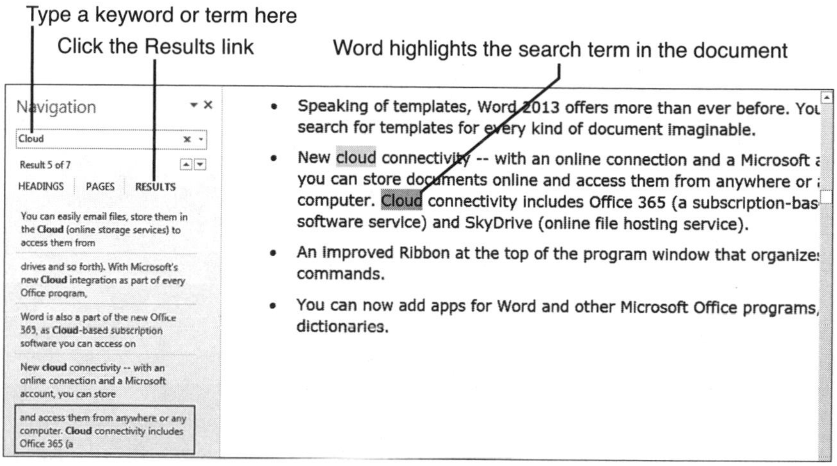

Type a keyword or term here
Click the Results link   Word highlights the search term in the document

FIGURE 17.25

You can use the Navigation pane to search for words or phrases in the document.

To close the pane, click its **Close** button (the **X** button in the upper-right corner), or deselect the **Navigation Pane** check box on the **View** tab.

 TIP   The **Navigation** pane is moveable—just click and drag its title bar to turn it into a free-floating box. To dock it again to the side of the window, double-click its title bar.

THE ABSOLUTE MINIMUM

If your Word project involves reference tools and lots of pages of text, you can find plenty of features to help you manage and build on the content. Here's a summary of your newfound knowledge:

- Use Outline view any time you want to plan out a document as a hierarchical structure, using headings and levels. Find the Outline view on the **View** tab.

- Word makes inserting footnotes and endnotes to cite sources, add explanations, and reference other information super easy. Look for these tools on the **References** tab.

- You can assign captions to figures and tables you insert to help clarify and explain. Look for the captioning tool on—you guessed it—the **References** tab.

- You can insert cross-references to other parts of your document, but the catch is you have to use reference "types" throughout your document, such as figures or headings, so you have something to reference to. Click the **Cross-reference** button on the **References** tab to get started.

- Pop in an index at the back of your document that refers the reader to the locations of all the important terminology you use in the text. Look for the indexing tools in the **Index** group on the **References** tab.

- Dress up the front of your document with a table of contents that lets everyone know what content you cover and where to find it. The table of contents tools appear on the left end of the **References** tab.

- Insert bookmarks in places you want to revisit in a flash, such as a heading or the last paragraph you were typing in when you had to stop and go eat lunch (after saving and closing the file, of course). Display the **Insert** tab to find the bookmarking tool.

- Word has a special pane you can use to quickly jump to parts of your document or even conduct a search. Find the **Navigation Pane** feature on the **View** tab.

18

IN THIS CHAPTER

- Learn how to use a digital highlighter pen.
- Leave notes with Word's Comments tool.
- Clean up repetitive mistakes using the Find and Replace tools.
- Finally find out what those wavy red lines are under all your text.
- Look up similar meanings with the ever-so-handy Thesaurus tool.

USING PROOFREADING TOOLS

Proofreading your documents is always an important step before you send them out into the world for others to view. Because we're not all trained editors, Word offers some handy tools to help us check over our documents for errors and other spots that need special attention. Sort of like grading your own papers at school, proofreading tools can help you sort out mistakes before they make it to a final printout or launch from your email account.

You can find a variety of tools to help you check over your documents, mark areas with special notations to yourself, and generally make sure everything's in order. They say you should never proofread your own work, but when you're all you've got, you might just have to do it yourself. Don't despair, though; Word has your back, as I'm about to show you in this chapter.

Highlighting Text with a Highlighter Pen

You can go over documents and highlight parts with a digital highlighter pen. This tool works just like a real highlighter you use to mark up textbooks, study materials, magazines, and printed documents. You can even control what color you use to highlight with—try doing that with a real highlighter pen.

When you activate the highlighter, the mouse pointer takes the shape of—wait for it—a highlighter pen! When you see this icon, you can start marking up your text. You might use this technique to draw attention to important parts of your document that you need to revisit, or to help another user notice the text. I daresay you can devise your own reasons for highlighting in a document, but after you see how fun this tool is, you might not need any reason at all.

Before you get started, I should at least warn you about the color you pick to highlight with; the palette offers several choices, but watch out for darker colors. Unless you are highlighting white text on a dark background, darker highlighting colors might cause some issues with legibility. If they do, just choose another color from the palette until you find one that works with your situation.

To use the highlighting feature, follow these steps:

1. Click the **Home** tab.

2. Click the **Text Highlight Color** drop-down arrow and choose a color from the palette (see Figure 18.1).

FIGURE 18.1

You can choose a highlighting color from the drop-down palette.

3. Click and drag across the text you want to highlight.

Word adds the highlighting color to the text, as shown in Figure 18.2.

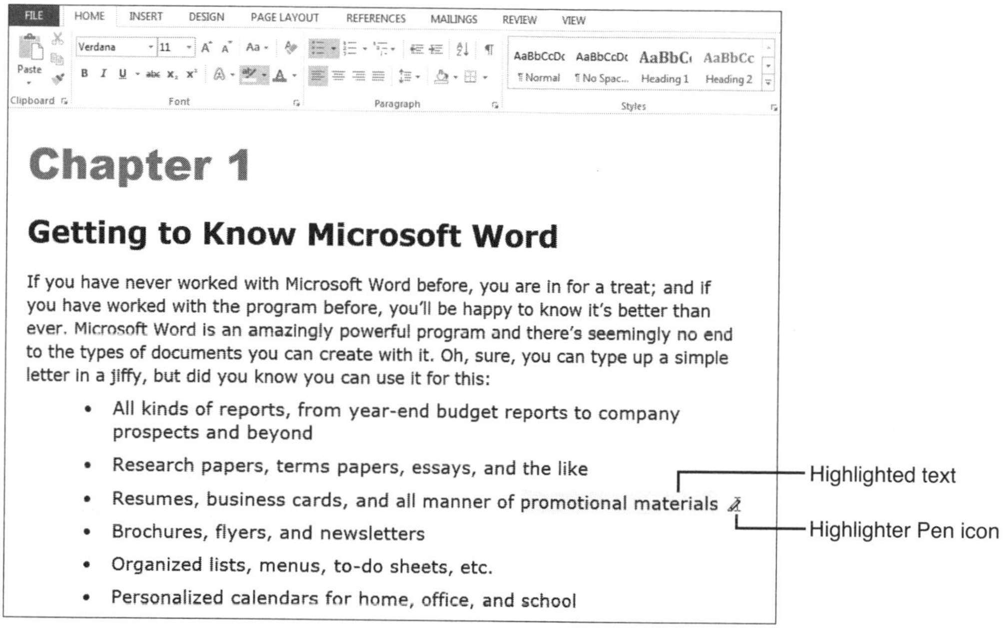

FIGURE 18.2

Here's an example of highlighted text.

The Highlighter Pen stays on until you perform another action or turn the feature off. You can turn it off just by clicking its button on the Home tab again.

To remove highlighting from text, select the highlighted text and display the tool's palette again, this time picking the **No Color** option.

Inserting Comments

Occasions might arise where you want to add a note to the text without inserting anything actually in the text, such as a reminder to check something later or a question about a certain fact or figure. You can use Word's **Comments** feature to add comments to your text. Word then tracks all the comments in the **Revisions** pane so you can revisit them in an orderly fashion. The beauty of adding comments is that they don't print out with the rest of the text (unless you tell Word to print them). Comments can apply to a word, a sentence, a paragraph, or the whole document.

Comments are particularly useful if your document is being edited by multiple users. Each person can respond to a comment, or start a new comment, and everybody's input includes their initials. Learn more about sharing and reviewing documents in Chapter 20, "Collaborating On and Reviewing Documents," along with using comments in the capacity of collaboration.

NOTE Word nabs each users initials from data gleaned during installation. If you're using someone else's computer, their initials appear in any comments you insert. To view or change your comment's initials, click the **File** tab and click **Options** to open the Word Options dialog box, and then click the **General** category to find the personalizing options.

To insert a comment, follow these steps:

1. Click where you want to insert a comment, or select the text pertaining to the comment.

2. Click the **Insert** tab.

3. Click the **Comment** button.

4. Word immediately opens the **Revisions** pane and places your name at the top of the comment as well as your initials next to the designated area in the document, as shown in Figure 18.3.

5. Type in your comment text.

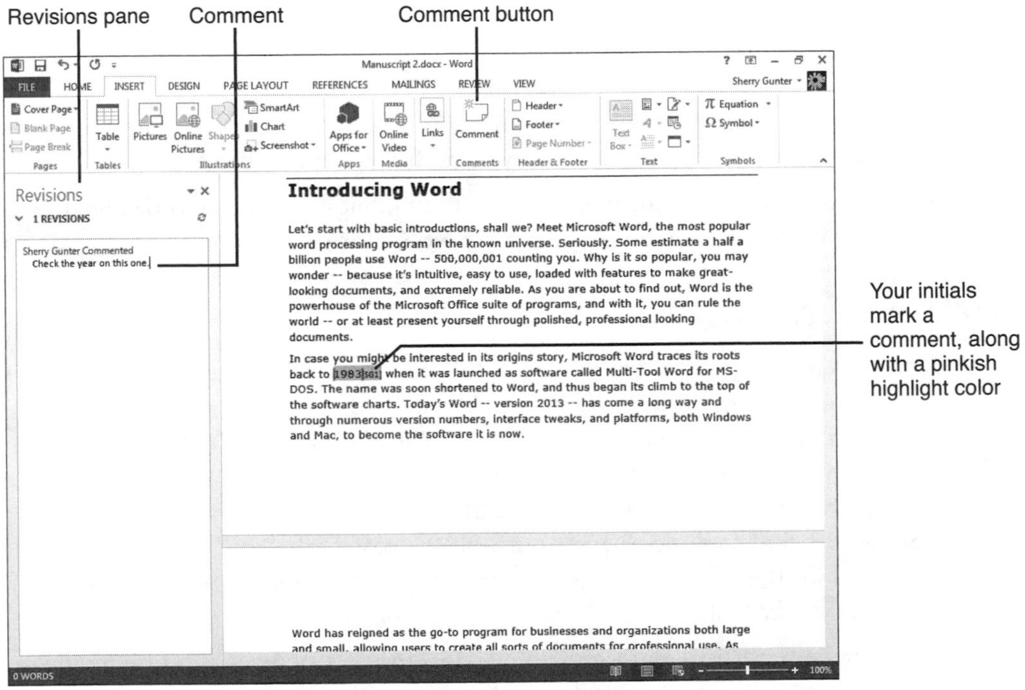

Revisions pane   Comment   Comment button

Your initials mark a comment, along with a pinkish highlight color

FIGURE 18.3

Word opens the Revisions pane when you add comments.

TIP You can also open and close the **Revisions** pane using the **Reviewing Pane** button on the **Review** tab.

You can close the **Revisions** pane, when finished. If the pane is closed, you can still view a comment simply by hovering the mouse pointer over the comment in the document, as shown in Figure 18.4. To edit the comment, right-click it and choose **Edit Comment**.

> looking documents, and extremely reliable. A
> powerhouse of the Microsoft Office suite of p
> world -- ugh
> docume Sherry Gunter, 3/4/2013 3:18:00 PM
> commented:
> Check the year on this one.
> In case igins
> back to 1983[SG1] when it was launched as so
> DOS. The name was soon shortened to Word
> the software charts. Today's Word -- version
> through numerous version numbers, interfac
> and Mac, to become the software it is now.

FIGURE 18.4

To quickly view a comment, move the mouse pointer over the comment.

TIP That's not all you can do with comments. When you're using them in conjunction with other collaborators, you can reply to someone else's comment, or mark a comment as done if everyone's finished with it. Learn more about collaborating on documents in Chapter 20, including using the **Comments** tools on the **Review** tab.

Finding and Replacing Text

Sometimes you not only need to find text in a long document, but also replace it with something else. For example, maybe you referred to the wrong person in a report or need to update the text with a different company name. Word's **Find and Replace** tools take the tedium out of making the same changes in several places. Whenever you find yourself about to change something manually throughout your entire document, stop and see whether Word's **Find and Replace** feature could do this work for you.

To start a find and replace operation, click the Ribbon's **Home** tab and look for the **Replace** button (it's located on the far right side of the tab). Click it to open the **Find and Replace** dialog box to the **Replace** tab, as shown in Figure 18.5. Click in the **Find what** box and type the word or phrase you're looking for in the document. Next, click the **Replace with** box and type in the replacement text.

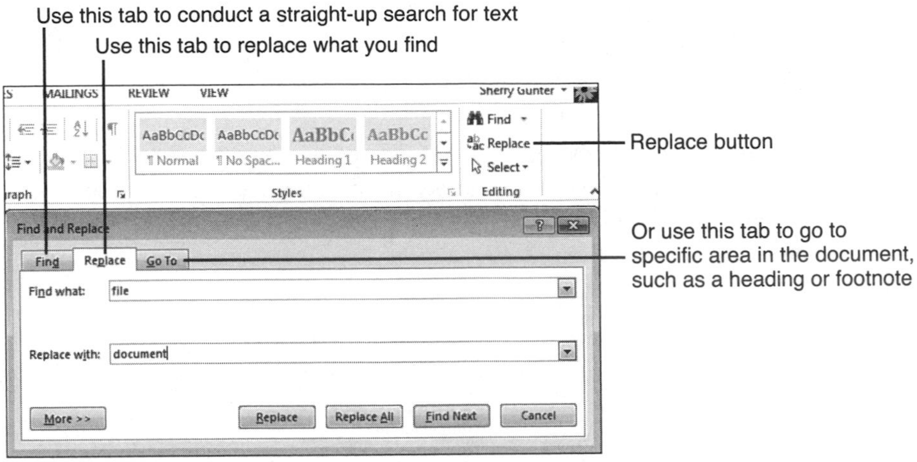

Use this tab to conduct a straight-up search for text

Use this tab to replace what you find

Replace button

Or use this tab to go to
specific area in the document,
such as a heading or footnote

FIGURE 18.5

Use the Find and Replace dialog box to conduct a search and replace mission in your document.

When you're ready to start searching and replacing, click in the document where you want to begin, like the very top, and click the **Find Next** button in the dialog box. Word moves you to the first occurrence of the text and highlights it in the document, similar to what's shown in Figure 18.6. To replace it, click the **Replace** button in the dialog box. (To replace all the occurrences with the new text, click **Replace All**.) To keep looking for more instances of the text, click **Find Next** again.

CAUTION Don't use **Replace All** unless you're *absolutely sure* you won't change something that shouldn't be changed. For example, if you confidently replace all instances of your company's old name with its new name in the annual report, you could accidentally change "In 2012, ABC Company became XYZ Company" to say "In 2012, XYZ Company became XYZ Company." Making yourself (or your boss) look stupid is never a good idea.

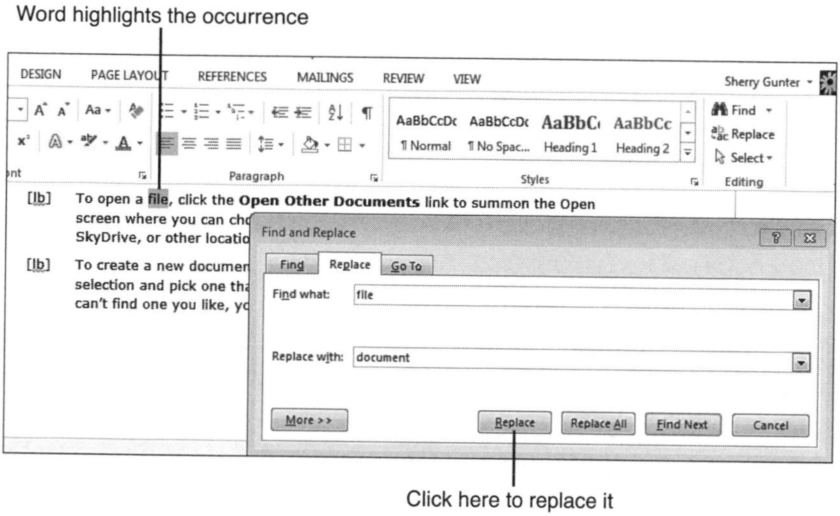

Word highlights the occurrence

To open a **file**, click the **Open Other Documents** link to summon the Open screen where you can ch... SkyDrive, or other locatio...

Find and Replace

Find | Replace | Go To

Find what: file

Replace with: document

More >>   Replace   Replace All   Find Next   Cancel

Click here to replace it

FIGURE 18.6

You can move through the document finding and replacing text while the dialog box remains open onscreen.

When you reach the end of the search, Word displays a prompt box; click **OK**. Lastly, click the **Close** button to exit the **Find and Replace** dialog box.

In the corner of the **Find and Replace** dialog box is a button labeled **More**. Click it to expand the dialog box and view some additional search criteria you can apply, such as matching case, whole words only, and so on (see Figure 18.7).

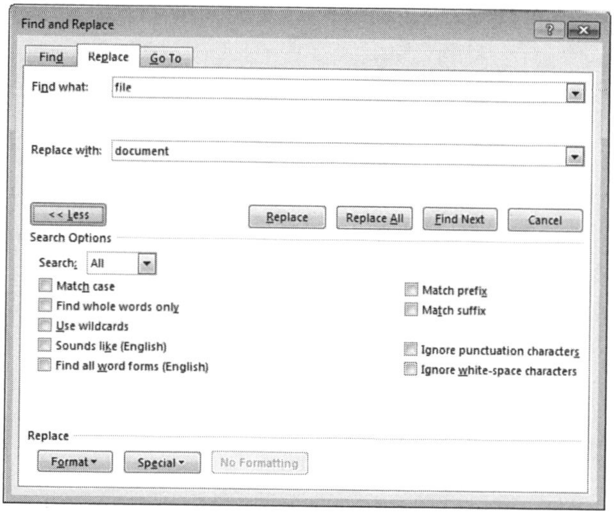

Find and Replace

Find | Replace | Go To

Find what: file

Replace with: document

<< Less   Replace   Replace All   Find Next   Cancel

Search Options

Search: All

☐ Match case
☐ Find whole words only
☐ Use wildcards
☐ Sounds like (English)
☐ Find all word forms (English)

☐ Match prefix
☐ Match suffix

☐ Ignore punctuation characters
☐ Ignore white-space characters

Replace

Format ▾   Special ▾   No Formatting

FIGURE 18.7

Expand the Find and Replace dialog box to view more search criteria.

If you would rather just look up a word or phrase rather than replace it with anything, use the **Find** portion of the **Find and Replace** tools. You can click the **Find** button on the **Home** tab to open the dialog box to the **Find** tools. You then type in what you want to locate and press **Enter** to jump right to it.

TIP The **Navigation** pane (explained in Chapter 17, "Tools for Longer Documents") also has a search feature you can use to look up terms in your document.

Checking Spelling and Grammar

One of the most important proofreading tools you can use is Word's Spelling and Grammar checker. It can help you correct spelling and grammatical issues that come up in your document. By default, the spelling and grammar checking functions are turned on when you start using Word. The Spell Checker underlines any problems it encounters in your text with a wavy red line. The Grammar Checker identifies grammar issues with wavy green lines. You can run a spell check anytime you want to review the document. The feature takes you through each problem, one at a time, until the check is complete.

To check your document, click at the top of the document, click the **Review** tab, and then click the **Spelling & Grammar** button. Word displays the **Spelling and Grammar** pane, shown in Figure 18.8, and highlights the first misspelling or grammar error in the document, along with correction suggestions; click the suggestion you want to apply. For example, in Figure 18.8, I need to change the misspelling of "smple" to "simple," so I highlight the word "simple" in the pane and click the **Change** button.

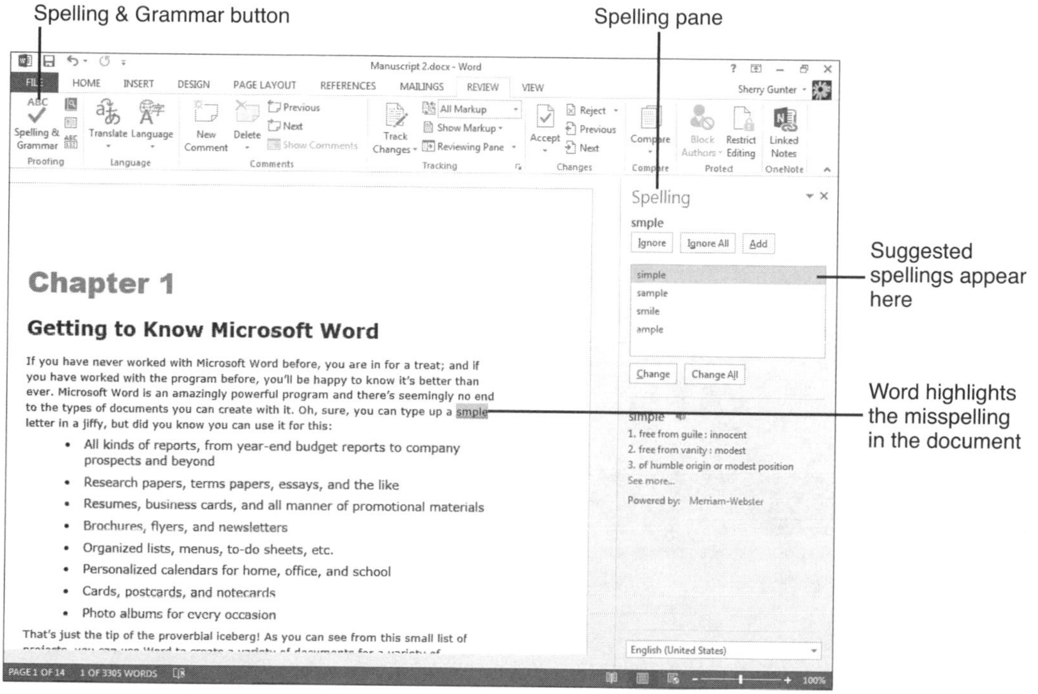

Spelling & Grammar button   Spelling pane

Suggested
spellings appear
here

Word highlights
the misspelling
in the document

FIGURE 18.8

The Spelling pane helps you check your document for spelling errors.

Here's what else you can do with the **Spelling** pane:

- If you know you've misspelled a word throughout, you can click the **Change All** button. (Be sure you're right before doing this!)

- If you know the word is correct, such as a person's name, click the **Ignore** button. If it appears throughout the document, click **Ignore All**.

- To add the word, such as a properly spelled name, to Word's dictionary, click the **Add** button.

- If you click outside the **Spelling** pane, like to fix something else in the document, you can click the **Resume** button that appears in the pane to restart the spell check.

- To close the **Spelling** pane, click its **Close** button.

Word checks the grammar of your document alongside the text, and if it encounters anything that looks suspicious, the **Grammar** pane appears, as shown in Figure 18.9. Keep in mind that not all the issues the grammar check points out are legitimate. For example, in Figure 18.9, it's trying to tell me I need to capitalize something in my figure caption. Like the **Spelling** pane, you can ignore the suggestion by clicking the **Ignore** button, or you can fix the problem with the **Change** button.

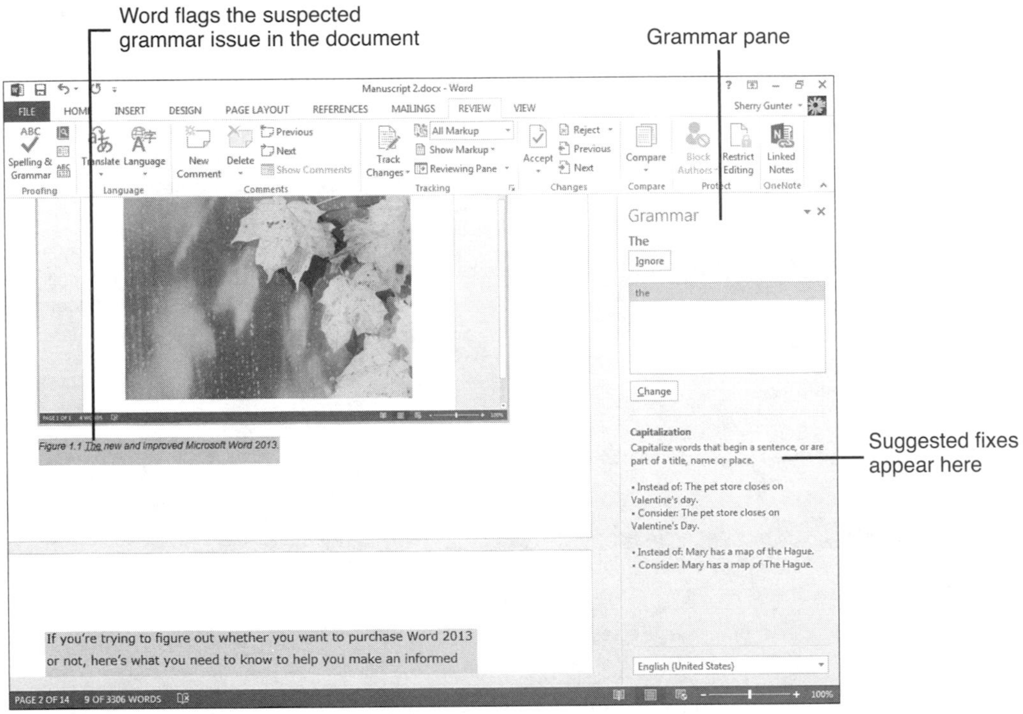

Word flags the suspected grammar issue in the document

Grammar pane

Suggested fixes appear here

FIGURE 18.9

The Grammar pane helps you check your document for grammatical errors.

> **NOTE** You can control how the spelling and grammar checking works, including whether it's turned on by default. Click the **File** tab and click **Options** to open the **Word Options** dialog box. Click the **Proofing** category to view all the options available. Click **OK** when you finish making your changes to the settings.

Using AutoCorrect

Word's AutoCorrect feature fixes spelling errors for you automatically as you type. You might have noticed it at work when you mistyped a word, such as changing **teh** to **the** without being prompted. This feature is turned on by default when you first open Word. AutoCorrect makes corrections based on suggestions from the Spell Checker. It also has its own list of many commonly misspelled words, and you can add your own favorite typos to the list. In addition, you can use AutoCorrect to automatically enter special symbols, long names, or phrases you type frequently.

To find your way to the AutoCorrect options, click the **File** tab and click **Options** to open the **Word Options** dialog box (see Figure 18.10). Click the **Proofing** category, and then click the **AutoCorrect Options** button.

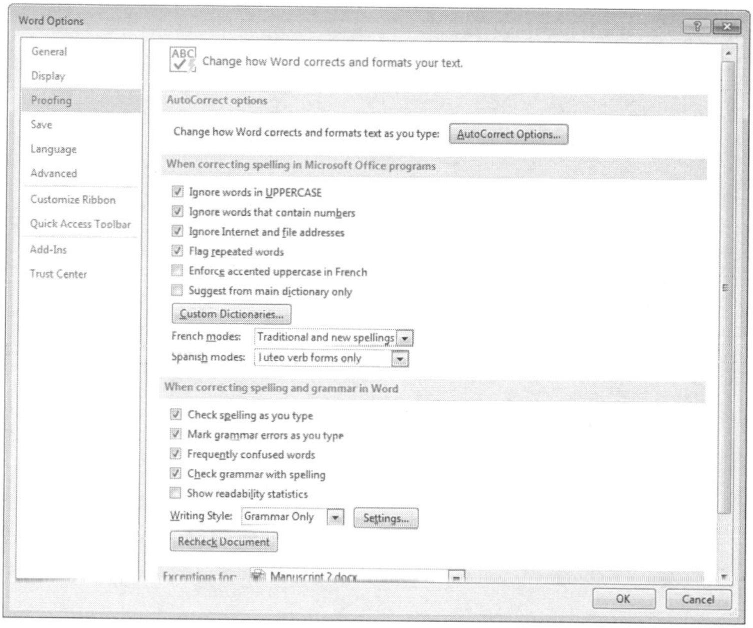

FIGURE 18.10

Find your way to AutoCorrect through the Word Options dialog box.

This opens the **AutoCorrect** dialog box, similar to Figure 18.11. The **AutoCorrect** tab lists all the associated options you can turn off and on, plus a pretty long list of commonly misspelled words that it checks for you as you happily type along. To add your own commonly misspelled word, click in the **Replace** box and type it just as you typically misspell it. Click in the **With** box and type the correction. Click the **Add** button and Word adds it to the AutoCorrect list. Click **OK** to exit the dialog box, and then click **OK** again to close the **Word Options** dialog box.

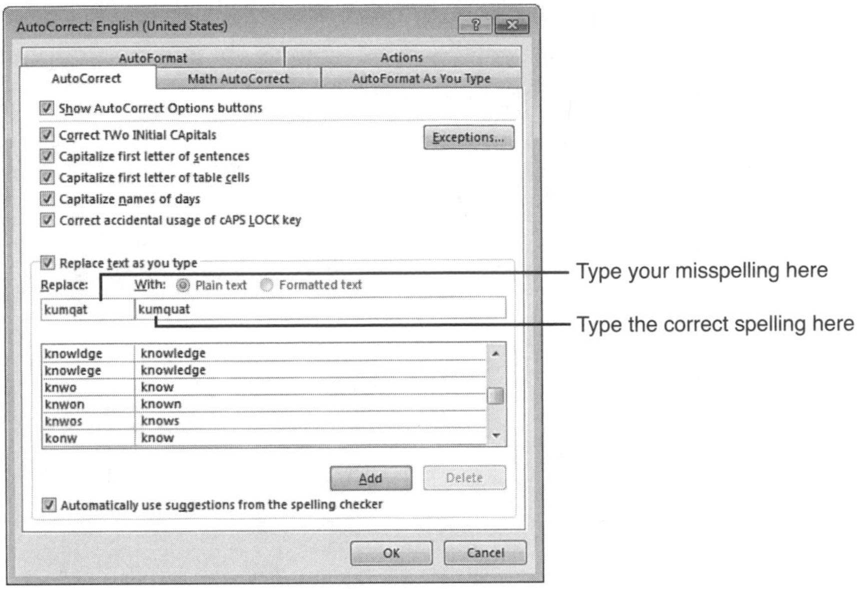

FIGURE 18.11

You can use the AutoCorrect dialog box to add your own common misspellings.

 TIP To turn off AutoCorrect, deselect the **Check spelling as you type** check box in the **Word Options** dialog box (see Figure 18.10).

If you find yourself typing in a long company name or similar phrase over and over again, you can turn it into an AutoCorrect entry. Designate an abbreviation for the name and the next time you type the abbreviation, AutoCorrect substitutes the full name. Brilliant idea, right? Here's how you do it—from the **AutoCorrect** dialog box, click in the **Replace** box and type the abbreviation for the long name. In the **With** box, type in the full name you want to swap the abbreviation for, and then click **Add**.

 TIP To remove a word from the AutoCorrect list, select it and click the **Delete** button.

Using the Word Thesaurus

Here's a common scenario (or at least it's common for me)—as you're proofreading your document you start to notice you've used a lot of the same words on a page and it's looking a little redundant, but you can't think of another word that conveys the same meaning. Luckily for you (and me), Word has a built-in Thesaurus feature to help you look up *synonyms*—words that mean the same thing.

To use the Thesaurus, follow these steps:

1. Select the word you want to look up.

2. Click the **Review** tab.

3. Click the **Thesaurus** button.

4. Word opens the **Thesaurus** pane, shown in Figure 18.12, listing synonyms. To replace the selected word with one from the list, move the mouse pointer over the right end of the word you want and click **Insert**.

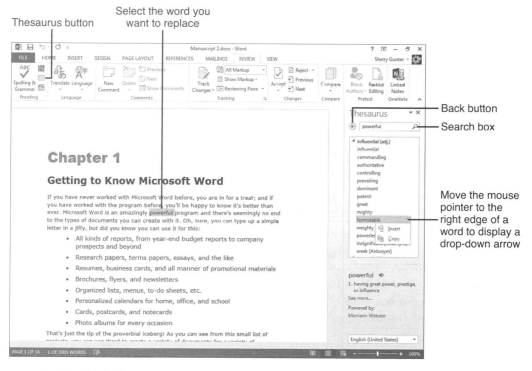

FIGURE 18.12

Use the Thesaurus pane to look up synonyms.

Here's what else you can do:

- To find more synonyms for a word in the list, click it.
- To return to the previous word's list, click the **Back** button.
- To look up a new word, type it in the **Search** box and press **Enter**.
- To exit the pane, click its **Close** button.

 TIP You can also right-click a word and choose **Thesaurus** to open the pane.

Researching and Translating Words

Just when you thought you had seen enough, here's another interesting feature I can show you—Word's language tools, or specifically, the **Translate** tools. You can use them in ways that help you communicate with others around the globe in languages such as Spanish, French, or Arabic. The **Review** tab's **Translate** button offers the following options:

- **Translate Document** Use this tool to translate the entire document and display it in an Internet browser window, with a little help from Microsoft's translation website.

- **Translate Selected Text** You can translate a paragraph, sentence, or phrase using this tool and the **Research** pane.

- **Mini Translator** Use this tool to quickly translate a word you point at with your cursor.

You can translate words and phrases and easily specify which language using the **Research** pane, and that's the method I'm going to show you. Start by right-clicking the word in your document you want to translate (you can also select a phrase and right-click, too). Choose **Translate** from the pop-up menu, as shown in Figure 18.13. Word opens the **Research** pane, shown in Figure 18.14. Click the **From** drop-down arrow to specify the source language (if needed), and click the **To** drop-down arrow to choose a language to translate to; in the example shown, it's Spanish. The results immediately appear in the pane.

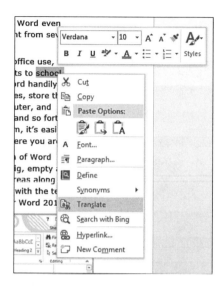

FIGURE 18.13

Right-click the word you want to translate.

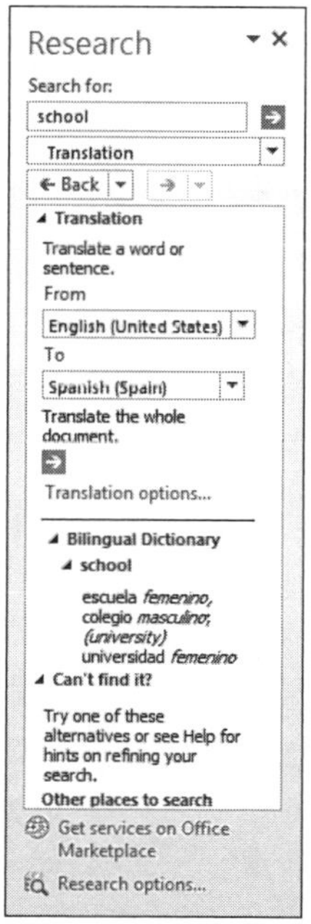

FIGURE 18.14

Use the Research pane to choose a language and view the results.

TIP To send the entire document for translation, click the arrow icon under the **Translate the whole document** heading in the **Research** pane. This opens a prompt box; click **Send** to continue to the website.

Checking a Document for Hidden Data

You can use Word's Document Inspector tool to check your document for sensitive information or hidden data. For example, if you plan on sharing the document with other users, you might want to remove any personal information from the file. Hidden data, also called *metadata*, includes elements such as comments, tracked changes, and information about who created the document. With the Document Inspector, you can control what type of content is inspected and see whether any issues need to be addressed.

1. Click the **File** tab.

2. Click **Info**.

3. Click **Check for Issues** (see Figure 18.15).

FIGURE 18.15

Activate the Document Inspector through the Info window.

4. Click Inspect Document.

5. This opens the **Document Inspector** dialog box, shown in Figure 18.16. Choose the type of information you want to check and click **Inspect**.

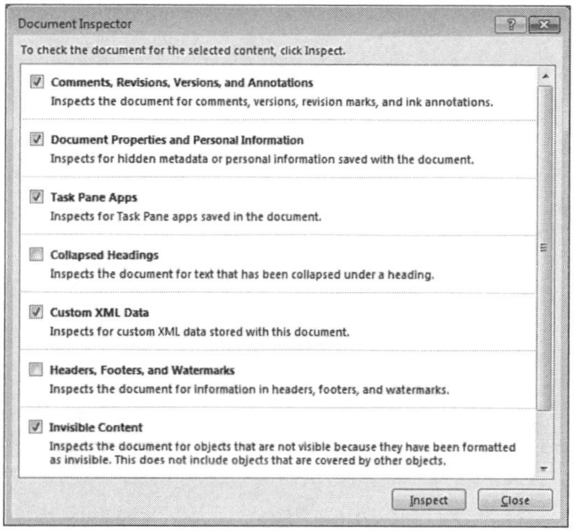

FIGURE 18.16

The Document Inspector dialog box.

6. The inspector checks the document and lists any potential issues you need to address, similar to what you see in Figure 18.17. Click **Remove All** to fix an issue.

FIGURE 18.17

The Document Inspector results.

7. Click **Close** to exit the dialog box.

CAUTION You cannot undo the effects of removing information with the Document Inspector. You can, however, restore the removed information by closing the document without saving the changes made by the inspection process.

THE ABSOLUTE MINIMUM

In regard to proofreading, a second set of eyes always helps, but when that's not available, you can use Word's many reviewing tools to help you check over documents. In this chapter, you discovered:

- You can use the highlighter pen, found on the **Home** tab, to draw attention to text with a highlight color.

- Insert comments to help you, or others, write notes about the document without printing them with the document.

- Use the **Find and Replace** dialog box to search your document for text and replace it with different text.

- Word automatically corrects misspellings using the AutoCorrect feature, but you can add your most common trouble words to the list to customize it to your peculiar spelling weaknesses.

- For a full-blown spelling and grammar review, activate the **Spelling & Grammar** button on the **Review** tab and pore over your document issue by issue.

- Whenever you need to find a word that's similar to another word, crack open Word's Thesaurus and look around for a substitute.

- Use the **Research** pane to translate a word in another language of your choosing.

- You can inspect your document for hidden personal data or sensitive information before you share it with others using the Document Inspector.

IN THIS CHAPTER

- Learn how to finally print out a document you've been working on all this time.
- Preview your files before sending them off to the printer.
- See how easy it is to print envelopes.
- Practice printing labels with one eye closed.
- Explore the secrets of mass mailing with Word's Mail Merge tool.

19

PRINTING DOCUMENTS

Okay, so you've made all these wonderful document files, perfected them with formatting, and proofread them so they sound super smart and professional. Now wouldn't you like to print them out? In this chapter, I'll show you how to preview documents before printing, how to adjust the printer settings, and how to print special things like envelopes and labels. As an added bonus just because I like you so much, I'm also going to take you through the top-secret steps for performing a mail merge—so you can see how fun it is to create mass mailings for business or pleasure. Well, mostly for business.

Previewing and Printing a Document

You can both preview and print from the same spot in Microsoft Word. Just open the **Print** window to see what I mean: Click the **File** tab on the Ribbon, and then click **Print**. Shown in Figure 19.1, the window features printer controls and options on the left and a preview area on the right. You can control how many copies you print, which printer you use (if you have more than one), and which pages print out, plus a whole lot more I'm going to tell you about.

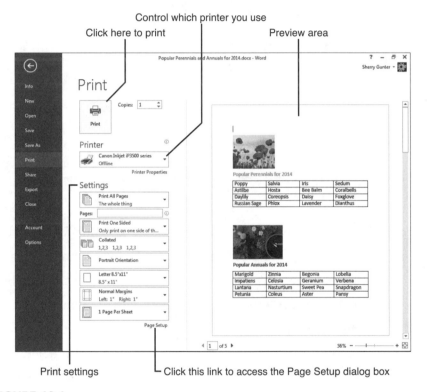

Control which printer you use

Click here to print

Preview area

Print settings

Click this link to access the Page Setup dialog box

FIGURE 19.1

You can preview and print from the same window in Microsoft Word 2013.

 NOTE You can add shortcut buttons for both printing and opening the Print window to your **Quick Access** toolbar—the toolbar that sits in the upper-left corner of the program window above the Ribbon. Click the **Customize Quick Access Toolbar** button (the arrow button at the right end of the toolbar). From the drop-down menu, click **Print Preview and Print** if you want to add a shortcut to the **Print** screen (refer to Figure 19.1). You can bypass the whole **Print** screen and go directly to printing if you add the **Quick Print** command to the toolbar.

Previewing Pages

Let's talk about previewing first. The preview area is scrollable, as you can tell from the scrollbar that appears on the far right side of the window. You can use the navigation arrows at the bottom of the preview area to display different pages. Of course, these are only helpful if you're previewing a document that's longer than one page. Click a navigation arrow button to move forward and backward among the document pages. To view a specific page, type its number in the box and press **Enter**.

Another nice control is the ability to zoom in and out to view a page. Drag the **Zoom** slider left to zoom out or drag it right to zoom in, as pointed out in Figure 19.2. You can also click either end of the Zoom bar to quickly zoom your view. If you zoom in, the horizontal scrollbar appears so you can move around to view different parts of the page. To return to full page view again, click the **Zoom to Page** button.

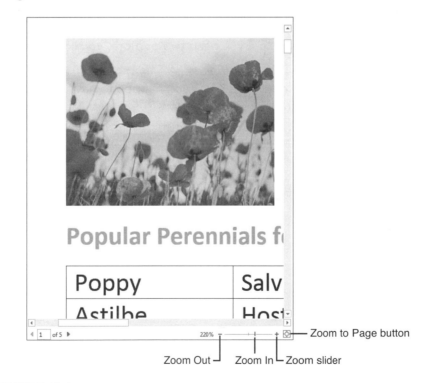

FIGURE 19.2

The preview area offers several controls you can use to check out your pages.

Managing Print Settings

If you're ready to print and you're confident all the settings are accurate as is, you can simply click the **Print** button (refer to Figure 19.1). That's all it takes, and the document is off and running to the printer. However, if you need to adjust a few things first, such as specifying how many copies to make, then let me take you through all the settings available.

 TIP   Before you get ready to click the **Print** button, you first need to make sure your printer is connected, turned on, and ready to go. If you have more than one hooked up, you'll have an opportunity to choose which printer you want to use. If you run into any kind of printing problems, most of the time it's a hardware problem, like running out of ink or paper. A printer pre-check can sometimes eliminate problems before they arise.

Next to the **Print** button, you can use the spinner arrows or type in a number for the amount of copies you want to print. This one's pretty self-explanatory. One copy is the default setting, so if you need two or more, you'll need to change the value.

To change the printer used for the job (if you happen to have more than one connected), click the **Printer** drop-down arrow (see Figure 19.3) and choose one from the list. The list also reveals options for faxing, sending the file to Microsoft's OneNote program, and so forth. At the bottom of the menu is a command for adding a printer, in case you just hooked up a new one that you want Word to recognize.

FIGURE 19.3

Change printers using the Printer drop-down menu.

Also at the bottom of the menu is the **Print to File** command, a holdover from the earlier days of word processing and DOS (which stands for disk operating system, one of the earlier personal computing platforms back in the '80s). When you activate this command, it saves the document's formatting and layout so a printing facility can print the file without needing to open it in its native application. You usually don't have to worry about this sort of thing these days. Saving a file to XPS or PDF format does the same thing, and almost anybody can read the file in XPS or PDF format.

If you need to view settings pertaining to your particular brand of printer, you can open the **Properties** dialog box, similar to what you see in Figure 19.4. To display the dialog box, click the **Printer Properties** link located just below the **Printer** drop-down menu.

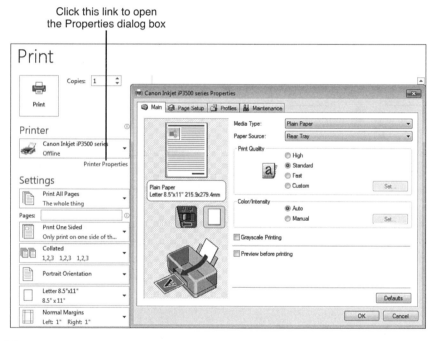

FIGURE 19.4

You can open a dialog box of properties for your particular printer.

You can control what prints using the first option listed under **Settings**, as shown in Figure 19.5. By default, Word assumes you want to print all the pages in your document and sets the option to **Print All Pages**. But if you click the drop-down arrow, you can choose to print just the current page, particular pages (which you then have to specify), or just the selected text (which you select in the document before flipping over to the **Print** window for printing). The menu also lets you choose to print extra document info, such as a list of styles used or file properties. The bottom of the menu lets you control odd and even page printing and whether any markup edit marks print.

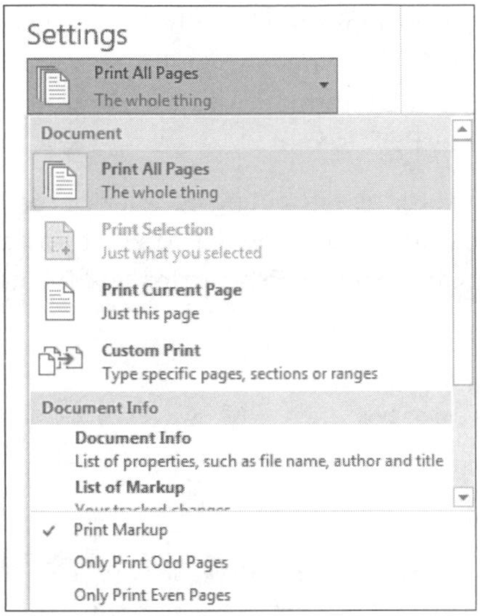

FIGURE 19.5

Control what prints using this menu.

If you need to print on both sides of the paper, you can click the next setting (see Figure 19.6) and instruct the printer on which paper sides are utilized or not utilized. Some printers can print both sides without any intervention, but others require some manual help to do this (such as home printers). You can choose the manual option and you'll be prompted when to switch the paper load for the second side's printing. The default setting, **Print One Sided**, does exactly as its name implies—just prints one side of the paper.

If you need to collate the pages for stapling together or binding, click the **Collated** drop-down arrow and choose whether to collate or not (see Figure 19.7). If you're making two copies of a 10-page document, for example, you can choose to print each set of 10-pages in order, which is the **Collated** option. If you want to print out two or more copies of each page at a time, such as two copies of page one, then two copies of page two, then choose **Uncollated**.

FIGURE 19.6

Use this menu to control which sides of the paper involves printing.

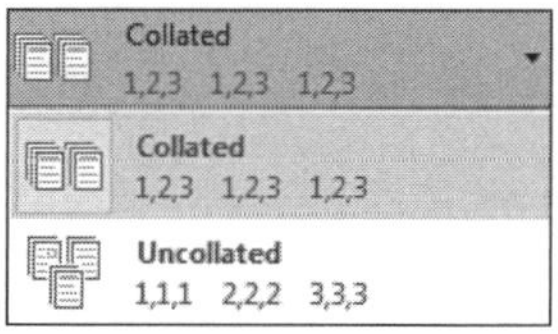

FIGURE 19.7

Need to collate your printouts? Use this menu to choose between collated and uncollated pages.

To change the page orientation, click the next setting (see Figure 19.8) and specify whether the page is taller than it is wide (portrait), or wider than it is tall (landscape).

FIGURE 19.8

Choose a page orientation.

If you need to specify a paper size, such as legal size, click the **Size** drop-down arrow and choose your paper size (see Figure 19.9). The menu list includes label sizes, business card sizes, envelope sizes, and more. Plus, you can click the **More Paper Size** command at the bottom of the menu and open the Page Setup dialog box to more paper size settings. Letter size (8.5" × 11") is the default setting.

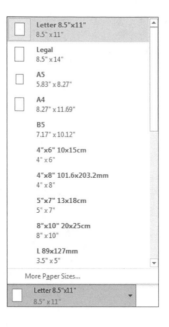

FIGURE 19.9

Need a different paper size? Choose one from this list.

TIP Have you ever wondered why some drop-down menus drop up instead of down? It's because of how much display space is available onscreen. If there's not enough room to display the menu in a downward direction, Word displays it upward instead.

Want to adjust your margins before printing? No problem. Click the **Margins** drop-down arrow, shown in Figure 19.10, and make a selection. You can learn more about setting margins in Chapter 9, "Formatting Pages." Careful, though; adjusting margins might create some issues for your pages, changing the layout and flow of text. Thankfully, you can preview everything you do in the preview area before committing the changes to a printout.

Lastly, you can fiddle with how many pages appear on a single printed page with the **Page per Sheet** drop-down menu, shown in Figure 19.11. Generally speaking, you only want to print one page on one piece of paper, but occasions might arise when you want to print 2, 4, 6, 8, or 16 pages on a single piece of paper. Naturally, the more document pages you print out on a single piece of paper, the smaller the pages appear and the less legible they are. But, hey, if you're into saving some paper, sometimes printing several document pages on a single printout might be helpful. The other option on the menu is to scale your document to fit a certain paper size, which might come in handy if you need to squeeze a document built on a larger paper size model onto a smaller actual paper for a printer.

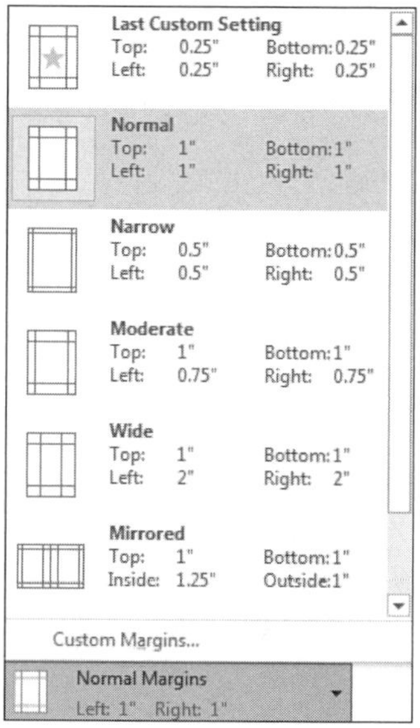

FIGURE 19.10

Use the Margins drop-down list to apply different margin settings to the document.

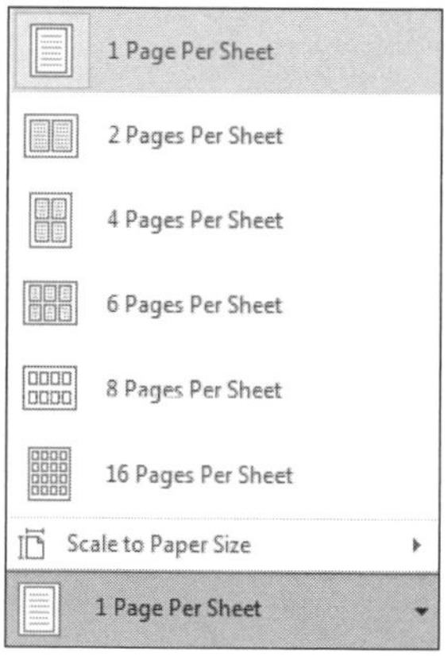

FIGURE 19.11

You can use this menu to print multiple document pages on a single printout page.

Any changes you make to the printer settings will remain in effect for any additional printing for the document, unless you change them again.

Controlling Page Setup

You can find plenty of tools for setting printing options before you actually get to the **Print** window. The **Page Layout** tab, for instance, lets you set margins, page orientation, and paper size with a click of a button. As you can see in Figure 19.12, you can click the **Page Layout** tab to view the settings, all of which are grouped under the heading **Page Layout**. You can set these options before you even begin building a new document, or you can assign them at any point of the document creation process. Just click the tab, then click a drop-down arrow to display a menu of choices.

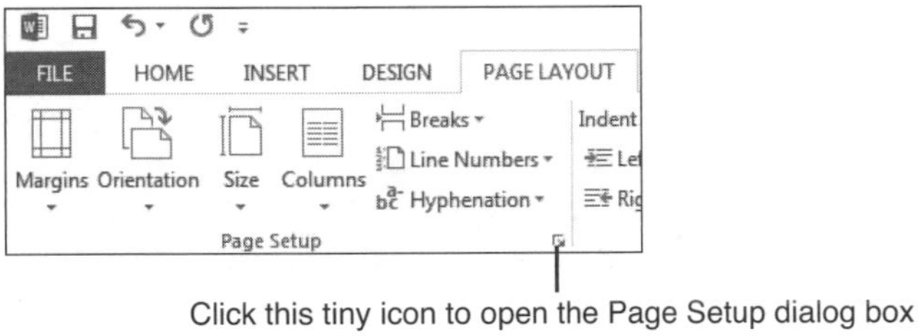

Click this tiny icon to open the Page Setup dialog box

FIGURE 19.12

You can find page layout controls on the Page Layout tab for setting margins, page orientation, and paper size.

The following Page Setup group commands can help you control aspects of your pages before printing:

- **Margins**—Click this button to view a menu of margin settings you can apply.

- **Orientation**—Switch between portrait and landscape page orientation using this button.

- **Size**—Specify a paper size, such as letter or legal, using this drop-down menu.

You can also adjust page settings through the Page Setup dialog box. Click the **Page Setup** icon (the tiny box with an arrow on it in the corner of the **Page Setup** group of tools) to open the dialog box, shown in Figure 19.13. The dialog box has three tabs: **Margins**, **Paper**, and **Layout**. The **Paper** tab lets you choose a paper size and source for your printer. Simply make your changes and click **OK** to apply them to the document.

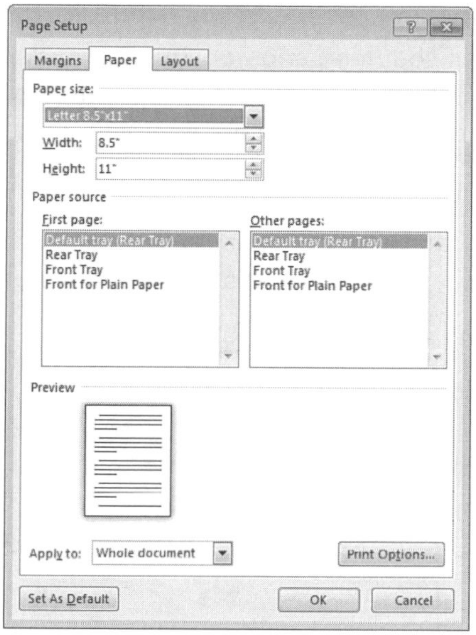

FIGURE 19.13

The Page Setup dialog box.

TIP You can learn more about setting margins in Chapter 9, as well as how to use the Page Setup dialog box to add headers and footers, and set vertical alignment options.

Printing Envelopes and Labels

Printing document pages is fairly straightforward; you click the **Print** button and away it goes. But did you know you can also print envelopes and labels with ease, too? Word has special tools for these very tasks, and I'm about to walk you through the steps for using them. Now go rummage through your desk drawer for some envelopes and labels and we'll put these features to work.

Printing Envelopes

You can grab the address information off of any letter you create in Word and turn it into a printed envelope. Using Word's **Envelopes** command, you can quickly whip up an envelope containing both the sender and delivery addresses, and control how the envelope prints out of your printer. Plus, you can change the font, envelope size, and position of the addresses on the envelope, such as moving an address to make room for a pre-printed logo on the envelope.

By default, Word is set up to process a standard size 10 envelope, which measures 4⅛" by 9½". If you need another size, you can specify one before printing. Also by default, Word assigns 12-point type for the envelope text, but you can change the font and size if you prefer something else.

Follow these steps to print an envelope:

1. Open the letter document containing the address information you want to turn into an envelope, similar to what's shown in Figure 19.14.

2. Click the **Mailings** tab on the Ribbon.

3. Click the **Envelopes** button.

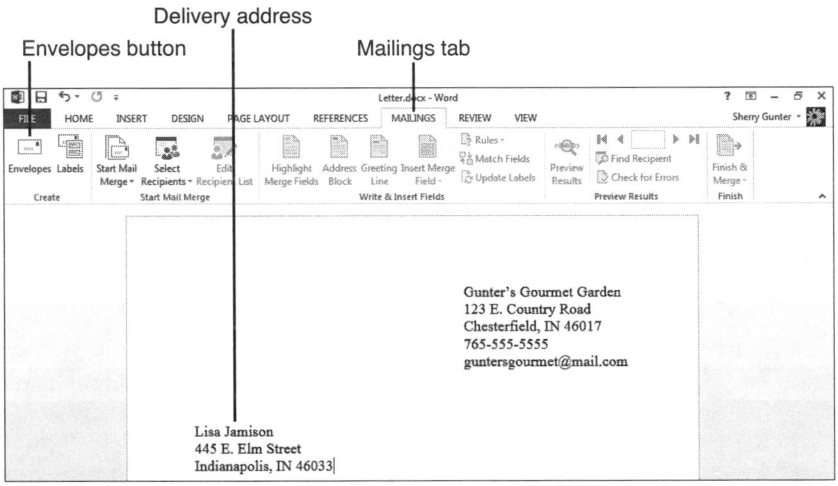

FIGURE 19.14

To make your way to Word's envelope printing feature, look for the Envelopes button on the Mailings tab.

4. Word opens the **Envelopes and Labels** dialog box shown in Figure 19.15, to the Envelopes options. (If the **Envelopes** tab is not already selected, click it.) Based on the letter document, Word guesses as to which lines of text comprise the sendee's address. To type another one instead, click in the **Delivery address** box and type another.

5. Click the **Return address** box and type in a return address, if needed.

6. Click the **Options** button to open the Envelope Options dialog box, shown in Figure 19.16.

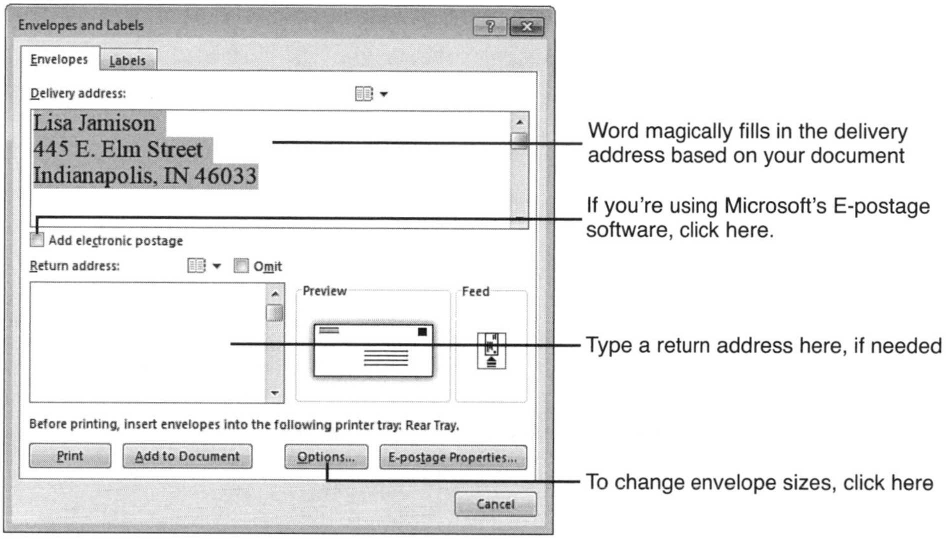

Word magically fills in the delivery address based on your document

If you're using Microsoft's E-postage software, click here.

Type a return address here, if needed

To change envelope sizes, click here

FIGURE 19.15

The Envelopes and Labels dialog box.

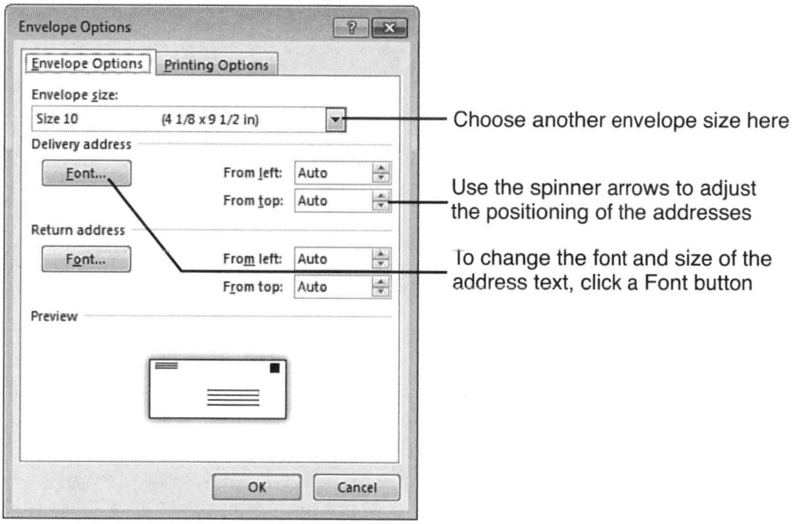

Choose another envelope size here

Use the spinner arrows to adjust the positioning of the addresses

To change the font and size of the address text, click a Font button

FIGURE 19.16

Use the Envelope Options dialog box to change the envelope size or reposition the addresses.

7. From the **Envelope Options** tab, click the **Envelope size** drop-down arrow and select a size.

8. If you need to control any positioning settings for either the delivery address or the return address, make your adjustments using the spinner arrows.

9. Click **OK**.

10. Click **Print** and feed your envelope through the printer per your printer's configuration.

Are you using electronic postage? You can print it out on the envelope as well, but only if you install the electronic postage software from the Microsoft Office website. Go ahead and click the **Add electronic postage** check box (refer to Figure 19.15) and Word displays a prompt box with some instructions for visiting the website to download the software. If you already have the software installed, you can click the **E-postage Properties** button to adjust the settings as needed.

If you need to tweak how an envelope is processed through your printer, such as changing the feed method or which printer tray to use, click the **Printing Options** tab in the **Envelope Options** dialog box and make your changes.

 TIP   Tired of typing in your return address for envelopes and labels? Why not add it to Word's customizing info so it's automatically added each time? Start by clicking the **File** tab and clicking **Options** to open the **Word Options** dialog box. Next, click the **Advanced** category, then scroll down the page to find the **General** options. There's a big text box located there labeled **Mailing address**. Type in your return address and click **OK** to exit the dialog box. Next time you use the **Envelopes and Labels** dialog box, the address is already there.

Printing Labels

Word also has tools to help you print out labels for addresses. You can print a single label or a sheet of labels. If you use label paper from a particular manufacturer, you can feed them into the printer, choose that manufacturer and label size, and print them from Word, too. When you create labels in Word, they're turned into a table with cell size matching that of the designated label vendor size you select. Most label paper is self-adhesive these days, and the entire sheet of labels is constructed of individual labels spaced out across the page. Your Word-based labels need to match the layout of your label paper, so you'll need to know the manufacturer and product number. Lots of label vendors are out there, including Microsoft, 3M, and Avery, so chances of finding a match among the labels listed in Word are pretty good. Even if you don't, you can designate your own new label size and layout.

You have the choice of printing a single label from your label sheet, which is handy so you don't waste label paper, or printing out a full sheet of the same label. You can also print out a sheet of different addresses. To do a full sheet of the same or different addresses, you instruct Word to create a new document. When you do, the addresses are all positioned across the page according to the label type you specify. To create a sheet of differing addresses, you can use this new document to type them all up. You can save the document to use over and over again.

Follow these steps to create and print a full sheet of labels:

1. Click the **Mailings** tab on the Ribbon.

2. Click the **Labels** button.

3. Word opens the **Envelopes and Labels** dialog box to the **Labels** tab, shown in Figure 19.17. (If the **Labels** tab is not already selected, click it.) If you're creating a sheet of the same address, click in the **Address** box and type the text you want on the label.

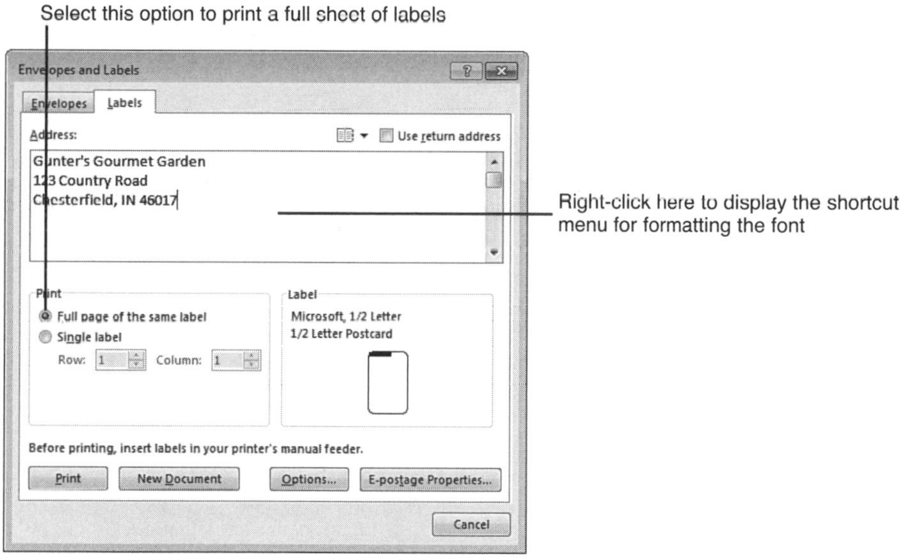

Select this option to print a full sheet of labels

Right-click here to display the shortcut menu for formatting the font

FIGURE 19.17

The Envelopes and Labels dialog box with the Labels options displayed.

4. If you need to apply any special formatting to the text, right-click in the **Address** box and choose **Font** or **Paragraph** to open the corresponding dialog box and make your changes.

5. To print all the same label, click the **Full Page of the Same Label** option.

6. Click the **Label** section to open the **Label Options** dialog box shown in Figure 19.18 (or click the **Options** button to do the same thing).

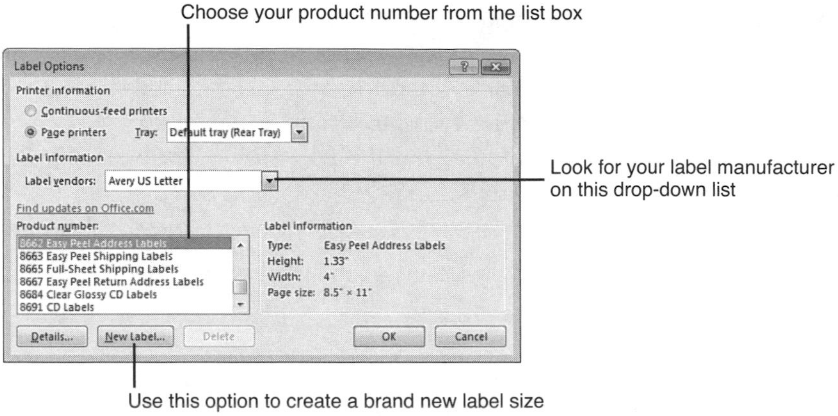

Choose your product number from the list box

Look for your label manufacturer on this drop-down list

Use this option to create a brand new label size

FIGURE 19.18

Use the Label Options dialog box to choose your label vendor and product number or style.

7. Select the type of label you're going to print on; if you can't find a match, choose **New Label** and enter the correct dimensions for your labels.

8. Click **OK** to return to the Envelopes and Labels dialog box.

9. Click New Document.

10. Word opens a new document with the label table in place (similar to what you see in Figure 19.19). If you're printing different addresses, this is the place to type them all up. Click in a table cell and start typing them in.

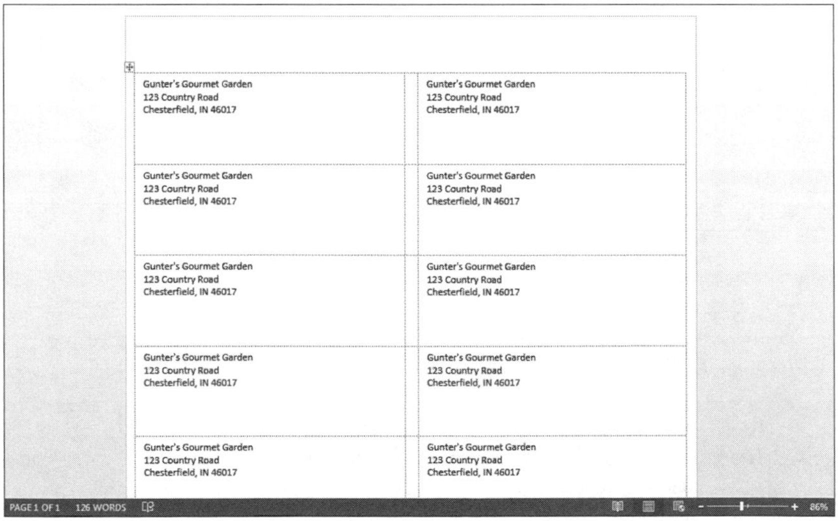

FIGURE 19.19

How about that—a new document filled with a label table to match your label manufacturer's label page layout.

TIP Saving the page is a good idea if you want to reuse the labels again. Click the **Save** button on the Quick Access toolbar or press **Ctrl+S** to save the file.

11. When you're ready to print the sheet, press **Ctrl+P** and feed your labels through the printer per your printer's configuration.

 TIP To avoid wasting your expensive labels, print a test set first. In step 11, use a blank sheet of printer paper rather than a sheet of labels. Place the newly printed page in front of a page of blank labels and hold the two sheets up to a light. If the printed text appears to be positioned correctly over the individual labels, you're ready to print on the labels. If not, adjust your settings and repeat the test until the printed sample and the labels are perfectly matched.

If you want just a single label, you can type it up in the **Address** box and click the **Single label** option, and then specify which label on the sheet to put it in before printing.

 NOTE You can grab mailing addresses from your contacts database, such as Microsoft Outlook. Click the **Address Book** icon in the Envelopes and Labels dialog box to start the process of using a contacts profile.

Using Word's Mail Merge Tool

Word's Mail Merge tool has been around a while now with various editions of Word, but it's still a pretty nifty feature even if it hasn't changed much through the years. Basically, you can use it to create mass mailings, such as form letters, invitations, or mass emails. You create a form letter in which you can insert personalized information, such as names and addresses, and end up with a customized letter to mail out. The Mail Merge Wizard walks you through each phase of the process, taking all the guesswork out of it. You can type up a form letter before you get started, or you can stop and do so when prompted. You can also choose to insert contacts and addresses from an existing table (database) or start a brand-new list.

The secret to personalized mail merge documents is designating merge fields. A *merge field* is preset information for automating parts of a document. Merge fields act as placeholders for information that is inserted later. For example, if your letter starts with a contact's address you can insert an Address Block field. If your form letter uses an opening salutation, you can insert a Greeting Line field that uses the contact's first name and a salutation. When you merge the form letter document with your list of contacts, Word grabs the data from the designated fields (such as a contact's address or first name) and inserts it into the document where you told it to.

To show you how this procedure works, we'll begin with an existing form letter I've typed up. To get things rolling, click the Ribbon's **Mailings** tab and click the **Start Mail Merge** button, as shown in Figure 19.20. We're going to use the Wizard for this procedure, which is simply a step-by-step walkthrough using a pane, so click the **Step-by-Step Mail Merge Wizard** option to open the **Mail Merge** pane, shown in Figure 19.21.

FIGURE 19.20

Start a mail merge using the Mailings tab.

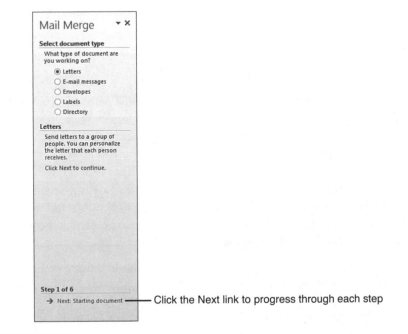

FIGURE 19.21

The Mail Merge pane walks you through each step.

Step 1, shown in Figure 19.21, is to select the type of document for the mass mailing. For this example, I'm going to choose **Letters**, but you can choose something else, if needed. After you make your selection, click the **Next** link at the bottom of the pane. Just so you know now, you can click the **Next** link every time you finish a step to progress to the next step.

Step 2, shown in Figure 19.22, asks you to specify a starting document. Unless you want to use another file as the form letter, leave the **Use the current document** radio button selected. You can also use a template or another document. Click the **Next** link at the bottom of the pane to continue.

FIGURE 19.22

Specify a document for the form letter.

Step 3, shown in Figure 19.23, is where it starts to get a little complicated. You need to choose your source for names and addresses—your contacts list. You can go several different directions here. You can use an existing database of contacts from a file or database, you can grab the information from your contacts list in Microsoft Outlook (if you happen to use Outlook), or you can type up a brand-new list of contacts. Just in case you don't use Outlook or have an existing list, let's build a new one. This route is going to take a little longer, but it's good practice and you just might need a separate list file for other activities on your computer. Click the **Type a new list** option and then click the **Create** button to open a window to start typing in names and addresses, shown in Figure 19.24. Of course, if you use an existing list or Outlook contacts, you'll be prompted to specify those files before continuing to step 4.

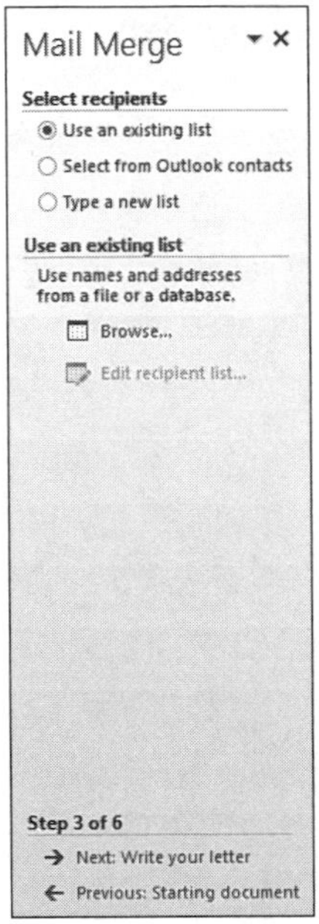

FIGURE 19.23

Choose the source of your contact data.

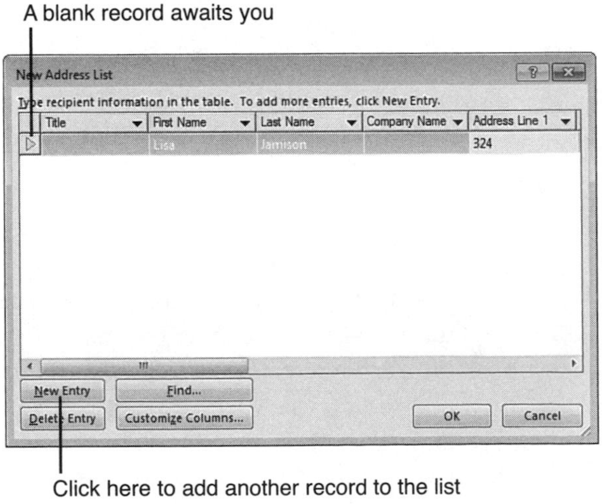

FIGURE 19.24

Use the New Address List window to build a brand-new database of contact information.

Meanwhile, back at the build-your-own list task, start typing in the first *record* (that's what they call a contact's information, in this case a row of entries). Click the **Tab** key to move from one column to the next. The default list format is pretty basic; each column represents a portion of the contact information, starting with title, first name, last name, address, city, state, and ZIP Code. After you finish entering all the data you want for the first contact, click the **New Entry** button and type in another. Keep repeating this procedure until you've completed your contacts list. When you're done, click **OK** (see Figure 19.25). Word prompts you to save and name the new list you just made, as shown in Figure 19.26. Word saves this data as a database file format (.MDB file extension). This file type can be opened in a database program, such as Microsoft Access, in case you were wondering.

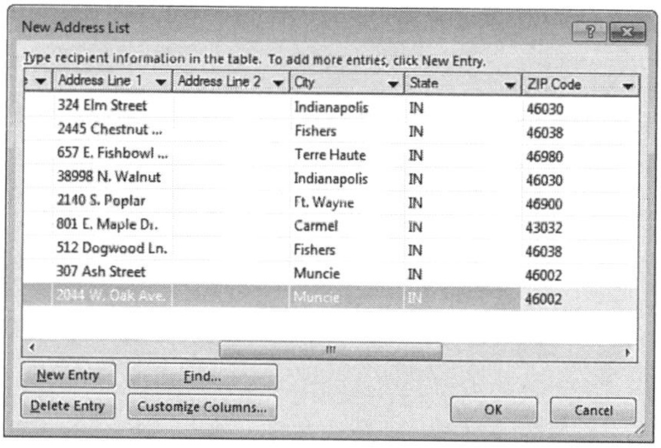

FIGURE 19.25

Click the OK button when you're done creating your list.

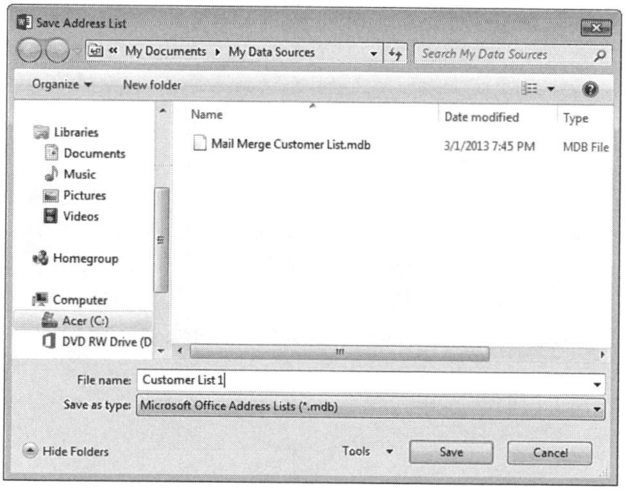

FIGURE 19.26

Word prompts you to save your list file.

TIP You don't have to use the default fields offered in the **New Address List** box. You can customize the bits of data you want to use for each record. To do so, click the **Customize Columns** button and start tailoring the record fields.

The **Mail Merge Recipients** box appears next, shown in Figure 19.27, listing everything again. This time, it's to tell you that everybody with a check mark next to their name is going to be included in the mail merge. You can take this opportunity to uncheck anyone you don't want included. Click **OK** to exit the dialog box. The newly created list (or at least its name anyway) now appears in the **Mail Merge** pane as your list source. Click **Next** to continue.

Data Source	✔	Last Name	First Name	Title	Company Name	Add ▲
Customer List 1	✔	Jamison	Lisa			324
Customer List 1....	✔	Noland	Candace			244!
Customer List 1....	✔	Goldman	Bob			657
Customer List 1....	✔	Wallace	Matt			389!
Customer List 1....	✔	Gunter	Tammy			214(
Customer List 1....	✔	Cousins	Edward			801
Customer List 1....	✔	Cannon	Jake			512
Customer List 1....	✔	Davids	Joshua			307

Mail Merge Recipients

This is the list of recipients that will be used in your merge. Use the options below to add to or change your list. Use the checkboxes to add or remove recipients from the merge. When your list is ready, click OK.

Data Source

Customer List 1.mdb

Refine recipient list

Sort...
Filter...
Find duplicates...
Find recipient...
Validate addresses...

Edit... Refresh

OK

FIGURE 19.27

Now you have a source for the contact information needed for your mail merge.

Step 4 involves adding the special merge fields needed to grab contact information. Using the current letter, click where you want to insert the address and click the **Address Block** link in the **Mail Merge** pane, shown in Figure 19.28. Word opens the **Insert Address Block** dialog box (see Figure 19.29), previewing a contact from your designated list. Check to make sure the information is what you want (in this example, I'm looking for the standard address info, three lines that include the person's name, street address, city, state, and ZIP Code). You can turn check boxes on or off for other options regarding the address information. Click **OK** when everything is to your liking.

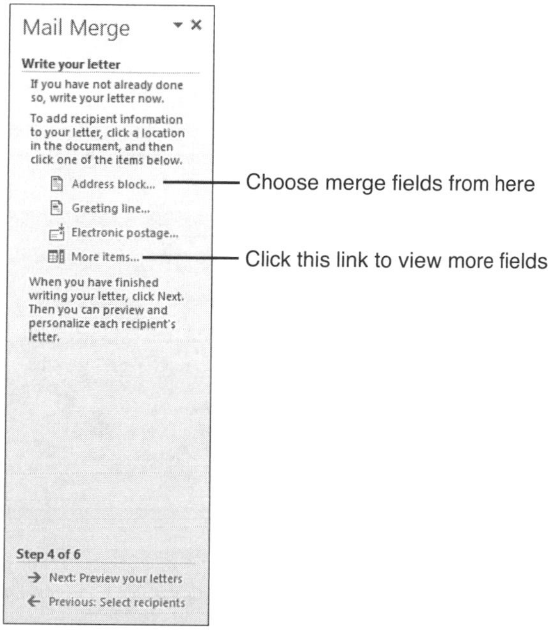

Mail Merge ▾ ✕

Write your letter

If you have not already done so, write your letter now.

To add recipient information to your letter, click a location in the document, and then click one of the items below.

　📄 Address block... ———— Choose merge fields from here

　📄 Greeting line...

　📑 Electronic postage...

　📇 More items... ———— Click this link to view more fields

When you have finished writing your letter, click Next. Then you can preview and personalize each recipient's letter.

Step 4 of 6

➡ Next: Preview your letters

⬅ Previous: Select recipients

FIGURE 19.28

Step 4 involves inserting merge fields into your form letter.

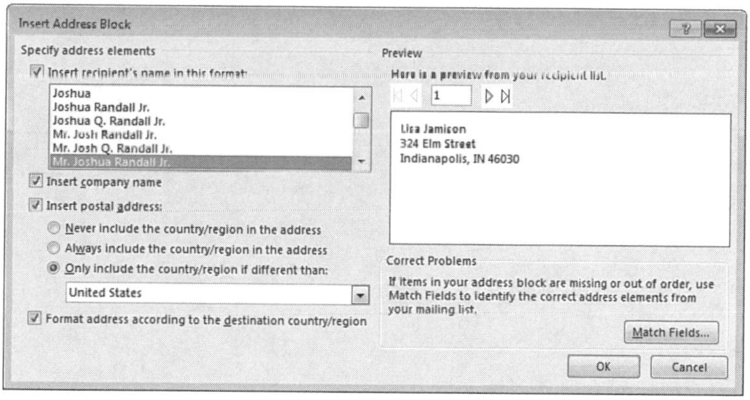

Insert Address Block

Specify address elements　　　　　　　　　　　　　Preview

☑ Insert recipient's name in this format:　　　　Here is a preview from your recipient list.

Joshua
Joshua Randall Jr.
Joshua Q. Randall Jr.
Mr. Josh Randall Jr.
Mr. Josh Q. Randall Jr.
Mr. Joshua Randall Jr.

　　　　　　　　　　　　　　　　　Lisa Jamison
　　　　　　　　　　　　　　　　　324 Elm Street
　　　　　　　　　　　　　　　　　Indianapolis, IN 46030

☑ Insert company name

☑ Insert postal address:

　○ Never include the country/region in the address

　○ Always include the country/region in the address

　◉ Only include the country/region if different than:

　United States

☑ Format address according to the destination country/region

Correct Problems

If items in your address block are missing or out of order, use Match Fields to identify the correct address elements from your mailing list.

Match Fields...

OK　　Cancel

FIGURE 19.29

The Insert Address Block dialog box.

Word inserts the field, as shown in Figure 19.30. You can continue adding more fields to your form letter in spots where you want to customize it, such as a greeting. Figure 19.31 shows the **Insert Greeting Line** dialog box where you can choose an opening salutation and control how you want the greeting to appear in the letter. A similar type of dialog box will appear for each field you add to your letter. After you've placed all your merge fields, click **Next** in the **Mail Merge** pane to keep going.

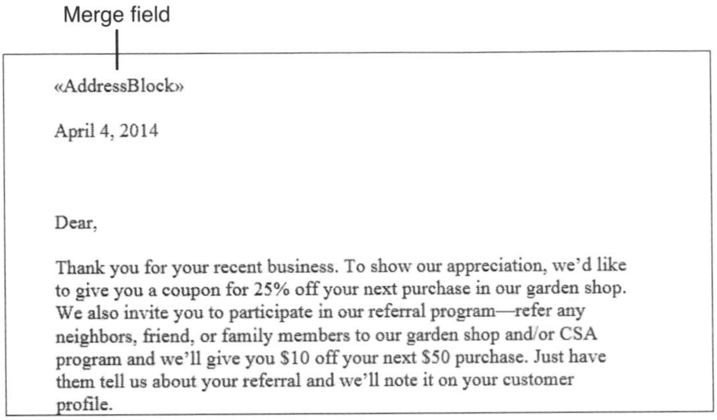

«AddressBlock»

April 4, 2014

Dear,

Thank you for your recent business. To show our appreciation, we'd like to give you a coupon for 25% off your next purchase in our garden shop. We also invite you to participate in our referral program—refer any neighbors, friend, or family members to our garden shop and/or CSA program and we'll give you $10 off your next $50 purchase. Just have them tell us about your referral and we'll note it on your customer profile.

FIGURE 19.30

Merge fields appear with special markings in your document.

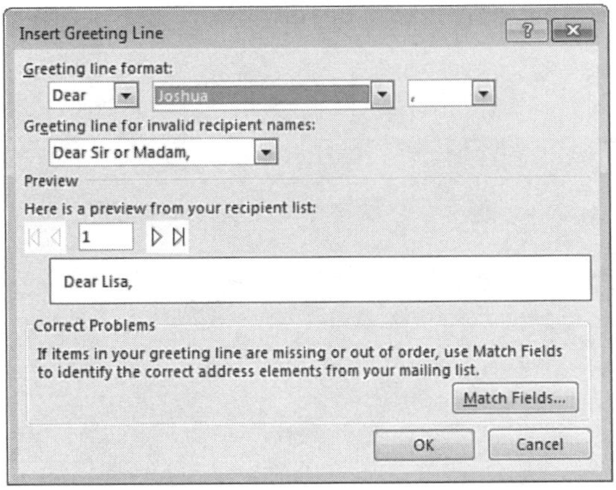

FIGURE 19.31

The Insert Greeting Line dialog box.

Step 5 lets you preview what your merged letter looks like with an actual merging of contact info into the letter, as demonstrated in Figure 19.32. You can use the navigation arrows in the pane to view different contacts' data in the letter. You can also use this preview time to make adjustments to your letter or merge fields. Notice the **Mailings** tab has a group of tools under the heading **Write & Insert Fields**. You can use the tools to add more fields, highlight them in the letter so you can see where they are, and more.

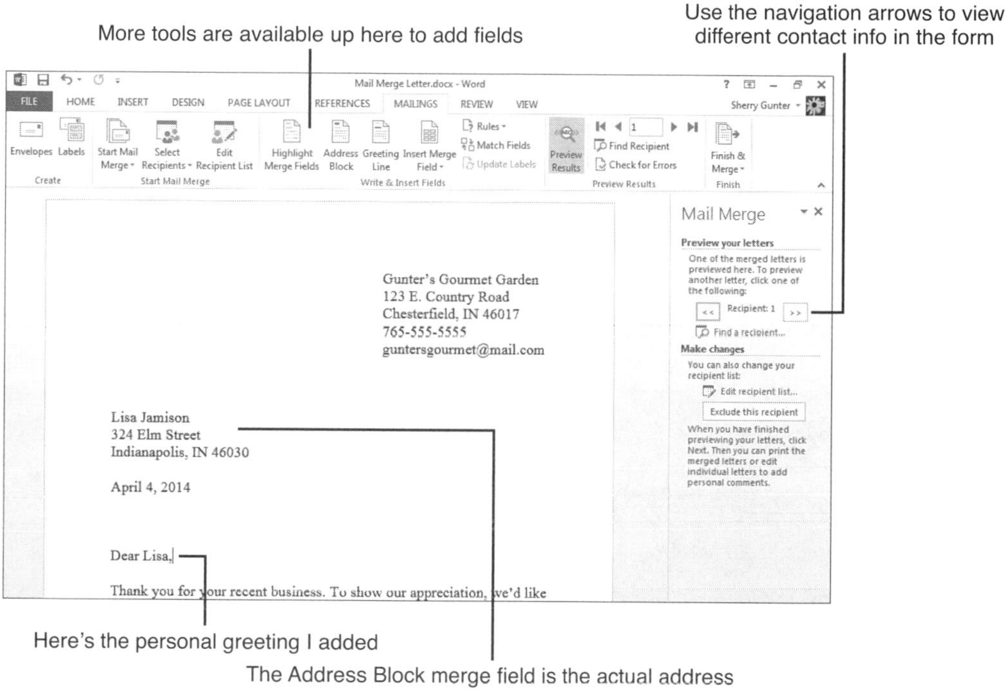

More tools are available up here to add fields

Use the navigation arrows to view different contact info in the form

Here's the personal greeting I added

The Address Block merge field is the actual address

FIGURE 19.32

Step 5 lets you preview your form letter with actual contact information inserted into it.

Whew, we're almost done. If everything's looking good and you're ready to merge, click the **Next** link at the bottom of the **Mail Merge** pane. Step 6, shown in Figure 19.33, instructs you on how to complete the merge. You can choose to print the letters directly, or open them in a new document file. Make your selection and away it goes. If you choose **Edit individual letters**, Word opens a new document with letters for each contact. If you go this route, a **Merge to New Document** dialog box opens and you can specify whether you want to merge all the records, or just certain ones. If you merge them all, you might end up with a very long document depending on how many contacts you're mailing.

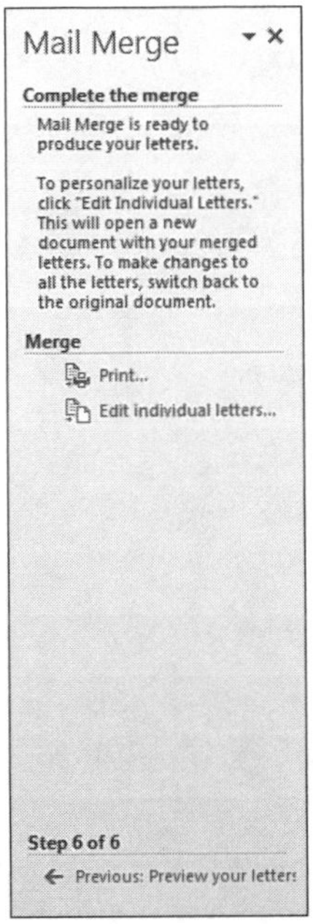

FIGURE 19.33

Step 6 is the last phase of the process; choose whether you want to start printing letters right away or view them all in another Word document file.

Well now, that was fun, wasn't it? I know it seemed a bit complicated, but it really beats having to type up individual letters. It's especially speedy if you already have a contacts list available and don't have to build a new one.

THE ABSOLUTE MINIMUM

You can print like a pro now. Here's what you picked up in this chapter:

- To print out a document, click the **File** tab and click the **Print** category. All the printing options hang out on the **Print** window.

- You can also use the **Print** window to do a final check of how your document is going to look when committed to paper.

- Printing envelopes is easy with a little help from the **Envelopes and Labels** dialog box.

- You can find a huge list of label vendors and label sizes to match your printer product; but if you can't, you can create a new label size to suit your situation.

- A mail merge takes a generic form letter and customizes it with information from a contacts list, such as names and addresses.

- Use the Mail Merge Wizard to walk you through the basic steps to create a form letter, add merge fields, and create a final merged mass mailing letter.

We've reached the end of the road in this quest to learn about Microsoft Word 2013. Hopefully, you now feel more confident and qualified to tackle just about any word processing task that comes your way. I would hand you a certificate of completion or something, but you're going to be so busy making documents now you won't have time to frame it or hang it up anyhow. So, let's just call it a job well done and part ways knowing you will always be my favorite reader. See you at the next Microsoft Word revision!

Index

A

access, restricting, 68

accessing SkyDrive from Word, WEB: 397-398

account name, 13

Add a Digital Signature, 68

Add-Ins tab, Ribbon, 24

Add Shape command, 200

adding
  apps, 50-53
  borders, 276-278
  captions, 299-301
  cells, 180-181
  color to text, 103-104
  columns, 176-179
  footers, 134-137
  headers, 134-137
  hyperlinks, WEB: 389-392
  Microsoft accounts, 41-42
  page numbers, 138-139
  picture styles, 276-278
  rows, 176-179
  services to Microsoft accounts, 47-50
  shading, 159
  special effects, 152
    drop caps, 152-153
    text effects, 153-154
    watermarks, 154-156
  text with Quick Parts, 88-89

adjusting pictures, 285
  correcting problems, 285-286
  removing backgrounds, 287-289
  tweaking colors, 286-287

alignment
  cells, 184-185
  controlling, 108

vertical alignment, changing, 132-133

alignment guides, 264

applying templates, 72-75

apps, adding, 50-53

Artistic Effects, 279
  applying to pictures, 281-282

ascenders, 121

assigning
  document protection, 67-68
  effects, 279-281
  styles, 150

attributes. *See* text formatting

AutoCorrect, 324-326

AutoFit command, 174

AutoFit Contents, 175

axes, charts, 207

axis labels, 208

B

backgrounds
  customizing (Microsoft accounts), 46-47
  removing from pictures, 287-289

bandwidth, cloud, 37

Bing Image Search, 241
  inserting pictures from, 244-246

Bing Video Search, 254

BMP (Windows Bitmap), 239

bold, applying, 96-98

bookmarks, inserting, 307-310

borders, 156
  adding, 276-278
  page borders, adding 158
  tables, 188-191
  text borders, adding, 157

Borders and Shading dialog box, 158

Borders tool, 157

breaks
  inserting, 139-142
  removing, 142

browsers, managing SkyDrive from, WEB: 394-397

bulleted lists, 118-120

C

captions, adding, 299-301

capturing screenshots, 250-254

cells
  adding, 180-181
  alignment, 184-185
  deleting, 180-181
  margins, 184-185
  merging, 181-184
  splitting, 181-184

Change Colors palette, 203

changes to documents, reviewing, WEB: 371-373

changing
  fonts, 98-100
  layouts, colors, and styles, SmartArt, 202-203
  markup display, tracking changes, WEB: 365-367
  point size, 100-102
  view modes, 29-31

character spacing, 125

chart area, 208

chart data, entering, 210-211

chart parts, 207-208

charts, 193
   chart parts, 207-208
   editing, 212-215
   entering data, 210-211
   inserting, 205, 209
   types of, 206

chart text, 208

check boxes, Ribbon, 23

checking documents for hidden
   data, 330-332

choosing style sets, 149

Citations & Bibliography, 299

Clear All Formatting
   button, 105

clip art, 240

Clipboard pane, cutting,
   copying, and pasting text,
   87-88

Close command, 17

closing
   documents, 65
   Word, 16-17

cloud, 36, WEB: 382
   bandwidth, 37

cloud computing, 36-38
   Microsoft, 38

cloud connectivity, 36

cloud storage, 36-38

cloud storage services, 36

collated printing, 338

color, adding to text, 103-104

colors
   changing (SmartArt), 202-203
   tweaking in pictures, 286-287

Colors dialog box, 104, 159

columns, 130-132
   adding, 176-179
   deleting, 176-179

comments
   inserting, 317-319
   tracking documents,
      WEB: 370-371

Comments feature, 317

Compare Documents dialog
   box, WEB: 373

comparing documents,
   WEB: 373-374

Compress Pictures, 287

context menus, 26-27

controlling page setup, 342-343

Convert Text to Table
   command, 165

copying
   data, 66-67
   text, 85
   text formatting from one
      place to another, 104-105

copying and pasting text, 86

copyright symbol, inserting, 93

correcting picture problems,
   285-286

Create Graphic group, 200

cropping pictures, 282-285

cross-references
   inserting, 301-302
   removing, 302

cursors, 82

custom indents, 111

custom tables, drawing,
   167-169

Customize Quick Access
   Toolbar button, 334

customizing
   Microsoft accounts, 42
      account pictures, 43-45
      background and theme,
        46-47
   SmartArt, 197-201

cutting and pasting text, 86

D

data
   copying, 66-67
   moving between files, 66-67
   pasting, 66-67

data categories, 207

data points, 207

data series, 207

data tables, 208

Delete Cells dialog box,
   179-180

Delete Columns command, 178

Delete key, 83

Delete Rows command, 178

deleting
   cells, 180-181
   columns, 176-179
   rows, 176-179

descenders, 121

deselecting text, 85

Design tab, 213
   Ribbon, 23
   tables, 190

diagrams, 193

dialog boxes, 27-29

digital pictures. See pictures

digital signatures, 68

Display for Review drop-down
   menu, WEB: 365

DNG (Digital Negative) file
   types, 240

.DOC, 72

Document Inspector dialog
   box, 331

document protection, assigning,
   67-68

document work area, 13

documents, 55
   checking for hidden data,
      330-332
   closing, 65

comparing, WEB: 373-375

emailing, WEB: 382-385

navigating with Navigation pane, 310-313

opening, 62-65

previewing, 334-335

printing, 334

managing print settings, 336-341

reviewing, WEB: 362-363

saving, 58-60

file types, 60-61

options, 62

sending as attachments, WEB: 383

sharing, WEB: 375-378

starting new, 56-57

structuring with Outline view, 292-296

tracking, WEB: 362-363

changing markup display, WEB: 365-367

comments, WEB: 369-371

reviewing changes, WEB: 371-372

turning on tracking, WEB: 363-364

turning into web pages, WEB: 386-388

viewing multiple, 65-66

.DOCX file extension, 60, 238

.DOT, 72

.DOTM, 72

.DOTX, 72

Draft mode, 29

dragging, resizing tables, 173-174

Draw Table command, 180

drawing

custom tables, 167-169

shapes, 218-221

Drop Cap dialog box, 153

drop caps, inserting, 152-153

E

Edit Hyperlink dialog box, WEB: 392

Edit Shape drop-down arrow, 226

editing

charts, 212-215

PDF files, WEB: 375

text, 82-83

effects, 219

assigning, 279-281

Effects, 279

emailing documents, WEB: 382-385

embedding videos, 254-257

Encrypt with Password, 68

endnotes, inserting, 297-298

entering chart data, 210-211

Envelope Options dialog box, 345

envelopes, printing, 343-346

Envelopes and Labels dialog box, 347

Eraser tool, 180

Excel spreadsheets, inserting as tables, 169-170

exiting Word, 16-17

external hard drives, 250

F

File tab, 23

file types, 60-61

.DOC, 72

pictures, 238-240

fill color, 219

Find and Replace dialog box, 319

finding

help, 14-16

templates, 76-78

finding and replacing text, 319-322

flash drives, 250

Flickr, 241

Flip command, 268

flipping graphics, 267-270

Font Color palette, 103

Font Color tool, 104

Font dialog box, 102

fonts, changing, 98-100

Font Size drop-down menu, 100

Font Size menu, 101

footers, adding, 134-137

footnotes, inserting, 297-298

Format Painter tool, 104

Format pane, effects, 281

Format Picture pane, 286

Format Shape pane, 224, 229

Format tab, 203, 213

Picture Styles gallery, 277

text wrapping options, 266

Format Text Effects icon, 229

formatting

borders, 156

page borders, 158

text borders, 157

pages. See page formatting

paragraphs. See paragraph formatting

shading, 156

adding, 159

shapes, 223-226

SmartArt, 203-205

special effects, 152

adding watermarks, 154-156

applying text effects, 153-154

inserting drop caps, 152-153

styles
  applying, 146-149
  assigning, 150
  choosing style sets, 149
  creating new, 151
text. *See* text formatting
themes, applying, 144-146

G

galleries, Ribbon, 22

GIF (Graphics Interchange Format), 239

Grammar pane, 324

graphic objects, 260

graphics. *See also* images; shapes
  effects, assigning, 279-281
  flipping, 267-270
  grouping, 270-276
  layering, 270-274
  pictures, 237. *See also* pictures
  positioning, 267
  rotating, 267-270
  sizing, 260-263
    alignment guides, 264
    with selection handles, 261
  SmartArt. *See* SmartArt
  text wrapping, 264-267

graphs, 193

gridlines, charts, 208

grouping graphics objects, 270-271, 275-276

H

headers, adding, 134-139

help, finding, 14-16

Help feature, 14-16

hidden data, checking documents for, 330-332

hiding Ribbon, 24

highlighter pens, highlighting text, 316-317

highlighting text with highlighter pen, 316-317

Home tab, 20
  Ribbon, 23
  Styles gallery, 149

hyperlinks, adding, WEB: 389-392

I

icons
  Layout Options, 205
  Paragraph icon, 23
  pushpin icon, 24
  Word, 12

images
  inserting from Internet, 240-242
  thumbnails, 241

indenting text, 110-111
  custom indents, 111
  setting indents with the ruler, 112-115
  simple indents, 111
  special indents, 112

indexes, creating, 302-305

Insert, 83

Insert Address Block dialog box, 354

Insert Cells dialog box, 179

Insert Chart dialog box, 206

Insert command, 178

Insert Greeting Line dialog box, 355

Insert Pictures dialog box, 201

Insert Pictures feature, 241

Insert tab, 20
  Ribbon, 23

inserting
  bookmarks, 307-310
  breaks, 139-142
  charts, 205, 209

comments, 317-319

cross-references 301-302

drop caps, 152-153

footnotes/endnotes 297-298

images from Internet, 240-242

pages, 139

pictures
  from Bing Image Search, 244-246
  from Office.com, 242-244
  from SkyDrive, 246-248
  your own, 248-249

Quick Parts, 89-91

Quick Tables, 165-166

sections, 139-142

shapes, 219

SmartArt, 196-197

symbols, 92-93

tables, 162-165
  Excel spreadsheets, 169-170

text box objects, 231-234

WordArt objects, 226-230

insertion points, 82

Internet, inserting images from, 240-242

italics, applying, 96-98

J-K

JPEG (Joint Photographics Expert Group), 238-239

key drives, 250

L

Label Options dialog box, 348

labels, printing, 346-349

layering graphics objects, 270-274

Layout dialog box, sizing graphics, 262

Layout Options icon, 205

Layout tab, Text Direction button, 185

layouts, changing (SmartArt), 202-203

leader characters, 115

leading, 121

legends, charts, 208

line spacing, 121-123

lists, 118-120

Live Preview feature, 145

lossless compression, 239

lossy compression, 239

M

Mail Merge pane, 350

Mail Merge tool, 349 358

Mail Merge Wizard, 349

Mailings tab, Ribbon, 23

managing
  print settings, 336-341
  SkyDrive
    accessing from Word, WEB: 397-398
    from your browser, WEB: 394-397

margins, 128-130
  cells, 184-185

Mark as Final, 68

markup display, changing, WEB: 365-367

master Document tool, 296

merge fields, 349

Merge to New Document dialog box, 357

merging cells, 181-184

metadata, 330

Microsoft, clouds, 38

Microsoft accounts, 39
  adding, 41-42
  customizing, 42

account pictures, 43-45
  background and theme, 46-47

services, adding, 47-50

signing in, 39-41

switching between, 41-42

Microsoft Word. *See* Word

mini toolbar, 26
  applying bold, italics, and underline, 97
  cutting, copying and pasting text, 87

Mini Translator, 328

moving
  data between files, 66-67
  text, 85

Multi-Tool Word for Xenix and MS-DOS, 6

N

navigating long documents with Navigation pane, 310-313

Navigation pane, 310-313

New Address List window, 352

new features, 8-9

numbered lists, 118-120

O

objects
  grouping, 275-276
  layering, 271-274

Office 365, 37

Office.com, 241
  inserting pictures from, 242-244

Office Store, 50

Office Web Apps, WEB: 398-400

Open dialog box, 64

Open page, 64

opening documents, 62-65

outline, 219

Outline mode, 29

Outline view, 292-296

Overtype, 83

P

page borders, adding, 158

PageDown, 83

page formatting
  columns, 130-132
  headers/footers, adding, 134-137
  inserting pages, breaks and sections, 139-142
  margins, 128-130
  page numbers, 138-139
  vertical alignment, changing, 132-133

Page Layout tab, 342
  Ribbon, 23

page numbers, adding, 138-139

Page Numbers feature, 138

page orientation, printing, 339

page setup, controlling, 342-343

Page Setup dialog box, 129, 343

pages, inserting, 139

PageUp, 83

paint format, 239

panes
  Clipboard pane, 87-88
  Format pane, effects, 281
  Format Picture pane, 286
  Format Shape pane, 224, 229
  Grammar pane, 324
  Mail Merge pane, 350
  Research pane, 328
  Revisions pane, 317-319
  Spelling and Grammar pane, 322
  Spelling pane, 323
  Styles pane, 150

Paragraph dialog box, 109

paragraph formatting, 107
  alignment, controlling, 108
  bulleted lists, 118-120
  numbered lists, 118-120
  spacing, 120-121
    character spacing, 125
    line spacing, 121-123
    paragraph spacing,
      123-125
  tabs, 115-117
  text, indenting, 110-115

Paragraph icon, 23

paragraph spacing, 120,
  123-125

pasting
  data, 66-67
  text, 86
    mini toolbar, 87

PDF (Portable Document
  Format), editing files,
  WEB: 375

Picture Border tools, 278

Picture Effects, 279

picture styles, adding, 276-278

Picture Styles gallery, Format
  tab, 277

Picture Styles tool, 278

pictures
  adjusting, 285
  Artistic Effects, applying,
    281-282
  borders, adding, 276-278
  colors, tweaking, 286-287
  correcting problems,
    285-286
  cropping, 282-285
  customizing Microsoft
    accounts, 43-45
  digital pictures, 237
  file types, 238-240
  inserting
    from Bing Image Search,
      244-246
    from Office.com, 242-244

from SkyDrive, 246-248
  your own, 248-249
picture styles, adding,
  276-278
removing backgrounds,
  287-289

placeholders, SmartArt, 197

plot area, 208

PNG (Portable Network
  Graphics), 239

point size, changing, 100-102

positioning graphics, 267

previewing documents, 334-335

Print Layout mode, 29

print settings, managing,
  336-341

Print to File command, 337

Print window, 334

printing
  collated, 338
  documents, 334
    managing print settings,
      336-341
  envelopes, 343-346
  labels, 346-349
  page orientation, 339

program window, overview,
  11-14

program window controls, 13

program windows, sizing, 13

prompt boxes, 29

proofreading, 315
  AutoCorrect, 324-326
  checking spelling and
    grammar, 322-324
  highlighting text, 316-317
  inserting comments, 317-319
  researching and translating
    words, 328-330
  text, finding and replacing,
    319-322
  Thesaurus, 327-328

protecting documents, 67-68

pushpin icon, 24

Q

Quick Access toolbar, 12, 25

Quick Parts, 135
  creating, 91
  inserting, 89-91
  text, adding, 88-89

Quick Print command, 334

Quick Tables, inserting, 165-166

R

raster, 239

RAW file types, 239

Read mode, 29, 32

red wavy lines, 83

References tab, Ribbon, 23

Remove Background tool, 287

removing
  breaks, 142
  cross-references, 302
  video, 257

Replace All, 320

repositioning
  shapes, 222-223
  tables, 186-187

requirements for Word, 7

researching words, 328-330

Research pane, 328

resizing
  shapes, 222-223
  tables, 186-187
    by dragging, 173-174
    Table Properties dialog
      box, 175-176
    Table Tools, 174-175

Restrict Access, 68

Restrict Editing, 68

restricting access to
  documents, 68

Review tab, Ribbon, 23

reviewing
changes to documents,
WEB: 371-373
documents, WEB: 362-363
Revisions pane, 317-319
Ribbon, 13, 20
Add-Ins tab, 24
check boxes, 23
Design tab, 23
elements of, 21-23
File tab, 23
galleries, 22
hiding, 24
Home tab, 20, 23
Insert tab, 23
Mailings tab, 23
Page Layout tab, 23
Quick Access toolbar, 25
References tab, 23
Review tab, 23
spinner arrows, 22
View tab, 24
rotating graphics, 267-270
rows
adding, 176-179
deleting, 176-179
ruler, setting indents, 112-115

S

Save As command, 58
Save As dialog box, 59
Save as type drop-down list, 61
saving
documents, 58-60
as web pages,
WEB: 386-388
file types, 60-61
options, 62
templates, 78-79
screen clipping, 252
screenshots, capturing, 250-254
Screenshot tool, 250
scroll bars, 13
sections, inserting, 139-142

selecting
table parts, 172-173
text, 84-85
selection handles, 75
sizing graphics, 261
Send a Link, WEB: 382
Send as Attachment, WEB: 382
Send as Internet Fax, WEB: 382
Send as PDF, WEB: 382
Send as XPS, WEB: 382
sending documents as
attachments, WEB: 383
services, adding to Microsoft
accounts, 47-50
shading, 156
adding, 159
Shape Effects, 279
Shape Styles gallery, 278
shapes
drawing, 218-221
formatting, 223-226
inserting, 219
repositioning, 222-223
resizing, 222-223
Shapes tool, 218
Share screen, WEB: 383
sharing documents,
WEB: 375-378
Show Markup menu, WEB: 366
signing into Microsoft accounts,
39-41
simple indents, 111
sizing
graphics, 260-263
alignment guides, 264
selection handles, 261
program windows, 13
shapes, 222-223
tables, 173, 186-187
by dragging, 173-174
Table Properties dialog
box, 175-176
Table Tools, 174-175

SkyDrive, 241, WEB: 393-394
inserting pictures from,
246-248
managing
accessing from Word,
WEB: 397-398
from your browser,
WEB: 394-397
sharing documents,
WEB: 375-378
SmartArt, 194-196
changing layouts, colors,
and styles, 202-203
customizing, 197-201
formatting, 203-205
inserting, 196-197
spacing, 120-121
character spacing, 125
line spacing, 121-123
paragraph spacing, 123-125
special characters, 93
special effects, 152
adding watermarks, 154-156
applying text effects,
153-154
inserting drop caps, 152-153
special indents, 112
spell checker tool, 83
Spelling and Grammar checker,
322-324
Spelling and Grammar
pane, 322
Spelling pane, 323
Spinner arrows, Ribbon, 22
splitting cells, 181-184
starting
documents, 56-57
Word, 9-11
Start screen, 10
turning off, 11
status bar, 13
stick drives, 250
stock photography, 240
strikethrough, 98

structuring documents with Outline view, 292-296

style sets, choosing, 149

styles
applying, 146-149
assigning, 150
changing SmartArt, 202-203
choosing style sets, 149
creating new, 151

Styles gallery, Home tab, 149

Styles pane, 150

subscript, 98

superscript, 98

switching Microsoft accounts, 41-42

symbols, inserting, 92-93

T

table of contents, creating, 306-307

table parts, selecting, 172-173

Table Properties dialog box, 186
resizing tables, 175-176

Table Styles gallery, 188-191

Table Tools, 171
resizing tables, 174-175

tables, 161
borders, 188-191
cells
adding/deleting, 180-181
alignment/margins, 184-185
merging and splitting, 181-184
columns, adding/deleting, 176-179
custom tables, drawing, 167-169
Excel spreadsheets, inserting, 169-170
inserting, 162-165
Quick Tables, inserting, 165-166

repositioning, 186-187
rows, adding/deleting, 176-179
sizing, 173, 186-187
by dragging, 173-174
Table Properties dialog box, 175-176
Table Tools, 174-175
Table Styles gallery, 188-191

tabs, setting, 115-117

templates, 72
applying, 72-75
finding, 76-78
saving, 78-79

text
adding with Quick Parts, 88-89
adding color to, 103-104
Clipboard pane, 87-88
copying, 85
copying and pasting, 86
mini toolbar, 87
cutting and pasting, 86
mini toolbar, 87
deselecting, 85
editing, 82-83
finding and replacing, 319-322
highlighting with highlighter pen, 316-317
indenting, 110-111
custom indents, 111
setting indents with the ruler, 112-115
simple indents, 111
special indents, 112
moving, 85
selecting, 84-85
typing, 82-83

text borders, adding, 157

text boxes, 234

text box objects, inserting, 231-234

Text Box tool, 231

Text Direction button, 185

text effects, applying, 153-154

Text Effects, 279

Text Effects palette, Transform category, 230

text formatting, 95
adding color to text, 103-104
applying bold, italics, and underline, 96-98
changing point size, 100-102
changing fonts, 98-100
copying from one place to another, 104-105
Font dialog box, 102

Text Highlighter tool, 104

text wrapping, graphics, 264-267

Text Wrapping tab, Layout dialog box, 266

themes
applying, 144-146
customizing Microsoft accounts, 46-47

Thesaurus, 327-328

thumb drives, 250

thumbnails, 241

tick marks, 208

.TIFF, 238-239

title bar, 12

toolbars, 26-27
mini toolbars, 26
Quick Access toolbar, 12, 25

tools
Borders tool, 157
Eraser tool, 180
Font Color tool, 104
Format Painter tool, 104
Mail Merge tool, 349-358
Picture Border tools, 278
Picture Styles tool, 278
Remove Background tool, 287
Screenshot tool, 250
Shapes tool, 218
Text Box tool, 231
Text Highlighter tool, 104
Track Changes, WEB: 362
Watermark tool, 155

Track Changes, WEB: 362
    turning on, WEB: 363-364
Track Changes Options dialog
    box, WEB: 369
tracking, 125
    documents, WEB: 362-364
        changing markup display,
            WEB: 365-367
        comments, WEB: 369-371
        reviewing changes,
            WEB: 371-372
        turning on tracking,
            WEB: 363-364
Tracking Options icon,
    WEB: 364
Transform category, Text Effects
    palette, 230
Translate Document, 328
Translate Selected Text, 328
translating words, 328-330
turning documents into web
    pages, WEB: 386-388
turning off Start screen, 11
turning on tracking,
    WEB: 363-364
types of charts, 206
typing text, 82-83

U-V

underline, applying, 96-98

vertical alignment, changing,
    132-133
video
    embedding, 254-257
    removing, 257
view modes, 29
    changing, 29-31
View tab, Ribbon, 24

viewing documents, multiple,
    65-66
views
    Outline view, 292-296
    zooming, 32-33

W

watermarks, adding, 154-156
Watermark tool, 155
Web Apps, WEB: 398-400
Web Layout mode, 29-31
web pages, turning documents
    into, WEB: 386-388
web servers, 36
Windows 7, starting Word, 9
Windows 8, starting Word, 10
Windows Live SkyDrive,
    WEB: 394
wizards, Mail Merge Wizard, 349
Word, 5
    closing, 16-17
    exiting, 16-17
    new features, 8-9
    overview, 6-7
    requirements for, 7
    starting, 9-11
WordArt objects, inserting,
    226-230
Word icon, 12

X-Z

YouTube, 254

Zoom dialog box, 33
Zoom slider, 32, 133
zooming views, 32-33

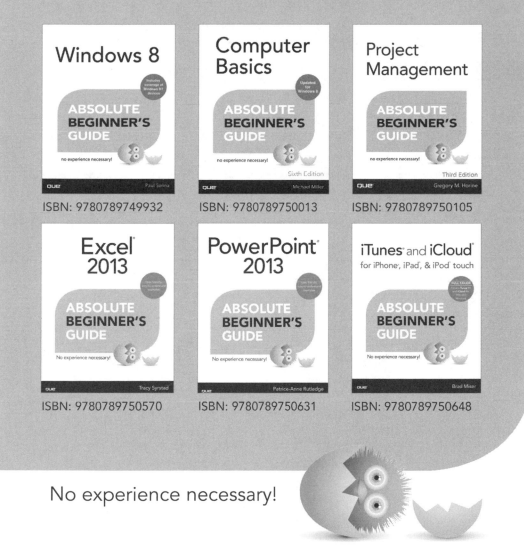

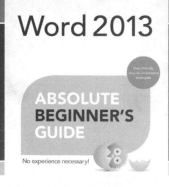

Word 2013
ABSOLUTE BEGINNER'S GUIDE
No experience necessary!

que   Sherry Kinkoph Gunter

FREE
Online Edition

Safari
Books Online

Your purchase of *Word 2013 Absolute Beginner's Guide* includes access to a free online edition for 45 days through the **Safari Books Online** subscription service. Nearly every Que book is available online through **Safari Books Online**, along with thousands of books and videos from publishers such as Addison-Wesley Professional, Cisco Press, Exam Cram, IBM Press, O'Reilly Media, Prentice Hall, Sams, and VMware Press.

Safari Books Online is a digital library providing searchable, on-demand access to thousands of technology, digital media, and professional development books and videos from leading publishers. With one monthly or yearly subscription price, you get unlimited access to learning tools and information on topics including mobile app and software development, tips and tricks on using your favorite gadgets, networking, project management, graphic design, and much more.

Activate your FREE Online Edition at
informit.com/safarifree

STEP 1:   Enter the coupon code: FPWCWFA.

STEP 2:   New Safari users, complete the brief registration form.
Safari subscribers, just log in.

If you have difficulty registering on Safari or accessing the online edition,
please e-mail customer-service@safaribooksonline.com

Addison Wesley   AdobePress   ALPHA   Cisco Press   FT Press   IBM Press   Microsoft Press   New Riders   O'REILLY

Peachpit Press   PRENTICE HALL   que   Redbooks   SAMS   SAS Publishing   vmware PRESS   WILEY   wrox